WHAT A PARTY!

WHAT A PARTY!

MY LIFE AMONG DEMOCRATS:

Presidents,

Candidates,

Donors,

Activists,

Alligators,

and Other Wild Animals

TERRY McAULIFFE

with Steve Kettmann

THOMAS DUNNE BOOKS ✹ ST. MARTIN'S GRIFFIN

New York

THOMAS DUNNE BOOKS.
An imprint of St. Martin's Press.

Photo inserts: McAuliffe Archive photos courtesy of Panoramic Visions, John Berry for the *Syracuse Post-Standard,* Larry Glenn for Photo Op, Alex Wong for Getty Images, Jocelyn Augustino, Christopher Briscoe, Addisu Demissie, Justin Paschal, Joe Reilly. Official White House photos credited to Ralph Aswang, Sharon Farmer, Bob McNeely, David Scull, and William Vasta.

www.thomasdunnebooks.com
www.stmartins.com

Design by Patrice Sheridan

LIBRARY OF CONGRESS CATALOGING-IN-PUBLICATION DATA

McAuliffe, Terry.
    What a party! : my life among Democrats : presidents, candidates, donors, activists, alligators, and other wild animals / Terry McAuliffe ; with Steve Kettmann.
        p. cm.
    ISBN-13: 978-0-312-37775-5
    ISBN-10: 0-312-37775-4
    1. McAuliffe, Terry. 2. Political consultants—United States—Biography. 3. Democratic Party (U.S.)—Biography. 4. Presidents—United States—Staff—Biography. 5. United States—Politics and government—1993–2001. 6. United States—Politics and government—2001– 7. Clinton, Bill, 1946– —Friends and associates. 8. Political campaigns—United States. I. Kettmann, Steve. II. Title.

    E840.8.M43 A3 2007
    324.2736092—dc22
    [B]

                                                                                2006032142

First St. Martin's Griffin Edition: February 2008

10 9 8 7 6 5 4 3 2 1

For my father, Jack,
who fought for the land of the free
and the home of the brave
as a soldier
and a Democrat.

AUTHOR'S NOTE

★ ★ ★

If you're in the market for a cautious, impartial, understated, pedantic—and boring!—look at American politics, put this book down right now and demand a refund. I've been passionate about politics and the Democratic Party my whole life, from the time I was a boy in Syracuse, New York, and I've always taken the view that if you are going to get in the arena and fight for what you believe, you might as well have fun doing it.

You've got to keep people laughing, even when you're also hoping to make them think—and to inspire them to action. I've done my best to present all the stories in this book in as accurate a light as possible. These are very serious topics to me. But I've also got to tell you: I am an Irish story-teller. My people came over from County Cork. We love Guinness. We love St. Patrick's Day. And we love blarney. This is my book and obviously I've done my best to make myself look good. Even if you think I'm full of it, I bet I can still make you laugh.

I've been lucky enough to have had a lot of great experiences and adventures during my twenty-eight years working in politics, starting with my work as the top fund-raiser for Jimmy Carter's 1980 reelection campaign and leading up to my four years as chairman of the Democratic National Committee. I try to give you an unfiltered insider's view of how things are really done in politics and why. I deal with our successes as a party and also with our defeats, and let the chips fall where they may. It's not personal. I have a lot of tough things to say, because it matters to me.

Here's another warning: If you're a Clinton-basher, I doubt you will like this book. A large part of the book deals with President and Hillary Clinton because they have been such a large part of my life. I'm honored to say they are both great friends of mine. You'll see them in these pages as you would one of your own best friends, whether I am telling you about Hillary playing mermaid with my five-year-old daughter, Sally, on vacation, President Clinton and I golfing in the pouring rain—or the time South Korean intelligence agents thought the President and I might be more than just friends.

I have a reputation for being hyperactive, and it's true—I love to be on the move and I can't keep still for long. To be honest, when I was approached about writing this book, I figured the whole thing would be a kick. I thought the project would take maybe a month or two of my time. But I was wrong. In the end, I put more than a year into the project. I waded through mountains of old newspaper and magazine clippings and voluminous daily briefings, and along with my coauthor, Steve Kettmann, I sat down to interview more than a hundred people, including all the top figures in the Democratic Party, to go over the details of experiences we've shared. We pulled our share of all-nighters working on the book, but it will all be worth it if I can not only entertain you but also inspire you to get involved in the political process—or at least think a little better of the people who do.

Every time I was down in my life when I was President, every single time, Terry was always there.

—BILL CLINTON, FEBRUARY 28, 2006

It is not the critic who counts; not the man who points out how the strong man stumbles, or where the doer of deeds could have done them better. The credit belongs to the man who is actually in the arena, whose face is marred by dust and sweat and blood; who strives valiantly; who errs, who comes short again and again, because there is no effort without error and short-coming; but who does actually strive to do the deeds; who knows great enthusiasms, the great devotions; who spends himself in a worthy cause; who at the best knows in the end the triumph of high achievement, and who at the worst, if he fails, at least fails while daring greatly, so that his place shall never be with those cold and timid souls who neither know victory nor defeat.

—THEODORE ROOSEVELT, APRIL 23, 1910

INTRODUCTION

★ ★ ★

I've never had more fun in politics than I did roaming around the 2004 Republican Convention in New York. Those smug, self-satisfied Republican delegates all stared at me like I was an animal in a zoo, but I felt like a kid in a candy store. Everywhere I went, the sight of me, the Democratic Party chairman, was enough to wipe the smiles right off their faces. I swear, you'd have thought Satan himself had shown up at the pearly gates, the way they were reacting.

"That's not that awful Terry McAuliffe, is it?" they'd say as I walked through Madison Square Garden.

"You bleeping commie!" I'd hear. "You're never going to take my freedom!"

"What are *you* doing here?" someone else would yell.

I had an escort with me, Detective Joe Sweeney and a detail of New York City police officers, but even if I'd been alone there would have been no holding me back.

"You're lucky I'm here!" I would shout. "I'm saving America!"

Growing up in Syracuse, New York, the youngest of four brothers, I got into so many fistfights that my nickname was Mad Dog. One afternoon, my brothers Johnny, Joey, and Tommy and I were cruising past Bishop Ludden High in our Dodge Dart convertible and Joey started taunting a group of high school kids. One barked an obscenity right back, so Joey stopped the car.

"Terry, you go get 'em," he said.

Only one problem: There were three of them and one of me. Plus, I was only twelve and a lot smaller than them.

"*What* did you say to us?" I asked, jumping out of the backseat.

Soon enough I got the living daylights beat out of me, and the whole time my brothers just sat in the car laughing their heads off. I wound up with a fat lip and a bloody nose, but so what? We were a loud, happy, close-knit family and we loved to mix it up. A week later we'd be cruising around in the Dodge Dart again and my brothers would throw me right back into another fight. I was brought up never to back down: *If you hit me, I'm going to pop right back up and hit you harder, every single time.*

So any Republicans who ever thought I'd run from a fight, they got the wrong guy. I was in my element, there at George W. Bush's 2004 Republican Convention. That first morning, I got up early and as I headed down to the lobby of the Sheraton, the elevator stopped on the thirty-second floor and I found myself eye to eye with a Republican delegate with his convention credentials flopping all over the place.

"You're Terry McAuliffe," he informed me, as if I didn't already know.

"Yes, sir!" I said.

"I don't give a damn if you were the last man on earth, I wouldn't ride the elevator with you," he said, all huffing and puffing.

"Sir, you have a great day," I said as the doors closed in his face.

It was like that all day. Other than Iowa Governor Tom Vilsack, who was also there to go on TV and counter some of the wilder Republican distortions, I felt like the only Democrat within a three-mile radius. I was like some strange species of animal that had somehow wandered loose from the holding pen. People were so blown away at the sight of Mr. Democrat there at their orgy of Democrat-hating, their mouths would literally fall open. I was creating such a scene, people kept coming over to have pictures taken with me so their friends would believe them later when they told the story about that crazy McAuliffe daring to set foot on their turf.

I took special pleasure in rattling their cages for the simple reason that I was good and ticked off. Earlier that year, I had really been giving it to Bush. I went on the ABC program *This Week with George Stephanopoulos* on Super Bowl Sunday and took a strong stand on how George W. Bush ditched his responsibilities to the uniform in a way that would have gotten him in serious trouble if he wasn't a congressman's son.

One of the big lies of the right is that Republicans have some kind of monopoly on patriotism and love of the uniform. Growing up in our house in Syracuse, patriotism was an even bigger religion than religion, and we were Irish-American Catholics, so you know that is saying something. We sat there at dinner every night, all six of us in our assigned seats, starting right at 6:30—except on Saturdays, when Dad took Mom out to dinner—and listened to my dad, Jack McAuliffe, regale us with stories from his time as a World War II army captain. He was in charge of all the big guns and always had to go ashore first on one of those LCMs to get the artillery in position before the battle, which meant his company could be blown to bits. Only a fool expected to survive even one battle.

Saipan, Okinawa—to us those weren't just the names of battles my father fought, they were windows into a world of service and dedication to your country. I talked to my dad every day on the phone right up until he passed away in front of the TV on New Year's Eve 2000. Jack went the perfect way, doing his favorite things, drinking a Scotch and watching a Syracuse grad, Donovan McNabb, quarterbacking the Philadelphia Eagles. The old man was my best friend and to this day his values are my values: patriotism, family, religion, and the Democratic Party. My father made sure I understood from an early age that what mattered most in life was getting out there and making a difference, working through the Democratic Party to make people's lives better and always standing up for your convictions.

So here the Republicans were in early 2004, attacking John Kerry on his war record. I was not about to let them use character assassination to destroy our nominee the way they had done to Mike Dukakis and so many others. These were the same people who attacked Bill Clinton for everything imaginable, going all the way back to when he was a baby. It was my job as party chairman to defend all the candidates against unfair attacks and we knew we had Bush dead to rights. My research director, Jason Miner, kept telling me that we had let Bush off way too easily in the 2000 campaign. Jason had spent years researching Bush's bizarre record of not showing up for his National Guard duty and we knew the facts spoke loud and clear. I had my staff brief the campaigns that we were about to launch our AWOL counterattack. So when Stephanopoulos said that the Republicans would try to paint John Kerry as "Michael Dukakis all over again," I was ready.

"George, I look forward to that debate when John Kerry, a war hero with a chest full of medals, is standing next to George Bush, a man who was AWOL in the Alabama National Guard," I told Stephanopoulos.

He asked me a few follow-ups and I kept hammering away.

"Listen, when George Bush struts around on an aircraft carrier wearing a flight suit, pretending he's some big military officer and saying, 'Mission

Accomplished,' he brings it on himself. . . . George Bush got out of college in 1968, the height of the draft. He used his father's contacts to get a spot in the Texas Guard. He then wanted to go work on an Alabama senate race. He went to Alabama for one year. He didn't show up."

My AWOL attack generated such intense buzz around the country that *Meet the Press* host Tim Russert went to the Oval Office on February 7, and asked the President directly if he could defend himself against the truth I'd spoken. Bush, true to form, had a thoughtful, credible reply ready, one he must have practiced repeatedly in his prep sessions.

"Yeah?" Bush said.

For some reason that wasn't enough for Russert.

"How do you respond?" he asked the President.

"I was—I served in the National Guard," Bush said. "I flew F-102 aircraft. I got an honorable discharge. I've heard this—I've heard this ever since I started running for office. I—I put in my time, proudly so."

Russert always does his homework. He let Bush talk about the fine people who have served in the National Guard and then he followed up.

"*The Boston Globe* and the Associated Press have gone through some of the records and said there's no evidence that you reported to duty in Alabama during the summer and fall of 1972," Russert said.

"Yeah, they're—they're just wrong," Bush said. "There may be no evidence, but I did report; otherwise, I wouldn't have been honorably discharged."

Listen, I don't know what it's like for a rich kid in Kennebunkport, but I grew up in a working-class family, and if I screwed up as a kid, I faced the consequences. My rowdy streak got me kicked out of the third grade, and I mean that literally. The teacher refused to teach a single day more if I remained in the classroom. But I didn't expect my parents to come to my rescue. I dealt with the humiliation of carrying my desk upstairs to another class and carried on. Bush was so used to going through life getting bailed out by family connections at every turn, he always expected to get bailed out for all his screw-ups. He figured he could skip out on his military service, just so long as the records were cleaned up later, the truth be damned.

Bush could not defend himself against my daily AWOL attacks for the simple reason that his past was indefensible. We had the administration on the run for six weeks and we saw how well our attacks were working when Bush went into free fall in the polls. His approval rating stood at 58 percent in an ABC News/*Washington Post* poll conducted January 15–18, 2004. The next poll, taken February 10–11, had Bush's approval rating down to 50 percent. Up until then, large numbers of Americans thought they could believe George W. Bush, but not anymore. Polls showed that 71 percent of Americans thought Bush was lying about his military service. We had made a major dent in what had been seen as Bush's biggest strength, the perception that he was truthful and had good character.

John Kerry loved what we were doing with the AWOL attacks. His staff called over to the Democratic National Committee (DNC) the day I made the first AWOL comments on ABC to thank us. But then on March 11, the day after Kerry won the nomination, his campaign manager called my COO at the DNC, Josh Wachs, and said I should back off.

"Tell the chairman no more talking AWOL," came the word. "No more of that. It's too partisan. The swing voters won't like it."

Josh was afraid to relay the message because he was so sure I'd be livid, and he was right to be worried. I was so mad I was ready to put my fist through a wall. I was also confused because Elizabeth Bagley, one of our top fund-raisers, had just talked to John at an event and he had emphasized to her how glad he was that I was taking on Bush with the AWOL issue so that he wouldn't have to do it. Several others told me they'd had similar conversations with Kerry.

I hated being muzzled on AWOL because I knew we were taking Bush and his political strategist, Karl Rove, out of their game. These guys were tough, ruthless, and willing to lie or cheat any way they could. After all, these were the same guys who orchestrated stealing an election back in 2000—Bush was never elected President, as I kept repeating on TV in 2001, he only became President when the U.S. Supreme Court intervened. The AWOL attack was the first time we had the White House reeling, and if you had them down on the mat, you did not let them up. But the Kerry campaign did. Then they compounded the mistake that July at our convention by committing the ultimate political malpractice by ordering all speeches scrubbed of any mention of George Bush by name or even of his scandalous record of incompetence.

The geniuses around John didn't even want me or any other high-ranking Democrats to go up to New York for the week of lies and distortions the Republicans were calling a convention. That is how gun-shy the Kerry campaign was. A sleazy campaign was organized against John by a bunch of Swift Boat veterans with axes to grind, which resulted in John's poll numbers taking a nosedive. Only then did the Kerry campaign change its strategy completely, and suddenly I was sent out there to unleash tough attacks on Bush day after day for the next three months. As part of that new strategy, the campaign also agreed to have me in New York during the convention.

No one could understand why the Kerry campaign was not fighting back harder against the Swift Boat smear, especially not John McCain, who despite being a Republican senator knew what it was like to be smeared by the Bush operation. They had gone after him before the 2000 South Carolina primary with such low-down tactics, it's a wonder McCain never punched Bush. The Bush boys put innuendo out there about McCain's time in a Vietnam prisoner-of-war camp, trying to make him out to be crazy. They attacked his patriotism, called him unstable, and alleged that he had an illegitimate child. It was a disgrace.

Given my lifelong respect for the military, I was amazed they would do that to a war hero. Any man who was brutally tortured for five years as a Vietnam POW deserves the respect of every American, but Bush operatives kept treating McCain with contempt. It took backbone for McCain to insist on a congressional torture ban in late 2005 over the objections of Bush and Dick Cheney, which ended up passing by wide margins in the House and Senate. Then, in a nauseating turn, Bush later declared in a "signing statement" that he was above the law and would ignore the torture ban whenever he felt like it.

Back in August 2004, McCain came up to me at the Republican Convention and we rode up the long, slow escalators together. He put his arm around me so he could get close and whisper. There were a lot of potential eavesdroppers around and he wanted to speak freely about John Kerry—and George W. Bush.

"Terry," he said. "What's the matter with your guy?"

I shrugged. What could I say?

"I like John," McCain said. "You know that. But he's looking like such a wimp. He's got to start fighting and defending himself."

"You know I'm all about fighting," I said.

Then McCain said something that really surprised me.

"My guy is no great shakes, but your guy looks like a wimp," he said.

The first day of the Republican Convention, Governor Vilsack and I were huddled with our briefers to go over a few issues before our ten o'clock press conference.

"Oh, and you might get asked a question about Matt Lauer—Bush was on the *Today* show with him this morning and said he couldn't win the war on terror," one briefer told us.

"Hold on!" I said. "Whoa, whoa, whoa. Stop the briefing. What did you just say?"

"Lauer asked Bush if we can win the war on terror," our briefer said. "And Bush answered, 'I don't think you can win it.' That was the quote."

Vilsack and I looked at each other in amazement. This was news to us.

"You're kidding me!" I said. "This is the biggest break we've had. Bush says he can't win the war on terror? That's his whole campaign. What are we doing about this?"

The campaign was giving Vilsack and me the green light to get out there and criticize Bush for this, but I knew that was the wrong decision. We needed our candidate leading the way on this, even if that was a departure from the usual political rule that you keep a low profile during the other party's convention. Our briefers were arguing that it would be pointless to have John Kerry respond directly. Their argument was that Bush would clean up his mistake quickly and rob any Kerry statement of impact. Vilsack and I respectfully disagreed. It was time for bold action, and if it paid off, it would pay off big.

"We've got to get ahold of Kerry right now," I said.

"Terry's right," Vilsack said. "This is too big. We've got to do something."

John was vacationing on Nantucket with his wife, and I knew the most important thing was to get him off that island. I didn't think it made sense for him to come to New York, where all the Republicans were gathered. My idea was to fly him to the site in Pennsylvania where hijacked United Airlines Flight 93 had crashed on September 11, after the heroic struggles of its crew and passengers.

"We have to get him in that farm field," Vilsack said, agreeing with me.

A dramatic enough setting like that would guarantee live TV coverage.

"George Bush says he can't win the war on terror," Kerry could say. "Well I *can* win the war on terror and I *will* win the war on terror as your next President!"

That would really shake up the race, shifting the dynamic wildly because, let's face it, the economy was a mess and the only asset Bush had was that people believed he was doing a good job of keeping Americans safe. The Republicans gave us an opening to gut Bush's No. 1 argument and to undercut the sleazy Swift Boat smears.

I tried to reach John on Nantucket that morning, but had no luck. Instead, I talked to John Sasso, a total pro who was heading up Kerry campaign operations at the DNC.

"We have to move quick, because Bush is going to clean this up if we give him the chance," I told Sasso, and explained what I thought we needed to do.

"Great idea, Terry. I'll get it to John and we'll do something," he told me. "Okay? We'll get back to you."

Vilsack was on the phone at the same time talking to a deputy campaign manager.

"This is the biggest break we've had in the campaign," Vilsack said. "They've been beating us up for the past month."

"Great, all done," I said after we both hung up. "What a huge break for us."

As we found out later, serious internal conflict had broken out inside the Kerry campaign that week and the top people were all distracted. I'll say it straight: They were too worried about saving their jobs to think first about beating George Bush. That day passed for me in a blur. I did dozens of TV and radio interviews and was itching to jump all over Bush for saying he couldn't win the war on terror, but I held off. I wasn't the one to be launching this missile at Bush, John Kerry was. John was the nominee. He fought in Vietnam.

I kept glancing down at my BlackBerry, expecting any moment to get word that John had made a big splash in the press with his response to Bush. I assumed he was already in Pennsylvania and that it was just a matter of time before we made Bush pay for this huge mistake. Man, this was going to be great.

Finally I sat down and watched the evening newscast and they reported the shocking news that Bush didn't think he could win the war on terror. Then they cut to Nantucket for John Kerry's reply. There was John in the water with his Windsurfer, and a reporter shouted a question, asking if he could win the war on terror. John smiled and gave a one-word answer, but it was so windy, you couldn't really hear what he said, and they had to put a subtitle at the bottom of the TV screen.

"Absolutely," it read.

That was our answer. That was our Democratic response. The next day Bush went to the national convention of the American Legion and cleaned it up. He stood with John McCain at his side and said, "Make no mistake about it, we are winning and will win" the war on terror. That was it. He took the issue away from us. We had our shot and we blew it. Instead of projecting an image of Democratic strength, with John Kerry standing near that hole in the ground in Pennsylvania and saying, "I will win the war on terror!" we'd given the American people a glimpse of him windsurfing and strangely out of it.

Just think for a minute how this would have gone if it had been John Kerry who said, "I don't think you can win it." Just imagine what Rove would have done with this. They would have had commercials up in an hour blasting John as an unpatriotic defeatist weakling, and they would have fired up their huge right-wing noise machine so that millions of people were all repeating the same buzzwords. They would have killed us.

We had an opportunity that could have sent Bush packing to his ranch in Texas, a one-term loser, and we botched it. I was still seething over that blown chance more than a year later when John Kerry and I finally had a chance to sit down for dinner in Washington. I was amazed to hear what John had to say about August 30, 2004, the day Bush said he couldn't win the war on terror.

"Nobody ever told me, Terry," John said.

In fairness, John's staff *had* urged him not to take his Windsurfer out, and what staff wouldn't have done that? But John's campaign manager had scheduled a ninety-minute meeting with him on Nantucket that day. She was afraid she was going to get fired and went up there to make her case to keep her job. So that day on Nantucket, John went into the water with his windsurfing board without having been told that Bush said he didn't think he could win the war on terror. He'd had no idea why the reporter asked him that question, and a year later he was still irate.

"That was one of the biggest mistakes we made in the campaign," John told me. "Nobody had briefed me. I don't know why I was on that island that day. I should have gotten off the island."

I mentioned my idea about going to Pennsylvania.

"I'd have gone to New York and made my statement right there at Ground Zero," John told me. "I'd have taken it right to them."

The lesson we Democrats all have to keep learning again and again is that it's not enough to be right on the major issues. Of course we have that on our side. We are the party of Bill Clinton, who I remind you had the highest job approval rating of any U.S. President when he left office. That was because Clinton got out of bed every morning thinking about how he could give the average Joe a shot at the American dream. The Republicans are the party of George W. Bush, who somewhere along the line stopped knowing the difference between truth and fantasy and as a result created an America that was much less safe than when he took office. Bush has presided over the most incompetent and least accountable administration in memory. He looted the treasury to give rich people like me tax breaks we don't need and that our grandchildren will still be paying off, along with the disastrous trillion-dollar war in Iraq. We Democrats are in tune with the American people on the issues, but being right doesn't mean a thing if we don't outwork the Republicans, outthink them, outorganize them, and outdiscipline them—because what we're fighting for matters that much.

The first step is to cut down on the distractions. Too often we're the party of distractions. We're forever losing our focus because we worry we're doing something wrong or are not united enough. Too many Democrats are in some way ashamed to be Democrats or are unwilling to accept that we are a big tent party that represents people of diverse backgrounds and perspectives and priorities, and yes, that includes entrepreneurs and owners of small businesses, too. I have nothing against individual Republicans. In fact, I have many good Republican friends. But the extremism of the Bush-Cheney years has given ordinary Americans every reason to be afraid and sickened: condoning torture, lying to Congress, making a habit of over-the-top secrecy and cronyism, handing important jobs to clownish amateurs who gave us the Hurricane Katrina mess ("Brownie, you're doing a heck of a job"), and the boondoggle of Iraq profiteering by U.S. contractors, and sending our soldiers into battle without body armor. It's a scandalous record and it's un-American what they have done to this country with their trillion-dollar war.

We Democrats are a political party, not a political machine run by Karl Rove and Tom DeLay and characters like Jack Abramoff, which is what the Republicans gave us in the Bush-Cheney years. Believe me, as more and more people fully understand the crimes and outrages of the Bush years, the country will take a fresh look at the Clinton years and remember fondly what it was like to have a booming economy and a country on the move. Republican operatives need to scare people witless and shove lies down their throats in order to win wide support. Democrats are on the side of truth and trusting in the basic decency of working men and women. We don't have to change who we are or how we think. We just have to make sure we stand up for ourselves and stand ready for the inevitable Republican smears and attacks, which they have to use because they know they can't win an honest debate. We have to stand behind our own people, the way my father always taught me.

Bill Clinton believed in reaching out to moderates and independents, as everyone knows, but he learned early that if you let Republicans get away with the dirty tricks that are a Republican invention, they will bury you. Clinton traveled to Florida in December 1981 for a state Democratic convention, where he fired up the party regulars with a message about fighting back against Republican smears and attack ads. "I said it was all well and good to let them strike the first blow," Clinton wrote in his book, *My Life,* "but if they hit us hard below the belt, we should 'take a meat ax and cut their hands off.' "

I know a lot of us on the Democratic side are talking about the importance of getting out there and fighting and that's great. If everyone from

Salon.com and the big names of the blogosphere to the leaders of the Democratic Party all agree we have to stay united and be tough and determined and not back down, then the Republicans have a lot to worry about. But it's easy to get fired up and talk a big game and it's a lot more challenging to get out the door and take action when the time is right.

As I'm writing this, it's late 2006 and the disaster of 2000 might seem distant to some people, but not to me. We won that election. The American people elected Al Gore to be the forty-third President of the United States. He didn't just win the popular vote, he won the electoral college—if Florida had not been taken from us. Governor Jeb Bush had promised his brother he was going to deliver the state, no matter what, and he worked with the state's official vote counter, who also happened to be the Bush campaign's state chair, Secretary of State Katherine Harris, to back up his word. The Republicans pulled so many tricks to rob African Americans of their votes, it was a national scandal.

The bigger scandal was that even in the aftermath of Election Day, with the outcome hanging in the balance, we did not fight hard enough. They sent down former Reagan Secretary of State Jim Baker, a tough SOB who knows how to get results. We dispatched former Secretary of State Warren Christopher, a very capable attorney but someone who was not suited for a street brawl. We should have sent down a take-no-prisoners fighter like Harold Ickes, my friend from the Clinton White House. We should have had our scrappiest, most determined people down there working to protect the integrity of the process. Instead, we let the Republicans outwork us and out-organize us. They flew down several dozen hoodlums from Tom DeLay's office who banged on doors and windows and actually shut down recount offices—and then crowed about it. Spike Lee did a ten-minute film for Showtime that sums it up: *We Wuz Robbed*. We should have called immediately for a recount of the whole state, since that would have been fair to everyone and easy to explain. Instead, we let them steal it from us. To me that episode was the defining moment for our party in the last twenty-five years.

Had we fought harder and smarter in Florida, just think of all the atrocities and travesties that America and the world would have been spared with Al Gore, not George W. Bush, as President—turning a $5.6 trillion federal surplus into a $4 trillion deficit, a trumped-up and fabricated war in Iraq, the development of six nuclear weapons in North Korea, Iran developing a nuclear weapon, Hezbollah firing thousands of rockets into Israel, and America's well-earned prestige around the world evaporating.

Senator Tom Daschle and Congressman Dick Gephardt, the Democratic

leaders in Congress, had been after me in December 2000 to run for chairman of the Democratic National Committee and I kept saying no. Vice
President Gore had also made a strong push to get me to be DNC chair, going back several years, and had even sat me down in the personal quarters
of the White House, along with the President, to try to get me to chair the
DNC. I resisted. Then the Supreme Court decision came down, stopping the
recount and handing the 2000 election to George W. Bush, a shameless mis-
use of judicial power, and after that I was so mad, I was seeing red.

I thought again about the DNC job and realized I had to do it. I was sickened by what happened in Florida. I was sickened that Al Gore had to pull out
of Ohio more than a month before the election because of a lack of resources,
then ended up losing the state by only 165,000 votes out of 4.7 million votes
cast, and that the Gore campaign didn't have the resources to run a full-
fledged campaign in his home state of Tennessee. I realized I couldn't rant
and rave about Democrats not fighting hard enough and then sit this one out.
I remember driving over to the Vice President's residence for lunch with Al
Gore three days after the Supreme Court ruling. I was still enraged. Gore
and I had a long, private lunch of tortilla soup and ham sandwiches, and I
told him I was determined to fight for the party.

"After what they did to you and this country, Mr. Vice President, it's
time to fight," I told Gore. "I'm running for chairman."

"Terry, if you're running, I'll endorse you," the Vice President said. "I'm
with you one hundred percent."

That was how I ended up being George W. Bush's toughest, most outspoken critic during the first four years of his presidency.

PART ONE

STEPPING INTO
THE RING

1

I remember walking home from Bellevue Country Club in Syracuse late one afternoon when I was fourteen years old, and with each step I was more depressed. I had just spent five hours caddying, lugging two heavy golf bags up and down hills for a grand total of eight bucks. I didn't mind the work. I've never minded the work. No, what had me distraught was the math. No matter how I turned it around in my head, it was clear I had already thrown my life away. I was going to have to face the cold, hard truth that I was a failure. What else could I call myself? There I was wasting my time, working for a measly two bucks an hour. I was never going to put any capital together at that rate!

"I've got to start my own business," I announced to myself as I walked the mile home from the golf course.

I was aware there were certain obstacles to starting a business at age fourteen. I could not open my own legal practice just yet, most likely, and I probably couldn't sell insurance either. I kept asking myself: What *would* people hire a young kid to do? One answer was house painting, but that just wasn't me. I'd leave that to other guys my age. Then, as I turned onto Dundee Road toward home, I saw an older guy in front of his house sealing his driveway. He was all sweaty and irritated-looking, but he was stuck out there. The winters in Syracuse are so brutal that everyone has to seal their driveways often by putting down a layer of hot tar emulsion liquid, which is dirty, nasty work.

"You know what?" I said out loud, walking faster now. "They'll hire a kid to do that. Nobody wants to do it himself and get that hot black tar all over you."

I didn't waste any time acting on my idea. I hurried home and typed up a letter announcing my new McAuliffe Driveway Maintenance business to all our neighbors. The next morning I handed those out all over the neighborhood, and by the end of that first day I had six jobs.

"Mom, can we go to Kmart?" I shouted across the house. "I've got to buy five-gallon buckets of tar!"

If you've never sealed a driveway, let me tell you, there's not much to it. You take a broom and sweep away any dust or debris, then dump the hot tar onto the driveway and smooth it out with a squeegee. I had a little red wagon to wheel the bucket of tar from job to job. I hired friends to help me and mulled over my biggest problem—tar. It didn't make sense to keep buying five-gallon containers at Kmart. The next step was Agway, a huge agricultural collective where I could buy fifty-gallon drums of concentrated tar. You had to dilute it, four gallons of water for every gallon of tar, so it went four times as far and you could increase your profit fourfold. The trouble was, those fifty-gallon drums were huge—and heavy. I was going to have to come up with a way to transport them.

"Hi, Uncle Billy," I said over the phone. "Listen, I need help."

Billy Byrne, my uncle, ran Byrne Dairy.

"I've got to start buying wholesale," I told him. "This retail is killing me. I need to move a lot more tar around. Do you have any old dairy trucks? Can I buy one?"

Uncle Billy was having a hard time keeping up with all this.

"Well, we've got that truck graveyard out there in Cicero," he said. "We'll talk about it and see what you want."

Billy said to call him back later, but I couldn't wait. My buddy Joey Hartnett drove me up old Highway 11 to Cicero, just north of Syracuse, and we found Uncle Billy's fleet of more than fifty old Byrne Dairy milk trucks all lined up and rusting with the keys in them. I had come prepared: I had a battery, a can of gas, spark plugs, and quarts of oil. We found a truck we liked and I put in a battery, replaced the spark plugs, added oil, and emptied some gas into its old tank.

"Keep your fingers crossed, Joey," I said.

I turned the key and the old dairy truck actually started. To this day I can still hear the rumbling of that big old engine and feel the hum of that big steering wheel vibrating in my hands. Man, the excitement was unbelievable. I was in business! This was the start of everything for me. The next morning, when my parents woke up, they saw that old Byrne Dairy milk truck sitting out front in the driveway. They were almost as surprised as my uncle was when I called him later that morning.

"I found a truck I liked," I said.

"We'll talk about it, Terry," he said. "Why don't you come down next week?"

"Uncle Billy, you don't understand," I told him. "I have the truck here at the house."

He was speechless. It had never dawned on him that I would head out to the lot on my own. There were liability issues, title issues—all kinds of things to think about. I just blew through all that. Uncle Billy was taken aback, but I think he respected that I was a young hustler. I got the title and license plates and we found some old brown house paint to slap on the truck. We put lettering on there, too, so anyone who saw us coming would know we were McAULIFFE DRIVEWAY MAINTENANCE.

Eventually I decided driveways were not enough.

"Excuse me, I'm here to see Mr. Higgins," I told the secretary at the Syracuse Savings Bank.

Tom Higgins was the president of the bank, and his parking lots were in bad shape.

"I'm sorry, Mr. . . . ?" the secretary asked me, trying not to laugh. "Do you have an appointment?"

I was sixteen years old, a skinny kid wearing one of my older brother's hand-me-down dress shirts with a big, ridiculous tie.

"No, I don't," I said. "I need to see him. This is very important. This is life or death for his business."

I was so serious, the secretary finally did laugh—and then she ushered me in to see the bank president.

"Mr. Higgins, let me tell you something," I said, not wasting any time. "You're a prominent businessman in this city. I want to show you what your business looks like."

He was ready to shoo me out of there in nothing flat, but I'd brought one of those cheesy photo albums with me and I think I'd piqued his curiosity. I'd prepared a nice portfolio of the potholes, cracks, and ruts in his parking lots.

"This reflects on your company, sir," I told Mr. Higgins as he flipped through the pictures.

Then he got to the second half and saw all the shots of smooth, dark, picture-perfect parking lots.

"This is what's happening with other banks," I told Mr. Higgins. "They are better looking. Your competitors are gaining a competitive edge against you."

I got the job. We repaved all the Syracuse Savings Bank parking lots. Then I went after fire stations and we started repaving them, too. The business just kept growing. Our phone at home rang at all hours, with people wanting their driveways sealed.

"McAuliffe Driveway Maintenance," my mother would say every time she answered our phone, like she was in an office.

One time my mother, Millie, was riding along with me in the passenger's seat when the rotted floor of the truck gave out and all four legs of her chair poked through and scraped the road as we drove along. You should have seen the look on Millie's face as she bounced up and down driving along the highway! Another time the old clutch gave out coming up a steep hill and I hit the brake, which sent the rear doors of the truck flying open. A freshly loaded fifty-gallon drum bounced out the back and accelerated downhill fast, flinging superthick black tar all over the place.

"I've got a big crisis," I told my dad from the first pay phone I could find.

He heard me out, and then surprised me.

"Terry, it's your business," he said. "You get all the profits. That means you deal with any issues that come up. Like this."

I couldn't believe how much thick, gooey tar was oozing down the hill. I put down cones to block off traffic, whipped out my trusty squeegee and spent a couple hours smoothing out the tar across the street and getting as much of the excess into the sewer as I could. It was miserable work, but every time I drove past that street I could smile to myself at how good it looked and get a reminder that when you start your own business, you have to clean up your own messes. No one else can do that for you.

My sister-in-law Patty, Tommy's wife, still laughs at the first impression I made on her. I took some of the money I made with McAuliffe Driveway Maintenance and invested in a snowblower and started my winter business. I would get up at four o'clock in the morning during the darkest, coldest days of winter and blow snow off driveways and sidewalks. I'd usually get paid with single dollar bills, which I'd jam into my pockets, and by the time I got home they would be a wet, crumpled mess. I would have been embarrassed to show up at my new bank, Syracuse Savings, to deposit money looking that bad. So instead I ironed each and every bill, spraying on a little starch for good measure. By the time I was done, those bills looked like they had just been wheeled out of the U.S. Treasury's Bureau of Engraving and Printing. The first time Patty met me, I was in the middle of ironing a big load of dollar bills and she just burst out laughing.

I always loved selling. The year I turned twelve I got a great idea for Valentine's Day. I went to see my mother at Quinlan's Florist, where she worked as a salesperson, and arranged to buy a thousand red roses at wholesale. Then, through my Dad, I was able to set up in the lobby of the big MONY office building, and spent the day selling single red roses for five bucks apiece. By the end of the day I'd sold all one thousand, bringing in five thousand dollars for flowers that had cost me a few hundred. That worked out so well that on St. Patrick's Day I did the same thing with green carnations.

If it involved talking, I usually did just fine. For the life of me I can't tell you how I talked my way into a job emceeing the summer concert series they had in Syracuse's parks, but it was one of the greatest gigs ever. The city parks department paid me for forty hours a week, even though it was only an hour or two per evening. They didn't seem to mind that I was not what you would call a musical expert—I have never so much as picked up a musical instrument, and I know as little about music as anybody you'll ever meet.

One time in the late 1980s, I was at a dinner party at Pamela Harriman's Georgetown house, standing there in the living room with Illinois senator Paul Simon—the one with the bow tie—talking about his run for President. Pamela came over and said she wanted to introduce me to someone, so I followed her across the room.

"Terry, I want to introduce you to Paul Simon," Pamela announced.

I thought she might be yanking my chain.

"Great, great," I said, shaking the man's hand, acting just as thrilled as can be that I was finally meeting him, whoever he was.

"Are you Senator Simon's son?" I asked.

He did a double take to see if I was messing with him, but could see I wasn't.

"No, not at all," he said.

We both stood there looking around the room. He seemed friendly enough, so I kept the conversation going.

"Well, what do you do?" I asked him.

"I'm a singer," he said.

"Really, a singer? Have you ever had a hit?"

"Have you heard of 'Bridge Over Troubled Water'?" he asked.

"Sure," I said.

"Simon and Garfunkel?"

"Oh yeah," I said. "My wife loves their stuff."

"Well, that's me," he said. "I'm Paul Simon."

That was how much I knew about music. For years my executive assistant, Justin Paschal, and my staff at the DNC tried to make me somewhat musically literate, arranging meetings for me with P. Diddy, Beyonce, and the Black Eyed Peas, but eventually Justin and the others just gave up. I never had any idea who they were talking about. I'm still like that. But back in Syracuse, emceeing those evening concerts, I didn't need to know much, just enough to step up to the mike at the portable bandstand and read from the list of big band classics they gave me, like Tommy Dorsey's "Boogie Woogie" and Glenn Miller's "In the Mood." The crowd was mostly blue-haired older ladies, and I loved to dance with the older gals. I've been told my singing sounds like a sick dog howling, but I was the Lawrence Welk of Syracuse.

★

I ALWAYS PLANNED ON getting my law degree and becoming a businessman, but my father was so passionate about politics, it rubbed off on me. He and I talked about politics from the time I was just a little squirt tagging along to local political events with him. My father, Jack, gave me a unique perspective on politics that has always stuck with me. He was treasurer of the Onondaga County Democratic Party for more than ten years and taught me about fund-raising from an early age. If you want to organize, if you want to put posters up all over town, you have to first raise the money to pay for it. Jack taught me young that money in politics was neither evil nor good: Money in politics was like gas in the tank, it was what you needed to get where you were going. If you had big plans to help people and to make a difference, you needed money to organize and to get people excited about your message.

Besides his work as a commercial real estate leasing agent, my father was always busy with some political event or campaign, including his own unsuccessful bid for the Syracuse City Council, which at that time was dominated by Republicans. I always loved going along with him to events, where he would usually take me up to the podium. I was with him on August 5, 1964, when Lyndon B. Johnson came to Syracuse to give a speech about the government of North Vietnam "flouting the will of the world for peace." I was only seven years old, and to me LBJ looked like a giant. Afterward, my dad brought me over to meet the President, and I was really nervous.

"How are you, young man?" LBJ asked me.

I moved my lips but no sound came out. *That's* never happened again!

"Great," I said finally. "Great to meet you, Mr. President."

My father was as thrilled as I was. He grew up in such a strong Democratic household that when FDR died in 1945, the family pulled all the shades down in the house and went into deep mourning. My father dedicated himself to the Democratic Party because he saw politics as a way to get involved and make a difference for the working men and women he knew in Syracuse. He understood that Democrats are the party of the people, and that was what made him such a big activist.

I worked my first fund-raiser when I was six. My father put me at the front door of the Persian Terrace Room at the Hotel Syracuse for the Onondaga County Democratic Party annual dinner and gave me firm instructions, which I always kept in mind later in life, much to the chagrin of many, many Democratic donors over the years.

"Terry, if they don't give you the money, they don't get in the door," my father told me. "No exceptions."

My dad taught me to go all out on every political race, no matter how small, and I took him at his word. A group of my buddies, including Duke Kinney, Marty Salanger, Joe and Steve Snyder, Jim Bright, Dave Mulherin, and Mike McInerney, had a great time with my campaign for student body president at Bishop Ludden High School. We dimmed the lights in the school auditorium, which was packed with more than a thousand students, and cranked up "Hail to the Chief." I drove up in a golf cart with a big PRESIDENTIAL LIMOUSINE sign, dressed in my best sweater-vest-and-tie combo. My buddies followed in another golf cart and were all dressed up like Secret Service agents with trench coats, sunglasses, and earplugs. We had put up so many signs, bumper stickers, and buttons all over the school, you couldn't move two feet without seeing "McAuliffe for President." I ended up with the highest vote total ever recorded at Bishop Ludden, a record that I'm told still stands and which probably had a lot to do with me promising free keg parties every weekend at the dirt road.

My dad loved sports, too, and was especially crazy about Notre Dame, which he graduated from in 1939. If my dad wasn't talking politics, he was talking sports or sitting in front of the TV watching sports. He was such a Notre Dame fan, my parents were married by Father Ted Hesburgh at the chapel on the Notre Dame campus. My big brothers and I were all sports-crazy and played whiffle ball in the driveway or wild football games in our neighbor's yard. When I was ten years old my big interest was boxing and I would go down to the YMCA and spar. I held my own, but I was never going to be dubbed the "Napoleon of the Ring" like my great-grandfather's relative, Jack McAuliffe, who was born in March 1866 in Cork, Ireland, where my family comes from, and moved to Williamsburg, Brooklyn, and learned from the great Jack Dempsey.

Jack McAuliffe, who stood all of five foot six, was Lightweight Champion of the World in the 1880s and 1890s, one of the last bare-knuckled boxers. He once boxed Jem Carney of England for seventy-four rounds in 1887, before a riot broke up the fight. Another time, he went sixty-four rounds in a title defense against Billy Myer, despite having broken his arm early in the bout, and battled to a draw. Jack McAuliffe was one of only a handful of champions ever to finish his career undefeated. Like all McAuliffes, he was a man of strong opinions and railed against "the modern powder-puff punchers."

★

My FATHER'S OTHER GREAT PASSION was war movies, no surprise for a former World War II artillery officer. The night I was born, six weeks premature, my mother was away for the weekend at a Catholic retreat in Skaneateles, near Syracuse, and as she was being rushed by ambulance to the hospital she pleaded with the nurses not to call my father.

"Oh no, don't disturb Jack," she told them. "He's watching *Thirty Seconds over Tokyo* and he's wanted to watch that for such a long time."

What a change from today where they expect fathers to be in the delivery room and cut the umbilical cord. They did call Jack, of course, and he was there in the waiting room when I was born. There were complications, and four or five times the doctor said my heart had stopped. Finally I was born and the doctor held me up for my mother.

"Oh, what a beautiful baby," she said. "Too bad he's dead."

But then the doctor whacked me and I started bawling, loud even then.

"Oh my God!" my mother said, she was so surprised. "It's a miracle."

My parents couldn't agree at first on what to name me.

"Jack, I think he was a miracle," my mother said. "We should have something miraculous. I think we should go for something from Notre Dame."

"Let's name him Knute Rockne and everyone can call him Rocky," Jack said.

"God no, we can't do that to this little boy," my mother said. "Let's call him Terry after Terry Brennan."

So they decided on Terry in honor of the Notre Dame football player who ran the opening kickoff back for ninety-eight yards and a touchdown on their wedding day. That day's game was their wedding reception—complete with hot dogs and beer.

My father hoped I'd go to Notre Dame, but he was also happy when I decided on Catholic University in Washington, D.C., where I'd earned a scholarship and started in the fall of 1975. Jack's friend John Mahoney lined me up with a paid internship working for our congressman, Jim Hanley, and every Tuesday and Thursday I took the number 80 bus down to the Cannon Office Building and did research, filing, and constituent correspondence. My first week working for Hanley, I was walking across the Capitol and met the Vice President, Nelson Rockefeller. Three years later, because of my work starting a program to tutor prison inmates, I was asked to attend a seminar at the American Enterprise Institute and got to meet Gerald Ford. We discussed apathy among the young at that conference, and the former President told me, "I could never sit on the sidelines," which I admired, because I never could either.

Ford was the third President I'd met—after LBJ in '64 and Jimmy Carter in '76. My father and I went to New York for the Democratic Convention that summer along with a group including Syracuse Mayor Lee Alexander and Tom Lowery, the Onondaga County Democratic chairman. Six of us wedged into one room in a little hotel, some of us sleeping on couches. The closest we got to the fancy hotels was taking a stroll through the lobby just to see what it was like to be where the action was. My dad and I were people-watching in the Sheraton, looking for big Democratic names, when rumors started flying, creating a hubbub.

"Carter is in there!" someone shouted. "He's coming out any minute!"

This was a huge kick for me, even if my father and I had to wait in the jammed lobby for more than an hour. Carter finally came down and I got a chance to shake his hand and say, "Hello, Governor." It might not sound like much, but I was thrilled.

★

THE SUMMER AFTER I GRADUATED from Catholic, my buddy Duke Kinney and I flew to Ireland and I went off on my own and zipped all over Europe on a Eurail Pass. I don't remember much about the flight back to Washington, but I'll never forget going to the baggage claim to pick up my backpack and watching the carousel go round and round without ever spitting out my backpack. The airline had lost it. I went home to the huge old house that about ten of us shared on Newton Street, a real Animal House. One of the guys in the house was a friend of mine from Catholic University, Tom Donilon, who was working for Hamilton Jordan on President Carter's reelection campaign. He hooked me up with an interview. Soon after I came back from Europe, I got a call asking if I would be interested in a fund-raising job for the Carter-Mondale reelection campaign. Tim Finchem was the campaign's finance director then; now he's commissioner of the PGA.

"You bet I would," I told Finchem. "When can I start?"

"How about tomorrow?" he said. "You'll be a national fund-raiser, traveling all over the country. We can pay you thirteen thousand five hundred dollars a year. Any questions?"

Ah, heck, I thought, *I can always go to law school.*

The airline still had not found my backpack, so I had to go down to the Carter-Mondale reelection headquarters in the only clothes I had, which were a white T-shirt, gray gym shorts, and sneakers. The place didn't look much better than I did. I got up to Finchem's office for my appointment and they didn't even have a chair for me. I got a look inside the office and there was nothing inside except a single desk in the middle with no chairs around it, and then I sat outside waiting. None of that bothered me. I was thrilled to be there and ready to wait all day, if necessary. I'd been out there awhile when a group from Florida arrived to talk to Finchem. The main guy was Carter's finance chairman for Florida, Richard Swann, and he seemed kind of mad at Finchem.

"Tim, you know I have an event with Rosalynn Carter coming up in September, or have you forgotten?" Swann said.

"No, no, I remember," Finchem said.

"So where is all this help you promised me?" Swann asked.

Finchem sat there scratching his head. I was craning my neck to watch as much of this as I could and Finchem saw me.

"There's a young kid out there," he told Swann. "McAuliffe. You can have him."

So they waved me into the room and I sat on the floor answering a bunch of questions. It was kind of a joke, but I just tried to sound serious and act confident about raising money, though I'd never raised a dime. Finally, Finchem turned to Swann.

"Will he do?" he asked him.

"Sure," Swann said, looking unimpressed. "Better than nothing."

"Terry, you're flying down with him to Florida," Finchem said.

I kept nodding and smiling, hoping no one said anything about my gym shorts.

"I'll meet you down there," Swann said. "You can stay at our house."

I was hoping Swann would be at the airport to meet me when I arrived two days later, but no such luck. I caught a cab and sat in the backseat staring at the meter the whole way to the Swann house in Winter Park, a suburb of Orlando. I ended up paying twenty-five bucks.

Jeez, I'm losing money already, I thought to myself.

Doris Swann and I hit it off immediately, even though Richard had forgotten to tell his wife that I'd be showing up with my suitcase and staying with the family for three weeks. She warmed up some pot roast and we popped open a couple of beers and made each other laugh trading stories about people we knew in politics. I met the dog and all four of their kids, including their oldest, Dorothy, who at the time had just turned sixteen. Richard got home late that night and couldn't figure out who his wife could be laughing with so loudly at that hour. He'd forgotten all about me.

After that I became almost part of the family. I arrived on August 30, and the fund-raiser at the Luau Hut at SeaWorld was only three weeks later, so Richard and I threw ourselves into the work and tried to make up for lost time. They gave me fat issues books that I read cover to cover, and I boned up on election law. Then they basically gave me a phone book and said: *Go get 'em,* and I would spend twelve hours a day on the phone. Lucky for me, I was a natural-born salesman. I could talk, Lord knows I could talk. If someone had a question I couldn't answer, I would say, "Well, we'll get back to you later on that issue, but are you going to raise us the ten thousand dollars?" I kept talking and we kept making money. In the end we cleared more than three times the goal for the event.

I was only twenty-two and it showed. I knew I had to do something about my wet-behind-the-ears look, so I started wearing fake glasses to make myself look older. They were just clear glasses, but I thought they made me look more dignified and professional. There is even a caricature on the wall at the Palm Restaurant in Washington showing me in those glasses in 1980. I still take a look sometimes when I'm in there, just to give myself a good laugh. My other trademark back then was the loud polyester suits I used to wear. Thank God no one got a match near me. I'd have gone up in flames.

Word spread quickly about what a great success the Luau Hut event had been. A lot of people in politics would have taken credit for themselves, but

Richard Swann wasn't that way. He kept telling everybody I'd done a great job. He and I were already close, working together and spending a lot of time at the house on Lake Virginia in Winter Park, waterskiing or just hanging out with the family.

Around this time I was down at the lake waterskiing with the Swann kids and Richard was home reading the paper. Doris came up from the lake and found him there in his study.

"Richard, I have figured out who Dorothy is going to marry," Doris said. "Who do you think it is?"

Richard kept reading his article.

"I'm talking to you," Doris said.

She ripped the paper out of his hands and tossed it onto the floor.

"Okay, who?" Richard said halfheartedly.

"I'm not telling," Doris said. "You guess."

"I don't know," he said. "The kid down the street? The school quarterback?"

Doris cut him off before he kept going.

"No, stupid," she said. "Terry!"

"Terry? Good Lord, he's old enough to be her father."

"Don't be silly," she said. "He's twenty-two and she's sixteen. By the time she's old enough to get married, it will be an ideal age difference."

2

★ ★ ★

I wasn't sure at first what to make of Chief Jim Billie of the Seminole Indian tribe. The Seminoles had earned a reputation as ferocious warriors in the 1880s when they lived in the Everglades and battled the U.S. government. In later years the Seminoles took to alligator wrestling, which proved a hit with tourists, but the tribe struggled with poverty. By the time I started visiting the Seminoles in 1980, they were enjoying some prosperity as the first Indian tribe in the country to offer high-stakes gambling. I asked Chief Billie if he was ready to write another check for Carter-Mondale. He smiled and told me he could maybe contribute $15,000, but it would depend on me.

"This time, Terry, I want you to take part in one of our ancient tribal customs," he said.

Great, he wanted me to smoke a peace pipe or do a rain dance. How tough could that be?

"Terry, we want you to wrestle an alligator," Billie said.

"Are you nuts?" I said. "I'm from Syracuse, New York. The most dangerous animal I've ever seen is a squirrel. I ain't wrestling no alligator."

"Oh, don't worry," Chief Billie said. "You only have to last three minutes and we'll bring you one that's drugged and toothless."

"Now we're talking," I said. "That I can do."

I'd had my first encounter with an alligator the year before and had not liked it. I was staying with the Swanns, and after dark one night I went for a run along the shore of Lake Virginia. I put my foot down on something solid and it moved! I could feel this huge, massive body jerk under my foot and the alligator's tail whipped around and hit my sneaker. I was lucky, though. The alligator was as scared as I was and scurried into the water. I screamed and dashed back to the Swann house at Olympic-record speed.

"I—I—stepped on an alligator," I told Doris Swann.

"You have to be careful," she said. "We lost our Irish setter, General, to one recently."

The Seminoles had an alligator-wrestling event coming up in three weeks and Chief Billie told me to mark the date on my calendar. I wasn't too worried about a drugged, toothless alligator, and for those three weeks I let my mouth get ahead of my brain. I told everybody in Washington about the alligator I'd be wrestling down in Florida with the Seminole Indian tribe in Broward County. I left out the small details that the beast was going to have no teeth and be dosed with tranquilizers.

Tom Donilon, the buddy who got me my first job in politics, called to tell me he had personally briefed President Carter, who thought that alligator wrestling for a campaign contribution sounded crazy.

"Stop him from doing it," Carter said. "We don't need the money that bad."

Tom dutifully passed on that message to me, but he knew me too well to think there was any chance he could talk me out of it.

Next came a call from the Vice President, Walter Mondale.

"Terry, what's this I hear about you and an alligator?" Fritz asked me. "Is this really happening?"

"Yes, sir," I said. "In about a week. It's fifteen grand for the campaign." He thought I was insane, but didn't try to change my mind.

"Good luck," he said.

The big day rolled around and Kevin Foley and I drove out to the reservation, where hundreds of people had shown up for the event along with several cameras, reporters, and *Newsweek* magazine. Chief Billie had a problem. Now that so many people had paid money to see me wrestle an alligator, his credibility was on the line. The people had a right to see real alligator wrestling, not a fraud perpetrated with a drugged, toothless beast.

"If you're going through with it, you've got to do the real thing," he told me. "That means wrestling Jumper, all eight feet and two hundred sixty pounds of him."

Now I really started to sweat. What had I gotten into? I had told so many people I'd be alligator wrestling, and the press and a big crowd were waiting to watch. My pride would not let me entertain any notion of backing down.

"Okay, Chief, tell me how we do this," I said to Billie.

He took me into his office and slowly walked me through the whole thing.

"You have to hold onto the mouth," he said. "An alligator's jaw muscles are so strong, he can bite down with a thousand pounds of pressure, but the muscles he uses to open his mouth are relatively weak, so your only hope is to keep that mouth shut and not let a thumb or finger slip in there. If he gets his mouth open, you're in for it."

He called out to someone who worked in his office and this guy came in and proudly held up his thumb and three fingers, showing where he'd lost one to an alligator.

"You also have to watch the tail," Chief Billie told me. "It's so strong, he can whip it around and snap one of your vertebrae."

This whole scene was becoming a nightmare. We left Chief Billie's office and the crowd that had gathered outside gave me a big cheer when they saw me walk out in my white Adidas T-shirt and sweatpants, pale and shaky. I smiled weakly and gave a big wave, but my smile faded when an old pickup truck pulled up with Jumper the alligator in the back. You could hear the noise before you even saw the truck, he was so loud. Jumper was thrashing around back there, banging on the metal with his tail. He had a burlap sack over his head and was madder than hell. It took four men to carry him out of the pickup and lay him on the ground two feet in front of me.

My first surprise as I straddled the beast was the smell. Oh man, that alligator reeked! You may think you've smelled bad breath, but until you've gotten up close to an alligator's snout and smelled the stench of decaying flesh emanating from its belly, you really don't know bad breath. I was terrified I was going to lose my grip and old Jumper would chomp down two of my fingers like Cheetos or whip me with his huge tail.

Chief Billie pulled off the burlap sack and slipped the noose off Jumper's jaws. I felt an instant of such raw terror, about a year's supply of adrenaline kicked loose all in that first second. I struggled to get my knees wedged on each side of Jumper so his tail couldn't hit me. I wrapped my hands around his mouth and held on as tightly as I could. My heart was racing so fast, I thought I might pass out. I only had to make it three minutes, but it felt like I'd been on Jumper for two hours.

Finally I felt Chief Billie's arm coming over my shoulder and grabbing the snout of the alligator and bending his head back to immobilize him. Billie told me to scoot off Jumper's back and scoot I did. The crowd cheered me like I was some kind of Roman gladiator. Billie and another Seminole tied his jaws shut again, and four of them carried him off to the pickup and back to the swamp.

As we watched the pickup drive away, I turned to Chief Billie and said, "Where's my check?"

Billie didn't waste any time. We went back to his office and he pulled out the checkbook and a bottle of whiskey. I accepted both. I felt I'd earned it.

I was so relieved to survive with all my fingers in place, I couldn't stop smiling, and now Chief Billie and I were buddies. *Newsweek* ran an article the next week about my three hair-raising minutes with Jumper, and six years later, *LIFE* magazine ran a huge picture of me sitting atop Jumper in a mud pit, the trousers of my suit rolled up to the knees, but this time with his jaws tied shut. For years my reputation as an alligator wrestler was the first thing people asked me about. Just to prove that alligator wrestling is risky even for an old pro, Chief Billie lost a finger to an alligator in February 2000 and preserved it in a little jar he carried around with him to show people.

"I love my daddy," Chip Carter said when he heard that I'd wrestled Jumper. "But I don't love him *that* much."

★

WE DIDN'T KNOW IT right away, but Jimmy Carter's reelection hopes probably went south on him the night in April 1980 when the attempt to rescue the U.S. hostages being held in Iran turned into a fiasco. There was a dust storm raging and one of the helicopters the military had sent in crashed into a transport plane, starting a fire that killed eight soldiers. When the news hit I was in San Diego with Carter-Mondale chairman Bob Strauss and national treasurer Evan Dobelle. I remember how devastated we were. The next day we found out Secretary of State Cyrus Vance, who had opposed the rescue attempt, had resigned in protest.

We were in a tough spot with Carter sticking to his Rose Garden strategy of staying at the White House and sending out the Vice President and First Lady to campaign for him. You need your biggest star to go out there and get people excited, and if you don't have that, it's like your legs are cut out from underneath you. All that year we ran into people who had been major donors for Carter in 1976 and never heard from any Carter people again. They were ticked off, too. That taught me how foolish it was to alienate your own supporters needlessly, never inviting them to see the President for a quick visit to boost their morale. I vowed to myself that if I was ever in a position to influence future Democratic Presidents, we would not repeat that mistake.

Mondale did so many events for us, I got to know him well and also got a chance to study his political style. Just like his fellow senator from Minnesota, Hubert Humphrey, Mondale believed passionately that the government was there to help people, and I loved talking to him about his years in politics. Fritz was in his own world in some ways, which led to a lot of laughs. One time we had a fund-raiser at San Francisco developer Walter Shorenstein's unbelievably beautiful old mansion in the Santa Cruz Mountains, and they went all out with the catering, the whole white-glove treatment with candlelight and you name it.

Fritz greeted a group of businessmen who had flown out to California for the event and, being Fritz, was just as nice as he could be to them and their dates for the evening. He asked them how they were doing and where they were from and so on, all in that good-natured Minnesota accent of his.

I thought I was going to bust a gut. Walter Shorenstein was sixty-five by then, but he and I got one look at these donors' dates and we could tell they were all hookers. Shorenstein didn't say anything and neither did I. We just smiled and waited until later when we could roar with laughter. The Vice President had no idea. He was chatting away, happy as could be. We were terrified he was going to invite them to the White House. But that was Fritz. He was from Minnesota and treated everybody like they were attending a church social in St. Paul.

I loved working with Walter Shorenstein, who had been a Democratic Party stalwart since the Johnson campaign in 1964. Walter arrived penniless in San Francisco after World War II, eventually owned or managed 60 percent of the commercial buildings in San Francisco, and funded the Joan Barone Center at Harvard in his daughter's memory. He and I had almost a father-son relationship for more than twenty years. I loved doing fund-raisers with Walter because he was never bashful about asking the people who did business with him to contribute to the Democratic Party. The man who distributed the millions of rolls of toilet paper to all his buildings was always good for a check, along with all of Walter's other vendors.

During Mondale's run for the '84 nomination for President, he was always looking for new fund-raisers. Nate Landow, a Maryland developer and top Mondale fund-raiser, brought Bob Farmer, another fund-raiser, on a trip to Texas so he could get to know Fritz. One morning after breakfast at the Holiday Inn in Fort Worth, where they were staying, Nate brought Bob up to Fritz's room for a chat.

"There's something I want to tell you, Mr. Vice President," Bob said.

"Whatever it is, Bob, I'm sure it's no problem," he said.

There was an awkward pause.

"Mr. Vice President," Bob said finally. "I want you to know that I've come out of the closet."

Bob waited to see if Fritz would react badly. He waited and waited. Fritz didn't have any reaction at all. He just looked very, very confused. Finally Bob left, eager to be on his way, and Fritz asked Nate what it was all about.

"What did he mean?" he asked, totally serious. "*Why* was he in my closet?"

★

I HAD LEARNED BY NOW that getting the commitments was often a lot easier than collecting, and I knew this was one area where my energy and persistence could pay off. I had a little trouble collecting on a commitment from T. A. Wilson, who had started at Boeing as an engineer and worked his way up to CEO. Wilson made a $5,000 commitment to me for a Rosalynn Carter event in Seattle and had not honored it yet, despite my calls to his office. We needed that $5,000. Once the commitment came in, we counted on that money. It's a good thing I don't mind getting up early. I hopped out of bed at four in the morning, studied my Seattle map, and showed up at Wilson's house before dawn and waited for him to come fetch his newspaper.

"Good morning, sir!" I said cheerfully when he came out in his bathrobe.

Wilson never knew what hit him. He could see there was only one way to get rid of me and came through with the checks. He actually laughed, he got such a kick out of my chutzpah. That story made the rounds, and soon people almost expected to see me turning up at all hours or showing up at their vacation homes, another move I started pulling that year.

One of my more unusual calls was to Florida Congressman Bill Nelson, who had made a commitment for $5,000 and had not paid up yet. This was in January 1986, just before Nelson was about to lift off on the space shuttle *Columbia*. I wasn't going to take any chances and talked my way through the switchboard at the Kennedy Space Center and somehow got ahold of Nelson.

"Bill, where's my five?" I said.

"Holy cow, Terry, I'm about to go up in the shuttle," he said. "Are you nuts?"

"Listen, I'm worried," I said. "Get me the five before you go up into space."

"Okay, I'll call my office," he said. "You'll get the money. Don't worry about it."

I got my money, and Nelson returned safely from that mission ten days later.

A highlight of my life was taking my parents to the White House on May 14, 1980, to a reception for key contributors. My dad had been working for the Democratic Party half his life and here he was, a few minutes away from shaking hands with the President of the United States at the White House. His favorite expression for years had been, "You always need to play in the *big ballpark*," and it didn't get any bigger than 1600 Pennsylvania Avenue. My mother was busy being proud of me. She was my biggest fan and kept close track of all the work I'd done roaming the country to shake loose contributions for the Carter-Mondale reelect. Finally our names were announced and we stepped up to smile and shake hands with President Carter and the First Lady. Both Carters looked a little tired, which was understandable given all their worries, but to me it didn't matter. I was just thrilled to be there. Then I looked over at my mother and saw she was frowning at Rosalynn for not being more enthusiastic.

Bob Strauss noticed, too.

"These are the parents of our best fund-raiser," he said to the First Lady.

Rosalynn didn't say anything and my mother was so mad, she about had steam coming out of her ears.

"Well, *he* loves *you* anyway," she said to the First Lady.

"Oh, I love Terry," Rosalynn said.

My mother stalked into the East Room and was as mad as a wet hen. I couldn't get her to calm down. Days later she was still talking about how annoyed she was.

As for me, I loved Rosalynn Carter. Because of the Rose Garden strategy, I had been working closely with the First Lady, traveling all over the country. In fact, the next day I had to call over to her secretary about something we had in the works.

"That was Terry McAuliffe," her secretary told Rosalynn. "You met his parents last night, I believe."

"I certainly did!" the First Lady said.

I guess my mom made more of an impression on Rosalynn than she knew. I never had much of a chance to talk to President Carter at that time because of the Rose Garden strategy, but years later Carter was one of the first individuals who endorsed me for DNC chairman, even though I was running against the former mayor of Atlanta, right there in his state, which was very important for me.

My first ride on Air Force One was that year, too. I was sitting in one of the forward cabins having lunch with Evan Dobelle when the President appeared and sat down next to me. This was my first in-depth discussion with a U.S. President. Carter spent the next thirty minutes quizzing me about my childhood, ambitions, and political views. I remember thinking to myself: *With all this man has on his mind, why is he spending so much time with me?* I asked the President how he felt the election was going and he told me that Americans were decent, hardworking folks and would ultimately make the right decision. I remember how relaxed and easygoing he was, sitting there with a sweater over his tie, sipping an iced tea.

After he'd gone back up front, I picked up the phone and called as many of my Syracuse friends as I could. They would say hello and hear: "This is Air Force One, please hold for Mr. McAuliffe." They loved those calls, which usually helped them get dates. You couldn't beat that for an ice-breaker down at the local bar: "I got a call from Air Force One today."

Four years earlier, the Democratic National Convention was in New York and my dad and I were so thrilled to be there that we waited in a hotel lobby for an hour to get a brief glimpse of the future President. This time I was back in New York for another convention and I was the party's chief fund-raiser, a fresh new face with a pocketful of podium passes. I had a blast with all my buddies from Syracuse down working for me. I was part of the inner circle now and had the event totally wired. Sometimes I couldn't believe I had come so far so fast. I half-expected to wake up and find myself back in the crowded hotel lobby with my dad, eager for any kind of glimpse of Carter.

We saw the polls showing the race to be neck-and-neck a week before Election Day and we thought we were going to win the thing, we really did. The last weekend before the election, the Iranian hostage situation jumped back into the news and that just killed us. Everyone was speculating that the hostages were going to be released any day, but it turned out to be another false rumor. The American people were sick and tired by then of having their hopes for the hostages raised and dashed. We were toast. Reagan swamped us at the polls and the Republicans took control of the Senate for the first time since 1952. I was in shock and as depressed about politics as I'd ever been.

The next month it was time for the annual meeting of the National Governors' Association. Harry Hughes, who was then the governor of Maryland, brought all the Democratic governors together to survey the wreckage of the defeat and to try to put their heads together to see where we should go from there as a party.

Exhibit A at that meeting was one of the big surprise losers of 1980, the young governor of Arkansas, Bill Clinton. No one had thought he was vulnerable, but he raised fees on the state car tags, and Carter put him in a terrible position by reneging on a promise not to send more Cuban refugees to Arkansas. Clinton was still looking shell-shocked that December and nobody was quite sure he would be able to overcome the tough loss, which made him the youngest ex-governor in U.S. history. How's that for a distinction?

Clinton sat me down that December to pick my brain on the Democratic Party's finances. It was the first time we met. Even though I was only twenty-three, I had been the chief money man for the party and the Carter campaign, and Clinton wanted to get my take on how we were doing, since he was being talked about as a top candidate for DNC chairman. He told me he wasn't ready to give up on running for governor again and would probably stay in Arkansas and take a job in a law firm. I remember having the same reaction to Clinton that a lot of people did. I thought he was energetic and had a big future. Everybody said, "This guy will be President of the United States someday." Your natural reaction when you hear that about yet another young up-and-comer is, "Sure thing, buddy." But with Clinton, you could see it. He was very smart and had tremendous magnetism. I guess I made an impression on Clinton, too.

"What is a sixteen-year-old kid doing being the finance director of the Democratic Party?" he asked Peter G. Kelly, the DNC treasurer.

I must have forgotten to wear my fake glasses that day.

★

REAGAN'S INAUGURATION hit us all like a kick in the gut, and not just for the obvious reasons. President Carter was racing the clock trying to free the hostages before Reagan was inaugurated, and it didn't look as if he would make it. Then Inauguration Day came and exactly five minutes after Reagan was sworn in, the U.S. hostages were finally released after 444 days in captivity. A former National Security Council (NSC) staffer named Gary Sick spent years investigating and put together a strong case that a deal had occurred between Reagan's people and the Iranians to sway the elections by delaying the release of the hostages—and in return for helping Reagan, the Iranians would be rewarded with weapons shipments from Israel.

Let me tell you why I'm sure the Reagan people had a hand in this. First of all, the arms transfers from Israel to Iran began almost immediately after

Reagan became President. Second, the main defense of the Reagan people was that it would have been too terrible a crime for Reagan to cook up secret deals with the Iranians in violation of U.S. law, but that is just what the Reagan administration did when it sold arms to the Iranians and used the profits to illegally fund the *contra* rebels in Nicaragua.

Finally, the key to Reagan's deal on the Iranian hostages was Bill Casey, a swashbuckling Cold War spy master who served Reagan as campaign manager and CIA director. Sick's sources told him that Casey met with the Iranians in a Madrid hotel in July 1980 and again several months later, and made the deal. I had no trouble believing Casey, a walking, talking Graham Greene character if ever there was one, had been able to hide his role in the deal with Iran, because I had it on good authority that he'd hid his role in illegally arming the *contras*.

In November 1986, as the Iran-Contra scandal was unraveling, I flew down to the *contra* camps with a group of congressional staffers on a trip paid for by a private group that supported democracy. Our first morning in Tegucigalpa, we were greeted at the airport by some American-trained pilots who would fly us to the *contra* camps in Huey helicopters. I won't say who they were working for, but let me put it this way: It was pretty clear these boys weren't retired Delta pilots. This was not going to be just any helicopter flight.

"We're going to be flying really low to the treetops," one of the pilots explained. "Don't be alarmed. This is to avoid SAM-7 antiaircraft missiles."

How low was really low? I'd find out soon enough.

"And finally, if we crash, remember one important thing," the pilot said. "Do not attempt to exit the helicopter until the blades stop turning."

That sounded like sensible advice to me. I strapped myself in up front close to our pilot, helmet and everything, and immediately started making friends with him and his copilot. Hey, when you grow up hearing war stories at the dinner table every night, the way I did, you're excited to be with these guys who are used to being in the thick of the action.

Once we neared Nicaraguan air space, the risk of getting shot down suddenly rocketed up from negligible to very, very plausible, and our flight veered from straight-ahead and businesslike to helter-skelter. My buddy the pilot jerked us hard left, so we rolled more than halfway over, and then jerked us hard right, so we rolled back over the other way. He would dip the nose to send us right down over the tops of the trees, and then we would drop down into a crevice between two mountains, and trees would be rushing by on each side of us. It was an unbelievable ride, like Disneyland for adults, and finally all I could do was laugh as I sat there holding on for dear life.

The copilot saw me laughing, and got a kick out of that.

"Man," he said. "You've got a big pair for a first-timer."

"Why—are—we—doing this?" I shouted over the clack-clack-clack of the rotor.

He grinned.

"See that hill back there with the rocky peak?" he asked me.

I twisted around and took a look back where we had just flown.

"Yeah?" I said, wondering where this was going.

"We were flying Director Casey along this same route a couple days ago," he told me.

Now he had my attention.

"Right back there, they locked on to us with a missile launcher," he said. "The warning lights went off and the alarm started beeping. Two more seconds and we'd have been vaporized."

The day I spent in the camps talking to *contra* leaders Adolfo Calero and Enrique Bermudez and meeting the troops happened to come just as the scandal was hitting the papers. As I was eating lunch with Calero, Attorney General Edwin Meese was confronting an obscure lieutenant colonel named Oliver North about his role in the affair. North admitted to taking money from selling weapons to Iran and diverting it to the *contras*. At first no one could believe Reagan had really gone to such extremes to curry favor with the Ayatollah Khomeni, one of America's biggest enemies. The facts soon became impossible to ignore.

"We did not, repeat, did not trade weapons or anything else for hostages— nor will we," Reagan said on national television. "Those who think we have 'gone soft' on terrorism should take up the question with Colonel Qaddafi. We have not, nor will we, capitulate to terrorists."

In fact, Reagan *was* soft on terrorism. When Hezbollah terrorists killed 241 U.S. marines in Lebanon, the Reagan administration took no action. All Reagan did was change the subject two days later by invading a small Caribbean island that nobody had ever heard of. Reagan tried to insist Grenada was of key strategic importance, and no one believed him; but for the most part attention shifted from the 241 dead marines. Not everyone was so forgetful: As longtime White House counterterrorism expert Richard Clarke reported in his book, Osama bin Laden would later cite the weak U.S. response to that grisly murder of the marines in Lebanon as a sign of weakness—in effect, a green light to take further terrorist action against us.

Few came out worse in the Iran-Contra scandal than the first President Bush. He was clearly trying to save himself from prosecution and scandal when he issued a series of pardons on Christmas Eve 1992 during his final days as President, just before Bill Clinton was sworn in. Bush pardoned six top officials, all to cover up his own involvement in the scandal, including former Defense Secretary Cap Weinberger and Bud McFarlane, the former national security adviser. This was not only a transparent effort by Bush to save his own skin, Bush was also interfering with Judge Lawrence Walsh's ongoing federal investigation. Judge Walsh was so outraged, he said that "the Iran-Contra cover-up, which has continued for more than six years, has now been completed." The pardons stopped two pending cases and nullified one conviction and three guilty pleas. One *New York Times* columnist, Anthony Lewis, was so appalled, he compared the first President Bush to Richard Milhous Nixon, dubbing him "George Milhous Bush."

When Reagan's Secretary of State George Shultz published his memoirs in 1993, he spilled the beans on how fast and loose Vice President Bush had been with the truth during the critical days of the Iran-Contra scandal. Shultz recalled pulling aside a Bush aide on November 8, 1986, to ask how the Vice President could possibly be claiming ignorance on TV. "The Vice President was in one key meeting that I know of, on January 7, 1986, and he made no objection to the proposal for arms sales to Iran, with the clear objective of getting hostages released in the process," Shultz wrote.

The Iran-Contra affair should be taught in detail to every high school student in America, so we can do a better job of learning from past mistakes. Cynical secret deals with our enemies to win elections will always come back to haunt their perpetrators later. It all started when Reagan's people schemed with the Iranians to deny Jimmy Carter an honest election. Once the Republicans started messing with the basic integrity of democracy, they were well on their way to stealing an election outright in Florida in 2000.

3

★ ★ ★

If I have an advantage over most people in Washington, it's that I've spent thirty years actively involved in Democratic politics but I'm not really of Washington. Sure, I show up with my wife every year at Sam Donaldson and his wife Jan Smith's great holiday party, and if I'm at my daughter's soccer game and run into Vice President Dick Cheney as he's out there to watch his granddaughter, I say hello and usually get a grunted "Hello, Terry" back. But I'm not of Washington in the sense that since the early '80s my work has taken me all over the country, and I've been lucky to have such a wide variety of experiences in and outside of politics, it's like I've lived several parallel lives. I've also had great luck in meeting fascinating characters who have become legends in their fields.

The first time I showed up in Los Angeles to raise money, I was a twenty-two-year-old kid from Syracuse who didn't know anybody. I figured I might as well put in a call to Lew Wasserman, the MCA-Universal chairman, who was the King of Hollywood. He started as a theater usher and worked his way up; by 1979 he was in his midsixties and had been on top for decades. He had helped the Carter campaign in '76, so I figured it was worth a shot, but I wondered if he'd even take my call.

"Mr. Wasserman, Terry McAuliffe," I said. "I'm working for President Carter. We have an event coming up. Can I come see you?"

"Sure, when do you want to do it?" he said.

This wasn't so hard! I showed up the next afternoon at 100 Universal Plaza in Universal City, a tall black glass tower, and went up to Wasserman's office and was ushered into the center of power in Hollywood. There was the man himself, with the big black glasses and white hair, waving me into his office. One amazing thing about Lew was that he never had a single piece of paper on his desk: It always looked swept clean. That was how he did business.

"Mr. Wasserman, I need you to raise one hundred thousand dollars," I said.

"Fine, I'll do it," he said. "What else you want from me?"

He'd caught me off guard. I'd thought I'd have to work a little harder.

"Am I chairing the event?" he asked.

"You can have whatever title you want," I said.

He asked me how long I was going to be in town, and when I said I'd be there for a few weeks, he insisted I stay in an extra room at his daughter Lynn's house, which I did, and got to know Lew's grandchildren, Casey and Carol. Lew Wasserman had been a great fund-raiser for the Democrats since the Kennedy administration and he'd seen plenty of young men like me come and go, but for some reason we really hit it off. He always told me he loved young hustlers because he still viewed himself as one, which I guess he was.

"Why do you never have any paper on your desk, Lew?" I asked him after we'd gotten to know each other better.

"Terry, let me tell you something," he said. "If I get a piece of paper here, I either throw it out or act on it. I don't let anything sit."

I've always followed that rule myself. At the end of the day you will never find papers on my desk. If you let things pile up, you'll always be playing catch-up. Another piece of advice Lew gave me was: Always return every phone call. That's another lesson I follow to this day. Sometimes in the heat of a presidential campaign I'd get backed up, but ultimately my call sheet would be clean.

Lew invited me to his house in January 1984, along with California congressman Tony Coelho and his wife, Phyllis, and Michigan Congressman John Dingell and his wife, Debbie. When we got there I was amazed to find myself at a small gathering of Hollywood legends. I'm the guy who didn't even know who the singer Paul Simon was and I have always been oblivious to celebrity, but I do like people who know how to have a great time, and the crew at Lew's house were world-class. This was when Johnny Carson was in his heyday with *The Tonight Show,* and after dinner he got up and did a monologue that was just like what he did on TV, except funnier because he could say anything he wanted. Carol Burnett got up and sang. I talked to Sidney Poitier, who started a national dialogue on race with his starring roles in *Guess Who's Coming to Dinner* and *In the Heat of the Night,* and he was a real gentleman. Debbie Dingell thought Cary Grant was the most charming man she'd ever met, and Kirk Douglas was just like he is in all his movies.

Tony sat next to Angie Dickinson, a real bombshell, who had starred in the '70s TV show *Police Woman* and who was very smart. The next year we were back at Lew's for another dinner and Angie was there again and was the life of the party. Placido Domingo sang for us and we all danced around the room. If you judge people by what kind of party they give and whether they can bring a group of people together for a relaxed, thoroughly enjoyable evening, Lew and Edie Wasserman were two of the all-time greats. I learned a lot from Lew about how to conduct yourself in business, politics, and life, and I feel lucky to have known him.

★

NEITHER DOROTHY SWANN nor I had any idea her mother had predicted we would end up getting married, and we'd have been awfully surprised to hear it back in 1979. A couple times when I was down in Florida on the fund-raising trail and Dorothy was going out with a group of her girlfriends, I would come along to have a few laughs, but it was like I was the big brother or cousin. They were high school kids and I was out of college, so it was as if we were from different planets.

Dorothy, who came from an old Southern family, was born in Durham, North Carolina, while her father was attending Duke Law School. She graduated high school in 1981 and went away to college at the University of Wyoming. Laramie was a long way from Winter Park. She loved the adventure of living in a different part of the country and the cultural contrasts to the world she'd grown up in. She ran across many gung-ho Republicans out there and got a kick out of the typical dorm-room décor: Reagan posters and "Welcome the MX Missile" bumper stickers. The college town had a lot going on, with its colorful and unique mix of academics, coeds, cowboys, oil and gas folks, and the truckers who rolled through on I-80 as they headed cross-country. Dorothy, of course, was a true-blue Democrat and environmentalist, and while she enjoyed teasing back and forth with her mostly Republican classmates, she found a few like her, too. When I saw Dorothy again that next summer, things were different.

Just as Jack had instilled his passion for politics in me, Richard inspired Dorothy. She decided to move to Washington her junior year in the hope of working on the issues she cared so passionately about. Once she transferred to Catholic University in Washington, we started dating, though with my heavy travel schedule it was hard to find time to spend together. One weekend in October 1983 we took a trip to Cape Cod. I had bought a condo in Dennisport, Massachusetts, with my brother Tom, and I wanted to inspect my purchase. No sooner had Dorothy and I arrived than the phone rang. It was Tip O'Neill, the Speaker of the House. Somehow he had gotten wind that I was on the Cape.

"Hello, Mr. Speaker!" I said, surprised as can be.

Dorothy shot me a knowing look.

"Terry, why don't you come golfing with me tomorrow?" Tip asked in that great old Boston accent of his.

"Okay, Mr. Speaker," I said. "Terrific. . . . Dorothy, I've got to go golfing with the Speaker tomorrow," I announced, hanging up the phone.

The next morning I got up early, took the car, and met Tip at Eastward Ho! in Chatham, leaving Dorothy in the condo. She had grown up around politics, and as long as I've known her she has always understood that my work was going to suck up a lot of my time.

Would I go golfing with Tip O'Neill? Of course I would! Tip was not only the biggest figure in the Democratic Party at that time, a legendary force in Congress, he was also a great storyteller and always fun to be around. Plus, he was Irish.

Everything out of Tip's mouth was Irish jokes or Irish stories, and I couldn't have been having any more fun if I'd been sitting in Limerick drinking Guinness with a bar full of leprechauns. Tip told me about the time he put together a good fund-raiser for Jack Kennedy and, late in the evening, the two men ducked into the men's room together.

"How did we do?" Kennedy asked him.

"About twenty grand, ten in cash, ten in checks," Tip told him.

"You keep the checks, I'll take the cash," Kennedy said.

That was sure a different era. (Definitely pre–McCain-Feingold!) Even if you had already heard Tip's stories or jokes, it didn't matter—the way he told them, they were still a riot. Tip had that big, white shock of hair and the big, bulbous W. C. Fields nose. He was like a walking caricature lifted straight from a political cartoon, but the thing about him was he never forgot who he was. He hated pretentiousness and taking on airs. He talked to everyone exactly the same, whether they were the elevator operator, or the person who cleans the toilets, or a CEO, or a President, or a lobbyist. The more downtrodden you were, the more time Tip had for you. He had huge hands and he would bear-hug waiters, waitresses, and busboys. I tell you, when Tip was in a restaurant, everyone in the place knew it.

Even at the peak of his power in the House, when Reagan and his advisers and half of Washington sat around discussing what Tip's next move might be, he always insisted on carrying his own luggage any time he was on the road. It was the damnedest thing. You'd be in an airport somewhere and there would be Tip O'Neill, instantly recognizable to everyone with that mane of white hair and the nose, shuffling through the terminal carrying his own bags.

Driving around Eastward Ho! with Tip that day on Cape Cod was a great adventure for me. That was Tip's favorite golf course, a breathtakingly beautiful layout near his summer house in Harwich Port. I couldn't believe my luck in having a day alone on the golf course with such a Hall of Fame Democrat, and I was so nervous on the first tee, I was sure I was going to hit my drive into the clubhouse. Tip put me at ease. He had the cigar going and the big, floppy hat on, and was just enjoying himself to the hilt. Tip only hit the ball about seventy yards at a time, but he was one steady golfer, hitting it straight as an arrow every time, driving seventy yards up, and then whacking it again, straight and true.

The only uncomfortable moments for me were in the golf cart. This was a hilly course and Tip was famous for being a big man. It's no exaggeration to say he barely fit into his seat. He would cut across a hilly fairway and I would get more nervous as the slope got steeper. I was sure the cart was going to flip over and send Tip and me rolling down the hill, golf clubs flying in every direction. Tip was always telling stories, and if I gave him any encouragement he was more likely to talk louder and to swing his arms, helping the story along. All it would take was one big jerk of his hand and there we would have gone, rolling down the hill. Years later I ran into Tip's daughter Susan and told her how jumpy I was in the golf cart that day.

"You *should* have been concerned!" she said. "He tipped it over on several occasions. Once he was out golfing with his friend John Griffin, and their cart rolled over and they tumbled all the way to the bottom of the hill. They were lucky the cart didn't crush them."

One thing Tip taught me was to never forget your roots and to always be proud of your hometown. That wasn't hard for me, because I loved growing up in Syracuse. In fact, whenever I went on TV as the DNC chairman, I always found a way to mention Syracuse, which I knew the people back home loved. They knew I hadn't forgotten them and never would, and to this day the Syracuse papers get a kick out of covering me as one of their favorite sons.

Tip O'Neill loved being from Boston. The man could not get three sentences out of his mouth without making some reference to his Boston Irish roots, and once he started with the stories and the jokes, there was no stopping him. The stories were Tip's way of reminding the people who came to Washington and accumulated power that they were only as good as their connection to the people back home. When Tip said, "All politics is local," the adage he made famous, he wasn't talking about some calculation or formula or political cliché—he was just describing life as he knew it.

The man also loved to play cards. He couldn't wait to pull out a deck, and then wanted to play for hours, making sure you were having as much fun as he was. I used to play gin rummy with Tip when we would go on campaign trips, and it would always cost me at least a hundred bucks. I never beat him and I'd been playing cards all my life. Back at the McAuliffe house on Overlook Drive in Syracuse, we would play "Pitch," a rowdy card game, into the late hours. We were so into our game of Pitch the night of my ninety-one-year-old grandmother Minnie's Irish wake, we couldn't find any paper and kept score on the back of her mass card, which Minnie must have loved, watching from above.

Tip and I finished up our round that afternoon and it just wouldn't have been civilized to do anything other than head into the clubhouse to play some cards. Now, understand, where other men might have tired of talking by that point, Tip was just getting his second wind. I felt like I was soaking up a priceless sense of perspective about politics, about people in general, and about all the crazy things you could count on happening sooner or later.

I just couldn't leave early that day, even though I was starting to wonder if Dorothy would have a shotgun ready for me when I finally headed back to the condo. So much for our romantic weekend.

"Terry, you've been gone twelve hours!" she said when I finally clomped into the condo in my golf spikes. "How long does it take to play eighteen holes of golf?"

"Honey, it was the Speaker!" I said. "You won't believe the afternoon I had."

I think, for Dorothy, that day was the perfect precursor for what her life with me would be like. She was just learning to love the ways of the Irish in Democratic politics. Eventually she forgave me, but she still teases me about leaving her stuck alone the entire day while I was off having the time of my life.

★

DOROTHY AND I MADE THE MOST of the rest of our time on Cape Cod that weekend and ran all over the place and saw as much as we could. It was her first trip to the Cape and she loved it. But only a few days later Richard Swann called and gave me some terrible, terrible news. Dorothy's mother had been playing tennis that morning and literally put the ball in the air to serve, and had a heart attack and collapsed. She was gone.

I was devastated. The whole Swann family was so important to me, and Doris and I had been great friends from that first night I showed up at the house in Winter Park and we ate pot roast and drank beer and made each other laugh. Nobody loved a good joke as much as Doris. She was just a very special person, someone I felt deeply about, and her friendship had meant a lot to me.

Richard asked me to find Dorothy and tell her the news in person. That was probably the hardest thing I've ever had to do. Dorothy was interning for Florida Congressman Bill Nelson that fall, answering phones, handling correspondence, running errands all over Capitol Hill, and greeting visitors to the office. I felt so awful, I had to stand outside the door of Bill Nelson's office for several minutes and try to get myself ready to face her. I walked into the office and spotted Dorothy sitting at the reception desk. A big smile came over her face when she saw me. She assumed at first that I was there as a surprise to take her to lunch. But almost instantly her smile faded. As soon as she saw my face, she knew something was very, very wrong.

"Terry, what is it?" she asked as I took her out into the corridor, where we could speak in private.

She had never seen me looking so stricken and assumed someone had died.

"My dad?" she asked me.

I couldn't even answer. I just shook my head.

"Not Christian?" she asked.

Her brother Christian was a competitive waterskier, ranked fourth in the world at one point, and accidents were not uncommon. I shook my head again and tried to speak, but it was like my mouth and jaw weren't working.

"Doris," I croaked, barely able to get the word out.

To be honest, I'd rather not remember those moments in too much detail; it was such a gut-wrenching, emotional time. The rest of the day passed in a kind of slow-motion blur, as if you weren't quite sure what was happening but had the sense that whatever it was, it would never end. I drove Dorothy back to her dorm right away, helped her pack, and then booked our flight down to Florida that afternoon. To give us more privacy I put us in first class, which Dorothy had never flown before, and I was glad I had. She seemed surprised I was getting on the plane with her, but I wasn't about to leave her alone that day.

After I got Dorothy home to Winter Park, I turned around and went right back to the airport to catch a flight back to Washington. I wanted to give the family some time to be alone together. Later that week, I flew back for the funeral and that was one of the saddest times of my life. Doris was forty-three years old and the mother of four children: Dorothy, at nineteen, was the oldest; her brother Christian was seventeen; her brother Campbell was thirteen; and the youngest, her sister Happy, was just eleven. Up until that day on the tennis court, Doris was a healthy, vivacious woman, bursting with energy. Staying there with the Swann family so soon after her death, it was like the whole house was in shock.

4

★ ★ ★

We Democrats had been reeling through most of 1981, Reagan's first year, and the talk all over Washington was that this Reagan Revolution was going to take back control of the House of Representatives in 1982, as the Republicans had taken back the Senate in 1980. However, the one thing standing in their way was Congressman Tony Coelho. Tony was the first freshman ever elected to head the Democratic Congressional Campaign Committee (DCCC), and he set about revolutionizing it. He brought a business approach to its operations and agreed to take the job only on the condition that he would have a say in how the money he raised would be spent. Once he took over, he made a major break with past tradition. Instead of handing out contributions to political buddies, the DCCC would now focus on competitive races and try to help challengers who could knock off Republican incumbents and gain new seats for us.

The experts all predicted that we would get blown out again in the 1982 congressional elections after our setback two years earlier. Everyone thought we were going to lose control of the House, but thanks to Tony we had the resources to do what we needed to do. On November 2 Tony invited me and several others to spend Election Night in the Speaker's suite of offices in the Capitol to watch the returns. What a night it was for us. We ended up stunning the experts and winning twenty-six seats in the House, one Senate seat, and seven governorships. Everybody was in great spirits. The Democrats were a force in Washington again, and the Speaker came over and put his big arms around me and thanked me for the money I'd help raise for the DCCC. We knew things were going to be different after that. Bob Michel, the Republican leader in the House, told *The New York Times* that night: "We're going to be at the mercy of Tip. It's a heck of an obstacle to overcome every time."

★

I DID MY BEST to avoid joining the Mondale campaign when they made their first big push to get me in the summer of 1982. I'd started as a full-time student at Georgetown Law School the year before, was raising money for the DCCC and the DNC, and had started several investment businesses. One of these companies was McAuliffe and Kelly Financial Services, started with my longtime friend Peter D. Kelly from Los Angeles. Peter also had a passion for politics and had served as the California Democratic state chairman. He and I had so much Irish blarney that we raised over $500 million for investment deals in our first six months of operation.

Bob Beckel, the campaign manager, asked me to write the fund-raising plan for Mondale's '84 campaign, and of course I was fired up to be handed such an amazing opportunity. What a great challenge for a twenty-five-year-old. Understand, people think of fund-raising as just sucking up the money that's out there, like a giant vacuum cleaner; but in practice you only succeed at raising money if you have a good, smart plan to energize people. Politics is a battle against your opponents and the money side is a big part of that struggle. Mondale and Jim Johnson, his campaign chairman, were asking me to be a key part of strategizing Mondale's approach to winning the nomination and the presidency.

But I had to think twice. The pressure was really starting to get to me. My ego said yes, do it, and I knew I would love the work. But that was one of the few times in my life where a voice in my head told me to back off and think about the long haul. You could say I was a little starstruck when I first got involved in politics. That was not the case anymore. I had no illusions about politics. I knew by then it was a tough, unforgiving world, where you were either up or down, and if you were down, no one remembered or cared that you were up a month or a year or a decade earlier. I was twenty-five and on a roll. That could change and change fast. I needed to equip myself to have a long haul in politics. Plenty of young hustlers had made their mark early in politics and then vaporized. That was not going to be me. I was in politics to make a difference and to fight for people like folks back in Syracuse. If I took on too much and became a flash in the pan, I couldn't do that.

That was why I buckled down and decided it was time to make some money. I knew that without financial independence I would be a slave to fate. I figured I only needed to lock away a few million in my early twenties and then I could do my political work as a volunteer. That would buy me freedom of movement and peace of mind. You have more power in political campaigns if they're not paying you and you don't have to worry about being fired. Plus, if you're not doing it for the money, you never find yourself having to choose between your beliefs and your next paycheck.

★

ONE TIME in October 1985, we went to visit one of our supporters in Southern California who had just built a state-of-the-art video conference center, one of the first ever. Marty Salanger, my buddy from Syracuse whom I'd hired to work for me at the DCCC, went down to their headquarters in Washington and got the video conference going and could see me sitting there in L.A. with Tip O'Neill and Tony Coelho.

"See you tomorrow in New York," Marty said at the end of the video conference.

Marty and I were going to run in the New York City Marathon together, but first Tip, Tony, and I were flying up to San Francisco for an event that night at the Fairmont Hotel. Tip had figured we would spend the evening in the Ben Swig Suite watching the St. Louis Cardinals and Kansas City Royals in Game 7 of the World Series. The starting pitcher for the Cardinals was former Red Sox lefthander John Tudor, and as I've said, with Tip everything was Massachusetts. But I wouldn't be seeing the game, because after dinner I was catching the red-eye to New York.

"Let me get this straight," Tip said. "You're flying all night and then running twenty-six miles?"

"That's right," I said.

"I wish I had your energy," he said. "Twenty-six miles is a long *drive* for me."

I had been running marathons for years, usually with my brothers, John and Tom, and still run them. I have run fourteen and three-quarters—some with training, some without; some with sleep, some without. The weekend before the 1980 presidential election, my Syracuse buddies, Bob Irving and Steve Snyder, and all the Carter fund-raisers who had worked for me came back to Washington after their events and I took everyone out for a wild night on the town along with my roommates Tom Flynn and John Murphy. The bars closed and we got back to the house around three or four and were looking for something to drink; all we could find was this stuff that tasted like black licorice. Even now, just thinking about that taste makes me wince. We all did shots, and around five I informed my buddies that I had to go upstairs and get a little sleep because in three hours I was running my first marathon.

I stumbled out of bed at 6:30 A.M., found my gym shorts and sneakers, and surprised myself with how well I did, finishing with a time of 3:02:50, which meant I actually ran my first marathon in under three hours, because the start was so crowded with more than six thousand runners lined up that it took me more than five minutes just to get to the starting line. This was long before the days when they would give you a computer chip to put in your shoe to track just when you start and finish. My friends, meanwhile, had finally stirred around 11:00 A.M. and made a pathetic attempt to come out and watch me finish. Only one problem: Right at the end of the Marine Corps Marathon is a steep hill that juts up about forty yards and ends at the Iwo Jima Memorial. I was trucking along near the finish and saw my buddies and shouted, but these guys couldn't even make it up the hill, that's how wrecked they were. I kidded them about that for years.

The toughest time I've ever had running a marathon was the weekend before the 1984 presidential election when I collapsed during the New York City Marathon and landed in the hospital. I hadn't trained much because of all the campaign work I was doing, and the day of the marathon was hot and humid. I stupidly let enthusiasm get the better of my good sense and wore a heavy cotton Mondale-Ferraro T-shirt that didn't breathe at all. This was the end of October, but it felt like summer with the temperature reaching 79 degrees and humidity topping out at an unbearable 98 percent. A forty-eight-year-old Frenchman who had already run four marathons collapsed during the race that year and died, a first for the New York City Marathon.

Race organizers urged everyone to ease up on their pace because of the stifling conditions, and most runners were smart enough to follow their advice; but of course I knew better. I was having a great time, pumping my fist for people who saw my red-white-and-blue Mondale-Ferraro shirt and yelled "Right on!" at me as I ran past. I kept tugging at my shirt, which was drenched with sweat and felt more and more as if it was smothering me. My breathing didn't feel right and my thoughts jumped around strangely. I knew I should back off my usual pace, but my whole life I've always just let it fly. When I run I never stop. I hate trying to slow down. It always feels like more work to slow down and then try to rev up again. The first twenty miles of a marathon are the easy part. People always talk about hitting the wall just before making it the full 26.2 miles, but that day in New York it felt more like I was hit by a truck, or like I was an NFL quarterback who had just been sandwiched between two onrushing three-hundred-pound linemen.

I was so overheated, my body temperature had climbed to 106 degrees. If you had asked me my name, I'd have had to guess at an answer. The one thing I knew was that I was determined to finish the race. I looked like hell, I somehow came to understand, and people started staring at me as if they thought my head was about to explode.

"Get him out of the race!" people shouted.

I heard, but the words were distant and incomprehensible and felt like they had nothing to do with me. I started weaving sideways back and forth, and I do mean weaving. I'd bump into someone on my right side, then kind of wobble back to my left, and then list toward the right again and then back to the left again. I was doing these big, wide S-turns but I was intent on keeping moving, even when someone tried to intervene.

"Get your hands off me!" I yelled. "I'm going to finish this race!"

I had totally lost my mind. The last thing I remember is coming down a hill and crossing a bridge into Harlem. There were thousands of people everywhere crowding around to watch the race. Just after the bridge you had to make a sharp turn, but I kept going straight and ran right into the crowd. That was the best thing I did all day, because everyone could see I had fried my brain and had a serious case of heat exhaustion. They rushed me by ambulance to Harlem Hospital with IVs stuck into me and plunged me into a giant tub of ice water. That's what they do in extreme cases to get the body temperature down quickly because every minute it stays that high it kills huge numbers of brain cells. Maybe I'm a little brain-damaged. Hey, that would explain a lot, wouldn't it? At least then I'd have an excuse.

★

I DON'T NEED TO spend much time talking about my law school days be-cause there isn't that much to tell. I don't recommend to anyone doing law school the way I did. I attended Georgetown Law as a full-time student even as I continued to work full-time, running four businesses as well as raising money for the DCCC, the DNC, and the Mondale campaign. So you get the idea that attending class wasn't my top priority, and I latched onto some-thing one of my professors told me: "The Cs hire the Bs, and the As teach."

No one worked full-time while they were a full-time student at Georgetown Law, but I did—and then some. It was a good thing they didn't take attendance. My second year I went out to San Francisco to organize an event and ended up missing four weeks of classes. I came back and found I had missed a pop quiz in Professor Paul Rothstein's class. I went to see him during his office hours to ask about making it up.

"Professor Rothstein," I said, pronouncing it "Roth*steen*," "I missed your pop quiz, so let's talk."

"First of all," he said, "it's 'Roth*stine*.' "

Second of all, I could forget making up the pop quiz.

"You get an F," he said. "See you at the next one."

I took nine days off from my fund-raising and business work and devoted it all to law school to get ready for finals. I had not read any of the materials or attended many classes. But fortunately these were such big classes, you could buy prepared notes called Gilbert's or Emanuel's. Those were my lifeline. To be honest, I found law school somewhat boring. How could it compare to playing cards with Tip or planning strategy with Fritz?

My last final of law school was Torts 2, which was unnerving, since I'd only been to a few classes and had never bought the textbook. It was supposed to be a four-hour exam. I studied about four hours and finished the exam in half that time. I might have taken longer, but I had a barbecue at my house that evening and was eager to get home. I can't tell you how relieved I was walking out of there. I think I aged ten years in those three years, but I was able to make it through, helped along by a great group of friends, especially John Boland, Chris Petersen, Charlie Graves, and Gordon Boelter. Thanks, guys! I also want to thank my assistant, Alecia Dyer, who did so much to help get me through it. She probably deserves the degree more than I do.

The next year, I took the bar examination and had to learn the law from scratch, since I had missed so much of law school. They make you wait forever to get the results and it plays all kinds of havoc with your head. I knew I had a good chance of passing, despite everything, since I was good at taking tests and had seriously crammed. I also knew failure was a real possibility. Then I'd have to go through the whole thing again.

I called to get the results and was put on hold and it felt like I'd have to wait forever. All the worries I had been trying to hold back jumped into my head stronger than ever and I started sweating bullets. It was the most excruciating five minutes of my life. Had I finally pushed it too far? Was my luck going to run out? Finally I heard a little clicking sound and she was back.

"Congratulations!" she said. "You've passed!"

I was euphoric. Ever since I was in grammar school I'd wanted to be a lawyer, and like everyone, I'd always worried about passing the bar. That was my last obstacle. Now I had checked that box and could move on.

★

MONDALE MADE A BOLD CHOICE for his vice presidential candidate that year, nominating New York Congresswoman Geraldine Ferraro, and after four years of Reagan, people felt an intense, pent-up frustration with having the right-wingers in charge of the government. We really felt like we were going to storm out of San Francisco after our convention and take back the White House. Then Mondale gave his speech.

"Mr. Reagan will raise taxes, and so will I," he said. "He won't tell you! I just did!"

People were turning to each other in the crowd and saying, "Did he just say what I think he just said?" or shaking their heads in disbelief.

The second I heard Mondale say that, I knew we were in deep trouble. Mondale *was* telling the truth, as Reagan's exploding budget deficits were going to mortgage our children's future. However, voters did not want to hear the truth and I knew that Reagan would eat us alive on taxes.

Mario Cuomo, the New York governor, gave an eloquent, powerful keynote address that was one of the best moments for Democrats that year, and he had everyone buzzing about him as a presidential candidate in 1988. That speech should have been all anyone was talking about after the convention, that and the exciting choice of Ferraro as the first-ever woman on a major-party ticket, but instead they were talking about our nominee promising he'd raise taxes. That was a convention of missed opportunity. We had a two-point lead after the convention in San Francisco, even after we said we were going to raise taxes, and could have had much more of a bounce.

I'm not sure how much it would have mattered in the end. Reagan spent the whole campaign talking about how it was morning in America, which actually resonated with people. Heading into November, the polls were showing that Reagan might win all fifty states. I kept seeing these gigantic, enthusiastic crowds turning out for Mondale's campaign appearances and figured the polls were wrong. They weren't. Reagan won every state except Minnesota and the District of Columbia.

5

★ ★ ★

We all have our habits we're trying to break, and for me it's going on Fox News. I can't help myself. I love it. Some of my friends tell me I need to cut down because the Fox people slant everything toward an extreme right-wing view, but I say: "So what?" I have a great time and it's a priceless opportunity to get our message out to people who don't usually hear from living, breathing Democrats. Plus, if you show up when they want you to talk about issues they think favor Republicans, they don't have much choice but to let you pipe up now and then on your topics.

Fox called me in April 2006, when Republican leader Tom DeLay announced he was resigning from Congress, and asked me to come on John Gibson's show. Of course I jumped at the chance. I was going to enjoy every second of this one. Fox sent a car over to get me and just as we were pulling up in front of the Fox News building, I saw a commotion in the street behind me. A motorcade had pulled up and dropped off a bunch of people. A scrum of men in suits was heading for the building. I scanned the group quickly and let myself hope, but no, I couldn't be that lucky, could I? Actually, I could be. That's right: It was Tom DeLay himself.

"Oh, this is too good," I said to my driver as I jumped out of the car, clutching the printouts I'd been reading, and racing after DeLay and his posse. Susan Molinari, the former congresswoman from New York, was right next to him, and the two of them were talking so intently, DeLay didn't spot me making a move on him. I caught him completely by surprise. There was a whole bank of TV cameras following his every move that day, and I ran right up and put my arm around DeLay's shoulder.

"Leader, how are you doing?" I said.

"Great, Terry," he said, grinning up at me.

At first I couldn't tell if he was actually smiling or just pasting on that fake-looking grin he pulled out for his mug shot.

"I've got all my anti-DeLay talking points," I said, holding up the papers. "Anything you want to add to this?"

That got a big laugh. DeLay really seemed to be in a good mood. The bank of TV cameras was capturing everything we said or did, and DeLay leaned in so we could talk without being overheard. But before he said anything, I jerked away and looked back at the cameras.

"Tom just told me he wants to become a Democrat!" I announced.

Everyone laughed at that, even DeLay.

"Boy, you've got to be a happy man today," I told him in a stage whisper.

"You have no idea," he said. "I've never been happier."

Part of that was an act, of course. There are times in politics when you have to suck it up for the cameras and put the best face on things, no matter how much you feel like you've been socked in the gut. But talking to DeLay face-to-face like that in front of the Fox News building that day, I had the feeling he really was happy or at least relieved. He had been stripped of his leadership position in the House and seemed ready for a change.

I headed up to Fox News and John Gibson threw me a real softball question. Yes, I said, it was important that the most powerful Republican in the House of Representatives was indicted in Texas for a money-laundering scandal and couldn't run for reelection because he knew any Democrat would beat him, but it was also important to see DeLay's demise in a larger context.

"This is all part of a pattern of a culture of corruption and incompetence of the government on the Republican side," I said. "This is just the beginning."

Gibson tried to say DeLay had outmaneuvered Democrats by ducking out of the race and denying us an issue, which was not much of an argument, but I guess that was the best that Fox News could come up with for a spin on such bad news for the Republicans.

"Tom DeLay was as good as it gets when you send out a fund-raising appeal," I said. "Don't think that the Democrats and others aren't still going to talk about Tom DeLay and the culture of corruption that went on. Two of his top aides have now pled. Obviously they were taking money and they were getting legislation. That affects all Republicans who are up this year in this election, not just Tom DeLay."

The end of DeLay's run in Washington put an end bracket on an entire era in Republican politics. They had set about building the mechanisms of political power, piece by piece, step by step, going all the way back to the 1950s and accelerating after their party melted down over Watergate. They were rewarded with eight years of Ronald Reagan and a slow reshaping of politics to their advantage. Newt Gingrich's spectacular flameout as Speaker of the House during the Clinton years, which I'll get to later, was an important sign of the limits of what the American people could stomach from extremist Republicans, but even after Gingrich went down the Republicans still had a huge advantage in organization, which they used to grab power as greedily as sailors on shore leave hit the nearest corner tavern.

Not until the administration of George W. Bush rotted before the eyes of the American people, betraying itself as corrupt and incompetent, did the Republicans face a real crisis in the political machine they built for themselves over decades. They let power go to their heads and forgot that in politics, you're only up as long as you take care of the needs of the working people you represent and not just your rich friends. But it's best not to overlook the example of how they built up so much power. There's no questioning the wisdom of their finding a way to look beyond short-term political crises, and instead focusing on where they wanted to be as a party decades in the future and building themselves a potent political apparatus.

*

I WAS ONLY IN FIRST GRADE, a little six-year-old, but I remember when our principal at St. Ann's School in Syracuse came in that terrible day in November 1963 and delivered the life-changing news that President Kennedy had been shot. He was dead. As little kids we couldn't grasp what it meant, and that was normal enough, but the adults we knew couldn't grasp it either. The shock and sadness were too big. Less than a year later, when Americans went to the polls for the 1964 presidential election, Johnson could run as John Kennedy's man, and that gave his campaign an emotional power—connected with the trappings of being President—that put the Republicans in an impossible position.

Barry Goldwater, the Republican nominee against LBJ, was an outspoken Arizona senator who had emerged in the late 1950s as a hero to conservatives with his vocal criticism of Eisenhower's "dime store New Deal" politics. "Extremism in the defense of liberty is no vice," Goldwater said in accepting the nomination, which scared a lot of people. Goldwater won only six states, but his candidacy energized hard-line conservatives. They followed his advice: "Let's grow up, conservatives! We want to take this party back, and I think someday we can. Let's get to work!"

Richard Viguerie was one of the conservatives who got to work. He would soon revolutionize the role of direct mail in politics. Walter Weintz, a circulation manager for *Reader's Digest,* sent out a mass mailing during Ohio senator Robert Taft's 1950 reelection campaign and included a request for money, making him the first direct-mail fund-raiser. Viguerie wanted to build on what Weintz had done, and in 1964 he paid a visit to the clerk of the House of Representatives, and sat down and copied a list of people who had donated fifty dollars or more to the Goldwater campaign. Over time Viguerie built that list of 12,500 conservatives around the country into a millions-strong resource for raising money and also for shaping the political debate. He energized small groups of voters over single issues and used that energy to align them with the Republicans.

Another important step the Republicans took after 1964 was to name a new RNC chairman, Ray C. Bliss. He had been expelled from the University of Akron for alleged ballot-stuffing in the May Queen contest and improperly helped tilt Akron's 1935 mayoral elections. Bliss took over as head of the Ohio Republican Party at a time when it was in total disarray and spent sixteen years rebuilding it step by step. He noticed that three groups in particular had shifted to the Democrats in large numbers for the '64 elections—African Americans, young people, and intellectuals. He worked hard to tone down the right-wing image that Goldwater projected and cultivated these three groups. That was basic interest-group politics, but he also put to work new techniques that helped him gain traction with these groups and with moderates.

"Mr. Bliss brought to the national chairmanship qualities that had succeeded in Ohio: acceptance of such new techniques as confidential polling, fifteen-hour workdays, tough-mindedness, discretion and the keeping of promises, a consuming desire to win elections and an eye for detail," *The Times* later wrote.

One of the biggest mistakes Nixon ever made was to force out Bliss, whose visionary work had helped elect him, and to install a series of chairmen who made little mark—Rogers Morton, later Nixon's interior secretary, and then Senator Bob Dole and George Herbert Walker Bush, whose job consisted mostly of trying to defend Nixon during the Watergate scandal. Not until Reagan chose Frank Fahrenkopf to head the RNC in 1983, in fact, did another RNC chair have the kind of impact Bliss did. Learning from Bliss's example, a series of RNC chairmen took the long view and concentrated on leaving some kind of legacy: Fahrenkopf, chairman from 1983 to 1989, made a priority of developing the voter files; Haley Barbour, a real character, took over in 1993, and put in state-of-the-art television studios; and then Jim Nicholson, the chair from 1997 to 2000, focused on developing the Republicans' Internet capabilities.

Nixon's resignation in August 1974, capping the Watergate scandal, pushed the Republicans to a whole new level of desperation. That was when the different strands really came together—the founding of *National Review* magazine eventually led to a whole network of conservative publications, from the Heritage Foundation's *Policy Review* to something called *The American Spectator,* which took under-the-table money from an ultraconservative named Richard Mellon Scaife and used it to send reporters out to do just enough digging to give the veneer of truth to wild, unfounded charges. That was how they cooked up the nonsense they put out against Clinton, alleging that he'd ordered the murder of political opponents and been involved with drug running, which they would then have Rush Limbaugh and other radio hosts talk up until they were ready to pass out (or in Limbaugh's case, maybe that's not the best way to put it).

Viguerie's direct-mail work led to a variety of Republican initiatives to identify specific interest groups, and to milk those groups for money they could use for still more direct-mail appeals. Democrats were either too complacent or too debt-ridden to take the same approach, and it really hurt us. The right-wingers had a whole universe of groups, from the John Birch Society to the Religious Right, that worked their core groups relentlessly and invested in becoming ever more scientific in the techniques they were using.

The Republicans also worked to develop dirty-tricks politics. Nixon moved up to the big leagues of U.S. politics in 1950, when he ran right over Congresswoman Helen Gahagan Douglas, a former Broadway actress known for her mix of brains and beauty, in the race for U.S. senator from California. Nixon not only smeared Douglas at every opportunity as the "Pink Lady," he accused her overtly and covertly of being a "fellow traveler" to Communists and distributed a reported half million pink flyers attacking her as "soft on Communism." That was all typical McCarthy-esque red-baiting. But Nixon also hired people to make anonymous phone calls to voters, asking, "Did you know Mrs. Douglas is a Communist?" and then hanging up. Nixon won easily, but in the battle of the quotes Gahagan Douglas had the last laugh. Nixon got mileage out of "She's pink down to her underwear." But Gahagan Douglas trumped him by dubbing him "Tricky Dick," which lives on to this day as the last word on Nixon.

The cheap-shot tactic of spreading disinformation through phone calls was the work of Nixon's campaign manager in that race, a Los Angeles attorney named Murray Chotiner who was not shy about explaining what he did. "The purpose of an election is not to defeat your opponent, but to destroy him," he later told the *Los Angeles Times*. Reagan's defense secretary, Cap Weinberger, explained in his memoir that it was often said, "Wherever you find Murray Chotiner, there is a trail of blood behind." Keep in mind, that was a Republican talking. Fast-forward a few years and a cocky young guy out of South Carolina would take that old Murray Chotiner dirty trick and give it a new name: push-polling.

Lee Atwater died in March 1991 of brain cancer. He was only forty years old and at the peak of his political power and influence. Since then his reputation has only continued to grow, but I'll be honest. I never much liked Lee Atwater and I have contempt for his style of politics. George H. W. Bush was President when Atwater died and *The Times* quoted him saying, "Barbara and I are heartsick about it. Lee was a very close friend to my sons and daughter as well as to Barbara and me. . . . [He] practiced the art of politics with zeal and vigor. I was very proud of him, proud to serve with him."

Atwater staked his career on the power of hate and fear. He believed in politics as a battle of who wanted it more, principles be damned, and that meant resorting to whatever slimy tactics you could dream up. Growing up in South Carolina, where Democrats were in a strong position, he formed his underdog rationalization of lying and cheating to win. "Republicans in the South could not win elections by talking about issues," he said. "You had to make the case that the other guy, the other candidate, is a bad guy."

Atwater was creative, I'll give him that, and we'll never even know half the stuff he pulled. But considering what he *admitted* to doing, the list has got to be amazing. For example, he was working on the Reagan presidential campaign in 1980 and, as *The Times* explained it, "a group of black ministers sought him out to express a desire to work for Mr. Reagan's nomination and obtain money for voter registration, Mr. Atwater replied that the campaign was 'broke,' but he suggested they try the big-spending Texas candidate, John B. Connally. As soon as the ministers left his office, Mr. Atwater relayed word to the third Republican campaign, that of Mr. Bush, that 'Connally's buying the black vote.' Soon the Connally and Bush camps were at each other's throats over charges of buying the black vote. Mr. Reagan remained aloof."

One of Atwater's ugliest moves was the Willie Horton ad against

Michael Dukakis in 1988 that helped Vice President Bush become President. The whole point was to scare people and to tap into racist stereotypes. Hate and fear—that was always the Atwater way. Later, facing death, he had regrets. "In 1988, fighting Dukakis, I said that I 'would strip the bark off the little bastard' and 'make Willie Horton his running mate,'" Atwater wrote in *LIFE* magazine. "I am sorry for both statements: the first for its naked cruelty, the second because it makes me sound racist, which I am not."

Atwater was a role model to Karl Rove. The two met in the 1970s when both were involved with campus politics. "Rove had never seen anybody quite like Lee, with his slow-cured manner and take-no-prisoners attitude," James Moore and Wayne Slater wrote in *Bush's Brain*. "He quoted Sun-Tzu. ('If your opponent is of choleric temper, seek to irritate him.') He was everything Rove wanted to be: the perfect political warrior."

More than anything, Atwater will go down in history as the man who invented push-polling. It's a term worth remembering, because you can bet the Republicans are going to pull more of this stuff in the coming elections. It's just like what Atwater explained about South Carolina when he was growing up. They can't win on the issues, so they have to find clever new tricks to make other people look bad. Push-polling has become a symbol of the whole attitude that Atwater espoused, and George W. Bush and his inner circle have embraced, which is the notion that you do whatever you have to do to win, no matter how harsh or ugly your tactics, and you don't care whether you destroy people's lives and reputations along the way.

To be clear, push-polling does not mean conducting public-opinion polls about a negative aspect of an opponent. For example, if John McCain is running for President in 2008 and an opponent calls people and asks, "Would it make you less likely to vote for McCain to know that in March 2000 he denounced Jerry Falwell as an agent of intolerance and then in May 2006 stood side by side with Falwell at his Liberty University?" that could be part of polling done to see how sensitive the public was to the hypocrisy of McCain's flip-flop.

The telltale sign of true push-polling is that no data is collected. There is no polling. Questions are asked, but only for the purpose of planting ideas in people's minds, which was what people connected to the Bush campaign did to McCain during the 2000 South Carolina primary. They posed as representatives of a polling company and asked people, "Would you be more or less likely to vote for McCain if you knew he had fathered an illegitimate child who is black?" Since McCain and his wife had in fact adopted a child from Bangladesh, the calls fueled rumormongering and badly hurt McCain, which understandably led him to lose his temper.

Over the whole sorry mess you could almost see Lee Atwater grinning somewhere, quoting his hero Sun-Tzu: "If your opponent is of choleric temper, seek to irritate him."

6

★ ★ ★

My first reaction when I heard that Dick Cheney shot his friend in the face while on a quail hunt in February 2006 was sympathy. I felt for Harry Whittington, the guy who got "peppered" with pellets from the Vice President's Italian-made 28-gauge shotgun, but also for Cheney himself. As any experienced hunter will tell you, accidents are going to happen out there. You dread that your day will come. But the more I heard about Cheney blasting Whittington in the face, the more the whole episode sounded fishy. Just imagine how it would have played out if Al Gore was out hunting in 1998, wheeled around and, with the sun in his eyes, shot another hunter in the face, putting him in the hospital . . . then waited twenty-two hours before informing the press! Even if you're a Republican, you have to admit: They would have had Al Gore locked up in Leavenworth before sundown. Cheney didn't even bother to tell his boss. He called the President's chief of staff and said there was an accident, but forgot to mention he shot someone.

The more we heard, the more it became clear that lying and misrepresenting were such second nature to these guys, they were honestly surprised when someone expected them to tell the whole truth. They kept saying Cheney was thirty yards away from Whittington when he fired, which we now know was questionable. First, the story was that not a drop of alcohol had been consumed, then it was "a beer." They couldn't get their story straight, which reminded the American people of all the whoppers this administration has told them.

From the twisting of intelligence before the Iraq War to the stonewalling about the White House leaking the name of a CIA operative to try to discredit an honorable man, the Bush administration engaged in a pattern of deception and pure incompetence that ran so deep and so wide it was just mind-boggling.

As unfortunate as the hunting incident was—and we're all relieved that Harry Whittington made a full recovery—at least it gave me great fodder for the speaking circuit, which I hit regularly, teamed up with former Republican National Committee chairman Ed Gillespie. All I have to do to get the crowd laughing is mention Cheney and hunting. That gets them right there. Then I mention the cockamamie story that Cheney only had "a beer" that day.

"C'mon, folks, I'm Irish," I tell the crowd. "If you crack one, you crack six. Look, he's out in the woods. He's got his camo gear on. He's all jacked up. You think he only had one beer?"

I give it a minute, and then add: "Let's be honest: The man was tanked!"

Once the laughter dies down after several minutes, and I can talk again, everyone wonders where I'm going with this.

"How do I know he was in the bag?" I continue, and by now the room is dead quiet, everyone is so curious to hear what I'll say next.

"Very simple. You hear all the time about people who shoot their business partners. You even hear about some people shooting their own wives. But let me be crystal clear. Folks, you never, ever, hear about a politician shooting one of their own *donors!*"

That brings down the house—and even Eddie can't resist doubling over with laughter.

★

I NEVER CRITICIZED CHENEY for being a hunter and never would, because I love hunting. I may not have grown up with it, but I've made up for lost time in recent years and have become an avid hunter. Among my more memorable trips were taking my son Jack wild boar hunting in Hungary with a group including Prince Andrew, and wild bird hunting with King Juan Carlos in Spain, who is a terrific guy.

I've become a pretty good shot, but the first time I picked up a gun it could have scarred me for life. That was back in November 1983, when a group of us headed down to the D-Dot Ranch, a 10,000-acre spread of wilderness south of Jacksonville, Florida, owned by James E. Davis, one of the four brothers who built the Winn-Dixie supermarket chain from a single store in Miami to become the largest chain in the South. The Davis brothers were huge conservatives, and Donald Regan, Reagan's treasury secretary, used to say: "When J.E. calls, I listen." That was true of congressmen, too, and when Davis invited a group down there that November, including Tony Coelho and John Dingell, the Michigan congressman and powerful chairman of the Energy and Commerce Committee, there ended up being twenty of us ready to spend three days hunting turkey and quail.

Understand, coming from Syracuse, the only turkeys I'd ever seen were the kind you unfold like an accordion and put down in the middle of your Thanksgiving dinner table. I'd never even held a gun, much less gone hunting. So, that first morning, we were out of bed before 5 A.M., and the first thing I knew, they'd thrown a shotgun in my hands. I'd have preferred a rifle, but apparently, I was finding out, you hunt deer with rifles but use a shotgun when you're going after turkey. I liked the feel of that shotgun in my hands, but I had one small problem. How was I going to load the thing? I had no idea.

They drove me out in the dark before dawn, stuck me in a tree stand, and left me there to do what I would. By this time I was a wreck, sitting up in a tree in the dark with a box of cartridges. I fumbled around with the gun for half an hour and finally got it loaded. I sat waiting for something to shoot and eventually spotted a few deer that had walked out of the woods and into a field. They were only about eighty yards away, so I figured I'd have no trouble knocking off a couple of them. I fired both barrels of the shotgun and the kick was so strong, I almost lost my footing. I looked up to see how many deer I'd felled and they all just stared back at me, as if they were surprised I was making so much noise. I reloaded and took careful aim and fired again, but no luck. They were just standing there laughing at me, probably thinking, *What idiot hunter thinks he can hit anything with a shotgun from eighty yards away?*

Before long there were birds flying all around me, darting into the trees behind me, or sometimes even landing on the tin roof just over my head. I heard one up on the roof and decided this bird was mine. When it finally flew over to the nearest stand of trees, maybe ten yards away, I saw it was a big black bird with a big red head, so even a first-timer like me knew that was a turkey. I pointed my shotgun and pulled the trigger and *blam!!* The black bird with the big red head didn't have a chance.

"I got me a turkey! I got me a turkey!" I started yelling.

Then I remembered I was out there all alone and would have to wait another hour before the pickup truck came to get me.

"I got me a turkey! I got me a turkey!" I started yelling as soon as I saw the pickup truck bouncing along the dirt road toward my tree.

There were two hunters in the pickup who hadn't got anything that morning, so I was feeling pretty good. Everyone scrambled down out of the pickup and went to take a look.

"Wow, look at the size of that thing!" Congressman Jack Brooks yelled.

"That is one big old turkey!" Bill Cable added.

Izzy, the old guy driving the truck, grabbed the bird and tossed it in the back, and on the drive back he radioed ahead to let them know we were coming. He was a grizzled old character who had to have been at least eighty years old.

"We've got ourselves a big one here," he said. "That's right, a big one, a big old turkey!"

This hunting thing was easy, I was thinking. Then we got back to the ranch house, and everyone was lined up out front to look at my turkey, including Dingell, who had been hunting since he was, like, six months old. The pickup pulled up and they all broke out cheering. Izzy took the bird to give it an official weighing in, and they were all yelling and howling. But something was up. The laughter was going on too long. This was not normal jubilation over someone shooting a turkey.

Finally someone told me the truth: I'd shot a turkey *buzzard,* which is a vulture, not a turkey. Luckily for us, a top law enforcement officer happened to be with us and he told us to feed the damn thing to the alligators, because even though there's no shortage of turkey buzzards, they are protected by the Migratory Bird Treaty Act. Those weekends at the D-Dot always included a lot of late nights of cigar smoking and storytelling, and late that night they were all still making jokes about my turkey buzzard. To this day people still kid me about it.

The next year, again thanks to Tony Coelho, I was back at the D-Dot with a different group that included Jack Warren, a big oil man from Texas who had been hunting his whole life and was an excellent shot. We were quail hunting, and everyone made sure to remind me of my turkey buzzard and to warn me that you have to be very careful when you are quail hunting. They are so quick, they can dart away from you in a heartbeat. It's easy to get disoriented and fire wildly. They gave me so many tips and warnings that I was very careful and bagged my share of quail without incident. But Jack Warren had his sights on a quail, and when it turned sharply just as he was about to fire, he jerked around to follow its flight and ended up emptying his birdshot into the radiator of the old yellow pickup truck. We were all kind of shocked and just stared at the sprinkling of holes in the front of the radiator. Then steam started gushing out and we could hear it hissing.

"Get in the truck!" we all yelled.

We wanted to get back to the ranch house before the old pickup broke down completely. Izzy radioed back that we were on our way.

"We've got ourselves an accident," he said.

That had them all in a state back at home base. They thought someone might have been shot. This was long before Cheney shot his friend in the face, but accidents are just a fact of life when you're quail hunting. Also, everyone remembered the year before and was wondering what McAuliffe might have pulled this time. So we drove up, steam gushing up out of that poor, abused radiator, and to this day everyone is sure I'm the one who shot the pickup. They all figured Jack Warren was just covering for me. The next year, when we showed up for another hunt, they brought me into the main lodge to look at the huge plaque they had mounted on the wall. There was the radiator chock full of holes.

★

MEN LOVE SPORTS because it's a great chance to hang out with the guys, give each other a hard time, tell stories, and just unwind. That's what hunting trips are all about. Early in 2003, the superlobbyist Tommy Boggs invited me along with a big group from Washington to spend a long weekend at his Tobacco Stick Lodge in Cambridge, Maryland, which is way out on the eastern shore of the Chesapeake Bay. Tommy, son of the former Louisiana Congresswoman Lindy Boggs and the former House majority leader Hale Boggs, learned Southern charm early, and he's the most generous and gracious host any sportsman could have.

Tommy loves to keep it interesting by inviting a lively group, and that time we were joined by none other than J. R. Ewing. He was looking good for a man of seventy-one and kept joking about how he was like the bionic man with a new liver. He had fake million-dollar bills printed up with his picture, which he would whip out and sign for you. Some of you may remember Larry Hagman as the actor opposite Barbara Eden in *I Dream of Jeannie,* but after playing a Texas oil man on *Dallas,* to me he'll always be J. R. Ewing, and he speaks his mind just the way J.R. did.

What stands out from our weekend at the Tobacco Stick Lodge was sitting there in a duck blind with J. R. Ewing, and a little excursion we made one night to a great old honky-tonk called the Barge because it floated on a raft. This was the dead of winter and there had to have been a hundred people in there hoofing like there was no tomorrow. They saw Tommy Boggs and all these other big hitters from Washington and couldn't have cared less, but they were doing cartwheels over having J.R. in their bar. They were hollering and hooting and making a big fuss over him, and let me tell you, he loved every minute. You could see him start to puff out his chest a little, proud of all the attention, and that was even before this beautiful, blonde bomber sashayed over to him on her high heels and gave him a look that would have melted butter.

"Can I buy you a drink?" she asked him.

"Why, shore," he said, turning around to wink at us and rubbing it in a little that we were all standing around talking to each other while he had beautiful blondes wanting to buy *him* drinks.

"I can't believe I'm really meeting you," the blonde told J.R. "You know what? You're my grandmother's absolute favorite."

His swagger evaporated and he came skulking back to us as we roared with laughter.

✦

I WAS HOOKED ON HUNTING after my first weekend at the D-Dot Ranch in Florida, and got to be a pretty fair shot. I know what you're thinking. Don't tell that to the turkey buzzard! Or the radiator! (It was Jack Warren, I swear, really.) Hunting stories are a lot like fishing stories: They tend to get stretched out. But I've got live footage of the time I went down to West Virginia as DNC chair during the 2004 campaign and ended up in a kind of shoot-off with the governor. It wasn't like I hadn't picked up a gun since the radiator incident or anything. I get out hunting a few times a year, and in 2004 my staff was eager to get me out there with my shotgun, so I did events in Michigan and Missouri when their hunting seasons opened. Nothing better than to have the Democratic Party chairman with a shotgun in his hand when people call us a bunch of wimps.

I decided to head down to Stonewall Jackson Lake in West Virginia in late September for an annual shooting event they have called Sportsman's Day. These good old boys thought it was about the funniest thing in the world that the chairman of the Democratic National Committee thought he could do a little shooting. Bob Wise, West Virginia's governor at the time, wanted to be a good sport and come along with me.

Stonewall Jackson Lake turned out to be a beautiful backdrop for what the good old boys hoped would be my coming humiliation, and when we pulled up in this huge field for the event I was amazed. It was like Guns 'R Us. There were all these different exhibits set up, everything gun-related you could possibly imagine, and it was like the whole crowd had been waiting for us.

"Chairman McAuliffe, Governor, come on over here," one of the organizers called out. "We've got our own little skeet range for you guys."

It was all set up and there was a knot of people there—TV cameramen and some local reporters with their notebooks and their pens held up in the air like a surgeon's scalpel, ready to slice. All the old guys in their hunting outfits crowded around to watch and they were all snickering. The chairman of the party! Wait till this wimp gets up there! I thought these guys were going to hurt themselves, they were laughing so hard.

They called me up first and the cameras started rolling. I called "Pull!" and they sent the first one up there. Bang! Nailed it. The second one flew up there. Nailed that one, too. I hit the third. And the fourth. And the fifth and the sixth. The governor couldn't even believe what he was seeing. Of the twelve they sent up there, I got eleven. The crowd was buzzing after that and now the governor had to go.

"Okay, Governor!" I called out with a big smile on my face. "Your turn!"

He knew he was in a real spot now because the last thing he wanted was to come out looking worse than the perceived wimp chairman of the DNC. The governor started firing and it didn't go as well. He ended up with a respectable seven. Then they brought us over for a competition on who could do a better job firing one of those old-time musket-type guns, where you actually dump the powder, tamp it down, and all that. I was first again. I stepped up, got the thing loaded, fired, and hit the balloon they lifted in the air about seventy-five yards away, all without any problems. The governor was up next and unfortunately the gun backfired on him. He was a great sport about all of it. Those folks would have elected me governor of West Virginia right on the spot, the way they were carrying on about what a great shot I was. We went to this big outdoor porch for a huge pig roast and I got up and gave a barn-burner of a speech, and I tell you, these boys were buying what I was selling that day, all because I can shoot.

*

BACK IN OCTOBER 1987, I visited the D-Dot Ranch again for another hunting trip, only that time Tony Coelho and the boys weren't kidding me about my *shooting*. I was about to fly to Rome, Italy, with Dorothy, and had confided to Tony that I planned to propose—and naturally, he told everyone. They were all goofing on me, toasting me and welcoming me into that happy club! Tony agreed on the spot to be my best man.

The trip to Rome was put together by the Catholic University Board of Regents—and included an audience with Pope John Paul II. Our group arrived in the beautiful, ornate Sala Clementina at the Vatican first thing in the morning for a private moment with the Pontiff.

The next day, we went back for a mass in the Pope's private chapel, and I secretly arranged to have the Holy Father bless the engagement ring that I planned to give Dorothy. That night, walking home from dinner back to the Hotel Excelsior, I pulled Richard aside to ask for Dorothy's hand in marriage, and he said he would be thrilled to have me as a son-in-law. I suggested to Dorothy that we take a walk down to the Trevi Fountain, where by tradition you throw three coins into the fountain and make a wish. I tossed the coins into the water and turned to Dorothy.

"I wish you would marry me," I said.

Lucky for me, she said yes.

Many friends gathered for a five-day marathon of wedding parties in the Orlando area, hosted by Swann family friends, leading up to our wedding day. Most of the out-of-town guests stayed at the Langford Hotel, an old Florida classic complete with tiki huts and potted palms, in downtown Winter Park. The night before the wedding, we were all gathered in the Ronald Reagan Suite at the Langford, where my parents were staying, which became party central. Kegs were rolled in and music was blaring. Around 4 A.M. I noticed that Dick and Jane Gephardt had quietly slipped off to bed. I was having none of it and called down to their room.

"I'm getting married today, Dick," I said. "This is no time to sleep. Get back up here."

Great trooper that he was, Dick got dressed and came back up, and as soon he walked in the door, one of my Syracuse buddies accidentally spilled a pitcher of beer on him. That didn't slow Dick down a bit. He stayed in the suite with all of us until the sun came up.

★

DEWEY BEACH DOESN'T RATE real high on most people's lists of top vacation spots, but it's perfect if you happen to be a fan of grungy bars with cheap beer, loud music, and a wide assortment of characters. I love spending time there. It's on the Delaware shore, as unassuming and unpretentious as any beach you'll find. Over the years it has developed into a big college party town, where you can always find live music and crowds of fun-loving young people. Just up Highway One is Rehoboth Beach, which has a boardwalk and attracts a bit fancier crowd; but Dewey Beach is just a little strip about a dozen blocks long between the beach on one side and Rehoboth Bay on the other. I've been renting a house down there almost every summer for more than twenty years and it's the kind of place where you wear shorts and a T-shirt all week long, even if you're going out to dinner, and so much beer gets spilled every night at the Bottle & Cork that your feet stick to the floor.

Late one night in August 1991, I was at my regular spot in Dewey Beach, the Waterfront bar and grill, with my friend Roberto Prats, who was later a Puerto Rico state senator and in 2004 only missed getting elected to Congress by a few tenths of a percent. At first Roberto and I didn't pay any attention to a nearby fight. The Waterfront was a real rocking place and it was all the same to us if some customers wanted to whale on each other. But this fight was a little unusual. The bouncer, a big, strapping guy with gold chains all over the place, got into it with a customer and punches were thrown. I think the customer might have ended up with a broken nose. Keith Monigle, the owner, was all in a state. He was a friend of mine and I was one of the honored guests he would let stay after hours as long as I wanted. I spent so much time at the Waterfront, Keith and his wife, Mary Beth, along with the bartender, D.J., flew down to Orlando for my wedding.

"I need your help, Terry," Keith said that night after hours. "One of my bouncers has just been arrested for disorderly conduct. He's a great kid. This isn't right."

Roberto and I agreed.

"You're a lawyer," Keith said. "Go get him out of jail."

I didn't have the heart to tell Keith I'd never been in a courtroom.

"You've got to go down there and help my bouncer," he said.

Roberto and I kind of stared at each other. He knew just how many beers I'd had, which, let me tell you, was more than a few.

"Listen, Keith, first of all, I've been drinking beer for several hours," I said. "Second, I don't practice any type of criminal law."

Keith brought another round and let me mull it over.

"It's the middle of the night," he said. "I have no other options. You've got to do something."

"Okay, let me go down to the police station and sort of get the lay of the land," I told Keith.

Roberto and I headed out the door in our shorts and flip-flops, and sauntered down to the Dewey Beach police station.

"Yes, I'm representing Johnny Hayes," I told the officer working the counter, trying to sound professional.

He looked unfazed at the sight of me and went to get Johnny. They brought him out to talk to me and he explained that he had seen a guy punch a woman in front of the bar.

"Guys just shouldn't punch girls," he said.

A couple of police officers were watching from across the street and when they saw Johnny throw a punch, they came over and arrested him.

The police officer told me Johnny had two options: He could set a normal court appearance in thirty-five days, which would have been awfully tough on Johnny, since he was going to be back in college by then. Or they could get the justice of the peace right now and he would hear the case.

"Let's get the justice of the peace!" I proclaimed. "Bring him down!"

I was fired up at that point, but the longer we waited for them to drag this old justice of the peace out of bed, the more I wondered what I'd gotten myself into. First of all, by this time it was moving in on 3 A.M. and no one likes being hauled out of bed at that hour. Second, I didn't practice law. Third, I had Roberto with me as my cocounsel and he was still only a law student. We walked into the courtroom, saw the justice of the peace looking down on us from up on his high chair, and then in came the arresting officers. One of the police officers kept staring at Roberto and finally appealed to the justice of the peace to take a look at the way he was having trouble standing up.

"Will you please ask that guy over there if he's been drinking?" the officer asked him, but to no avail.

I was starting to get nervous.

"Are you licensed to practice in Delaware?" the justice of the peace asked me.

"No, Your Honor," I told him in my best courtroom voice. "However, I am a member of the District of Columbia Bar, and I'm also licensed to practice before the United States Supreme Court."

This, believe it or not, was the God's truth. I am a member of the Supreme Court Bar. Now, you might be wondering: How does a person who barely attended his law school classes become a member of the United States Supreme Court Bar? Well, basically, you just need to have two members of the Supreme Court Bar write letters on your behalf. Congresswoman Eleanor Holmes Norton, who taught my civil rights class at law school, was my main sponsor.

But this justice of the peace we'd dragged out of bed at 3 A.M. in Dewey Beach didn't know any of that. He was impressed and it showed. He kind of sat up higher in his chair and the whole tenor of the proceeding changed. You could tell he couldn't wait to tell his buddies that he'd had a lawyer in front of him who practiced before Justices Rehnquist and Stevens and all the rest.

The police presented their case and I was a bit nervous, as I didn't want to lose my first—and only—court case. Then it was my turn. I put Johnny the bouncer up on the stand and asked him what had happened.

"You think I want to get into a fight?" he said, gesturing to his gold chains. "I don't want to fight anybody. I could get my chains ripped off."

He seemed to feel this was the most reasonable defense in the world.

"Your Honor, he broke my gold necklace and he hit a girl!" he said.

I needed to establish that the bouncer wasn't just some twitchy, hulking thug, itching to crack skulls left and right, but Johnny's credibility was not the key to my defense. My approach was to raise questions about the police officers who had arrested him. I think I saw Perry Mason do something like that once.

"How far away were you?" I asked the first officer I put up on that stand.

He admitted he was across the street. I nodded and let the implications of that fact sink in with the justice of the peace, who clearly felt he was watching some kind of master of the legal profession in action.

"And the incident in question occurred at about what time, to the best of your recollection?" I asked the police officer.

"It was after one o'clock," he said.

"After midnight," I said. "So it was dark outside and the only light was coming from a single street lamp approximately fifteen yards away from the defendant at this time?"

"That's correct," he said.

I was having a great time. I tore down their case piece by piece. It seemed pretty clear that I had raised enough doubt about their credibility during the forty-five minutes of the trial that the outcome was settled, but you never know. The justice of the peace reappeared after deliberating in private and we waited to hear his ruling.

"Not guilty," he said as he pounded the gavel.

I'm telling you, you'd have thought I was Paul Newman at the end of The Verdict, the way we carried on. We stormed out of the courtroom and went back to the Waterfront and everything was on the house, of course. Keith insisted on personally cooking up Roberto and me a big batch of lobsters, and we feasted on that and drank beer until sunrise. Dorothy thought I was nuts when I crawled into bed laughing my head off.

"What happened to you and where have you been?" she asked me.

"Honey, you are not going to believe what I've done this time," I said, sliding into bed. "I'll tell you in a couple of hours when I wake up."

7

★ ★ ★

Our doorbell rang on Christmas morning, 1993, and right away I thought: Who could that be? Dorothy and I were married in October 1988 and, by that Christmas season five years later, we were a family of four. Dori, our oldest, was born in June 1991, named for her late grandmother, Doris, and Jack, named for his grandfather, came along in February 1993. The kids had already ripped open their presents that Christmas morning by the time we had our surprise visitor, and I waded through a sea of crumpled-up wrapping paper and discarded bows and ribbon and opened our front door to see who could be there.

"Merry Christmas, Terry!" Dick Gephardt greeted me, flashing that Midwestern apple-cheeked grin of his.

"Dick!" I said.

Dick could have been showing up at 4 A.M. and I'd still be thrilled to see him. He and I carry on like brothers and spend most of our time together laughing, which is why he's such a good friend of mine that he was in my wedding. Dick was carrying a big box with Christmas wrapping and a giant bow. The box looked like it was moving.

"Hi, Dick," Dorothy said, coming over to the door, and I could tell she was in on some secret.

"Come on in!" I shouted.

Now the kids were really getting into this. Dori and little Jackie came over to the box Dick had brought in with him, and both pulled back when they heard the box whimper. They weren't scared, just startled. They were back an instant later and ripped the thing open, and there was Bailey, a tiny golden retriever puppy. She was just the cutest little puppy, and of course the kids and Dorothy all went nuts. I slapped Dick on the shoulder and kidded him about how we'd have to lay newspapers all over the house until little Bailey was housebroken.

"We took care of that," Dick said, flashing the apple-cheeked grin again.

I was amazed, but they really had.

"Every kid should have a dog, Terry," Dick had been telling me ever since Jack was born that February. "We always had dogs growing up. That's a big part of childhood. You don't want them to miss that."

"You're right, Dick," I'd always say. "I'll get around to it."

But I never found the time. I wouldn't have known where to look. Where do you go to find the perfect puppy? But sometime around Thanksgiving that year, Dick called Dorothy to get her approval.

"Don't tell Terry, but as a surprise I want to get you guys a dog for Christmas," Dick told her.

A lifelong dog lover like Dick was not going to drop just any mutt off on us. Dick and his wife Jane drove four hours down to West Virginia and picked up Bailey, then drove four hours back to Washington and kept Bailey at their house for a month. Dick and Jane looked after the puppy, housebreaking her, and Dick even gave her baths in his bathtub. That's the kind of guy Dick is. You don't find many like him in Washington.

The Times ran an article about Dick in February 1987 that kidded him for having "what colleagues have called an air of unmitigated wholesomeness about him."

"You know what Dick Gephardt's weakness is?" Oklahoma Congressman Dave McCurdy told *The Times,* joking about what a perfect-looking Dick-and-Jane couple he and his wife were. "His dog's not named Spot."

Dick and I had already been through a lot together by that Christmas. Dick had run a great race for President in 1988, and I will always be proud of the hard work we did on his campaign. We all knew it was going to be tough, since no congressman had been elected President since James Garfield in 1881. People kept telling Dick after the '84 election that he could be the one, and he started to talk seriously about running for President, but I wasn't so sure that was the best idea. I liked Dick right off the bat, from the first time I met him in 1983, but I was also tired of watching Democrats lose presidential races to Republicans. I was on the lookout for a candidate who had the eloquence and star power to make everyone think the same thing: *This man will be a great President.*

The potential candidates for President in 1988 made their bids for my help the year after the '84 elections. Since there was no instant front-runner in the race, the way Mondale had been in '84, it was wide open and everyone thought he could be the one. I'd have lunch with Senator Joe Biden one day and he'd be asking me to work for his presidential campaign, and then Gary Hart and I would meet for drinks and he'd be making his pitch, and on and on it went.

My early choice was Mario Cuomo, the New York governor. If Cuomo was going to run, he had my support. It was that simple. I'd flown to New York in '83 to have breakfast with Cuomo, and we sat there and talked politics for two very lively, very intense hours. Not only was Cuomo a natural for the national stage as New York governor, but he was also brilliant. He was the most exciting and knowledgeable politician around, I thought, and since he was from my home state and a Catholic, I'd most likely be for him if he was in the race. That put me in the same position as a lot of us, stuck trying to figure out what Cuomo was going to do when the man himself didn't know.

Dick told me in July '85 that he was definitely running for President, and early on I agreed to help him raise a little money, but I said I still had to keep my options open to see if Cuomo would run. Dick desperately wanted to have me as his finance chairman and started calling me morning, noon, and night, most every day, for several months. I was impressed by his persistence and flattered by the attention. He called so often, it got to be a joke at our house. Whenever the phone would ring we would say, "Must be Gephardt." Dick knew that my early loyalties were to Cuomo, but that didn't deter him. After several months I couldn't take being badgered by Dick anymore.

"If you promise never to call me again, I'll be your national finance chairman," I jokingly told Dick over lunch.

The next day, February 19, 1987, Mario Cuomo announced he would not be a candidate for President, surprising everyone, including his own wife.

★

DURING THIS PERIOD I kept very busy with my different businesses and with new challenges that kept cropping up. David Wilmot, the dean of admissions at Georgetown Law School, asked me in 1987 to join seventeen others on the board of the newly chartered Federal City National Bank in Washington. The next year, the small bank was in trouble and the board met to sort out the crisis. A group of board members led by Stu Long, who owned bars all over Washington, decided they needed me, the youngest member of the board, to take over. Stu, Washington businessman Art McZier, and Dick Nelson, the manager of the Hyatt Hotels in Washington, spent the weekend urging me to take the job, saying I was the only one who could save the bank.

By that time I had already started a dozen companies and had my own law firm and venture capital companies, but I was intrigued by the idea of being elected one of the youngest bank chairmen ever. Joe Kennedy was just twenty-five when he took over the Columbia Trust Bank in 1912 as bank president. Later I almost shared another distinction with Joe Kennedy when Bill Clinton asked me to become ambassador to the Court of St. James, but Al Gore's 2000 convention got in the way.

If I'd have known what these guys on the bank board were asking me to do, I would have told them to jump off a cliff, but on January 18, 1988, three weeks before my thirty-first birthday, I was elected chairman. We immediately restructured and hired a new president, Clyde Smith, and went to work getting the small bank back on track. Those were bad years in the banking industry, as the Bush 41 administration, reeling from the savings and loan crisis, set about closing as many small banks as possible. They wanted to consolidate the industry and create megabanks, ignoring the useful purpose community banks serve for smaller businesses and the little guy. In Washington alone there were six small banks started in the 1980s, and only two survived.

Early in my tenure as chairman, a new team of young, inexperienced bank regulators showed up, and the federal bank examiner dropped a bombshell.

"We're going to send in the liquidation team," she told me.

"I'm new to this job," I said. "I can save this bank. If you want to shut us down and cost the taxpayers millions of dollars, I'm putting you on notice that we're not going quietly."

It took a lot of convincing, but eventually they gave us more time. I think of that as probably the roughest five years of my life, working my tail off in another unpaid job, but also as one of my sweetest triumphs in business. In the end we were able to rally the board members and bring in enough new business to keep the bank afloat long enough to salvage the situation, and successfully merged the bank in May 1993.

★

IF ANY CONGRESSMAN was going to pull it off and win the presidency, I thought Dick Gephardt had a shot. Born and raised in St. Louis, the son of a milk truck driver, he had a work ethic and great Midwestern values. He'd been a star legislator since he was first elected to Congress in 1976, and always fought to make sure that American workers had a level playing field in the world economy.

Given the skepticism about a congressman making the jump to the White House, we were running into brick walls with donors all the time. Basically Dick needed someone like me, an upbeat, crazy, happy-with-life guy who was up all the time whether the news was good or bad. We ended up second in money among Democrats, behind only Massachusetts Governor Michael Dukakis, but the ups and downs of a campaign are enough to drive most people bonkers. The phone rang in our office in early 1987, and it was Dick calling from a plane with some unbelievable news.

"We can raise a million dollars at an event in Louisville, Kentucky!" he told me.

Dick was with a group of businessmen including one we'll call Bebe, a former fund-raiser for a Kentucky governor, who was telling Dick he would organize a Louisville event and bring in a million bucks. Now let me tell you, it's a lot easier to raise money for a governor. They have all kinds of business to hand out, road contracts, construction jobs, you name it. But it's a whole different story when you run for President. I was never going to contradict Dick, but when he said we could raise a million on this event, as a fund-raiser your first reaction was to discount that tremendously. We budgeted it for $100,000.

The event was scheduled for mid-May, just before Memorial Day, and as it approached I took to joking with my finance director, Boyd Lewis, about the million bucks we were going to be raking in on this Kentucky event. Hoo boy! It was going to be great! We'd laugh over that awhile and then get back to work. But then Boyd got a call from Bebe and passed the word to me that the event had pulled in $220,000. We were euphoric! It wasn't a million, but that was a nice heap of dough. I was especially pleased because Bebe said he'd FedEx all the checks up by Saturday, which meant we could go ahead and issue paychecks to our staff a few days early so they could all go out and enjoy the three-day holiday weekend. They'd all been working their tails off, living hand to mouth, and really needed to let off some steam.

"Go ahead and issue the checks," I told the campaign manager, Bill Carrick.

So, as I was getting ready to leave the office to go to Dewey Beach for the weekend, Finance was everybody's hero. They were stopping by my desk to thank me, and making jokes about how many cases of beer they'd be able to carry home. That Saturday morning I was talking to Boyd on the phone from my rental house in Dewey Beach. We went over the numbers real quick, the way we always did, and then I was going to walk down to the beach.

"Did you get the package from Louisville?" I asked Boyd.

"No, it didn't come yet," he said.

This was around eleven o'clock in the morning.

"Well, when does FedEx come?" I asked Boyd.

"Sometime around now," he said. "They'll get here."

I puttered around the house a while and at noon the phone rang again.

"No FedEx yet," he said.

"Well, that's weird," I said. "Have you called Bebe?"

"No, I'll call him and call you back," he said.

A few minutes later the phone rang.

"He says more checks came in, about twenty thousand dollars more, so he wanted to wait and send them all together," Boyd told me. "We'll get them by FedEx at four o'clock."

I got a full afternoon out of Dewey Beach and was back at the house at five o'clock when the phone rang again.

"No checks," Boyd said.

Now I was getting a little nervous. Keep in mind, we had just issued our payroll checks and we needed the money from Kentucky to cover them. The one thing you can never do in a presidential campaign is bounce checks. Once you do that, word will get out in a heartbeat and it will be like blood in the water for the sharks. Your campaign is over. You can't survive that.

Boyd suggested I call down to Louisville.

"What's the deal?" I said. "You said the checks would be here."

"Terry, great you called," Bebe said. "A few more checks showed up, about six more. It was too late for FedEx to get there today so I put them all on Delta Dash and they'll arrive at the airport at 7:10 tonight."

"Okay, great," I said.

Boyd sent his assistant, Sage Smith, out to the airport to go to the Delta gate to meet the flight and collect the checks.

"Sage is at the airport," Boyd told me when he called at eight o'clock. "The plane is in. There's no package."

This was getting very serious. Boyd and I kept calling Bebe down in Kentucky, but he was unavailable, and in fact to this day we have never heard from him again. Now it was time for full-out panic. I worked the phones all day long and into the night the rest of that weekend, calling finance committee members around the country and pulling out all the stops.

"I don't care what you have to do," I said. "You go to your neighbors. You try anyone you can. But you get checks in here. It's now or never."

Somehow we got enough checks by Wednesday to cover all the paychecks and save us a major embarrassment.

"What happened in Louisville?" I asked Dick later.

"Terry, this was a very weird event," he said. "I got up to speak and nobody stopped talking to listen to me. Everybody was just standing around in gym shorts, drinking beer and laughing and talking among themselves."

Here's what we finally put together: Bebe promised Dick a one-million-dollar event and couldn't sell tickets to his fund-raiser. He was desperate to save face and got wind that there was going to be a party at a restaurant in Louisville with free beer. So Bebe took Dick up to this restaurant where a huge crowd had shown up to drink the free beer.

"It was packed," Dick remembers. "I mean, you couldn't move. I thought, 'This is the greatest.' There were all these young people in cutoffs. I was all pumped up and gave a really fiery speech. But it wasn't quite what I expected. They didn't seem to understand what was going on too much. They didn't seem to care that I was even in the room."

The event had nothing to do with "Gephardt for President" and no one gave a penny to the Gephardt campaign. That had to be the craziest stunt ever pulled in fund-raising.

★

GARY HART WAS CONSIDERED the 1988 front-runner, based on his strong showing in '84, but no one thought he was a lock. Cuomo, if he ran, loomed as the next-strongest candidate, but his intentions were unclear. Dick was dismissed as a "dark horse" in a big pack of question-mark candidates that included Bruce Babbitt, Dukakis, Al Gore, Jesse Jackson, and Paul Simon, and it was a given Dick would have to finish in the top three in the Iowa caucuses and in the top two in the New Hampshire primary to have any chance. Dick knew better than anyone how important Iowa was, and had his mother Loreen live in Des Moines for a year to work on his campaign. By the last few days before the vote in Iowa, just a month after political professionals had been writing off our campaign, Dick was suddenly dubbed the front-runner.

Sure enough, Dick won the thing! But in a stroke of bad luck, the news coverage was all about the Republicans, since Vice President Bush had shocked everyone by coming in third place behind Bob Dole and Pat Robertson, showing that Bush wasn't the lock for the nomination everyone had been expecting. Eight years earlier in Iowa, Bush had pulled in 38,000 votes, but after eight years as Vice President he mustered only 21,000. Johnny Apple, writing in *The Times,* called it a "stunning" result and a "surprisingly feeble showing" for Bush.

Our strategy in the Gephardt campaign was built around winning Iowa and then using that bounce to go up to New Hampshire and knock off Dukakis, who had a big edge there as governor of a neighboring state. But once Gephardt won in Iowa, he was everybody's target. We had hoped Simon would have been knocked out after Iowa, but he had just enough money left to come to New Hampshire and launch a series of negative ads against Dick. We had to pivot, and instead of going after Dukakis, we had to fight Simon for second place, which we ended up getting.

Thanks to Tom Daschle, Dick was resurrected and won big in the South Dakota primary, finishing with 44 percent to 31 percent for Dukakis and 8 percent for Gore, although Dukakis cut into our coverage when he won the Minnesota caucuses the same day. The big contest after that was Super Tuesday, when twenty states and one territory would all have their Democratic primaries or caucuses on the same day. We had to reach out to 46 million registered voters in those mostly southern states, compared to only 1.5 million voters in Iowa, and the only way was buying TV ads. That was going to be expensive and we were living hand-to-mouth.

"All right, Bill, how much do we need for Super Tuesday?" I asked Bill Carrick, the campaign manager.

It was my job to raise the money and his to spend it.

"Terry, we need $1.1 million," he told me.

We were sitting in his office for our weekly meeting and I let him think he'd shocked me for a minute. He was always asking for more than we could give him and we would go through this whole song and dance until we worked our way around to a more realistic number. This was the first time the number he gave was less than what we could give.

"Bill," I said. "How about if I give you $1.6 million?"

"It's over!" he said. "We've got it. We've won the primaries. We're going to win the nomination."

The other campaigns decided they had to stop us. We were coming up to the industrial states like Michigan, where Dick was going to do great. Neither Dukakis nor Gore wanted to take the chance that Gephardt would do well on Super Tuesday and use that as a springboard into Michigan and the other industrial states. So they both went after him. Dukakis and Gore pulled a pincer movement on us with both campaigns going heavy with anti-Gephardt ads. Taking heat from two sides like that, we melted.

A week before Super Tuesday, Dick's pollster called and said, "We're ahead in every state." Four days later, Dick remembers, the pollster called again and said, "We're behind everywhere except Missouri." Gore had a very effective ad of a guy who looked like Dick on a trampoline doing flip-flops, and that really cut into Dick's support and turned Dukakis's big war chest into an important factor.

"We were riding high in the saddle and four days later we were dead," Dick says. "That's the way it works in politics."

I argued that we should focus our spending on Dick's home state of Missouri and one or two others, like Oklahoma and Texas. But no, no, no, we had to go for a knockout blow. We spread our money out and bought television ads in several states we shouldn't have, like Florida. Congressman Claude Pepper helped us in Florida, but we never should have wasted our precious resources in a state the size of Florida, when the Dukakis campaign was outspending us overall two to one. Missouri, where Dick had started out as a city alderman in St. Louis, ended up being the only bright spot for us: Dick won there with 58 percent of the vote, but everywhere else was a disaster for us.

We knew we were dead after that. The only question was whether to fold up our tent or fight awhile longer. I remember we had a secret meeting down in South Carolina in a little cabin way out in the woods to talk about the future of the campaign. We had Michigan coming up, which would have been great if we weren't so far in debt by then.

"Well, let's try to make a stand in Michigan," one faction was saying.

"Look," I said. "We don't have the money to go make a stand in Michigan."

The mood in the cabin in the South Carolina woods got a little more tense.

"But let's do this," I said. "Let's put a bare-bones operation together in Michigan and then we can keep fund-raising, and whatever we raise will still be matched by federal funds. That way we can start paying down our debt and pray for a miracle."

So we decided we would keep going at least through Michigan, but instead of using it to pay down the million-dollar debt we'd run up by then, our political team spent an additional $2 million in Michigan. Jesse Jackson won the Michigan caucuses, with Dukakis a few points behind, and Dick way back in a distant third. That was the end. Dick had a press conference to announce it was over, and to thank everyone. Someone asked if he would be running for President again in 1992. A huge crowd of us, several hundred strong, gave him a big hand and just kept clapping, not letting him go on.

"I don't think Jane was clapping," Dick said, smiling at his wife, standing next to him with their three kids.

I knew better than most why Jane might have been cautious about Dick running again. Even after we closed up shop in Michigan, the bills kept coming in, and when I added them all up I found out Dick was $4 million in debt. That was a lot of money in 1988. Someone had to go to Dick and give him the bad news, and I wasn't about to hand that job off to anyone else. A lot of people walked away from this man as soon as that campaign was over. I didn't spend the money, but I was his finance chairman and I was his friend and this was no time to make myself scarce.

"Dick, let me tell you something," I said. "I started with you, and I'm going to finish with you. I'm going to stay with you right to the end until we finish this debt off."

Boyd Lewis and John O'Hanlon, another one of our fund-raisers, made the same vow to Dick and stayed on, and we spent the next year and a half flying all over the country whittling that debt down dollar by dollar. We knew Dick had to get this monkey off his back or he could forget about running for higher office again. John Glenn, the senator and former astronaut, ran for President in 1984 and ended up almost $3 million in debt. Glenn wrestled with that debt for many years and to this day may still not have paid it off. As I've said before, the one thing you always have to have as a fund-raiser is certainty that your candidate is going to win, so you can pass that on to people and they can have the feeling of backing a winner. That gets difficult when your candidate has already lost. And let me tell you, paying off a debt of a failed presidential candidate who is a member of Congress, not a senator and not a governor—that is one huge challenge. Your base of donors has already reached their maximum contributions, so you have to go out and find new thousand-dollar donors.

I knew the only way to get Dick's debt down was to attack it, and we had luck negotiating some of it down, settling for fifteen to twenty cents on the dollar, and raised enough to cover the rest. It took eighteen months of miserable work, but we freed him from that burden, and that cleared the way for Dick later to become House Majority Leader and to run for President again. I'd do the same thing again in a heartbeat. Loyalty was one thing my father taught me young back in Syracuse, and old Jack would have given me an earful if I'd tried to shirk my responsibilities to Dick. The only hope we had was that people loved Dick and thought he would run again in 1992.

"You've got to help Dick," I would say. "He's got a great future. We've got to get him ready for '92."

Dick was thinking hard about running again in '92 and we had a whole series of meetings in my office. I was in favor of him running, since you never know what can happen in this business. But I think for Dick it was a searing experience to have that debt hanging over his head, and he was not eager to repeat it. A group of us would meet to talk strategy and analyze the race, and none of us liked what we were seeing. This was at a time following the Gulf War when the first President Bush was up around 90 percent in the polls.

"What the heck," I said. "You can't win if you're not in there."

We went around the room to see what everyone thought and over and over it was the same: "We just can't beat Bush."

In February of 1992, when the Clinton campaign was faltering, many of Dick's advisers kept calling him and trying to get him to change his mind and run. It got so bad that one of Bill Clinton's top campaign officials asked for a secret meeting with Dick to urge him to get in the race, and the three of us talked it over. I was against Dick jumping in late. I'm a strong believer that once you've made a decision, you've got to stick with it. I spent an hour and a half after the meeting with Dick making clear how strongly I opposed this. You should run for President because you have a vision for what you can do for the country, not because your advisers suddenly smell opportunity.

Gephardt had made the decision in the summer of 1991 not to get into the race and wanted to focus on his responsibilities as House Majority Leader, where he knew he could immediately make a difference. Bush was so high in the polls, and a Democrat had not won since Jimmy Carter in 1976. There was so much pessimism, it overwhelmed a lot of Democrats who didn't believe Bush could be beaten. It took someone with an unusual ability to tune out the negative and focus on a positive vision of the future even to take on that race, which is why I'm so glad that Bill Clinton decided that it was finally time to live up to what people had been telling him since he was a boy and run for President of the United States.

8

★ ★ ★

I'd known for years that Bill Clinton was that rare figure who could really take us places as a party, and Election Night 1992 was one of the all-time great moments in my life. Clinton had ousted George Herbert Walker Bush and was bringing a freshness and energy to Washington that had people everywhere excited about the first Baby Boomer President. I had cochaired a national event for the campaign in Little Rock that September with Molly Raiser and Tony Coelho that raised $5 million, and was thrilled to be witnessing history the day of Bill Clinton's Inauguration, which I knew Dorothy and I would be talking about for the rest of our lives. "We must invest more . . . and at the same time cut our massive debt," Clinton said in his fourteen-minute Inaugural speech. "It is time to break the bad habit of expecting something for nothing."

The President had a small diplomatic pickle on his hands his first month in office with South Korea, where on February 25, Kim Young Sam was inaugurated as the first civilian president in thirty-one years. Bill Clinton was always very alert to potential problems in foreign policy, even early on when he had not yet earned the reputation as a statesman that in June 2000 would make him the first sitting U.S. President ever to be awarded the prestigious Charlemagne Prize in Aachen, Germany.

Clinton appreciated even in 1993 how important South Korea would be in helping us deal with the regime in North Korea, still led at that point by

Kim Il Sung, the so-called Great Leader and former buddy of Stalin, who presided over what might be the least free country in the world. We had 40,000 troops in South Korea, including 14,000 along the DMZ, guarding against another North Korean attack like the one that started the Korean War on June 25, 1950.

Clinton's problem was that South Korea was hosting the three-month Taejon Expo later that year, with more than one hundred countries participating. It was an event planned to mark the centenary of the World's Columbian Exposition of 1893 in Chicago, but Congress had not agreed to fund any U.S. participation. During the Bush 41 administration, people at the U.S. Information Agency said that so much government money was wasted, Congress would not fund these international expos and fairs anymore.

The South Koreans put pressure on the Clinton administration to participate, since without us the first official international exposition to be held in a developing country would have been a failure. That would have been a major slap in the face to South Korea. Dick Gephardt advised the President to take quick action and to appoint me to rescue the event, which was going to run from August 7 to November 7, and they fast-tracked my appointment through the White House and Senate.

On March 19, I was sworn in at the U.S. Information Agency as commissioner general, and was soon given the rank of ambassador by the President. I immediately flew to South Korea and was sworn in as U.S. ambassador to the Taejon Expo. A big part of my job was raising money to fund the U.S. presence, and we ended up pulling in $3.4 million from the private sector, so that not a dime was charged to taxpayers. Our biggest sponsor was Amway.

I also had diplomatic responsibilities associated with smoothing over the awkwardness after we almost stiffed the South Koreans and didn't show up for their big event. Given all the appointments the administration had to cover, the President did not announce his choice of Emory president Jim Laney to be ambassador to South Korea until July 3, and Jim did not start until October.

I lived in South Korea through a good part of 1993, staying in Seoul and taking helicopter rides south to Taejon with my deputy, Kevin Allen. We made an interesting duo, since Kevin was the son of Ronald Reagan's national security adviser, Richard V. Allen. We did events all over South Korea to build up interest, and spent months preparing for the U.S. National Day as part of the Expo. I had to give a big speech in front of thousands of people and it was all very formal and well choreographed. Just as Dorothy and I were walking up, surrounded by dignitaries and thousands of people, one of the South Korean protocol people pulled her aside.

"You can't do that," he told her.

She had no idea what he was talking about.

"Do what?" Dorothy asked, puzzled.

"You cannot walk next to the ambassador," the South Korean told my wife. "You need to be two steps behind him."

If I hadn't been trying my hardest to be diplomatic, I'd have laughed in this poor bureaucrat's face. There was no way in a million years anyone was going to put Dorothy in a position like that.

"That ain't gonna happen with my wife," I said. "She's going to walk right with me."

★

AMWAY WAS MAKING a big move into South Korea at that time, which was why they were our top sponsor. All of a sudden you had thousands of women out selling Amway products to their friends and neighbors or church groups, and that was a shock to the entire culture. Women in South Korea in general did not work. But these Amway-selling women were making a living and enjoying feeling independent, and they were recruiting their friends and family to sell Amway, too. So many complaints were raised about the rapid spread of this network, the government actually stepped in and arrested a group of Amway employees, including the company's top executive in South Korea, an American named David Ussery, Avon Japan's former chairman of the board. David was a great guy, and they hog-tied him and frog-marched him off to prison in early July.

Luckily for Ussery, he had been nabbed a week before Bill Clinton was due to arrive in South Korea as part of a six-day tour of Asia that was his first trip abroad as President. Now remember, Jim Laney had been chosen as ambassador but wouldn't be in South Korea until October. So I sat down with the attaché at the embassy and we cooked up a plan to get David Ussery freed without having to strong-arm the situation or embarrass anyone.

The President arrived for a two-day visit, and immediately started charming the host South Koreans and the tens of thousands of U.S. soldiers. He walked out onto the Bridge of No Return separating North and South Korea, stopped near the white line dividing the two countries, and said, "Some day this will all be one country again."

That night Kim Young Sam hosted the President and First Lady at a lavish State Dinner at the Blue House, the South Korean counterpart to the White

House. Clinton was coming off a successful visit to Japan and had done a great job that day of connecting with the U.S. troops, who cheered wildly when he borrowed a saxophone from a member of the Army Band and started riffing. We were having a great time at dinner when someone came up to me.

"You have an urgent call from the U.S. Embassy, Mr. Ambassador," I was told.

An urgent call! I walked over to take it.

"Mr. Ambassador, the situation with David Ussery is becoming critical," the attaché at the embassy told me. "He's been held a week now and they're still binding his wrists and ankles with rope. Please make sure you give the President a thorough briefing on the situation tonight."

"I'll do that," I said, hanging up and walking back to the table.

Soon we got word that Ussery was being released. Our plan had worked to perfection. We had staged the urgent call to me at the state dinner, knowing full well that South Korean intelligence would listen in and pass every word on to the South Korean president. We also knew that the last thing they wanted was for President Clinton to make a public issue of Ussery's imprisonment. That was to be avoided at all costs. So they knew they had to release Ussery fast, before Clinton was forced into action on his behalf, and that was exactly what they did.

"President Clinton's two-day visit to South Korea was devoted almost entirely to demonstrating to Seoul and Tokyo that Washington was committed to stopping North Korea from building nuclear weapons," Gwen Ifill wrote in *The New York Times* that July 12. " 'When you examine the nature of the American security commitment to Korea, to Japan, to this region, it is pointless for them to try to develop nuclear weapons,' Mr. Clinton said. 'Because if they ever use them, it would be the end of their country.' "

Unfortunately, the Bush 43 policy of no interaction with North Korea, just because Bush and his advisers were determined to do the opposite of whatever Clinton had done, leaves us in a threatening situation today. On Bush's watch the North Koreans have developed at least six nuclear weapons and now have the capability to deliver them and potentially to hit U.S. territory. Heck of a job, George.

*

OUR OLDEST SON, JACK, was born in February 1993, and at that time everyone was talking about health-care reform. Bill Clinton had given a speech exactly one month before Jack's birthday announcing the President's Task Force on National Health Care Reform with the First Lady as chair. He

declared that the administration would push to control health-care costs
and provide health care to everyone. Unwisely, as we now know, he also
vowed to present his plan for health-care reform to Congress within one
hundred days.

Dorothy was in labor at Georgetown Hospital and I was there lending
moral support. Just to be friendly, I started talking to the anesthesiologist
and her OB, Dr. Mark Reiter, and before you knew it we were really getting
into it over health care. Dorothy was suffering through the pain of labor and
the doctors and I were having a heated argument.

"Do you want socialized medicine?" the anesthesiologist asked me, his
voice rising.

"Of course not," I said. "However, there are thirty-seven million unin-
sured people in this country with no access to health care. Is that fair?"

I was almost shouting by then and began to worry that in his first moments on earth, poor little Jack was going to have his mind seared for life
with this health-care debate.

"And last year we spent $45 billion on administrative costs," I said.
"That's not providing health care. That's pushing paper. You call that efficient?"

We were making so much noise that we got kicked out of the delivery
room by a nurse who made Nurse Ratched look like Mother Teresa.

"Okay, guys, you're out of here," she insisted and we walked out into
the doctor's lounge to slug it out there. Jack McAuliffe is still proud to this
day that as he came into the world his father was down the hall fighting for
the little guy.

★

MY BUSINESS BACKGROUND helped me when I went to work as chairman
of the DNC Business Leadership Forum the first year of Bill Clinton's presidency. When I stepped down in February 1994, Vice President Gore flew to
Florida for our annual weekend retreat down in Boca Raton and presented
me with a plaque saying: THE GREATEST FUND-RAISER IN THE HISTORY OF
WESTERN CIVILIZATION. We built the BLF up from just 132 members when
I started to 620 members when I resigned, and smashed all records for fund-
raising. We needed to change the image of our party and bring in some pro-
business people, and I went out and signed up young entrepreneurs and
small business people all over the country. They loved Clinton and Gore,
and understood what they were trying to do to reduce a bloated federal bu-

reaucracy, eliminate thousands of meaningless federal regulations, and provide incentives to spur economic growth.

One of my favorite months of the year has always been March because of St. Patrick's Day, and that's when I head to New York City for the annual Big East basketball tournament. The McAuliffe men have been making the tournament a yearly tradition ever since the Big East was founded in 1979, and I tell you, my thirteen-year-old son, Jack, can't wait until he's old enough to be included—and I'm sure it will be the same with Peter, once he's old enough to figure it out. It was always a great chance to spend time with my dad and my brothers and cheer on Georgetown, my alma mater, and Syracuse, my hometown team. A group of us always rode up together, including Washington journalists Al Hunt and Mark Shields, both great basketball fans. We always took the 7 A.M. train so we could get up there in time for the noon start and catch four games that first day.

The 1994 Big East started out on a high note when Georgetown blew out Boston College in the first round. That was also the year that Donyell Marshall scored forty-two points in a game for Connecticut. I hated to duck out on the Big East early, but I had to fly to Cleveland on March 12 for a DNC meeting, where I was elected finance chairman. I got up on the podium as briefly as I could and then hopped a cab back to the airport and flew back to New York for more of the Big East.

I had been in the Oval Office for photo ops before or just to poke my head in for a look around, but two months after the Big East, in May 1994, I had my first full-fledged meeting there to go over the DNC budget with the President, DNC chairman David Wilhelm, chief of staff Mack McLarty, deputy chief of staff Harold Ickes, and political director Joan Baggett.

I was respectful and deferential, as you'd expect of someone during their first real meeting in the Oval Office, but nobody could expect me to stop being myself. That budget had been loaded up like a tanker. The DNC was being used as a dumping ground for people who had to be taken care of one way or another, and it was draining money away from what should have been our spending priorities. When the conversation turned to political consultants, I went off on a tirade.

"Many of these consultants should be working for free!" I said.

Everyone knew I was a full-time volunteer.

"These consultants are making tons of money and they're ripping us off for hundreds of thousands of dollars a year!" I exploded.

I went on and on and the President just sat there looking at me and smirking. On the way out of the meeting Harold Ickes looked over at me and shook his head slowly.

"You were pretty damn blunt," he said. "Not many people go into the Oval Office and talk like that."

"Harold, I'm serious about this," I said. "The donors don't want us to waste our money on a bunch of consultants."

★

HEALTH CARE SHOULD HAVE BEEN an issue that brought the country together, but instead it was splitting us apart. As is often the case, that was largely the result of a high-priced lobbying campaign. Insurance companies were making a fortune with the old system and didn't want it changed, so they paid for a series of TV ads starring "Harry and Louise," supposedly two regular Americans talking health care. The Health Insurance Association of America spent $17 million on the ads, which were so slick and manipulative, they struck a chord with the general public and prompted 286,000 calls to a toll-free line in the first six months after they started airing in September 1994.

Dan Rostenkowski, then the chairman of the House Ways and Means Committee, blasted the ads, saying, "Your messages are becoming the Willie Horton of the health-care campaign—they're increasing the heat of the debate without adding any light."

They had successfully—and incorrectly—convinced every American that they could no longer go to their own doctor, but would be assigned one by some big governmental health-care organization.

The White House knew it had to fight back against these ads and decided to turn to the DNC, which up until then the Clinton administration had not used. Former Ohio Governor Dick Celeste was charged with rounding up $10 million for an ad campaign countering what the health-insurance lobby was putting out there, but Dick and his team had trouble raising the funds. There was some thought to asking me to take this on as well as my duties as DNC finance chair, and I was all for it.

"We've got to counter these ads," Hillary Clinton said in a meeting with her staff that April. "We need to raise ten million bucks."

"Who could we get to do it?" asked Mandy Grunwald, Hillary's media consultant, who would end up producing the ads.

Someone suggested me.

"No, no, he's already got enough to do as finance chairman," Harold Ickes said. "He's got his hands full."

"Look," said Hillary, "if Terry says he can do both, he can do both."

The Clintons ended up learning some important lessons over the health-care campaign, starting with a new awareness of just how far entrenched special interests would go to resist change and how successfully clever opponents can get the media to go along with a false story line. The Clintons' plan was nothing revolutionary. The idea was just to make health care universal, make it affordable, make it more competitive, and improve the quality. If different insurance companies had to offer the same benefits and compete on quality, the result would be better, cheaper health care. That was a worthy goal, but the administration made some mistakes in its communication strategy, and the press twisted everything they were doing way out of proportion. We were all learning lessons about how effective some people could be at manipulating the press.

"I didn't get that," Hillary says now. "I was a little girl from Chicago. I went to college, I read these newspapers, I lived in Arkansas. I sort of figured that what we read was a fact. I was shocked to find out otherwise."

The health-care fight ended up establishing a real bond between Hillary and me. We held a series of meetings to discuss the progress I was making and got used to working together. Neither one of us could believe the extreme scare tactics that were being used against us on health care. Democrats had been working for health-care reform since Harry Truman, but people were trying to make us out as socialists because we thought all sick people, not just rich ones, have a right to see a doctor. We all knew what this was about. The Republicans wanted at all costs to stop Bill Clinton from getting a big political win on his signature issue.

I threw everything I had into raising $10 million to level the playing field and instructed my finance director, Laura Hartigan, to make this the top priority of the DNC fund-raising operation. Laura had grown up in Chicago in a strong family of Irish Catholics, all of them fiery redheads. Her father, Neil Hartigan, had served as Illinois' attorney general and narrowly lost a race for governor. As finance director, Laura did a magnificent job of managing and organizing the fund-raising staff, and put together a list of prospects for us to go after for the health-care campaign.

One of my first prospect meetings was up in Connecticut with Skip Hayward, the chairman of the Mashantucket Pequot Indian tribe. The Pequots operated Foxwoods Casino and were raking in the money, reportedly a million bucks a day, so I thought they could write us a check for half a million. Laura and I flew up to meet Skip and he sent out a huge white limo to meet us on the tarmac, and I think it was even longer than the private plane the Pequots had sent to fly us up from Washington.

Skip met us out in front of the casino and couldn't have been friendlier. Now keep in mind, people always knew why I was visiting. If I came to see you, it was pretty clear I wasn't there to give you a dental checkup—though it might be as painful. Skip took us on the longest casino tour you could imagine. He had us down in the bingo parlor and was explaining every last detail of how it all worked. The whole time I was trying to find an opening to ask Skip for that half a million bucks, but he never gave me a chance to say two words.

He offered Laura and me drinks and that was just fine with me. One thing I always teach young fund-raisers is: Never say no when someone offers you a drink. Rule No. 1 is get the drinks going early so everyone is loosened up and feeling good. Rule No. 2 is don't let them drink so much that they later forget their commitment.

One of the best young fund-raisers I've ever trained was Peter O'Keefe, who still works with me on a number of projects. I remember one time in 2002, we went to Boccaccio, a great old Italian joint in Baltimore, to have lunch with Peter Angelos, the Orioles owner.

"Would anyone like a glass of wine?" Angelos asked.

"No, thank you," Peter said.

"You bet I would, and Peter will have one, too," I said. "Why don't you join us?"

I told Peter later: You never turn down a drink, especially when you're going to ask for a million bucks. We drank and got the million. And Angelos remembered the commitment.

That night up at Foxwoods Casino in Connecticut, it soon became clear that we were going to have to knock down a few drinks before we ever got an answer out of Skip on the half million. All through dinner I was talking about how important the health-care program was for the future of our country and how much it mattered to the President and Hillary. This went on for two hours and every time I would ask for the money, Skip would find a way to distract me or change the subject before I could get an answer out of him. He was good, very good. Not too many people can put me off that long.

"Let's go to the show!" Skip said around ten o'clock.

Laura and I still had to fly back to Washington and were itching to get out of there, but what choice did we have?

"Let's go!" I said.

So we settled into a booth right up front in this huge nightclub with more than a thousand people crowded in there, and they brought out a magnum of champagne and popped the cork. We were all carrying on and having a good old time, but I was starting to get a little nervous that this show was going to end without me getting my commitment.

"Skip, I need that five hundred grand," I said. "Are you going to do it or aren't you?"

For a minute he just smiled and thought about how to answer.

"You know, Terry," he said. "If you get up on stage and sing a song, I'll give you the five hundred grand."

"Give me a microphone," I said without missing a beat.

Someone brought out handheld mikes and I hopped up on stage with Laura and walked over and asked the orchestra to fire up "Will You Still Love Me Tomorrow?" We gave it our best, but to be honest, we sounded like two sick dogs being beaten with a cat-o'-nine-tails. People were yelling, booing, catcalling. If we'd have gone on much longer, who knows what they would have done? But for $500,000 I didn't mind humiliating myself for five minutes.

I walked back to our booth and handed Skip the mike. He and his wife and all his aides were doubling over, they were laughing so hard.

"Congratulations, you got it," Skip said.

"Great," I said and without breaking stride, walked right out of there, and hopped back into the big white limo with Laura, and on to the airport. We laughed the whole way back to Washington. I called the First Lady from the plane.

"Fire up the ads," I said. "I just got us our first five hundred grand, and you're never going to believe what I had to do to get it done."

★

I THINK THE PRESIDENT liked that I had guts and was passionate about breaking out of the pattern of business as usual. Later that year, my name kept coming up in White House discussions of who ought to head up fundraising for the 1996 reelection campaign.

"Why are you having Dick Gephardt's top money guy as our finance chairman?" the Vice President asked.

"Al, because he's the best," the President said.

PART TWO

FIGHTING HARD FOR
THE PRESIDENT

9

Bill Clinton and I had a lot to discuss on Election Night 1994, but when the President pulled me aside around ten o'clock and took me up to the Truman Balcony, the two of us sat there awhile just working on our cigars and taking in the view. When Clinton told me later that he loved every minute of his eight years in office, he was telling it like it was. Even in the worst moments—and Election Night 1994 was one of them—the President always found a way to share with you his sense of awe and wonder at where life had taken him. We sat in big lounge chairs there on the Truman Balcony, the President drinking his usual Diet Coke, me with my usual beer, and looked down the sloping south lawn of the White House toward the Washington Monument and Jefferson Memorial, which looked so close you could touch them.

"Doesn't it look like Thomas Jefferson is looking right at us?" the President said.

To us this was the best view in America. What a great country if the White House was open to a couple nobodies like us, a kid from Syracuse whose dad was a local real estate agent, and a kid from Hope, Arkansas, whose dad was killed in a road accident before he was born. That night was my first time out on the Truman Balcony alone with the President, and I was hoping Bill Clinton would have enough time left in office that I'd get a few more chances to sit out there with him and plan how we could make a real difference for the American people in the future.

"You know, Mac, we've done all right," the President said. "Not bad for two kids from the sticks."

Clinton and I had often been at the same functions in the decade-plus since our first meeting in 1980 after he'd become the youngest ex-governor in history. "That's my Ripley's deal," he likes to say. Up until that night on the Truman Balcony, we hadn't spent much time alone, but even then it was obvious we had a way of feeding off each other. I'm a very upbeat person. It's just my nature. That was something Bill Clinton and I shared. He loved my positive energy because it fired up his own natural optimism.

Earlier that night at the reception downstairs, the President was dejected and angry. Everyone at the White House was moping around like they were at a wake. Only when we got up on the balcony did Clinton focus on the future. As I did my best to find a silver lining, his mood started to improve. The way I saw it, there was good news and there was bad news in the election results. To start with the bad news, Newt Gingrich and his sham "Contract with America" had led an absolute rout of Democrats. We had lost both the House and Senate. As President Clinton put it in his book, *My Life,* "(W)e got the living daylights beat out of us, losing eight Senate seats and fifty-four House seats, the largest defeat for our party since 1946."

So what was the good news? Again, that Newt Gingrich and his "Contract with America" had led an absolute rout of Democrats. I was sure their victory was going to be *our* victory. It was just going to take awhile. Gingrich was one heck of a salesman. Say what you will about the man's character or basic decency, he could sell. But the worst thing that can happen to a master of the art of bull is to fall in love with your own image. It's like when pro athletes start thinking they really *are* that guy the image makers back at shoe company headquarters in Oregon have planted in everyone's heads. Gingrich was going to plump up like a Thanksgiving turkey and revel in his power. He was going to get overconfident. That would hurt him. Worst of all for Gingrich, he was actually going to have to pass some of this extremist legislation he'd been hawking so breathlessly all over the country. Once people got a load of the crazy things Newt and the posse who rode in with him had in mind, they'd sour on the whole lot of them.

People ask me all the time what the trick to fund-raising is. They always want to hear that there is some secret. But it's simple enough and I'll spell it out in black and white: As a fund-raiser you're selling belief. You're selling vision. You're selling hope. You're selling dreams.

"I really believe one reason people gave Terry money is that he wasn't just raising money, he made it fun, he made it part of the fight," Bill Clinton says. "It wasn't just: I'll take your money and let somebody else fight. He made you feel like you were involved in it."

There was not a lot of holiday cheer for Democrats at the end of 1994. Everyone was talking about how the voters had handed Bill Clinton a stunning setback. We had one major executive out in California who had planned a big DNC fund-raiser for us in late November, and he called me the day after the election and said he was canceling on us. This was not *Profiles in Courage*. It sickened me to see so many people heading for the hills on Bill Clinton. You've got to stick with your friends through good times and bad.

Newt Gingrich ended up flaming out in a hurry and looking ridiculous. All you have to do in Washington to get a laugh in some circles, even to this day, is recite, "Suddenly the pouting sex kitten gave way to Diana the Huntress. She rolled onto him and somehow was sitting athwart his chest, her knees pinning his shoulders." That was the famously bad passage from a novel Gingrich published in 1995 with a collaborator. I'm not making this up. Who could? But in the weeks after that November's elections Gingrich was considered a hot story. To a certain extent, you understood. The election result was a rebuke of historical proportions and Gingrich had helped make it happen. Still, something weird was going on. A congressman might stand equal with the President, the way Tip O'Neill did with Ronald Reagan, but in terms of prestige and maneuverability, the President always comes out ahead. Even so, the media was going nuts over Gingrich and gladly tossing any sense of perspective out the window. *Time* magazine put a rampaging elephant on its cover with the headline STAMPEDE! and took a mean-spirited swipe at one of the President's best qualities by adding: "The Republican romp lets President Clinton really feel the voters' pain."

★

FOUR DAYS BEFORE CHRISTMAS, Dorothy and I dressed up in black tie and headed to the White House for a Christmas party that was not as festive as we'd hoped. It was always a magical experience to be inside a White House decorated for the holidays with a spectacular Christmas tree up to the ceiling in the Blue Room, and a seventy-pound replica of Bill Clinton's childhood home in Hope, Arkansas, made of gingerbread and chocolate and featuring Santa on the roof and Frosty the Snowman in the front yard. Everyone had fun, but in a subdued way, and even a relentless optimist like me had trouble jacking people up, which presented me with a problem. If I couldn't pump up the guests at a White House Christmas party, how was I going to get anywhere with the President at the meeting we had scheduled for the next morning?

I was waiting with Harold Ickes, the deputy chief of staff whose father was one of Franklin Roosevelt's top advisers. We were ushered into the Oval Office for the meeting and as we started to walk inside, the President held up his hand.

"Just Terry," he said. "Harold, I need to talk to Terry alone."

This was the first time I was alone with Bill Clinton in the Oval Office. I like to think of Clinton as the Babe Ruth of American Presidents: Not only one of the greatest ever, but also a man of remarkably diverse talents. The Babe could hit home runs like no one else, and he was also a great pitcher. Clinton was one of the best pure campaigners ever, and he was also one of the best political strategists the Democratic Party has ever seen. That day in the Oval Office he broke down in detail what had gone wrong and why he felt so bad for the Democrats who lost because he had not been able to do more for them. Clinton needed to pressure quite a few members to get his budget passed and that was the right thing to do: Over time it became clear to everyone, especially a lot of skeptics in the media, that the budget Clinton pushed through that year was the key to taming the deficit and giving us surpluses that powered eight years of the greatest economic expansion this country has ever seen. That budget passed by a single vote, and some Democrats in Congress supported it knowing that it could spell defeat for them.

I think it helped Clinton to go through his analysis with me one more time to see if there might be anything he had missed. He kept a close eye on me as he talked about low turnout among Democratic base voters helping to explain the wide margin of Republican victory, as opposed to the normal swing expected for midterm elections two years after a new President takes over. I nodded and said "Yes, sir," and Clinton mentioned that up until that year we had held on to a lot of old Dixiecrat seats in the Old South with candidates who had been in office forever and a day, but who were finally retiring. Then he went over how the National Rifle Association, the rich and powerful gun lobby, had defeated about a dozen of our members who had voted for the Brady Bill and the Assault Weapons Ban. The NRA pumped more than $70 million into targeting Democrats and even bragged about how much money they'd spent. The Brady Bill was named for Jim Brady, Ronald Reagan's spokesman, who was seriously wounded when Reagan was shot, and his brave and determined wife Sarah campaigned for that bill for ten years before it finally passed. That vote was the right thing to do.

The President had just signed a bill that would get rid of 90 percent of the deficit, but the American people barely realized it. All through the Reagan years, people heard Republican leaders talk about the need to stop adding hundreds of billions of dollars in new debt every year, but Reagan ran up the biggest budget deficits in U.S. history, which climbed to an unheard-of 6 percent of GNP. So when President Clinton talked about doing the hard work of slashing the budget, people were trained by their experiences under Reagan and Bush 41 not to believe it. In fact, only after three years of budget-cutting under Clinton did a majority of Americans finally answer "Yes" when they were asked, "Is the deficit going down?"

Clinton's rundown on the elections was just a warm-up for what he really wanted to ask me: Would he have the resources to mount a campaign? Was it as bad as everyone out there was telling him?

"Mr. President, no one has talked to more donors than I have," I said. "They'll be there for you. They need you back off the mat. They need to see you back out there fighting. Get the hell out of the White House. It's like a morgue in here. You should get out there and see the people and tell them where you want to take this country. They're not mad at you, sir, they just need leadership. They're dispirited and they need you to be the First Cheerleader. I can't tell them the direction you want to take this country. I need you to do that."

Dorothy and I had our annual Christmas dinner party the night after that meeting with Clinton, and by then everyone seemed to know I was going to be Clinton's finance chairman for the reelection campaign, though no formal decision had been announced. That night our group included the Gephardts, the Coelhos, Doug Sosnik and his wife, Fabiana Jorge, former DNC chairman Chuck Manatt and his wife, Kathy, and Father William Byron and Monsignor William Kerr, the priests who married us. At the end of the night, as everyone was getting their coats, Dick Gephardt pulled me aside to let me know he was all for me working on the President's reelection campaign.

"He's lucky to have you," Dick said. "And you know what? He's going to win."

★

THE DAY AFTER CHRISTMAS everyone was clacking about a Rick Berke *New York Times* article saying GEPHARDT'S STAR RISES IN '96 SCENARIOS. "While no prominent Democrat is publicly making the case for Mr. Gephardt, he is the subject of behind-the-scenes chatter on Capitol Hill among Democrats who fear that President Clinton's popularity will not rebound and believe that Mr. Gephardt would be a logical alternative should the President decide not to seek reelection—whether by his own choice or because he is forced into early retirement," Berke wrote.

Forced into retirement? Were they all nuts? I had just talked to Dick at my house three days earlier and I knew there was no way on earth he was running. The one potential threat Clinton and I both took seriously was the possibility that New Jersey senator Bill Bradley, the former NBA star, might hop into the race. Bradley had always been talked about as a strong presidential candidate and an independent-thinking Democrat, and the fact that he later challenged Al Gore for the nomination in 2000 showed that he would not have hesitated to take on Clinton for the '96 nomination if he sensed opportunity.

I was not about to let that happen. We were going to show strength early and shut down a potential Bradley challenge before it could even get started. I knew President Clinton would not only be able to run for reelection, he would win. Hands down. Case closed. But sometimes I felt like the only voice of optimism in a sea of naysayers.

Many Washington pundits were writing Bill Clinton's political obituary after the 1994 midterm election. That November 13 on *This Week with David Brinkley,* Sam Donaldson said: "I just frankly think that for the next two years the President ought to enjoy life. Go on Air Force One, throw some parties, pursue pleasurable companionship of men and women that he enjoys in this town."

David Brinkley was right with Donaldson.

"Inspection trips on the beaches and such," he suggested.

I'll never forget how stunned I was watching ABC that morning and hearing these respected newsmen suggesting Clinton ought to just get on Air Force One and fly around the country for the next couple years because there was no way he could even run again. It was disconcerting, but at the same time I loved it because I knew we were going to have the last laugh.

"I was actually encouraged by what Sam said," the President says now. "That got my competitive juices flowing. They had to pronounce me dead ten or fifteen times in the '92 election, so I began to adopt a rule of thumb that whatever they said was the opposite of what would happen. If they'd said I could still win, I'd have been scared to death."

Clinton needed some time to get back into a fighting mood. I showed up back at the White House for breakfast with the President two days after Christmas and was shocked at how depressed the mood was. I got off the elevator on the second floor and it was dark and eerily quiet. The butler called out, "Mr. President," and he appeared out of the bedroom, looking solemn as we walked down to the Treaty Room for breakfast. The President looked as down in the dumps as I'd ever seen him, which surprised me because he'd seemed fine when I'd talked to him in the Oval Office five days earlier. I knew he'd had no meetings over the holiday weekend, so he must have spent twenty hours a day on the phone calling people who were depressing him. I knew I had to move and move quickly. If I was going to pull off the aggressive fund-raising plan I had in mind, I would need an upbeat Bill Clinton. I had to change the mood of this breakfast fast.

"Let me be crystal clear, sir," I said. "Since we met in the Oval Office last week, I've made my round of calls all over the country and I can tell you they still love you out there."

Clinton looked up at me with that hangdog look of his and didn't seem at all cheered up by what I said. This was going to take extreme measures.

"Don't worry about money, Mr. President," I said, slamming my fist down on the coffee table for emphasis and sending a fork flying through the air.

He had been sort of slouching down in his lounge chair, and I don't know if it was the two pots of coffee we were well on our way to guzzling, my booming voice, my fist pounding the table, or the fork tumbling past the President's ear, but at that point he came to attention.

"I'll make a promise to you right now," I said. "We'll raise the money faster than it's ever been done in American politics."

I slapped my knees for emphasis and sat back. For a good half minute we just stared at each other, neither of us sure what to do next. I did my best to eat my scrambled eggs and bacon using my spoon, because I wasn't about to start crawling around on the floor looking for my fork.

The whole time the President was looking at me as if he thought I was crazy. He followed my every move as if the way I spread butter on my toast was going to give him some important clue. In the weeks since the election he had spent so much time analyzing what he had done before the election to cost him what votes with which bloc of voters, he was in some kind of overdrive of analysis and had trouble downshifting. He wasn't ready to hear any good news.

"If you give me the time, we'll get the people motivated and you can get back to finish the work that people first elected you to do," I told the President. "People voted for you in 1992 because you gave them hope."

Clinton was coming closer to smiling now, but you could see the worry fighting to reel him back in. A part of him wondered if he was crazy putting a big part of his reelection hopes in the hands of this nut.

"Let me ask you something, Mr. President," I said. "Have I ever lied to you before? Have I ever not met a commitment?"

I had my eyebrows hiked up for emphasis and he knew I was dead serious about this.

"No, Mac," he said.

"Well, I ain't gonna start now," I said.

He tried to say something, but I wouldn't let him.

"We're not going to talk about it anymore, Mr. President," I said. "It's done. I'll put the plan together."

That was when it finally hit Bill Clinton that I would back up what I was saying. Once that sank in, a burden was off him. You could literally see his physical posture change. Years later he told me it kind of embarrassed him that I'd seen before he had how and why he was going to win and win handily in 1996.

"Terry was the first person I talked to who thought that now that the Republicans had won this majority, they would actually try to do what they said and the people would hate it," Clinton remembers. "He figured out that Republicans winning on such a radical platform would actually help me get reelected and he thought that long before the conventional wisdom said so. He instinctively knew what we later learned."

The President finished up breakfast that morning in late '94 and turned back to the campaign.

"What do I need to do?" he said.

"Mr. President, the first thing I need is time on your schedule for you to personally look your past supporters in the eye and say, 'I'm running for reelection and here's why you need to support me.' Nobody else can do that but you, Mr. President.

"Two, you ought to call and thank all the people who helped us this year.

"Three, when you're out jogging or golfing, you need to include supporters with you and spend time with them in a leisurely atmosphere."

"No problem," he said. "Just put it in a memo and send it down to Nancy."

He put his arm around me and walked me down the long corridor from the Treaty Room past the Yellow Oval and back to the elevator. The President kept saying he couldn't thank me enough, and now the bounce was back in his step. I could tell from the twinkle in his eye that the fire had been reignited.

I went straight back to my office and called in Laura Hartigan and we started writing the fund-raising plan for the Clinton-Gore reelection campaign then and there. I was so jacked up after the breakfast, I didn't want to waste any time. I told Laura we were not going to put together just any fund-raising plan, we were going to put together a plan that would shatter all records.

The next day I received a call from Hillary, thanking me profusely for everything I had done to cheer up the President and to get him back in a fighting mood.

"I'm sick and tired of all the negative people around Bill bringing him down," she said. "We've got a lot of work to do for the American people over the next two years. We need Bill in fighting shape."

That night I went out to dinner with Harold Ickes, who would be the key man coordinating all the reelect activities from the White House, and his assistant, Janice Enright. He and I did not know each other well in the beginning, but he soon became my strongest advocate and supporter. He was one of the most loyal friends anyone could ever have, and if I ever needed to go into a foxhole, I'd want Harold there at my side. A fellow New Yorker, he was a tough, no-nonsense lawyer with a long civil rights background. We finished up our dinner that night and ended up talking another three hours about our vision for the campaign.

Later that week I drafted a memo putting down what the President and I discussed at breakfast and faxed it to Nancy Hernreich, the President's director of Oval Office operations. The memo was just a few lines, nothing controversial. A candidate was going to spend time with his supporters. What a shocker that was! I was careful how I worded the memo because the Clinton White House leaked like a sieve, and the only question in my mind was how many minutes it would take before a copy of this memo would be hand-delivered to *The Washington Post*. Little did I know that this would become the infamous Lincoln Bedroom Memo.

★

THE NEXT MONTH, I was expecting to meet the First Lady down in Puerto Rico for my last event as DNC finance chairman. Puerto Rico was always a wild place for fund-raising, going back to my first visits there for the Carter campaign, when we raised $300,000 and Evan Dobelle and I actually had a gun pulled on us in one meeting with a disgruntled fund-raiser. I always had fond memories of Puerto Rico because the people were friendly and colorful, we raised a ton of dough, and it was the first time I got a chance to spend some time with Jackie Kennedy. She was a goddess to them and rightly so. She was such a great lady, as charming and gracious as anyone

I've ever met. Our last day on that visit in 1980, Evan and I thought we'd save a little time by heading to the airport in Jackie Kennedy's motorcade, and she ended up inviting us to ride in the car with her. I'll never forget it.

I was looking forward to getting out of Washington for this January 1995 Hillary event and figured we would take care of business in a hurry and have some time to relax in Puerto Rico with a group including the First Lady, Dorothy, my team of Peter O'Keefe and Laura Hartigan, and my old friend Tony Coelho. It was near freezing when I left Washington and in the nineties when I arrived in San Juan, which hits you like a hot towel. The police were waiting to take me straight to the governor's office at La Fortaleza, which sits on this ledge of land looking out at the ocean. Charles V of Spain had the palace built in 1540 as a fortress, and it's the oldest governor's mansion in the hemisphere.

Governor Pedro Rossello greeted me like an old friend, which I was, but right away there was all kinds of drama. Puerto Rico's two parties were squabbling and somehow that had created complicated problems with the $250,000 fund-raiser we had all been working our tails off to get organized.

"Terry, the event's off," the governor told me. "I'm not doing it. I'm not playing all these games."

That was just Puerto Rico. Politics there are always complicated.

"Terry, I'll still get you some money," the governor told me.

We had no option but to roll with it. That meant calling Hillary in Washington.

"Don't get on the plane," I said. "The event's off."

We were all booked into this spectacular resort called El Conquistador, with suites perched atop a cliff looking down on the Caribbean, a really fun, sprawling property where you could get lost for a week. Dorothy was due in that afternoon, and we figured we'd make the best of a bad situation and try to enjoy ourselves since everything had been paid for already and this was the kind of place you didn't visit every day. They didn't have anything like it back in Syracuse, I'll tell you that.

No sooner had Dorothy arrived and the five of us had hit the beach and ordered up a round of piña coladas when a waiter came out and tried to talk to me in a heavy accent. It took a few minutes before I deciphered that El Presidente was calling for Mr. Magooloff.

I put my glass down and hustled up to the suite to return the call to Operator One at the White House.

"Where are you?" the President asked.

I told him I was down in Puerto Rico and gave him a recap of the craziness with the canceled event.

"Terry, I need you back here for a meeting tomorrow morning at eleven o'clock," the President said.

"I'll be there, sir," I said, knowing that my plans for a romantic weekend were out the window.

This resort was almost an hour from the airport, so I had to get up at 3:15 to leave in time to make a 5 A.M. flight to Miami and connect to a 7 A.M. flight to Washington. Dorothy wasn't going anywhere, not with the Golden Door Spa at her disposal with all the amenities, so I left her behind with Pete O'Keefe in our beautiful suite overlooking the ocean.

"Peter, you be careful in here now," I told him as I went out the door at 3:45.

I hurried from National Airport and rushed in through the White House front gate just in time for the meeting. Besides the President and Vice President, you had a group including the chief of staff, Leon Panetta; deputy chief of staff Harold Ickes; Ron Brown, the commerce secretary; and Mickey Kantor, the trade representative. That was the meeting where they decided they would need a new team running the DNC. After a tough loss like what we'd suffered in November, change was inevitable. The question was: Change to what? Who should become the next DNC chairman? And who would replace me as DNC finance chair, now that I was moving on to the reelection campaign?

The meeting dragged on for two hours and felt ten times that long. There was a raging debate over whether the next chair should be Senator Chris Dodd of Connecticut or Congressman Bob Torricelli of New Jersey, who was actively campaigning. The President finally wrapped up the discussion by turning to me to get my opinion.

"Mac, who do *you* want?" he asked.

"Mr. President, as far as the money is concerned and putting the reelection campaign together, don't worry about it," I said. "I've got that covered. You make the decision based on what you think is in the best interests of the party. I'm fine with either one."

They wound up making one of those decisions by committee that never quite work out in the end, opting to have two chairmen. Chris Dodd would become general chairman and head up the communications end of the job, and Don Fowler, the former chair of the South Carolina Democratic Party, would become national chair and deal with political organizing and fund-raising. As with most political decisions, the President turned to Harold Ickes and said, "Make it happen," and that ended the meeting.

Both Chris and Don were excellent choices. No question that Chris would do a great job on TV pushing the Democratic message, and there was no greater Democrat than Don Fowler. He had spent his whole life working in the trenches for the Democratic Party. But I always believed it was important to have one leader in charge.

Now that the DNC issues were out of the way, it was up to Harold and me to put the operation together to show the world that Bill Clinton was a political juggernaut who was a lock to become the first two-term Democrat since FDR, and we were going to do that in style.

10

★ ★ ★

I took over as Clinton-Gore finance chairman in early 1995, and unveiled my fund-raising strategy at a large meeting in the Map Room on March 20 with the President and First Lady, the Vice President, and all the top advisors. My approach was to think big and bold and to back it up, and if anyone didn't like it, they could just get out of our way and watch us do it.

I made my presentation and explained how we were going to open up reelection campaign headquarters on April 14 and come out smoking and wrap up our legal maximum of $43.2 million in record time, far earlier than anyone had ever done it. I deliberately scheduled our kickoff event in New Jersey to send a strong message to Senator Bill Bradley, who was thinking about running. This wasn't going to be any secret. Doug Sosnik and I later went up to Senator Bradley's office and I told him we were going to do our first event in New Jersey, rent the biggest hall in the state, and raise more than a million bucks. I went through the whole plan and Bradley stared at me as if he thought I was full of it and then started making fun of my plan.

"You think you can raise a million dollars at one event in New Jersey?" the senator asked me.

"I don't think," I said. "I know."

"I doubt it," Bradley said.

"Want to bet?" I shot right back.

The plan was that after the New Jersey event we would have million-dollar fund-raisers in Little Rock, Chicago, Miami, Denver, San Francisco, and Los Angeles. I predicted we would raise more than $12 million in our first quarter, something that had never been done before, and everybody would be talking about how strong the Clinton-Gore reelection campaign looked.

Everyone in the Map Room meeting besides the President and First Lady thought my plan was way too aggressive. They stared at me as if I couldn't possibly be serious, but no one wanted to be the first to speak after I'd finished. Finally Leon Panetta and Mickey Kantor decided to voice their concerns.

"Well, Terry, that is a very aggressive plan you've outlined," Leon said nervously. "But what if things aren't as good as you say? What if you go out with this aggressive plan and you fail?"

This kind of wet blanket treatment did not faze me in the least. To me there was nothing worse than having a winning hand and playing it like a loser.

"If we get embarrassed, we're dead," Mickey said. "If you fail, then the President is ruined."

Why did they want to talk about failing? Weren't we there to figure out how we were going to *win*?

That was when Hillary spoke up.

"I've got one thing to say," the First Lady said. "Why is anyone in this room asking Terry McAuliffe a question about money?"

★

DURING OUR PLANNING MEETINGS, the staff tried to get me to use a smaller venue for the big New Jersey kickoff event on June 22. Elaine Howard, our director of events, worked hard to change my mind.

"Why are you so insistent that we go to the Garden State Convention Center?" she asked me.

"Because there's nothing bigger," I said.

Another key rule of fund-raising is: Always use a smaller room than you think you need because you want your event to look crowded. We knew there would be several hundred reporters at this event, all of them ready to bury us if it did not go well, and we were taking a big gamble with the aggressive strategy I had laid out. The Clinton presidency was on the line. But if you risk nothing, you win nothing.

Just three days before that big fund-raiser in Somerset, New Jersey, I'd been over at the Mayflower Hotel in Washington with Harold and Doug for the kickoff finance board meeting with a couple hundred top fund-raisers from all over the country who had all agreed to raise $100,000. I could pump them up with one of my speeches, but I needed Harold and Doug as the White House political operatives to walk them through a practical strategy of how we were going to win in '96. I wanted a nice bright map glowing with all the states we were going to win to give Bill Clinton another four years.

"Terry, what do you want me to say?" Doug asked. "I can't give you a map today that shows how we can win two hundred seventy electoral votes."

"Well then, make it up, Doug!" I said. "Whatever you do, make sure you motivate these people."

Keep in mind, this group had decades of political experience and they made it their business to know if they were being snowed. I opened the meeting, and before I introduced Sosnik, I got everyone fired up by saying we were going to win.

"And now Doug is going to tell you how," I said.

"I am?" Doug said.

That got a few nervous laughs and I gave Doug a look as if I were ready to strangle him.

Sosnik gave his PowerPoint presentation, showing state by state how it was all going to come together, and the meeting ended on a high note. The point was: Sometimes you just have to believe. You can't always map out every detail of a strategy, but you know when you have the goods. The details can be worked out later. That New Jersey fund-raiser was going to be the big test: It would either happen the way I'd planned and laid out for everyone in the Map Room and we would be on our way, or the naysayers would have their day.

You should have seen it when the President and First Lady walked into that old cavernous hall in New Jersey on June 22 and the place was absolutely jammed—a total sellout. The Vice President was there with Tipper, and seeing all that Democratic firepower lined up onstage together for only the second time since the 1993 Inauguration had everyone jacked up. The convention center was no deluxe facility, with its cement floor and cavelike acoustics, but we had it all decked out in red, white, and blue, and the place looked great. Everywhere you turned, you saw that people were fired up about taking the fight to the Republicans. That was when everyone knew: *This is for real! Do not count this man out!* We sent a message to everybody around the country: *We're still here and we're still fighting.*

Earlier that day the President and First Lady toured Ford's Edison Assembly Plant wearing black union jackets with Bruce Springsteen's "Born in the U.S.A." cranked up for full effect. I'd seen Springsteen for the first time in a tiny gym in Georgetown in October 1976, back before he and the E Street Band became famous. I loved his energy and the way he gave a voice to regular, hard-working Americans in his songs.

"Give 'em hell, Bill!" an autoworker shouted to the President at another plant he and the First Lady visited that day.

"You help and I will," Clinton said.

That night we boarded Air Force One just before midnight and celebrated the successful kickoff of the campaign. The President changed into a golf shirt, and came back to join Laura Hartigan and me for a late dinner of chicken sandwiches. He presented me with a box of cigars as a thank-you and entertained us with stories all the way to Little Rock.

Once we collected $1.1 million at that New Jersey fund-raiser, it pretty well stifled all talk of Bradley challenging Clinton for the nomination. We were on a roll after that and rattled off million-dollar fund-raising events in succession and made it look easy. From Little Rock we went on to Chicago and Philadelphia. We flew down to Florida and out to California. At the same time we had cranked up a blockbuster direct-mail operation that was going to raise half of our total. Soon everyone was talking again about Bill Clinton as the Comeback Kid, and that in turn fired up everyone working with us.

"It proved we weren't dead," Bill Clinton says now. "It was really important to send a message to everybody else, but it was also important to me and to our whole team. That's one thing McAuliffe always got instinctively. If he hadn't raised the money, all the rah-rah in the world wouldn't have worked, but the point is, if you hadn't had the rah-rah, you wouldn't have raised the money. If you hadn't had people sort of looking up and thinking up, we wouldn't have made it and it was critical. By early 1995 we were smoking again."

Once we were on a roll again we never had much to worry about from a primary challenge and our attention shifted to the Republican side. Word was making the rounds that Colin Powell, the former chairman of the Joint Chiefs of Staff, was being encouraged to run for President as a Republican. Clinton was concerned enough about that scenario to ask me what I thought. I told him no way. Too many people I knew had talked to Powell and said he was definitely not running. Powell would agonize over his decision, but sometimes you can just look in a man's eyes and know he doesn't want it. That left Senator Bob Dole as the likely front-runner. Nothing against Dole, a good senator, a war hero, and a master of the sharp one-liner, but the twenty-three-year age difference meant that by comparison Clinton would seem even younger and more dynamic, playing to our strengths.

By that September we were wrapping up with a final fund-raising swing through California, and the President was still amazing us all with his energy level. We had a fund-raising dinner in Denver and a freak snowstorm grounded us on the tarmac.

"Let the press plane take off first," the President said.

We ended up sitting there on the tarmac in Air Force One for three hours playing cards, and by the time we arrived at the Fairmont Hotel in San Francisco it was four or five in the morning California time. We all got an hour or two of sleep and then the President started the next day with an event at 7:00 A.M. We did other events in San Francisco and Oakland and flew down to L.A. for two more fund-raisers. Clinton played the saxophone and worked the crowd at a youth event. By this time it was 2:00 in the morning and the President was like the Energizer Bunny—still going, still going, still going.

"You know, sir, you're on your forty-fifth hour," I said. "I think you've done your duty. You can go to bed now."

The next morning, September 21, I shocked everyone by announcing to the press that we were shutting down the Clinton-Gore fund-raising operation nearly fourteen months before the election because we had already raised the maximum legal amount. Nothing like this had ever happened before in American presidential politics. It took us only five months of fund-raising to reach the maximum and we were done, leaving the playing field open for the Senate and House candidates and the DNC. I had never worried about '96, knowing full well that if we just got our people energized we were off to the races. Now more and more people were starting to understand how right I had been, and we didn't hear a peep out of the talking heads who ten months earlier had said Bill Clinton was politically dead—and should spend his remaining time in office flying around the country on Air Force One.

★

NEWT GINGRICH WASN'T THE FIRST Republican to let a little Washington power go to his head and cloud his judgment and he won't be the last. I'm not sure he really believed all the stuff he was saying, but he got caught up in the crazed notion that he was some kind of political revolutionary who had changed the American system of government forever. He truly seemed to think he was entitled to every bit as much respect and deference as the President of the United States because as Speaker of the House he was somehow the equal of Bill Clinton. Forget that Newt was elected Speaker with only 228 votes in the House of Representatives and Clinton was elected President with the votes of 44 million Americans. And last I checked, they hadn't found room for a Speaker of the House on Mount Rushmore.

Gingrich was his own worst enemy and hurt his credibility after Yitzhak Rabin's funeral. Clearly one of the major highlights of the Clinton presidency was September 13, 1993, when Yasser Arafat and Rabin stood together in front of the White House and shook hands. The hope and promise of that sunny day were soon shattered. An extremist Israeli law student assassinated Rabin in November 1995 as the prime minister was leaving a huge peace rally in Tel Aviv. We were all deeply shaken up, no one more than Bill Clinton, who had just seen Rabin ten days earlier. I remember seeing the President then and talking about the tragic loss. He was just devastated. I have not often seen Bill Clinton at a loss for words, but that was one time.

"This son of David and of Solomon took up arms to defend Israel's freedom and laid down his life to secure Israel's future," Clinton said at Rabin's funeral in Israel. "Now it falls to all of us who love peace and all of us who loved him to carry on the struggle to which he gave life and for which he gave his life."

The President wanted time to himself on Air Force One during the long plane ride back to Washington after that emotional trip to Israel, but he was in the middle of a standoff with congressional leaders over the budget, and decided to take some time during the flight to speak to Gingrich and Senate Majority Leader Bob Dole. There are photos that prove it, including one that Hillary Clinton reproduced in *Living History*. However, Gingrich somehow felt the President had not shown him proper respect and was really upset that he didn't get to leave Air Force One through the exit up front.

Then with the budget standoff at a critical state later that month, Gingrich said that the President's alleged "snub" on the funeral delegation's flight back from Israel had driven him to grind the country to a halt by shutting down the federal government. Gingrich, who must not have noticed the White House photographer snapping pictures on the flight, embarrassed himself by complaining that Clinton had not met with him. "This is petty," Gingrich said, hitting the nail on the head better than he seemed to know. "You've been on the plane for twenty-five hours and nobody has talked to you and they ask you to get off the plane by the back ramp. You just wonder, 'Where is their sense of manners? Where is their sense of courtesy?' "

The press was all over Gingrich after that and rightly so. The New York *Daily News* put a caricature of Gingrich in diapers on its cover with the blaring headline: CRY BABY! Even Republicans were embarrassed and Virginia Congressman Tom Davis admitted: "We look like idiots."

We'll never know if the public would have sided with President Clinton on the government shutdown even if Gingrich had not made their choice so easy. The important thing was that the President's statesmanlike handling of the difficult budget talks earned him the lasting respect of the American people. He surged in the polls and Gingrich dropped, and the President's budget discipline paved the way for the economic boom of the Clinton years.

Hillary flew to Iowa in early February 1996, a couple of weeks before the presidential caucuses there, and walked into a dental hygienist convention at a hotel in Des Moines. She was amazed at the reception she received.

"All these woman saw me and they started jumping up and down and screaming and saying how much they *looooooooved* the President," Hillary remembers. "That was when I knew we were all right. So I called Bill.

" 'I think you're going to be okay,' I told him. 'Don't worry about Iowa.' "

★

EVEN I HAVE TO ADMIT that in recent years it has gotten more difficult to be an American in other countries. I'm Mr. Positive. I like everybody. I always find a way to make new friends wherever I go. But by 2006 I would be getting out of a taxi in Cairo or rounding a street corner in Dubai or having lunch in Beijing, and it would hit me: We really have turned the whole world against us. People in other countries don't hate individual Americans—not in most cases anyway—but just being an American walking around in a foreign country has become a much less comfortable experience than it was a few years ago. As DNC chair I kept warning people about what would happen if the Bush-Cheney-Rumsfeld cabal were allowed to carry on with their shoot-first, ask-questions-later approach to inflicting their will on the world. Now we know. They have truly poisoned the well. George W. Bush has been the best friend anti-Americanism ever had. He'll be firing up our enemies for generations to come. The man couldn't even dream of addressing a crowd in a foreign country for fear they'd shred him to pieces.

Contrast that with the mood in Belfast in late 1995 when Bill Clinton flew into town to headline the annual tree-lighting ceremony and even brought a fifty-foot-tall white pine Christmas tree flown all the way from Nashville,

Tennessee. You stood there in front of Belfast City Hall and looked out at the sea of more than 100,000 grinning, bundled-up Irish all inching forward toward the President with that surging magnetic force you see every once in a while at a great rock concert, like Bruce Springsteen or U2, but it was more magical than that and really took your breath away.

This was the first time an American President had visited Northern Ireland and everyone felt the sense of history in the air. There was a current of emotion that was so electric, it gave you goose bumps. I'd say a good quarter of the people in the crowd were holding up American flags. They were not just thrilled to be welcoming Bill Clinton, son of Virginia Cassidy, daughter of Ireland a couple of generations removed, they were also open and gleeful about celebrating American values. It was spectacular.

I was walking through Belfast City Hall beforehand with Bill Daley, son of the legendary mayor of Chicago, and we bumped into the President just before he went onstage.

"Isn't this incredible?" he said to us with a big grin. "Can you believe this?"

Even then you could hear the gigantic crowd yelling and screaming out front, sounding like it must have been half a million people, the way they roared. I had never seen Bill Clinton more fired up or happy. He was ecstatic about the trip.

Many people thought the President was crazy when he gave Gerry Adams a visa in 1994 and again in 1995, and invited him to come to the White House for a St. Patrick's Day celebration. The President, working with former Senate Majority Leader George Mitchell and Senator Ted Kennedy, wanted to bring peace to Northern Ireland and end the years of terrible violence between Catholics and Protestants. Many in Washington snickered. The idea of Bill Clinton reaching out to the leader of Sinn Fein, the political arm of the Irish Republican Army, was almost treasonous to some. Clinton truly believed Sinn Fein might be serious about negotiating to get rid of IRA stockpiles of weapons. The President had his eye on history and didn't care what anyone said. He always believed that when you negotiate, you have to negotiate with all sides. If you're going to get a lasting agreement, you have to have everyone sitting at the table with you. That's how you get true dialogue and compromise and ultimately a meaningful agreement. George W. Bush didn't see it that way, which was the No. 1 complaint you heard about him when you traveled around the world.

Clinton's vision had paid off in spades by that night in Belfast, and the people of Northern Ireland were in a mood to celebrate the stirring progress in the peace process and the difference it had already made in their lives. Up onstage with the Clintons that electric night were two students, one Catholic and one Protestant, who had won a contest to see who could write the best letter to President Clinton. The First Lady read the letters aloud to the crowd as Cathy Harte and Mark Lennox stood watching.

" 'My name is Cathy Harte and I am a twelve-year-old Catholic girl,' " Hillary Clinton read. " 'I live in Belfast in Northern Ireland and I love it here. It's green, it's beautiful, and, well, it's Ireland. All my life, I have only known guns and bombs with people fighting. Now, it is different. There are no guns and bombs.' "

Mark Lennox, the Protestant boy, was fifteen, the same age as Chelsea.

" 'We will have to change our ideas and work for change,' " the First Lady read from Mark's letter. " 'Change must mean changing our own understanding of each other. . . . Some people want to destroy peace and the peace process in Northern Ireland. We must not allow this to happen.' "

I tell you, it all clicked into place beautifully that night. The Lord Mayor of Belfast, Eric Smyth, stepped up next and led the foot-stomping crowd in a loud countdown. Everyone chanted together and then the President threw the switch and this amazing fifty-foot-tall Christmas tree flickered to life. The crowd roared.

"As I look down these beautiful streets," Clinton said, "I think how wonderful it will be for people to do their holiday shopping without worry of searches or bombs, to visit loved ones on the other side of the border without the burden of checkpoints or roadblocks, to enjoy these magnificent Christmas lights without any fear of violence."

The closing was my favorite part of the speech.

"Ladies and gentlemen, this day that Hillary and I have had here in Belfast and in Derry and Londonderry County will long be with us as one of the most remarkable days of our lives," the President predicted and he was right. "May you remember the words of the Lord Mayor, 'This is Christmas. We celebrate the world in a new way because of the birth of Emmanuel: God with us.' And when God was with us, he said no words more important than these: 'Blessed are the peacemakers, for they shall inherit the Earth.' "

It was perfect. There's just no other way to put it. Marcia Hale, an assistant to the President, Chicago mayor Richard Daley, and I were standing next to novelist Pat Conroy, author of *The Great Santini* and *The Prince of Tides*. I turned to look at him late in the President's speech and tears were sliding down his cheeks.

"Pat, can you write this?" Marcia asked him.

"Yes, and I will," he said.

The cease-fire was fifteen months old at that point, and all over town, everyone was talking about how it was the first Christmas in memory that people in Belfast felt comfortable going downtown to shop. The Secret Service had set up two-inch-thick bulletproof glass in front of the President, due to the obvious security concerns, and he was given strict instructions to stay behind the glass. At the end of his speech Clinton couldn't help himself. He stepped out in front and waved to the crowd. It drove the Secret Service crazy, but they loved it in Belfast.

"Watching Ireland fall in love with President Clinton and his wife, Hillary, was a magical experience," the *Irish Voice* reported. "Clinton's trip was one of substance. The Irish were not falling in love with a symbol of their own emigrant success, but rather with an American who had gambled on bringing peace to Ireland after a quarter century of conflict. The Irish— Protestant and Catholic ordinary folk—were not about to forget."

I tell everybody that trip was one of the greatest moments I've ever had in politics. Everywhere we went huge crowds turned out and broke into ecstatic cheers of "We want Bill! We want Bill!" You had millions of people on the streets cheering President Clinton and cheering America, and it was spectacular.

"In President Bill Clinton, Ireland has seen more than a charismatic who aroused tumultuous emotions on the streets of Belfast, Derry, and Dublin," the *Irish Independent* wrote. "It has seen an authentic world leader."

The day after the Belfast tree-lighting, we were in Dublin and went to a great pub on Camden Street called Cassidy's. Supposedly there was some kind of connection with the President's relatives on his mother's side, and from the look on his face you definitely thought he was coming home. We got there and it was just jammed and we had senators, congressmen, and the Irish foreign minister Dick Spring all wedged together having pints of Guinness.

We had a black-tie dinner that night in Dublin Castle and then had to get moving. Word had even gotten to the President about our flight over from Washington on our Air Force jet, which was loaded up with just about every prominent Irish-American in the country, I think. Halfway over the Atlantic the captain came on with an announcement.

"This has never happened in the history of the United States Air Force," he said. "We have no more alcohol on this aircraft!"

We loaded up for the flight back and all we did was raise our glasses and sing the whole way. Pat Conroy and Governor Hugh Carey of New York were telling stories to a group including New York congressman Peter King and Florida Senator Connie Mack, and we all had a great time together, Democrats and Republicans, and when we got back to Washington the papers were filled with rave reviews.

Maureen Dowd, the *Times* columnist, said the Irish had given Clinton "the two best days of his presidency. . . . In Ireland, he was Jack Kennedy and the World Cup rolled into one. It was the presidency Bill Clinton had dreamed of, but never experienced. . . . In Ireland, the prodigal son of the Cassidy clan was celebrated as a statesman, a saint, an angel of peace, a ruddy handsome devil 'with a bottomless bucket of charm,' the most powerful man on earth and 'King Billy.' "

Back in Washington, Clinton said, "It was just absolutely overwhelming. I don't know if in my life I'll ever have a couple of days like that again."

11

★ ★ ★

We were all gathered up in the presidential suite at the Excelsior Hotel in Little Rock on Election Night 1996 when the networks announced we had won. Bill Clinton was the first Democrat since FDR to win a second term! I let loose with a big crazy Irishman yell and was giving high fives to everyone in sight when the First Lady came rushing over from across the room, and gave me a bear hug.

"Woo-hoo!" I screamed right in her ear.

She rubbed her ear as if I had broken her eardrum, but then she broke into another wide grin, and you could see how relieved and proud she was. We'd made history and more than anyone other than the President, she knew how much we'd had to overcome.

"Terry, I think you've made me deaf," Hillary said as she walked away, which I took as a compliment.

It wouldn't be the first time I'd made someone deaf! The First Lady couldn't hear out of that ear for three hours, but then there was so much noise up in that suite with everyone carrying on, I'm not sure any of us could hear quite right that night.

Earlier that day on Air Force One, somewhere over Missouri, Chelsea had led everyone in the Macarena, a popular dance that year. Both her parents took part, though spokesman Mike McCurry informed the press that his boss had danced "in a presidential manner." That summer at the Democratic Convention in Chicago, the DNC hosted a "Party of Champions" for eight hundred people at Michael Jordan's restaurant, and I led a whole group in the Macarena, or as they all started calling it, the *Macker*-rena.

The President was not there that night, but the First Lady was, and she showed off her moves. She likes making the joke that doing the Macarena, she looks like someone swatting at a swarm of mosquitoes. I disagree. I think she pulls it off beautifully. Tipper Gore came out and joined in, too, and the Vice President came out as well. He was a good sport and made fun of himself by standing there stiff as a board as Tipper and Hillary and I did the Macarena around him.

On Election Night in Little Rock, they'd closed off all the streets and put up giant outdoor screens to keep everyone informed of the election results. Tony Bennett, Mr. "I Left My Heart in San Francisco," was up on the stage and, as *The Washington Post* reported, vendors were selling "Hillary Is A Babe" T-shirts. It was a total carnival atmosphere with people everywhere doing the Macarena, and it seemed like the whole city had dissolved into one great party.

This was not only four more years, this was the American people saying they couldn't care less about the fake scandals Republicans had schemed to cook up and promote through a thousand different plots. The Comeback Kid had done it again. Down in front of the Old State House the street was so packed with people in Clinton buttons and party hats waving flags, no one could move, and when the President started his victory speech, the crowd yelled so loudly you could barely hear him.

"I would not be anywhere else in the world tonight," Bill Clinton told the crowd in Little Rock.

I was thrilled that we had pulled it off and also very, very ready to take a break from politics. Once the election was behind me, I was eager to enjoy some time at home with my young family, which had grown with the addition of our third, Mary, who was born in August 1994. I'd also bought a home-building business down in Florida with my friend and partner, Carl Linder, who was a great American success story, having dropped out of high school and gone on to build a billion-dollar insurance and banking empire as well as owning the Cincinnati Reds. This was one of the largest home-building companies in central Florida, building more than one thousand homes a year. We bought it out of receivership, restructured the management, and sold it for a nice profit several years later.

★

I ALWAYS LOOKED forward to the annual Army-Navy Game, which was coming up the first Saturday in December, but that year I had mixed feelings about going. I was eager to take a break from politics, but the Vice President had his presidential run in 2000 to think about and really wanted me to take over as chairman of the Democratic National Committee. I got wind that he had been putting pressure on the President to ask me to take the job. Only later did I found out how much pressure.

"You know, you owe it to me," Gore told the President. "If I'm going to be elected, I've got to have a good party."

On the one hand I was excited about the challenge, but on the other I also knew it wasn't right for me at that time. First of all, any time your party has control of the White House, being chairman is a miserable job. You have no autonomy or power; you're just expected to do whatever the White House political operation tells you to do, and you're not really a spokesman for the party since obviously the President has that job covered.

A bunch of us piled into Air Force One to fly up to Philadelphia for the Army-Navy Game on December 5, and I was with the President all afternoon and he didn't say a word about the DNC. The game itself was a classic that year, even though it was a rainy, downcast day. I always rooted for Army, out of respect for my dad, and I was sitting there with Ed Rendell, then the mayor of Philadelphia, and he kept offering me beers and I kept saying no. I wanted to remain as sharp as a tack in case the President hit me with the DNC job on the way home, which I had been tipped off to expect. I remember cheering like mad as Army scored on a seventy-yard run by fullback Ty Amey and ended up winning, 34–30, and we all got back on Air Force One for the quick flight to Washington. I kept looking at the large digital clock on board, which ticked down the remaining minutes of the flight, and when we got to "15:00," I figured I could relax and finally ordered that beer. Just as the steward put the beer in front of me, Bruce Lindsey came walking into the cabin. Bruce has been one of the President's closest confidants for forty years, a down-to-earth, calming influence, and I was usually glad to see him—but not this time.

"Terry, the boss would like to see you," he said.

I got up and left my untouched beer behind as everyone laughed.

"See you later, Mr. Chairman," Andrew Friendly, the President's aide, yelled out.

I walked as slowly as I could up to the President's private cabin, trying to chew up more time, and, of course, Bill Clinton was not in any hurry to ask me to do something that he knew I didn't want to do. He had a way of circling a topic.

"What do you think about this DNC chair thing?" he asked.

"I just don't think it's right, Mr. President," I said.

He knew I wanted no part of it. After all, I was the President's top fund-raiser, and if they sent me over there with the alleged DNC/Asian fund-raising scandal swirling about, that was going to be bad news for him and for me. Even though I wasn't involved in the alleged scandal, I was the President's close friend and the press would want to include me in every negative story.

I talked with Clinton about my home-building business and how much I wanted to spend more time with Dorothy and the kids. I kept waiting for him to make the hard sell, but as the landing gear came down and Air Force One touched down at Andrews Air Force Base, I realized his heart wasn't into pressing me on this. He knew how hard I'd worked and how I felt about this. He also knew that Dorothy was dead-set against it.

All through this period the papers had been heating up with speculation that I was a top candidate for DNC chairman. *The Wall Street Journal* floated the idea on November 8, and ten days later *The Washington Times* ran a hilarious piece calling me a front-runner for the job and saying it was a done deal. *The Washington Post* reported in mid-December that the White House was "trying to persuade" me to take the job, but that I was reluctant, and quoted someone at the White House saying, "In most people's eyes, McAuliffe is the first choice and the second choice for the job." *The White House Bulletin* quoted a "source" who actually made a pretty fair point: "No matter how reluctant McAuliffe might be, if the President says, 'You need to be part of this legacy, and you can't walk away from me now,' there's no way Terry McAuliffe will turn him down."

True enough, and the week after the Army-Navy Game, the President and Vice President called me in for a late-night meeting in the President's study on the second floor of the residence, the Treaty Room. There were two armchairs on either side of the couch, and they put me on the couch so they could work on me from each side. It was around midnight when we started and after 2 A.M. when I left, so for two hours I had the Vice President on my left and the President on my right banging my brains in to become chairman of the party. How could a kid from Syracuse resist this kind of pressure?

"I just don't want to do it," I kept saying. "I'm chairing the Inauguration. I've raised a lot of money. I just want to take a break."

I'll be honest with you, it's hard to keep saying no to the President and the Vice President. I was starting to feel that I was somehow unpatriotic, and I'm the guy who sings "God Bless America" in the shower. The one thing I did say was that if I was ever DNC chairman, I would go in there with the mission of rebuilding the party, making a mark with a technological overhaul and giving the party the tools to fight the Republicans on their terms, if need be. I would want to make a lasting impact the way that Ray Bliss had as RNC chair.

"Okay, let's end the discussion," I said. "I don't want to do it. However, if you can't find anyone else, I'll do it. But I want the both of you to commit to me that you will both continue to work hard to find someone else."

I looked at the Vice President.

"Are you going to keep looking?" I asked him.

"You bet, Terry," he said.

The President said he would, too. I got up to leave and as soon as Gore closed the door behind me, leaving the two of them alone, I was just sure Gore and Clinton were giving each other high fives and celebrating that it was a done deal. As I rode the elevator down from the residence all I could think was: *I've been had. They're never going to look for anyone else.*

I pulled into our garage around 2:30 and Dorothy was waiting up for me. As soon as she saw my face, she knew I'd caved.

"You gave in, didn't you?" she said.

What could I say? I could tell that for the first time in our marriage Dorothy was really disappointed in me. A day or two later she was at home around five o'clock in the afternoon, helping the kids with their homework and dealing with the usual chaos that takes over the house around then when the phone rang.

"Dorothy, this is Al Gore," said a voice. "I'd like to talk about Terry running for DNC chairman. The party really needs him, and I need him."

She couldn't believe it was the Vice President calling her. He'd never called her before.

"This would be a great thing for Terry," Gore told her.

Dorothy did not agree, but she heard out the Vice President. She'd always liked and respected him, and wanted very much to see Gore as President; she just didn't want it to be at my expense. She listened and listened. Al Gore can be very thorough when he's making a point. Finally she had to speak up.

"I just don't think it's a good thing for Terry," she told him firmly. "I'm sorry. I just don't think it's the right time."

Gore made his case again, talking about how positive this could be for everybody.

"Tell me you believe this is good for my husband, Mr. Vice President," she said.

When I got home that night, Dorothy told me the Vice President had called to lobby her for half an hour and I was amazed—and impressed.

"That's smart, very smart," I said.

The Vice President knew how much I respected Dorothy's advice and that if she was dead-set against me taking the job, I probably wouldn't do it. That night the phone was ringing constantly with different people calling to give me the latest on this or that person who was also being talked about for the job. None of them sounded likely to satisfy Al Gore. I didn't like the way this was looking at all.

The next night, getting dressed for a White House Christmas party, Dorothy and I were going over the names we'd heard mentioned as possibilities, trying to figure out who else might make sense.

"I'm going to say something to the President," Dorothy said. "You've been out on the road constantly for four years and you deserve some time with your family."

We got to the party and Dorothy looked beautiful, but she was pretty nervous. In later years the four of us went on vacations together and Dorothy and the President are great friends now, but back then she wasn't as comfortable asking for his help. One of the little traditions we had at White House Christmas parties was at some point in the evening the President would be dancing with the First Lady and I would be dancing with Dorothy and we'd switch partners.

"May I dance with your beautiful wife?" Clinton asked me that night.

"Absolutely!" I said. "If I can dance with your beautiful wife."

I always had such a good time dancing with the First Lady, and she made me feel comfortable even though she was a great dancer and I was a klutz. She didn't even complain the many times I stepped on her feet with my size 13Ds. That night I was especially grateful to her for staying out of this whole DNC thing. She wasn't pressuring me at all one way or the other. Everybody in Washington was talking about this, and she figured there were enough people involved and she would give me a break. To Hillary, it was always family first.

Dorothy didn't waste any time with the President because you never knew when he would be called away. It was a slow song, which made it easier to talk.

"Please don't do this to my husband, Mr. President," Dorothy said.

She was looking right into his eyes and he could see how serious she was about this. She mentioned names of some other possibilities for the job.

"Well, none of them will be as good as Terry, but I hear you," Clinton said.

The President later said that once Dorothy stared up at him with those big blue eyes and said she was asking for his help, he knew he couldn't deny her.

"I'll never forget Dorothy looking at me," he says now. "She made me feel like I had sentenced Terry to death or denied him the right of habeas corpus. You know I'm a sucker for her anyway. Everything she wants, I'm for. I roll for her any time."

Clinton talked to Gore the next day and that was basically the end of it. I was home free and called Al Gore and said I just could not do it, but that I would be there for him in a big way in 2000. He was very gracious and accepted my decision. He was always a class act.

★

ONE OF THE PROUDEST MOMENTS I ever had was as cochairman of the Inaugural Committee, which was a lot of work because for the first time ever we weren't taking any corporate contributions. Normally anyone can give anything they want for the Inauguration, but that year we decided to ban all overseas contributions and limit contributions to a hundred dollars each. It ended up costing $21 million and that's a lot of money to raise a hundred bucks at a time. I didn't have to wrestle any alligators, but did get stuck shooting a commercial for the QVC shopping channel in front of the Pennsylvania Avenue reviewing stand, which was probably my lowest moment in American politics. QVC had a reach of 58 million households and in one day generated a quarter of a million dollars selling memorabilia. Mark Weiner, a longtime party supporter and a close friend who has always been there for me, was pushing me to do it to increase our sales, but I was hesitant. I called Clinton to see what he thought.

"My mother watched QVC all the time!" the President told me. "Go for it."

We had no trouble pulling together a star-studded lineup for the twelve black-tie galas, but did have some difficulty with the competition for high school bands. This, obviously, was a subject dear to the President's heart, given his lifelong love of playing the sax and all those summers he spent at band camp.

The President called me up hotter than a pistol on January 8 after he read an article in *The Washington Post* about the high school band from Cody, Wyoming, whose ninety-four members spent ten months raising $100,000 to make the trip for the Inaugural parade, thinking they were the only Wyoming band in the running. But a Jackson Hole jazz and concert band had been chosen instead, and Clinton personally intervened to invite the "Broncs" Band from Cody. Once the good news was passed along, band director Derek Spitzer had the kids out practicing again, even though in Cody it was down to 20 degrees outside. "I didn't hear a single complaint," Spitzer told *The Post*.

The Thursday before the Inaugural weekend, *The Post* ran a story: POLAR WEATHER WON'T STOP WEEKEND. It dropped down to seven degrees the two days before the Inauguration and we were worried no one would come out for the two days of musical performances, interactive technology, and children's entertainment we were setting up in seven huge tents on the Mall. Just to be sure, I went out there in the bitter cold to do a stand-up for CNN in my shirtsleeves, telling everyone, "Come on down! Everything's great. And Barney is going to be here!"

To me, all the work and all the preparations and even the President's Inaugural speech in which he spoke out against "petty bickering and extreme partisanship" were all just a prelude to the big event, the parade down Pennsylvania Avenue starting at 2:15 that afternoon. The chairman's car leads the parade and I'll never forget what it was like up there with my father, Jack, riding shotgun, and a whole phalanx of police motorcycles leading the way and the President following behind. I think for my father that day was an absolute dream come true, looking out on all of Washington lining the streets to wave and cheer. My father always wanted to play in the big ballpark and this was better than sitting on the Buffalo Bills bench during the Super Bowl.

Our lead car was the first to pull up in front of the reviewing stand, and as we got out the President stopped his limousine and walked the last couple of blocks. Chelsea joined her father in going without a coat, despite the biting cold, and the people took up a loud chant of "U.S.A! U.S.A!" We were the first ones up in the presidential box and looked back to see the President, Hillary, and Chelsea walking toward us, and the crowd going wild. Somehow the crisp winter air made it even more exciting, and my dad and I just looked at each other and smiled, thinking: *It doesn't get any better than this*. The Clinton and Gore families warmly embraced us that day. Tipper Gore and her three daughters welcomed five-year-old Dori and three-year-old Jack as they ran up to the front row of the presidential reviewing stand and camped out to watch the parade. They took turns passing two-year-old

Mary back and forth throughout the parade. Even the President and Vice President took their turns baby-sitting and pointing out various passing floats to the kids. What a day for a dad and an American.

That night I ran around giving toasts at all the different balls and galas, and I was on such a tight schedule to make them all, we had to interrupt Meat Loaf. He was just about to start a new set and they brought him over to meet me, which was pretty funny, since I had absolutely no idea who he was and he had absolutely no idea who I was. He didn't look much like a rock star, but then, I guess I didn't look much like anyone's idea of the chairman of the President's Inaugural.

Three days later I held a thank-you party for the Inaugural staff, and as a surprise I had Clinton and Gore drop by to show their appreciation, which really had everyone fired up. I called the Vice President up to the podium and said I had a surprise for him. I presented him with a big blue placard showing that there were only 1,458 days remaining until *his* Inauguration on January 20, 2001. You should have seen the smile on Gore's face as he went to give me a bear hug!

Two and a half weeks later a small group organized a surprise fortieth birthday party for me at the Hay-Adams with the President, my mother and father, my family, and a small group of close friends. Millie had just lost all her hair after an illness and had a wig on, which kept sliding all over her head. She looked like Carol Channing, which was funny because she always thought she sounded like her. One time she was at a Broadway show, talking to a friend, and a man in the next row heard her voice and asked if she was Carol Channing. "Hello Dolly" became her signature song, and any time there was a piano in the room, whether at weddings, wakes, or dinner parties, she would belt out her version of it. That night at my birthday party, the President was sitting to my right and Millie was to my left, and when they sang a duet of "Hello Dolly," it came through in stereo.

The dinner at the Hay-Adams was a fun, small family affair, and they really surprised me. After it was over, someone suggested we go over to the Mayflower and have a drink at the bar. We got over there and the place was rocking with about five hundred people there to celebrate my birthday with me, my second surprise of the night. The Vice President flew through a snowstorm to make the party and he grabbed the mike and he and Tony Coelho led the crowd in singing "Happy Birthday" to me.

It was a great way to celebrate my first forty years. What a hell of a ride it had been from the time they pronounced me dead at birth to my first Onondaga County Party fund-raiser when I was six years old to the driveway-sealing business I started at age fourteen. I'd been working like a Tasmanian devil in politics ever since I started fund-raising for Jimmy Carter in 1979, and loving every minute of it. I had a beautiful, healthy family, I'd had adventures all over the world I never could have imagined, and felt I'd made a difference in people's lives by working for the Democratic Party. I was finally ready for a break from the rough-and-tumble of politics after twenty years.

12

★ ★ ★

Dick Gephardt and I had a great skiing vacation out in Telluride, Colorado, in late February 1997. I found it funny: You could pick up the paper every week and read about how I was going to have such a difficult choice to make between Gephardt and Gore going into the 2000 election, but I already knew Dick would never run in 2000. Al Gore had put in his time as Bill Clinton's hard-working second in command and it was his turn. Dick was not about to take on an incumbent Vice President of his own party.

I was at the little airport in Telluride on February 23 on my way home from the ski trip with Dick and Jane when I ran into Mark Warner, later the governor of Virginia, who had actually worked for me at the DNC in 1980. There had been a spate of stories in the paper about alleged fund-raising irregularities at the DNC during the '95–'96 election cycle.

"Terry, I'm amazed that you're Clinton's finance chairman and your name has not been in any of these stories," Mark said to me that day at the airport.

"Mark, that wasn't the Clinton-Gore campaign, that was the DNC, which I'd left two years before there were any issues," I said. "So there's no reason my name should be in any of these stories."

If it had been a movie, everyone would have complained that the timing was too unbelievable: Not five seconds after I said that to Mark, my beeper went off and I looked down and it said: *Urgent, call Cheryl Mills, White House.*

Cheryl Mills was the deputy White House counsel and I was baffled why she would be trying to reach me. She'd never called me before.

"Terry, I want to alert you that the press will probably be calling you," she said when I phoned her back.

I was baffled.

"It's about a memo that you wrote," Cheryl said.

Ever since I first got started in politics, I've always followed the *Washington Post* rule: Assume any memo you write to anybody—especially to the President of the United States—is going to show up in *The Washington Post* someday.

"What memo could possibly be controversial enough to make news?" I asked Cheryl.

She read the memo aloud and I recognized it right away as the one I had written just after my breakfast with the President in late December 1994, when he was dejected after the midterm loss. I was still baffled. There was nothing in there for anyone to get excited about.

"Okay, I'm fine with that," I said. "So what?"

"Well, unfortunately for you, Terry, the President turned the memo over and wrote a note to Nancy Hernreich on the back saying, 'Ready to start overnights right away,' " she said.

Thus the famous Lincoln Bedroom Memo.

"Okay, but it doesn't have anything to do with me," I said. "He didn't write that note to me. I didn't even get a copy of the memo back."

"Terry, I know you didn't get it back," she said. "I'm just letting you know this is going to be news."

Next I called Doug Sosnik. If I ever get my own late-night television show, Sosnik would be my sidekick. He always has the perfect line.

"Doug, have you heard about the memo?" I asked him.

"We've all heard about the memo, Mac," he said.

"Really, you think this is big news?" I asked him.

"Oh yeah," he said. "We're talking networks."

"Networks?"

I was going to be all over the three national network news broadcasts. I flew home from Telluride, arriving early on the morning of the twenty-fourth, and still was having a hard time sorting this out. Understand, this was like a Star Chamber. I had written a simple memo more than two years earlier and had never seen it again or heard a word about it. Now it was about to become one of the biggest stories of the year. I didn't determine where the President met people or when. I couldn't have cared less if he met supporters at McDonald's. I just needed him to eyeball people and say: *I am running again and I need your help.* They had to hear it from him.

I was still hoping the White House would be able to kill this story. That was how naïve I was. That first day back in Washington was quiet enough and I thought maybe I'd dodged this bullet. Early the next morning I walked down my driveway and kind of stood back and kicked open the newspaper to see if I'd find my picture staring back at me from the front page. Good news. No McAuliffe headlines. Just something about LIVESTOCK CLONING. I hopped into my Jeep and drove down to M Street for a nine o'clock meeting.

My assistant Alecia Dyer called and told me that Associated Press reporter John Solomon had called to say he urgently needed to speak to me. He was about to move a story saying that I wrote a memo to the President recommending that he use the Lincoln Bedroom for fund-raising.

"Tell him I'm going into a board meeting and I'll call him in an hour," I told Alecia.

I parked in the garage and was walking into the meeting when Alecia called back to tell me Solomon was going with the story with or without comment from me. I called him myself to tell him he didn't have his facts straight.

"I've just talked to someone in the White House who has seen the memo and says that you recommended the use of the Lincoln Bedroom," Solomon told me.

"John, let me be crystal f—— clear," I said. "I'm telling you it's just not true. I have never written the words 'Lincoln Bedroom' in my life. If you go with your story, I guarantee you—I *promise* you, John—you will be forced to do a retraction within the hour. Trust me on this."

"Okay, Terry, I'll get right back to you," he said.

Steam was coming out of my ears as I stepped into the meeting to join the video conference in progress. I couldn't blame Solomon. He was doing his job. What had me furious was that someone in the Clinton White House had actually called this reporter and fed him lies. What great, loyal, committed, stand-up Democrat was responsible for this? (John, the statute of limitations has passed. I'll buy you dinner at Café Milano if you tell me who it was.)

Not five minutes after I'd hung up with John, Alecia called to tell me the story had just hit the wires. Now John was in my doghouse for blowing me off.

I drove back out to McLean for a noon birthday party for my son, Jack, who turned four that day. We had about thirty kids running around the house screaming and yelling, and all I could think about was this damn AP story, which was now turning into a huge controversy.

This was what they had all been looking for. Now they thought they had the President's buddy and finance chairman involved in the fund-raising scandal. But sure enough, once I'd called Cheryl to raise holy hell, the White House released the memo and just as I had promised, John Solomon had to set the record straight and report that I had nothing to do with the Lincoln Bedroom. However, nothing could stop the frenzy that Solomon had unleashed.

"Terry, don't come down to the office," Alecia told me. "There are cameras everywhere downstairs. They're staking you out and walking up to people on the street with pictures of you, asking if they know you."

Thanks, John. However, I did get to stay and have some more birthday cake with Jack.

Wolf Blitzer invited me on CNN that Saturday night to talk about the controversy, and a lot of people were telling me not to do it. I said: Screw it. One, I wanted to defend myself. Two, people needed some perspective on the Clinton-Gore fund-raising operation I ran, which was limited to individual contributions of $1,000 or less. In fact, our average contribution was $98. I didn't care if many of the DNC people were ducking and hiding. I was going to set the record straight.

Wolf kept asking me questions as if I should be embarrassed.

"Wolf, I was the finance chairman," I told him. "The President didn't ask me to be the CIA director. He didn't ask me to be the secretary of state. It was my job to go out and prepare for the President's reelection and energize people."

So often in Washington a scandal dynamic starts to take over and the press gets all heated up over something. That's the time you want to keep your head and stay calm and ask yourself: Have you done anything wrong? If you know you haven't and you have nothing to hide, the camera picks that up. I was proud of the work that the Clinton-Gore finance team had done.

At one point, Wolf said, "even though the appearance [is] . . . that it smells."

I wasn't going to let Wolf have that one.

"How does it smell?" I asked him, fighting right back.

It's all in how you handle yourself. I knew I was right. Later on that same show, after my appearance, CNN showed the results of a new poll, which found that by a margin of three to one, Americans thought Clinton administration fund-raising was nothing different from what other presidents have done.

The whole fuss over the Lincoln Bedroom was another example of how a little misinformation was so often turned into a blunt object to pound away at the Clinton administration. The President had invited around 800 people for overnights and of those, only 200 had given him money and all of those were close friends. Unlike other Presidents, who had estates in Kennebunkport or 1,600-acre spreads in Crawford, Texas, called the "Prairie Chapel Ranch," Bill Clinton owned no house of his own, and the only place for him to invite old friends to spend time with him was at the White House. Of course, many of these friends were supporters, and Clinton had them over for late nights of conversation and card-playing because he found them fascinating and energizing, and he loved the opportunity to learn from people. And for your information, Clinton, like all Presidents, personally paid for any expenses incurred by his guests, as opposed to official visitors.

The idea that someone who had given him money in the past would somehow be *barred* from an invitation—that was just crazy. Clinton loved staying up all night long, if you'd stay up with him. But he was just raked over the coals for inviting people to the White House. Not a single person came forward to say that he was solicited for money and promised a night in the Lincoln Bedroom.

The Republicans flailed away on the Lincoln Bedroom, carrying on as if Bill Clinton were disgracing the White House. Then George W. Bush became President—I still won't say he was elected—and what do you know, he started having his donors over to the White House, too. In his first year, the Associated Press reported, the Bushes had 160 overnight guests at the White House, including donors who had raised at least $100,000 for the Bush campaign in 2000, as well as many other contributors. So how did the Bush administration handle the awkward fact that the Bushes were doing the same thing Republicans had criticized the Clintons for? Simple: they refused to tell the truth. A White House spokesperson claimed she didn't know if overnight guests had been in the Lincoln Bedroom or another bedroom. "They sleep in a variety of guest rooms in the White House," she said, stonewalling shamelessly. But reporters just let it go. Imagine if the Clinton administration had tried to short-circuit the Lincoln Bedroom stories with that approach.

A fever took over Washington that summer. The Republicans planned Senate hearings on campaign finance. This was big stuff for the Republicans. They were all worked up with a lot of wild speculation about how the Chinese government was allegedly controlling the U.S. government through some elaborate scheme of spreading money around. The Republicans were just sure they had all the details sorted out, the way conspiracy theorists are always sure of that, but the cold, hard truth was it didn't add up. Their real goal with their ridiculous fund-raising investigations—an absolute farce considering the Republicans had more fund-raising abuses than the Democrats—was to cripple the Democratic Party financially. Their over-the-top investigations and requests for millions of obscure documents cost the DNC more than $18 million in one year, including more than $4 million just for copying costs. That's a whole lot of trees taken down. Maybe it was their secret plan to clear some more land for oil drilling.

My deposition before the Thompson committee ended up falling on June 6, 1997, which happened to be the day that my six-year-old daughter Dori's kindergarten class was having a special tour of the White House. They even got to meet Socks, the First Cat, and brought home postcards with paw prints.

"It's a big day!" I kept telling everyone that morning at the White House. "I'm headed up to my deposition to the Senate committee."

Peter O'Keefe was working at the White House then and told me it was much different when he went in for his deposition. He was so nervous, his stomach was doing cartwheels, and he couldn't even think about eating. Not me! I looked forward to going to this deposition, and was having a great time that day, throwing little Dori up in the air and laughing.

"Aren't you getting deposed today?" Peter asked me.

"You bet I am," I said. "I can't wait. We're going to go have some real fun."

This was pure political theater and I was in my element. I remember riding to the Hart Senate Office Building with my lawyer, Richard Ben-Veniste, a lawyer's lawyer with a distinguished career, including having been chief prosecutor of the Watergate Task Force at age thirty. This was a relationship destined for collision. Ben-Veniste's rule was that clients never talk, and all I ever wanted to do was talk. The whole way over to the deposition that morning he was explaining how we wanted to keep this quiet. He told me he had arranged to sneak me in through a back door and I looked at him like he was crazy.

"No way," I said. "We're going in the front door."

So we walked right in the front door of the Hart Building and stepped into the elevator, which was packed with tourists.

"Folks, let me introduce myself," I said. "My name is Terry McAuliffe and I am being deposed by the Senate Governmental Affairs Committee to-

day. I was the President's finance chairman. Do you know how much of
your taxpayer dollars they're wasting on this witch hunt?"

I asked if they all wanted to come along with me to the deposition
room, but Ben-Veniste put his foot down. For some reason he wasn't too
keen on me bringing a whole group of tourists into the deposition room.

"They are not coming!" he said, folding his arms over his chest.

I was talking to people the whole elevator ride up and by the time the
doors opened, Ben-Veniste was ready to explode.

"That's it!" he said when we got off. "That's it! You're on your own.
You can represent yourself."

We walked into the hearing room, still bickering, and I was carrying on
like I was running for mayor. I kept talking to everyone in sight.

"All right, let's get at it, boys!" I said. "Let's get down to business."

This was a sham and a political witch hunt, and I was going to give it the
deference it was due. I figured what the heck, why not carry on a little and
show them I wasn't afraid? I knew I hadn't done anything wrong, so what
could they do to me? Nothing.

I got sworn in and then started beating the living daylights out of this
young guy asking me foolish fund-raising questions, Gustavus A. Puryear
IV, Esquire, who was one of the nine attorneys there.

"Do you have any objection to those lawyers remaining here today?"
Gus asked me.

"The more the merrier!" I said. "Bring 'em on. Glad to have them."

Gus didn't know what to make of me. Obviously he had never raised a
dime in his life. Normally a deposition was a solemn affair. People were
nervous and uptight. They were worried about getting drawn into a perjury
trap. They were careful in their answers and deferential to their questioners.
Deposing me was a new experience for Gus. I was sick and tired of the way
young White House and DNC staffers were being terrorized and bankrupted
by these people and I was also fed up with the way Democrats were ducking and hiding and looking for someone else to blame. I'd had enough of
our usual Democratic circular firing squad, and it was time to fight.

Early on Gus asked if I was somehow involved in the planning for the
Clinton-Gore reelection campaign.

"Gus," I said. "I *was* the planning!"

I wasn't going to take any guff from this kid, no matter how many
ridiculous questions he asked me. I went in with the attitude that I was going to tell the truth and if that included my giving an honest accounting of
what Bill Clinton had meant to this country, great.

Gus asked me about my breakfast meeting with the President following the 1994 midterm elections.

"We talked about the Republicans . . . who had just won the House and the Senate and this 'Contract with America,'" I said. "We were concerned that elderly people could be thrown on the streets and that Medicare and Medicaid and education. . . ."

I went on a twenty-minute dissertation on the successes of the Clinton-Gore administration and Gus began to roll his eyes.

"You smirk, but let me tell you, this is what the people were worried about out there," I said.

Now Gus looked defensive.

"I noted a slight smirk on you, Gus, but that's what it was about," I continued. "I am about positive. I'm talking about the future of our country and that's what I talked to Bill Clinton about."

I had the feeling that Gus had not done his homework in preparation for this deposition. He seemed to think that under pressure I'd want to shift blame and start talking about how people at the White House, not the reelection campaign, had really made the key decisions. He would not have had to ask many people to find out that he was barking up the wrong tree.

"As people will tell you, I have a certain style of management and leadership," I said. "I didn't need any oversight. No one was second-guessing me. I did it. I ran it. . . . I take full responsibility."

I couldn't believe how many people came to the mistaken conclusion that having coffees at the White House was my idea. It wasn't, no more than having sleepovers in the Lincoln Bedroom was my idea. My only recommendation was that the President needed to reconnect with his past supporters to get them excited about the upcoming campaign.

How dense could Gus be? What political candidate doesn't meet with his supporters?

"My simple motive was as every United States senator, every United States congressman, every governor, every mayor, when they get ready for reelection or election, they sit down and meet with their key supporters and sort of get them revved up or energized and why they should support them," I told Gus. "That was the goal, simple as that."

Now I was on a roll and shifted the focus to Senator Fred Thompson, Gus's boss.

"I would have you ask every senator on this committee, ask your chairman, Senator Thompson, who may or may not run for President, that at some point, he is going to sit down with his top supporters and get them energized to support his candidacy," I said.

"Did you ever tell a DNC donor or a potential DNC donor that if they had made a fifty-thousand-dollar contribution to the DNC, you would put them in a luncheon at the White House?" Gus asked.

"I have been doing this business for eighteen years," I said. "I've never said 'For this you get that.' . . . Did we recommend, Gus, people whom we hoped would be helpful or had been helpful? You bet. . . . As I've always said, I could have cared less if those first ten coffees were done at McDonald's. It didn't matter to me. I needed people to see the President and get his vision for the future. . . .

"I traveled three hundred days a year, not talking about coffees or lunches or dinners, I talked about Bill Clinton and what he meant to this country. . . . When the Republicans shut this government down several times, it was Bill Clinton who stood tall on that and said we're not going to allow the elderly and the homeless to be treated this way because that's not what this country is all about, and that's why ninety-nine percent of the people did what they did for Clinton-Gore and for the DNC."

It went back and forth like that for hours.

"Did you ever in the course of encouraging or soliciting a person to make a contribution to the Democratic National Committee, whether on the Committee staff, whether working at the Committee or not, mention the possibility of attending an intimate event at the White House, such as a luncheon or a coffee?" Gus asked.

"If they thought for giving money and that was the reason they were getting invited, no," I said. "I told people to give money to help Bill Clinton win the reelection. I can't say it any differently. It's not like a movie theater we were running over there and you bought tickets to it. . . . I want to make a key point here, Gus. I didn't invite people. The White House invites. I recommend."

"And in the course of telling people to give money to help Bill Clinton, did you ever mention the possibility that they may meet Bill Clinton on intimate terms at the White House?" Gus tried.

"Generally, the people whom I dealt with, Gus, I knew them all well," I said. "They all knew Bill Clinton. They didn't care about going into the White House. They knew him. These people were with him, trudging through the snows of New Hampshire in 1991. If you look at my Clinton-Gore list, this wasn't these people, arms dealers and all this other wacky stuff that you read about. These are people that were with the President when no one else was in

1991. These were not like unknown characters, and the people who came to those coffees, no, Gus, *past* supporters, p-a-s-t. . . . Many of them had supported the President when he ran for governor of Arkansas. It's a different whole deal that I ran."

I knew Gus wanted to put me in a corner and squeeze me. They were hoping to make me look bad in my deposition and then they could read some of my quotes into the official record of Fred Thompson's Senate committee investigating campaign finance. There was a problem with that strategy of theirs, however. If they wanted to read any of my deposition into the record, the Democratic senators had the right to demand that they introduce all of the deposition. The way I kept talking about Bill Clinton and all the great things he had done for this country, I knew they were never going to be introducing this deposition into their record.

If I had a theme that day, it was how proud I was of the work we had done to help reelect Bill Clinton and Al Gore. In fact, over the course of the four-hour deposition, I said I was "proud" twenty-two times. I also said "Gus" forty-nine different times. It just rolled off my tongue, like, "Okay, Gus."

I had nothing against the guy. I tried to be friendly and twice I even gave him book recommendations, suggesting he read *The Choice* by Bob Woodward.

After I'd left the DNC to head up the Clinton-Gore finance operation, a DNC fund-raiser named John Huang had become the center of the controversy. Naturally Gus hoped I would tell him that Huang and I used to hit the sauna together every Tuesday afternoon.

"Did you ever meet John Huang?" he asked.

"You and every reporter in America have asked me this question," I said. "He went to the DNC, I believe from the press reports, in December 1995. I had been out of the DNC for over a year basically and I had left Clinton-Gore. So he was not a factor in any of the things that I did."

Gus asked me what procedures we had for vetting the checks.

I said he'd have to ask staff and the lawyers about that, but explained: "We were sensitized to the issue because, you know, the Republican National Committee had that horrible instance of Mr. Kojimami, or whatever his name was, the deadbeat dad who sat next to Reagan or Bush and, you know, hadn't paid his child-support payments. . . .

"I mean, look at the Dole for President Committee. Let's use that as an example. You got this guy, Simon Fireman, who was the vice chairman of finance, not some little low-level fund-raiser, top-shelf guy, takes two hundred thousand dollars in cash and hands it out to his employees and has them write checks. . . . And now this guy, Fireman, has got a bracelet around his leg, and he's running around his home in Massachusetts. . . . You've seen a story in the *L.A. Times*, six straight stories in a row about Congressman Burton and all the crazy people that gave him money."

I had Ben-Veniste so wound up before we even entered the deposition, he really gave it to Gus.

"You guys are not getting along," I said at one point.

That was my way of kidding my attorney. I knew this kid Gus had no chance going up against him.

"Don't play those games," Ben-Veniste told Gus a little later. "It's silly."

"Well, while we're on the topic of playing games, I mean, if he saw this document and it refreshed his recollection about events at the DNC in preparation for his deposition, what privilege am I invading?" Gus asked.

"What privilege are you invading?" Ben-Veniste asked, incredulous.

"Exactly," Gus said.

"Did you ever hear of the attorney-client privilege? . . . If you want to hit the books, you can look it up."

Gus never really recovered his composure after that. He looked calm enough, but his questions were nothing more than a nuisance.

"We're not going on a fishing expedition of every time I went to the White House for a meeting," I scolded him. "If you have something to ask me, ask me."

"I'm merely taking up something that you said earlier, Mr. McAuliffe," Gus said.

"Okay," Ben-Veniste said. "Take up another subject. That's not an appropriate question."

"None of your business," I told Gus.

"None of my business what meetings stand out in your mind at the White House when you were at Clinton-Gore '96 or at the DNC?" Gus asked. "Is that correct?"

I had him hot under the collar now.

"Yeah," I said. "I'm telling you that if you have specific questions about meetings I had at the White House, great, ask me about it."

"I'm just asking—" Gus attempted.

I cut him off.

"My discussion with the President about his golf game is none of your business," I said.

"Is that what discussions stand out in your mind?" Gus asked.

"He didn't say that," Ben-Veniste said.

"That's hypothetical," I added.

"I'm not asking a hypothetical question, with all due respect, Mr. McAuliffe," Gus said.

"I think we ought to break for lunch," Ben-Veniste said. "We're getting silly here."

★

THEY WERE SO HAPPY to see me leave that day. As Ben-Veniste and I were heading out, we overheard one of the deposers say there was no way they were going to call this lunatic before the committee.

"We ain't putting *this guy* in front of a TV camera," he said.

Too bad! A month later Doug Sosnik was up for his deposition and started talking to the stenographer during a break.

"God, how many of these things have you done?" Sosnik asked the guy.

"I don't know, two hundred and twelve so far," he said.

"That has to be awful," Sosnik said. "Any stand out?"

"You know this guy McAuliffe?" the guy asked.

Sosnik tried not to laugh.

"I know him very well," he said. "Why?"

"Oh, he was the best," the stenographer said. "He killed them."

To me, that was the greatest compliment I'd ever received. I couldn't wait to tell the President, but by the time I got back to him, Sosnik had already told him and he was roaring with laughter.

"Mac, I wish I had a hundred of you," the President said.

13

★ ★ ★

I almost felt bad for Senator Fred Thompson, the Republican chairing the hearings on campaign finance in July 1997. He knew he had a weak hand but had to go ahead and play it with that same serious, worried look that has made him a sought-after actor from *The Hunt for Red October* to *Law & Order*. Thompson first made his mark as chief minority counsel to the Senate Watergate Committee. He was the one who came up with the question, "What did the President know and when did he know it?" which, just by being asked, was the beginning of the end for Nixon. Thompson was one smart cookie, and he had also worked as a shoe salesman and a truck driver along the way, which told you something. He just didn't have anything to work with when it came to the Senate Governmental Affairs Committee hearings.

The Republicans on the committee thought they were going to feast on their first witness, Richard Sullivan, the former DNC finance director. Based on a deposition Richard had given, word spread among Republicans that his testimony before the committee was going to be devastating for Democrats. I knew better. To me, it was always clear that the whole thing was going to be a washout. Since the Republicans had courted some of the same characters, it kind of cut down on how much leverage they had. Still, you never knew for sure, and all around Washington everybody had their own pet theory about how the hearings were going to work out.

One of the unfortunate aspects of politics is how fast friends desert you in times of trouble. The press put Richard Sullivan right in the vortex of the fund-raising scandal and he was suddenly a pariah. No one wanted to stand by him. No one wanted to talk to him. But Richard had worked for me on and off the last ten years, and I had been his chief sponsor for Georgetown Law School. I wasn't about to desert him now.

I gave him a call before the first of his two days of testimony and did my best to buck him up.

"You know what, Richard?" I said. "If you want, I'd be honored to sit up there with you to give you support."

He jumped at the offer and said he'd love to have me there. The next morning as I was driving in to the capital to sit with him, my phone rang and it was Richard.

"My lawyers think it's a bad idea to have you sit by me," he said. "They think it would be too much in your face."

"Well, that was the whole idea!" I said. "But maybe they're right. Good luck. Knock it out of the park, and I'll take you and the team to dinner afterward."

Richard did great. Instead of coming across before the committee as the sinister, conniving, lecherous, deceitful political operative they wanted to portray him as, he came off looking like a Boy Scout. He was calm and composed and articulate before Fred Thompson's hearing. Senator Pete Domenici kept reading from Richard's deposition and trying to get him to crumble. It didn't happen.

The coffees "were really fund-raisers, weren't they?" Domenici asked.

"Senator, the coffees helped us with our fund-raising . . . but they were not fund-raisers. The coffees were a tool in helping us motivate and energize the people that we needed to motivate and energize," Sullivan said.

"Now, for the first time since you've been here I really believe you are spewing words calculated to confuse the issue," Domenici said.

That was senator-speak for Domenici being frustrated that there was nothing he could say. Michigan senator Carl Levin got tired of the Republican senators trying to make an issue of sleepovers in the Lincoln Bedroom, given what Republicans have pulled. Levin reminded them, for example, of the official White House stationery that was mailed out during the Bush 41 administration tastefully embossed with the message: "Benefits Based on Receipts," no doubt in tastefully smaller type.

After I'd left my role as DNC finance chairman in 1994, they'd tried to save money by not rehiring the check-vetting team that we took with us to Clinton-Gore. That, to me, is an essential part of fund-raising. I've never had a single check returned in my nearly thirty years of fund-raising and that's because I make sure we do our homework. The DNC decided they could do without the vetters and the result was that some shady characters got through the cracks.

Thompson had raised a stir the day before Richard testified by announcing he had information about "the existence of a Chinese plan to subvert our election process." Boy, that sounded dramatic. But unfortunately the information was classified, Thompson said, so he couldn't pass it on. Gotcha, Senator. We'll make a note of that. But if Thompson was sitting on some explosive information, you would think he'd have had more luck scoring points with Richard Sullivan in the hearing that day.

Time magazine was devastating to Republicans in its article on the first week of the hearings, using the headline NOT READY FOR PRIME TIME and adding NO WONDER THOMPSON WANTED TO LOWER EXPECTATIONS: WEEK 1 PRODUCED NEITHER LIGHT NOR HEAT NOR GOOD VISUALS. *The New York Times* explained: "Midway through his four-hour performance, Mr. Sullivan had Democrats crowing over the dearth of firsthand testimony he offered to corroborate the sensational Republican charge that there was a China-directed plot to compromise American policy by way of the Clinton campaign's hunger for money."

The Times didn't know the half of it. I watched the hearings in my office that day and bellowed out to anyone who would listen, "Richard is doing great. Thompson can forget about running for President if he plans on using these hearings as a springboard."

That night the mood was electric at the Palm, a Washington restaurant that is a real landmark for political types. If you've done anything in politics, they've probably got a caricature of you somewhere at the Palm. The steaks are excellent and you always have a great time talking to the crazy assortment of people you run into there. Tommy Jacomo, the general manager, opened the Palm in 1972 with his brother Ray and has hosted every President since Nixon. Tommy has some Muhammad Ali stories you have to ask about if you ever get in there. He'll tell you.

Richard was the guest of honor that night for our dinner with young fund-raisers Jay Dunn, Scott Freda, and David Jones, as well as Scott Pastrick, the former DNC treasurer, celebrating Richard's successful testimony. The Palm was packed and we were seated in the back corner near the caricature of me in the glasses I used to wear in my twenties to make me look older. We were attacking our steaks and breaking down the day's events one more time when Freda came back from the men's room with a huge grin.

"You're not going to believe who's sitting up front," he said. "Fred Thompson."

"No way!" I said and threw my napkin down.

It was Thompson and Mike Madigan, the chief Republican counsel on the committee.

"This is too good to be true!" I told the guys, clapping my hands together before I hopped up out of my seat. "I gotta go say hello."

Everyone at the table loved the idea except poor Richard.

"Mac, are you crazy?" Richard said. "I've got to testify again tomorrow."

I just laughed and walked the ten yards over to Thompson's table, and it was like one of those E. F. Hutton moments: Everything froze. People stopped talking midsentence and stared at me. This was the kind of thing people came to the Palm to see, Clinton's top money guy confronting Thompson when he was right in the middle of presiding over these hearings. No one had any idea what I'd do. They thought I might start yelling or throwing chairs. You could hear people murmuring, "What is he *doing*?"

But I was smiling the whole way over, and why not? This was going to be fun! I slid up next to Thompson and his counsel, and without breaking stride I reached out and grabbed a chair from the next table and sat down. Just as I was pulling up the chair I spotted John, a waiter I knew, walking past.

"John, let's get a round here for the three of us!" I said, and turned back around and held out my hand to shake the senator's hand.

Once I'd ordered a round of drinks, they knew there was no getting rid of me without a little conversation first.

"Boy, Senator," I said. "Ole Sully, he kicked your ass today, didn't he?"

Madigan broke out laughing. He couldn't believe I'd even sat down, much less ordered drinks and started talking that way to a United States senator.

"Man, you got guts," he said.

"Hey, I saw what I saw," I said.

Thompson was amazed when I first walked up, but before long he was laughing right along with me. We were just a couple of old grizzly bears playing with each other and we both knew it, but that didn't mean we couldn't enjoy ourselves.

"I hope you guys are going to call me up," I said. "I can't wait to get up there and talk about Bill Clinton and everything he has done for this country."

We all knew there was no way they were going to call me before the committee.

★

IF YOU WERE THE CLINTONS or anyone who worked for them, you could count on being badgered, bullied, and bankrupted by a relentless combination of congressional subpoenas, hostile grand jury depositions, and highly misleading leaks to the media. The Republicans thought they had devised the perfect political perpetual-motion machine, both creating the appearance of scandal with all their petty investigations and trying to capitalize on the nearly universal disgust with the nonsense going on in Washington. But they were too clever by half. They were trying to manipulate the American people, and the American people were too smart for that. They threw everything they had at us and none of it stuck.

It sounds like a story with no heroes, just a lot of unhinged Republicans willing to pull out the stops and the Democrats they victimized, but in fact there were heroes: the grand jurors. The Republicans seemed to forget that our American justice system calls for real people, not paid political hacks, to sit in the courtroom and use their honest judgment. These people knew a farce when they saw one.

If the Republicans wanted to come after me, that was fine by me. I could take the heat. But their method was to drag in every junior staffer they could just to intimidate them. To call it a fishing expedition would be an overstatement. At least when you're fishing, you have a chance of catching something. This was all show, all bluster. They had nothing and they knew it. The Clintons and I could handle it when they came after us, but hundreds of other people whose names will never make it into a book had to hire lawyers and were financially ruined. They came to work in government to do good things for people and were so badly treated, it was unfair and wrong.

The Republicans went after people like Aprill Springfield, who started out as an intern in Hillary's White House office and worked her way up. Her job was basically carrying papers from place to place with no idea of what was in any of them, but Ken Starr subpoenaed her, brought her in, and had one of his pit bulls give her a going-over. What kind of person does something like that? It was hardly a surprise when one of Ken Starr's henchmen was convicted of stalking. I'm serious. In May 2006 Robert Ray was charged with stalking his ex-girlfriend. She told him to get lost four months earlier, but he wouldn't take no for an answer and would continually show up to harass her. Sound familiar?

I'd like to see all of Starr's former lackeys locked up somewhere, but some of them have actually been appointed as federal judges. That fits in with the Bush administration strategy of covering up incompetence with promotions. Amazingly enough, Bush nominated one of the men who had badgered this 1999 college grad, Aprill Springfield, when she was called in to testify before the Senate committee investigating Whitewater. His nomination came before the Senate and ninety-six senators lined up to vote for him. Only one opposed him: Senator Hillary Clinton. She came back to her office after the vote and Aprill Springfield rushed over to thank her, throwing her arms around the senator and getting emotional.

"Thank you so much for voting against that evil man," she said, bursting into tears. "He was so mean. He was so unfair. That man should not be a judge."

Or the Republicans would go after someone like Labor Secretary Alexis Herman, a distinguished public servant whose honor and dignity were an inspiration to many. Unfortunately, Attorney General Janet Reno had caved under pressure time and time again, and made baffling decisions on when to appoint independent counsels. Let me lay it out: I'm all for the way Jack Kennedy did it. He appointed his brother to be attorney general. You need someone in that job who knows the ways of Washington and won't be bullied by a gang of political zealots.

The list of Reno's bad calls was way too long. How about Ken Starr? Robert Fiske had already investigated this two-bit land deal called Whitewater and determined nothing was amiss, but even so, Starr was given the job of carrying on the investigation, and he turned it into a witch hunt and a shameless waste of taxpayer money. Lawrence Walsh, the Iran-Contra independent counsel, spent $47.4 million on his investigation of a scandal so serious it forced Bush 41 to pardon former defense secretary Cap Weinberger and five others. Starr somehow found a way to top that, spending more than $52 million. Five independent counsels spent more than $110 million of taxpayer money in pointless investigations of the Clinton administration, according to the GAO.

How about the investigation of HUD Secretary Henry Cisneros? What a farce that was. He pled to a misdemeanor charge in 1999 and paid a small fine, and in 2001, Clinton pardoned him, so there was no crime. But independent counsel David Barrett's investigation dragged on for ten full years and cost the taxpayers $21 million before it was finally shut down in April 2006. Cisneros was a superstar of the Democratic Party, an important Hispanic leader, and the Republicans kept this investigation open, wasting taxpayer dollars, so that he could not run for the Senate or governor of Texas. He was approached about running for DNC chairman in 2005 and begged off, saying he couldn't even consider it because of the cloud of the continuing investigation.

Janet Reno hemmed and hawed over whether to appoint an independent counsel to investigate Alexis for some obvious sham charges and then did it anyway, even though Reno herself said that her investigation "developed no evidence clearly demonstrating Secretary Herman's involvement in these matters and substantial evidence that she may not have been involved." The whole case against Alexis was so weak, it was a joke. Some crazy guy who had dated a friend of Alexis's claimed the woman gave Alexis cash. They had nothing to back up this character's wild allegations, but they turned it into a whole rigmarole and even had the President of the United States testify under oath for an hour in September 1999 to independent counsel Ralph Lancaster and two of his lawyers. Isn't that great? We had our commander in chief taking an hour from his duties as the most powerful man in the world to take part in a cockamamie witch hunt that would go nowhere.

I couldn't wait to defend Alexis. They subpoenaed me on the thinnest of pretexts. I'd chaired an event with almost a thousand people attending and this crazy character was allegedly one of them. I'd never even met the guy. Once again, my lawyer and I did our usual routine before I showed up in front of the grand jury. Richard Ben-Veniste may be expensive, but he is one heck of a good straight man. I'd be rubbing my hands together in the backseat, saying "Let me at 'em!" and poor Ben-Veniste would tell me one more time in that soothing lawyer voice of his that our goal was to say as little as possible and get in and get out. Every time he said it, I roared with laughter. As if!

So we got to the district courthouse and I busted in through the front doors and I was there in this big marble hall bellowing hello to everyone in a voice that echoed in every corner. I was talking to guards and clerks and anyone I could.

"You're a Democrat, right?" I kept asking.

I walked into the grand jury room and left Ben-Veniste waiting outside because no one is allowed to bring counsel inside for a grand jury proceeding.

"Do you swear to tell the truth, the whole truth, and nothing but the truth, so help you God?"

I may have had contempt for the whole witch-hunt atmosphere, but putting your hand on a Bible and being sworn in was as serious as it got, and I was very solemn. I took my seat and one of Lancaster's prosecutors started the questioning with almost a pained look, as if we were all somehow imposing on his time.

"Do you have counsel present outside?" he asked me.

I took a long, slow look at this guy.

"Are you out of your mind?" I thundered. "At six hundred and fifty bucks an hour, do you think Richard Ben-Veniste would miss this opportunity?"

The grand jurors all broke out laughing, and it took awhile before everything settled down. I knew right there I had that grand jury.

"This is a witch hunt against this woman!" I exclaimed at one point and I saw several of the grand jurors nodding along with me.

The three lawyers were all white and the grand jurors were mostly African American and they knew about the great work Alexis had done. They knew she deserved admiration and respect, not cheap gutter tactics.

"It is a disgrace what's being done to this woman, this woman of distinction," I said, flailing in the air. "This government is lucky to have people like Alexis Herman and Bill Clinton and all they have done for this country."

I was very respectful of the grand jury, but I made it perfectly clear how unfair I thought this attack on Alexis was. The grand jurors nodded their heads in agreement. Lancaster ultimately agreed, because charges were never filed.

I knew it was a grand jury, but I just couldn't help myself and as I got up to leave, I turned to the grand jurors and thanked them.

"Make sure you vote for Al Gore!" I said. "Keep this country free and safe."

They all started clapping and a couple of guys stood up and cheered. I've never heard of anyone getting a standing ovation at a grand jury, but I guess there's a first time for everything.

14

★ ★ ★

Former Miramax boss Harvey Weinstein told Hillary in late 1997 that he'd like to arrange a special screening of his latest movie, *Good Will Hunting,* at Camp David, the rustic presidential retreat in Maryland's Catoctin Mountains. "What a great idea," said the First Lady. Soon the screening was set for January 1998, and the Clintons invited Dorothy and me to be there along with director Gus Van Sant, producer Lawrence Bender, Robin Williams, and two young actors who had written the movie. I'd never heard of either of the two young actors, of course, but when I mentioned to Dorothy that they were on the guest list, she told her girlfriends that we were going to be having dinner with Matt Damon and Ben Affleck. We were excited about our first weekend together at the historic presidential retreat.

Camp David can really cast a spell with its woods and spectacular views, its sprawling layout of old cabins with names like Hickory, Hemlock, Dogwood, Walnut, and Red Oak, and most of all its air of history. The Clintons preferred to stay in Washington most weekends during the first term because Chelsea, who was still in high school then, liked to be there with her friends, but once the President started making regular visits to Camp David after Chelsea left for college, he loved it up there and always wanted to have a lot of people around.

"Mac, who should we have up this week?" the President would ask me. We were looking forward to playing cards, watching some football, and exploring the 134 acres of land in our golf carts or on bikes, and having a fun weekend, which, let's be honest, is usually the main reason the President goes to Camp David. Presidents need to unwind, too.

"Without Camp David you'll go stir crazy," Pat Nixon warned Nancy Reagan.

Camp David actually started out as a small group of cabins called Camp Hi-Catoctin built in late 1938 along with a swimming pool and dining hall by the CCC and WPA. FDR's doctors wanted him to escape the summer heat of Washington and in April 1942 he visited Camp Hi-Catoctin, 1,880 feet high and cool, and declared, "This is Shangri-La." At a cost of $18,650 he had the camp converted into a presidential retreat he called Shangri-La.

Winston Churchill visited in February 1943 and raved about the fishing and stopped at the Cozy Tavern for a drink and to play the first jukebox he'd ever seen. President Eisenhower came often and in 1953 renamed the place Camp David after his five-year-old grandson David.

Nikita Khrushchev, the little spark plug of a man who led the Soviet Union after Stalin, was nervous when Andrei Gromyko brought him the Americans' proposed itinerary for his September 1959 trip to the United States.

"*K-e-ntp-David?* What's that?" Khrushchev asked suspiciously, according to William Taubman's biography.

"All Gromyko could offer was a translation: 'Camp David.' Khrushchev demanded: 'What sort of camp is it?' Why hold talks there rather than in the capital itself? Only after inquiries were made in Washington was Khrushchev reliably informed that Camp David was the president's dacha in Maryland," Taubman wrote.

Eisenhower and Khrushchev slogged through tense talks on the Berlin crisis and took time to tour the grounds, including the newly installed two-lane bowling alley. The meetings ended in a surprise agreement on Berlin and an improvement in U.S.-Soviet relations referred to as "the Spirit of Camp David."

President Nixon invited Brezhnev to Camp David in June 1973 and presented him with a dark blue Lincoln Continental, which the Soviet premier immediately took for a spin, barreling along the narrow country roads at high speed and scaring the heck out of Nixon, who sat white-knuckled in the passenger seat. "At one point there is a very steep slope with a sign at the top reading, SLOW, DANGEROUS CURVE," Nixon wrote in his memoirs. "Even driving a golf cart down it, I had to use the brakes in order to avoid going off the road. Brezhnev was driving more than fifty miles an hour as we approached the slope. When we reached the bottom, there was a squeal of rubber as he . . . made the turn. After our drive he said to me, 'This is a very fine automobile. It holds the road very well.' 'You are an excellent driver,' I replied. Diplomacy is not always an easy art."

Nixon spent a lot of time at Camp David, making more than 120 visits just in his first term, and refurbished the President's four-bedroom Aspen Lodge and put in a putting green near the fish pond that had first been stocked with rainbow trout for Ike.

It was under Jimmy Carter that Camp David really hit the big time. As *Time* reported in February 1978: "When Anwar Sadat signed the guest book at Camp David's presidential house, Aspen Lodge, he was checking in at the world's most exclusive and elaborate political retreat." Few thought Carter had a chance of presiding over an important breakthrough between the Egyptian leader Sadat, who stayed in Dogwood Lodge, and the Israeli leader, Menachem Begin, who stayed in Birch Lodge. But after twelve difficult days of negotiations, some conducted in armchairs around the two-story fireplace in Aspen Lodge, the historic Camp David Accords establishing peace between Egypt and Israel were reached.

*

THE WEEKEND OF the *Good Will Hunting* screening turned out to be the calm before the storm in early 1998. Saturday morning, January 10, *The New York Times* had excellent news for the President: 370,000 JOBS ADDED TO ROLLS IN DECEMBER. The President's unpopular decision to tame the deficit early in his administration had paid off in a way that every working American could understand. In sharp contrast to the net job loss in the early years of the George W. Bush administration, the economy under Clinton was booming. "Riding a strong economy, the nation's employers added 370,000 new jobs to their payrolls last month—far beyond expectations—and at year's end, employment reached record levels," *The Times* wrote that morning in January. "Not since the government began to compile employment numbers, starting in 1948, has such a large percentage of Americans worked."

The way to get around Camp David is to drive golf carts, and I always had a great time ripping through the trails at full throttle just like Brezhnev before me. One weekend the next year, Hillary and I were leaning against the front of a golf cart and talking, and little Jack, who was only six years old then, accidentally hit the gas and the cart hopped forward and rolled right over the First Lady's foot and knocked her over. I about died. I was thinking: *Oh my God, what if my son had killed the First Lady?* Talk about a career-ender! First I screamed in her ear on Election Night 1996, leaving her temporarily deaf, and now this. The McAuliffes were definitely hazards. However, Hillary, the ever-resilient hostess, scrambled right back up and dusted her slacks off. Poor Jack was a wreck, worrying how the First Lady was going to react, but she didn't miss a beat.

"Has Bill been teaching you to drive?" she joked.

Jack turned bright red, and Hillary and I continued our discussion at a safe distance.

Up at Camp David that weekend in January 1998, Dorothy and I had settled into our cabin and signed the guest book, which listed everyone who had ever stayed there, and in doing so became a part of history, joining the likes of Mikhail Gorbachev, Maggie Thatcher, Bobby Kennedy, Clark Clifford, and the Dulles brothers. I headed over to the sports complex for my daily workout and noticed a crowd in front of the chapel, including Harvey Weinstein, who was there with the movie people getting a quick tour of the grounds. I went over to say hello and started introducing myself around.

"What do you boys do?" I asked two young men in the group.

They seemed surprised by the question.

"I'm an actor," said the blond one.

"Really?" I said. "An actor? That's got to be a lot of fun."

"Well, yeah, it is," the young guy said, laughing.

"Terry McAuliffe," I said, shaking his hand.

"Matt Damon," he said.

"What about you?" I asked the other one.

"Ben Affleck," he said.

A little later Dorothy and I ended up driving around with Robin Williams and his wife, Marsha, and exploring. Now, I was never a big TV watcher, but even I knew the TV show *Mork and Mindy* from the '70s and '80s. Back then you always heard people trying to copy Robin Williams's crazy style of comedy, bouncing all over the place like a nuclear-powered Ping-Pong ball, but no one could pull that off except Robin. We found him very entertaining and all weekend we would hear him doing his improvisations or breaking off into peals of laughter. Sometimes you couldn't see Robin, just hear his voice resonating from out of the woods, and that cracked us all up. Ben Affleck joined Robin, Marsha, Dorothy, and me for a quick tour of the skeet range and then we took a look inside Marine One, which was resting gracefully in its hangar.

It was playoff season in football and the President and I couldn't wait to plop down in front of the big-screen TV in Laurel Lodge. Bill Clinton and I both loved sports and we were always talking about college basketball and football, his two favorites. Everyone knew that Bill Clinton could talk politics like no else around, he was so knowledgeable and insightful, but he was almost as much of a virtuoso talking about sports. He always knew everything about the two teams squaring off and even if he was doing four things at once, he always followed every detail in the game with a laserlike focus.

That Sunday at Camp David, the early game was John Elway and the Denver Broncos against Kordell Stewart and the Pittsburgh Steelers in the AFC championship. While most of the guys watched the game, Robin Williams was off in the other side of the lodge, crawling on his knees and doing strange animal imitations that had everyone cracking up. He did it quietly, too, so we could concentrate on the game. Matt Damon and Ben Affleck joined us, and I did my best to get them involved in conversation with the President. The young guys were real sports fans and we all had a great time watching as Denver jumped out to a big halftime lead. Late in the game, Elway was under pressure on third-and-fifteen and drilled a bullet pass for a first down with 2:46 left. The Broncos ran out the clock and were on their way to the Super Bowl—and soon we were on our way to dinner.

★

THE GREAT THING ABOUT THE WHITE HOUSE style in the Clinton years was that they loved the elegance but they also loved to have fun. Dinner that night was a formal five-course dinner with the White House stewards serving us, but we had about twenty of us gathered at one big table and everyone was dressed casually. Dorothy was seated next to the President and his old friend National Security Advisor Sandy Berger, and I was across the table next to Hillary. Matt Damon was sitting next to Secretary of State Madeleine Albright, who had just arrived, and the two of them really hit it off, carrying on a long discussion that bounced all over the place. It was entertaining to see Hollywood meet D.C.

The stewards started us off with some kind of soup, which was good because you can eat soup and keep talking without slowing up. Then they brought out the second course, and about the time the White House staff was taking away those plates there was a small commotion and Ben Affleck stood up to go meet someone who was arriving late.

"Who's that?" I asked Hillary.

"That's Gwyneth Paltrow, the actress, you idiot," she said.

We got up from the dinner table and milled around a little, then posed for a big group picture. Dorothy practically knocked over Madeleine Albright as she rushed over to grab the seat next to Matt Damon. Then it was time for everyone to get in their golf carts and ride over for the screening. I always loved movie night at the White House and this was even better, all of us tucked in at Camp David for the weekend, the staff handing out bags of popcorn. I loved the movie, too. As a kid from Syracuse, I enjoyed a story about two kids from the South Side of Boston.

The way the little theater at Camp David is set up, everyone sits on couches or overstuffed chairs and in the front row are two love seats. Affleck and Paltrow were sitting on one, and the President and Hillary were on another, looking very cozy with the President's arm draped over the First Lady's shoulder. For the rest of us, though, it was a little hard to watch without being distracted. Affleck and Paltrow didn't come up for air the whole time. I guess they'd already seen the movie.

Sean, the shrink played by Robin Williams, tells a story early in the movie about shocking his buddies by giving up a big Red Sox game to go talk to his future wife, saying, "I gotta go see about a girl." The movie ends with Damon's character running off to California and leaving a note, explaining, "I gotta go see about a girl."

Once the movie ended, the lights came on and the President stood up and told everyone how much he liked the romantic ending.

"That sounds like me in the summer of 1971," Bill Clinton said. "I decided I had to go see about a girl. I turned down a job working in the South for the McGovern campaign and drove out to California with Hillary instead. Best decision I ever made, too."

★

SOME OF THE GROUP peeled off after the movie and called it a night and some of us were just getting started. The bowling alley at Camp David has to be one of the most fun places to bowl in the world. There are just two lanes and it gets kind of stuffy down there, but you're bowling side by side with past Presidents. Nixon had his friend Bebe Rebozo spring for a one-lane bowling alley underneath the White House, and Nixon would bowl game after game by himself late at night there and at Camp David. Henry Kissinger must have gotten tired of hearing about the bowling.

"I just shot 120," Nixon said one night at Camp David.

"Your golf game is improving, Mr. President," Kissinger said.

"I was bowling, Henry," Nixon replied.

That would have placed Nixon in second that night, behind my 123, but on the night Apollo 10 flew past the moon in May 1969, Nixon left Aspen

Lodge all alone for more late-night bowling and rolled a 204, his best game ever. Jimmy Carter used to average in the 160s. President Clinton was normally a very good bowler, but that night he was devoting most of his energies to coaching Dorothy and Madeleine. The last time the secretary of state had bowled was forty years earlier as a high school student in Denver, and the President walked her through the steps several times, Diet Coke in hand. "With the President serving as my personal instructor, I remembered how to release the ball without injuring myself or alarming the Secret Service," Albright recalled in *Madame Secretary.*

Once the President had Albright squared away, he was over giving Dorothy the full treatment with pointers and advice. He analyzed her foot placement, her backswing, the weight of the ball she was using—everything. Neither Madeleine nor Dorothy was knocking down many pins, but to this day Dorothy still fondly recalls that presidential tutorial on bowling. By two o'clock most everyone was ready to go to bed. A couple of people in the group were so tired, they had actually dozed off in their chairs. We all walked up from the little bowling alley and people got into their carts to drive back to their cabins.

"Mac, you want to come in for one game?" the President asked me.

He wanted to play cards, but the First Lady and Dorothy gave their customary responses, rolling their eyes.

"Not me," said the First Lady. "I'm going to bed."

"Not a chance!" Dorothy said. "I'm going to bed, too."

So it was just the President and I back at Aspen Lodge, the presidential cabin, and we got into a great game of Upwords, the three-dimensional version of Scrabble, which was always one of the President's favorites. I'm no match for the President with his command of the language, but as always we'd be playing and talking and the time zipped away. He was drinking Diet Coke and I was drinking coffee, and the next thing you knew, you started to notice the blue jays and snowbirds twittering outside, and you looked out the big picture windows and you could see the woods out there because it was already getting light. I finally got back to my cabin at 7:15 A.M.

"What have you been doing?" Dorothy asked me.

"Playing Upwords," I said.

We had to be up and dressed within forty-five minutes, but that was how Bill Clinton liked it. He loved life and always wanted to squeeze a little more out of every day, especially when he was sitting around enjoying himself, and he could chew on a cigar and do a crossword puzzle and play Upwords and maybe watch some sports on TV, all at the same time. Forty-five minutes later, there Clinton was, chipper and ready to go through another whole day. The man just had an amazing energy level.

★

THAT MONDAY MORNING, all the movie people had to get up early to catch a flight to Chicago, where they were going to appear on Oprah Winfrey's show. Before the rest of us left, the President asked if I would go for a walk with him and the two of us set off. You couldn't walk side by side with the President in the crisp mountain air at Camp David without thinking about Churchill, Khrushchev, and Gorbachev strolling down the same trails.

"These legal bills are really killing me, Terry," the President said. "These nuts are trying to bankrupt me. They want to put me in the poorhouse before I get out of the White House."

It was obscene what was happening to him. At a time when Al Qaeda operatives were in the United States organizing a terrorist act so twisted and sick that it would become a true national trauma, Ken Starr and Louis Freeh had FBI agents fanning out all over America, harassing people to make up stories about the Clintons. In order to defend themselves, the President and Hillary had run up $3 million in legal bills fending off all these insidious attacks. It was all part of a Republican plan to use money as a weapon against a politician they feared. They wanted to bankrupt Bill Clinton just as they had bankrupted the DNC.

I wasn't too concerned about any more legal bills for Clinton, because I knew the only other thing coming up was the President's deposition five days later in a sexual harassment case brought against him by a woman named Paula Jones. Clinton told me there was nothing to it, so I figured his legal ordeal would soon be over.

The Jones case represented the tip of the iceberg of the campaign of character assassination a group of extreme right-wingers had organized against Bill Clinton. They knew he connected with the American people and they knew that unless they pulled out all stops of decency and respect for the presidency and used every dirty trick they could to undermine him, he was on his way to going down in the history books as the next FDR. The rabid-dog mentality was so out of hand that Jack Abramoff's business partner, disgraced Republican lobbyist Michael Scanlon, another convicted felon, later wrote an e-mail about Clinton, saying: "This whole thing about not kicking somebody when they are down is BS—Not only do you kick him—you kick him until he passes out then beat him over the head with a baseball bat—then roll him up in an old rug—and throw him off a cliff into the pound surf below!!!!!"

Another compassionate conservative!

If you look hard enough, you can always find unflattering episodes in anyone's life. There were Republican Presidents who carried on affairs that were well known to everyone in Washington, and not a peep of it ever made it into the press. I'm not going to name names here. But everyone in Washington knows exactly whom I'm talking about.

By that weekend at Camp David, Clinton's insurance no longer covered his legal expenses in the Jones case and as a sitting President he could not accept legal services for free. The nut jobs organizing against Clinton thought they could undermine the choice of the American people, but they were wrong. Plenty of people were ready to stand by the President against these thugs and I was proud to be one of them. We were going to put together a new Legal Defense Fund and we were going to take the fight to these people and win.

"We will take care of it, Mr. President," I said. "I am not going to allow you to leave the White House bankrupt. You have worked too hard and done too many great things for the American people to let Ken Starr bankrupt you."

He thanked me and we kept walking.

"Mr. President," I said. "I gotta tell you, I just don't like this deposition thing. Let's settle it. Whatever it takes, I'll raise it. If it's a million, it's a million. Let's move on."

★

I WAS OUT IN CALIFORNIA a week later skiing at Lake Tahoe with Dorothy, Laura Hartigan and her husband, Jeff Jenkins, Peter Kelly, Ari and Martha Swiller, and a guy named Tom Scott, who was a big Republican and was in my face all the time about Clinton. That stuff never bothered me. We were having a spectacular time flying down the slopes carving up the mountain and decided to take a break in the lodge and get some lunch.

Some wives would probably go nuts if their husbands were always having long discussions with waiters, but Dorothy actually gets a kick out of me wanting to connect with everyone I meet. She knows that's just the way I am. I love to talk to people and hear their stories and I love to kid around with waiters and elevator operators and the other people you run into in the course of your day. I knew the first names of all the butlers at the White House and always asked them what was new. That day at Lake Tahoe the waiter and I were talking back and forth throughout the meal. He had no idea who I was and that was fine with me.

"Did you hear the news?" he asked us at one point. "Something about Clinton and an intern?"

I had not heard the news.

"Yeah, sure, buddy," I said. "Stop listening to those wackos on crazy TV shows."

He wasn't backing down.

"That's what everyone is saying," he said. "It was on CNN."

I gave him a good tip anyway and didn't think twice about CNN. We hit the slopes again and inched forward in line for the ski lift.

"Hey, Terry McAuliffe!" someone else in line shouted all of a sudden.

It was a Republican I knew vaguely.

"Mac, you are *ruined*!" he said. "Your career is over."

"What are you talking about?" I said.

"They are reporting that Bill Clinton was involved with a former intern," the Republican said.

"This is the craziest thing I've ever heard," I said.

My phone was ringing all day and finally I took a call and found out *The Washington Post* had just reported on the front page that the President was allegedly involved with a former White House employee named Monica Lewinsky. I'd never heard the name and neither had Laura Hartigan. This sounded like a bogus story all the way. There was no way it was true.

I put in a call to Doug Sosnik at the White House.

"What's going on, Doug?" I asked.

"Everybody is a little guarded now because they're going to be under oath," he said. "Honestly, I don't know anything. I know as much as you."

"Wow, this is crazy," I told Doug. "I'll give you a call tomorrow."

"If we're still here," Doug said, not missing a beat.

15

★ ★ ★

The worst day for me during the hell we all we went through in 1998 was September 9, when Ken Starr loaded up two vans with eighteen boxes of documents each and sent them rolling up to the Capitol, claiming they provided "grounds for impeachment." Like everything Starr did in his out-of-control investigation, this was furtive and sleazy. He threw in videotapes and page after page of salacious sexual detail, all just to get people talking and to try to undermine the President of the United States because Starr, a Republican, wanted to hurt the Democrats. I sat there with Peter O'Keefe watching CNN's live coverage of these two dark blue vans driving up Pennsylvania Avenue on their way to Congress and felt sick to my stomach.

Charles Bakaly, Starr's grandstanding, unethical spokesman, showed up on the East Front of the Capitol for a press conference in which he said that the office of the independent counsel "has fulfilled its duty under the law." Hearing him say that had me ready to start throwing chairs through the window. Duty had nothing to do with it. Zeal and hate did. "Responsibility for the information that we have transmitted today, and for any further action, now lie with the Congress, as provided for by the Constitution," Bakaly said.

How *dare* he talk about the Constitution. Starr was a runaway train who had thrown aside any last shred of decency or perspective. He was charged with reinvestigating a failed land deal that lost the Clintons money and he somehow converted that into a sex obsession. The 445-page report he sent to Congress as the "Whitewater independent counsel" had 581 references to sex and only four to "Whitewater." If that isn't perverted and twisted, I don't know what is. The report read like a cheap paperback novel, loaded with passages that were both lurid and sophomoric. What a waste of taxpayer dollars! I would almost have respected Starr if he had come right out and admitted this was a partisan witch hunt, but instead he would stand there, pasty-faced and sweaty, and mumble about duty and the Constitution as if he were somehow neutral. What a crock.

That night I took Peter, Jay Dunn, and Richard Sullivan to dinner at the Capital Grille over at Pennsylvania and Sixth. A group of Republican congressmen were at the table right behind me carrying on like sorority girls on spring break. I tell you, they were giddy. I had my back to them, knocking back a beer, when someone walked in and the Republican congressmen got so excited, they started hooting and hollering.

"We've got him now!" the new arrival called out. "We've got the son of a bitch! We've got Clinton!"

The new arrival came over and started high-fiving the Republican congressmen. *High-fiving!* Can you imagine? It would have been a despicable display even if this new arrival had been a software salesman from Wichita or a mechanic from Van Nuys. I turned around to see who could be carrying on so joyfully at the pain this sad, sorry spectacle was causing our entire nation and was forced to do a double-take.

The man high-fiving the Republican congressmen and crowing over getting that "son of a bitch" Bill Clinton was none other than Charles Bakaly, Ken Starr's spokesman, a glorified con man with slicked-back hair and a slicker grin. This was supposed to be the office of the "independent" counsel and they were working in lockstep with the Republicans in Congress.

So just who was Bakaly and how did he come to be working for Ken Starr? An interesting story. Bakaly was a conservative Republican who had worked in the Reagan White House as an advance press aide. Back in early April 1998, Starr had the unbelievable gall to claim that his hate campaign worked "in the realm of facts and law, and not public relations." That, like much out of Ken Starr's mouth, was flat-out false.

Starr was flying back from Little Rock that March and sat in seat 24A talking to Bakaly about coming to work for him.

"I would really like to get your views on how to nurture relationships with individual reporters," Starr told Bakaly, as reported later by Al Kamen in *The Washington Post.*

Starr wanted to work individual reporters and get them "away from the pack," and Bakaly recommended having reporters over to his house. Starr, always a witty guy, said it might be difficult for him to have reporters over for "libations."

"Starr also wondered if it would be 'best to have surrogates do that so I don't have to get involved,'" Kamen reported.

What a shocker, then, that Chuck Bakaly was later up on charges of lying about leaking grand-jury testimony to one or more *New York Times* reporters as Starr's "surrogate" and only narrowly avoided serving six months in prison. The one who should be up on charges is Ken Starr. As for Bakaly, a judge cleared him of the charges in October 2000, but even *The Times*—the paper he'd leaked to—made clear what a low-life cheat the man was.

"Mr. Bakaly gradually disclosed to the Federal Bureau of Investigation that he had provided *The Times* with some documents in connection with the article, and that he may have inadvertently confirmed some information for (Don) Van Natta," *The Times* reported.

What a joke. *May have inadvertently confirmed* secret grand-jury testimony! Who knows what planet Judge Norma Holloway Johnson was on? And she was appointed by Jimmy Carter, too. Alan Gershel, one of the prosecutors, was so incensed about Bakaly's pathetic verbal backflips in court, he said, "Lies upon lies. Like a house of cards, they eventually came tumbling down."

★

THE ISSUE IS NOT whether Bill Clinton made a horrible mistake. He did. I was with him through this entire period and I can tell you the man went through deep anguish over the mistake he had made and its consequences. I was scheduled to join the President, Hillary, and Chelsea for their August 1998 family vacation to Martha's Vineyard to play golf with the President, but at the last minute I was scratched.

"I love you like a brother, Terry," Hillary told me. "You're not coming."

"Fine with me," I said. "I hate golf anyway."

The President gave his four-hour deposition to Starr's grand jury on August 17, and admitted that he had engaged in wrongful conduct. Even after that he still had to endure countless questions designed merely to badger him. This was a political witch hunt, not an investigation.

That night the President sat back down in the Map Room and spoke to the nation. I was traveling to Norfolk, Virginia, to spend several days on the magnificent aircraft carrier the U.S.S. *John F. Kennedy.* For years the Department of the Navy had been inviting business leaders to see their men and women in action.

"I must take complete responsibility for all my actions, both public and private," Clinton told the nation.

"Now this matter is between me, the two people I love most—my wife and our daughter—and our God," he said. "It's nobody's business but ours. Even Presidents have private lives."

I sat there and debated whether I should call the President, knowing that he had given a disappointing speech. I was sure he knew that he hadn't done well and I finally decided I needed to call him.

"How do you think I did, Mac?" Clinton asked.

"I don't think it was your best night, Mr. President," I said. "You looked angry. You're at your best when you're calm and in control and tonight you could tell you were angry. However, we need to move on."

That was one night when I wasn't the chief cheerleader. The Clintons began their Martha's Vineyard vacation the afternoon after he gave the speech, and the President was like a man in exile. He spent his time walking alone on the beach with his dog, Buddy, hanging his head. Golf was out of the question. He hardly talked to anyone. He told me later that he slept on the couch and Hillary basically did not say a word to him that entire trip.

It's easy for people who weren't close to Clinton that awful summer to say the President's anguish was all some kind of show. To that I reply: Anyone who thinks this man didn't go through tremendous personal turmoil doesn't know. He was in absolute anguish and it was sometimes excruciating just to talk to him. He was in a personal living hell because of what he had done to his wife and his daughter. That was the way he described it to me: "An absolute living hell."

★

FORMER SOUTH AFRICAN PRESIDENT Nelson Mandela may be the most remarkable man alive. If anyone had reason to give in to anger and bitterness, it would be Mandela. He was a leader of the African National Congress, formed to resist South Africa's racist apartheid government, and spent eighteen years doing hard labor at the notorious Robben Island prison just off the South African coast. Mandela emerged after his prison years to be the least bitter person I've ever met.

When you are with him he exudes warmth and compassion. There is not an angry bone in his body. For years now any time I've had the feeling that things were tough, I think of Nelson Mandela and my perspective shifts. This man spent eighteen years breaking up rocks and living in a cramped little cell and he decided he did not want to be a captive anymore, once he was freed—not of hatred, not of anything. Clinton loved Mandela and admired him deeply.

"I know you did a great thing in inviting your jailers to your inauguration, but didn't you really hate those who imprisoned you?" Clinton asked Mandela when the two visited Robben Island in March 1998.

"Of course I did, for many years," Mandela told him. "They took the best years of my life. They abused me physically and mentally. I didn't get to see my children grow up. I hated them. Then one day when I was working in the quarry, hammering the rocks, I realized that they had already taken everything from me except my mind and my heart. Those they could not take without my permission. I decided not to give them away."

Then Mandela told Clinton, "Neither should you."

That September, Mandela came to the United Nations in New York to deliver a farewell address before the nations of the world, and he also visited the White House for a reception in his honor. During his White House remarks, which were interrupted repeatedly by applause, Mandela spoke up for Bill Clinton as a man and as a leader, calling him a friend of Africa and of black people everywhere.

"Few leaders of the United States have such a feeling for the position of the black people and the minorities in this country," Mandela said. "We have often said that our morality does not allow us to desert our friends and we have got to say tonight, 'We are thinking of you in this difficult and uncertain time in your life.'"

Mandela was speaking for all of Africa and in a sense for all of the world community in saying he hoped the United States would move on from this scandal preoccupation to work to solve the world's problems. Soon, President Carlos Menem of Argentina, President Vaclav Havel of the Czech Republic, and King Hussein of Jordan were also making eloquent statements on behalf of the President.

Clinton would often talk to me about how much he admired Mandela and how much he tried to emulate him in not carrying hate. We all hear people setting similar goals for themselves and usually good intentions are no match for human nature. The following year I was shocked to realize just how deeply forgiveness ran in Clinton's nature. I showed up at the White House on August 1, 1999, a scorcher of a Sunday that hit 100 degrees in Washington, and spent a little time out at the swimming pool with the President and Hillary before we headed over to the Army-Navy Club for some golf. As soon as we pulled out of the White House in Clinton's limo, we were stopped dead by a huge crowd of summer tourists at the corner of Fourteenth and Constitution, thousands of people fanning out in every direction. The President always had his little cooler full of Diet Cokes below the presidential seal stitched into the backseat of the limo. We both grabbed Cokes for the short ride to Army-Navy and I thought about a news report I wanted to ask Clinton about.

It might not quite fit with the lessons of my Catholic faith, but I don't mind admitting that I couldn't have been happier when the news broke on July 30, 1999, that Linda Tripp had been indicted by a Maryland grand jury. You bet I was happy! I'm not saying I didn't feel sorry for Tripp, obviously a sad, pathetic person. But mostly I felt exultation. Tripp shamelessly manipulated Monica Lewinsky and pretended to be her confidante, all because Tripp was secretly recording their phone conversations and scheming against the President with fellow right-wing wackos like Lucianne Goldberg, trying to squeeze out a book deal. To me, friendship and loyalty are sacred. Tripp's deceit made me sick. She was indicted on two counts of illegally taping phone calls—which she did even after her lawyer advised her that in Maryland secretly taping calls is illegal.

"Did you see the Linda Tripp thing?" I asked the President as we inched along in the limo toward Army-Navy.

"You know, Mac, I've got to tell you, I really feel sorry for that woman," the President said. "She's really had a rough life. She had a really, really bad marriage and she got divorced."

My thoughts were racing, but I held my tongue.

"It wasn't her fault, Mac," he said. "I hope it's behind her. She didn't mean to do it, Mac, I know she didn't."

A part of me wanted to shake him. I wanted the President to be as mad at Tripp as I still was. Then I thought of Mandela and the advice he gave Bill Clinton, telling him not to hate his enemies. I had always known that Clinton had a wonderful gift for seeing the best in people. No matter what, he found a way to believe in their good qualities. I thought he might make an exception for some of his enemies, people who had schemed against him and hurt the country in the process, but no, the man refused to give in to that. Sitting with me in the backseat of his limo, the President could have said whatever he wanted. He could have cursed Linda Tripp. He could have launched a long tirade and kept it up halfway around the golf course. But no, he was worrying about Linda Tripp. He was wishing her well. And even that wasn't enough. He started to work on me, trying to persuade me that I should feel bad for her, too. I wish I could say he convinced me.

★

HILLARY WAS VERY HONEST in her book about the pain her husband caused her that year and her soul-searching about her marriage. I saw that pain up close and went through my own disappointment and anger that the President had made the mistakes he had. Hillary has always been a fighter and even during the worst of the impeachment stuff, the idea never crossed her mind that Bill Clinton should resign. It never crossed his, either. They looked at impeachment for what it was, a power grab by an out-of-control right-wing cabal helped along by world-class hypocrites like Newt Gingrich and Tom DeLay.

The Republicans threw everything they had into turning up the heat on impeachment because the politics of personal hate are all they have, but as the November 1998 elections approached it was clear the Republicans' strategy had flopped. Republican overreach and abuse of power was so extreme, it brought the voters back to the Democrats. People everywhere were saying and thinking: *What Bill Clinton did was not right, but these hate-filled people trying to bring him down are a whole lot worse.*

We knew that the 1998 congressional elections gave us a great opportunity to take the wind out of the sails of the drive toward impeachment. If the Republicans won seats, they would feel empowered to continue their political witch hunt. If we could pick up seats and break historical precedent, we were sure we could shut down this charade. I worked with the President, Senator Bob Kerrey, the chairman of the DSCC, Jonathan Mantz, DCCC finance director, and Dick Gephardt on a massive unity fund-raising drive across the country, doing three events to raise a total of $13.6 million for House and Senate races. The President worked tirelessly, not only raising money but also traveling the country and doing 116 political events.

We went into Election Day with the experts all predicting we would lose seats in the House, and that was consistent with history. I stopped by the Vice President's residence for an Election Night party and then went over to the White House, where the plan was for about twenty of us to eat some pizza and watch the election returns in the movie theater. It didn't work out that way. The President was on his way to join us when he stopped by Chief of Staff John Podesta's office and sat down at his desk and started clicking around with his computer.

This was the first time Bill Clinton had ever used a computer on Election Night, and he was so excited that he could follow results precinct by precinct all over the country. Talk about a kid in a candy store. He had instant access to early returns and this was a man who knew every congressional district by heart. He could sit there and look at the results and tell us exactly how many seats we were going to win. Clinton never left Podesta's chair that whole night. We could not have pried him away if we tried. Instead, we moved the pizza and the people to Podesta's office and followed the returns from there.

Around midnight the mood in the room changed dramatically as it became clear that we were actually going to pick up seats in the House. I called Dick Gephardt and told him that I had someone who wanted to talk to him, and handed the phone over to the President, who congratulated him warmly. We ended up picking up five seats in the House, the strongest showing for the party of a President six years in office since James Monroe in 1822. We held even in the Senate and were able to defeat the two key figures in the Senate's Whitewater investigation, Al D'Amato of New York and Lauch Faircloth of North Carolina.

Political Director Craig Smith and I were the last ones with the President that night. Craig left around 2:30 A.M. and the President and I savored the historical result for another twenty minutes and then finally decided to call it a night. He put his arm around me and walked me down the long, dark hallway from Podesta's office back to the lobby.

"Mac, I can't thank you enough for all that you've done," he told me.

"Mr. President, I think we have finally shut impeachment down," I said.

It was a stunning achievement made possible by the work of many people, including someone we had not seen that night—Hillary Clinton. She was superstitious about Election Night and hated to watch early returns. Instead, she watched the movie *Beloved*, starring Oprah Winfrey, and only found out later about the result she had helped bring about with her tireless work on the road that year, doing dozens of events in twenty-seven states.

As I was driving home in my Jeep that night, smoking a cigar the President had given me, I was so happy that we could finally put the nightmare of impeachment behind us. I could focus on getting the library built and the Clinton foundation started, which would allow Bill Clinton to continue his life of public service after he left office, working on such issues as HIV/AIDS, global hunger, childhood nutrition, and the urban enterprise initiative. I was just sure there was no way the Republicans would move forward on impeachment after this election. How wrong I was. We soon found out that Gingrich and the Republicans were moving full speed ahead with impeachment despite the clear wishes of the American people, as conveyed in the election results and in exit polls that showed six in ten Americans wanted the impeachment sideshow to stop. Erskine Bowles talked to Gingrich that month and asked why he would intentionally inflict such harm on the country even though the people were strongly against pursuing impeachment and would make Republicans pay a political price.

"Because we can," Gingrich told him. "This isn't about the American people. This is about what we can do."

How wrong he was. This *was* all about the American people.

★

EVEN THOUGH IMPEACHMENT was back on the front burner, the President still had to attend to his duties as chief executive. The Republicans might have been obsessed with continuing the impeachment farce, but the President was getting back to work for the American people, soon leaving Washington for a five-day trip to Japan, South Korea, and Guam that would include attending the Asia Pacific Economic Cooperation conference in Japan and two days of talks with Japanese Prime Minister Keizo Obuchi. Clinton continued on to South Korea, where I met him in his suite in the afternoon shortly before we attended another state dinner at the Korean Blue House.

The President held a press conference with President Kim Dae Jung and was pleased when Kim issued a strong defense of Clinton, much as Nelson Mandela had done at the White House. As we walked down the steps with Kim Dae Jung afterward, the President asked Sandy Berger, Doug Sosnik, and me to ride with him in his limousine. We said good-bye to President Kim at the bottom of the steps with rows of South Korean military in full dress uniform standing at attention nearby.

From there we drove off for an unscheduled visit to the six-story-high Seoul Citizens Hall to attend a strange Ed Sullivan–type variety show that was being shown live on South Korean television. The President stood backstage during a set by his brother, Roger Clinton, who finished up "On Shaky Ground" and then introduced "my brother, President Bill Clinton." The President stepped out on the stage and hugged his brother and shook hands with the members of his rhythm-and-blues band. I'm not sure anyone in the audience spoke enough English to understand anything Roger was saying. I spotted a guy in the front row directing the crowd of four thousand people; he would wave his arms and all four thousand people would stand at once and cheer.

We got back to the Presidential Suite at the Hyatt at 10:30 and, of course, Clinton wasn't about to miss this opportunity to play Upwords. Sosnik, the chief of staff on the trip, was having none of it and went to bed early. We started a game and then another and another. I would have headed to bed around 1 A.M. or so, but I knew better than to even try. Clinton kept telling stories, and by the time I left to stumble back to my room, almost asleep on my feet, it was 4:40 in the morning.

There had to have been fifteen assorted U.S. and South Korean Secret Service all standing watch outside the door of the Presidential Suite, and I mumbled hello to one of the American agents I knew and went back to my room to get a couple hours of sleep. The next morning I went back to the President's suite for an early breakfast and on the way in, all the Korean Secret Service were giving me strange looks and my friends in the U.S. Service were snickering. I walked into the suite and the President and Doug Sosnik were laughing so hard, they nearly had tears rolling down their cheeks.

"I'm sorry, Macker," Sosnik said and laughed some more.

Finally I got it out of him. A member of the Korean Secret Service had pulled aside one of his American counterparts early that morning and asked some delicate questions about the President.

"Is there something we need to know about President Clinton?" the Korean agent asked. "He was alone in his suite last night until almost 5 A.M. with a good-looking younger man."

I couldn't wait to get back home to the States to tell Dorothy that one.

★

THE HYPOCRISY INVOLVED in the persecution of Clinton was unbelievable. People who live in glass houses should not throw stones, and these Republicans were prime offenders. First, Gingrich announced all of a sudden on November 9 that he was stepping down as Speaker of the House and would not run for reelection, giving the cover story that he did not want to be "an excuse for divisiveness and factionalism." Only later did it come out that Gingrich, who had served his first wife with divorce papers while she was in a hospital being treated for cancer, had called his second wife while she was visiting her mother and given her the news that their relationship was over. So he wished his mother-in-law a happy eighty-fourth birthday and then told his wife that for years he'd been having an affair with a congressional staffer more than twenty years younger than he was.

Judiciary Committee chairman Henry Hyde led the impeachment bandwagon against Clinton in the House. Later, stung by press reports of his cheating on his wife for four years with a married woman with three kids, Hyde tried to excuse himself for his "youthful indiscretions," even though he was forty-one years old at the time in question and broke up a marriage.

Thanks for the moral leadership! I was forty-one at the time and I don't think I would have gotten away with going home and telling Dorothy I'd been having a four-year-long "youthful indiscretion."

What a fine crew of moral exemplars to be sitting in judgment of Bill Clinton. You'd think these guys would have figured it out, but no. They embarrassed themselves by voting for impeachment and what happened? Bill Clinton's approval ratings jumped. Within days after the House impeachment vote on December 19, he was up 10 points in a Gallup poll to an all-time high of 73 percent, beating Reagan's all-time high by five points. Gallup also found that public disapproval of the Republicans jumped 10 points in the wake of the House vote.

The Senate vote on impeachment coming up in January or February 1999 was going to be the key test, and the American people had offered a clear verdict: More than two-thirds said the Senate should not vote for impeachment. The senators might have learned from their House colleagues, but oh no, conservative Republicans wanted to drag this out. They were going to lose the vote, as soon became clear enough, but they wanted to keep the whole thing going as long as possible.

I was at my health club in Tysons Corner, Virginia, working out one Sunday late in January 1999, when one of the attendants came over to tell me I had an important call. It was Senator Tom Harkin, one of the leading fighters on health care and education. I loved Tom Harkin because on my birthday he always sent me a bottle of Irish whiskey. No one else did that. He wanted my help in getting the right person to deliver the all-important speech wrapping up Clinton's defense before the Senate impeachment vote.

"Listen, we need Dale Bumpers," Harkin told me. "Bill Clinton has to ask him. I don't know how to get him. We have to get a better defense going in the Senate and he's the best one to relate to these Republican senators. But if we are going to do this, we have to move very quickly. We're running out of time."

I told Tom I'd get right on it. I loved the idea. Bumpers, the former Arkansas senator, was an eloquent speaker well liked by other senators. I called Operator One at the White House and in a few minutes I was on the line with the President.

"Spectacular idea," he said. "Tell Tom Harkin I'll call Dale Bumpers immediately."

Clinton tracked Bumpers down in a day or two and he agreed to give the speech. Bumpers did a superb job on the Senate floor, too, taking a tough line against Clinton but putting the charges and Starr's out-of-control investigation in historical perspective. "Javert's pursuit of Jean Valjean in *Les Miserables* pales by comparison," Bumpers told the Senate. "I doubt that there are few people, maybe nobody, in this body who could withstand such scrutiny. . . . But after all of those years and fifty million dollars—of Whitewater, Travelgate, Filegate, you name it—nothing. Nothing. The President was found guilty of nothing, official or personal. . . . The American people now and for some time have been asking to be allowed a good night's sleep. They're asking for an end to this nightmare. It is a legitimate request."

We needed to hold only forty-five Democratic votes in the Senate, and after Bumpers gave his riveting speech on January 21, we knew we would make it. It would be three more weeks before the vote ended this nightmare.

I knew everything was all right again the next Tuesday, February 16, when the President and I got out on the golf course again for the first time in three months, just like in the old days. The President could finally allow himself a round at the Army-Navy Golf Club with his brother-in-law, Tony Rodham, and me. It was the first time he'd golfed all year. He made up for lost time, enjoying the unseasonably warm February afternoon, and for the first time in months he was able to relax.

★

My attitude was: This man is my friend. He made a mistake and yes, I had been mad at him about that, but above all he was my friend, and my parents brought me up to be the kind of man who always stands by his friends. Anyone can stand with you when it's easy sailing. I tried to be there for the President in any way I could during that tough time and the best was always when we could hit the golf course.

Through this whole period, we talked all the time on the phone and over rounds of golf, but we never had a direct discussion of the matter. We still had a lot of work to do, but mostly, he needed a close friend, someone he could talk to on a personal level to relax and get away from the swirl and pressure of all that was happening around him. He maintained a separation. The other big reason we didn't talk about it was that just about everyone in the White House had been subpoenaed and the President was trying to protect me and keep me from having to go before the Starr grand jury. I was never subpoenaed, which is amazing because when you look at the White House phone logs, as Starr and his pack of jackals did, you saw that night after night the President was calling me around midnight for long talks.

Nobody is perfect. I know I'm not and I've never met anyone who was. The President finally did raise the subject on the golf course on a beautiful afternoon in June 1999. It was only the two of us and we'd just putted out on the seventeenth green at Army-Navy.

"Mac, what did you think about the whole thing?" the President asked me.

"What thing, sir?" I said.

"You know, about the whole thing?" he asked.

"Sir, let me be blunt," I said. "Boy, you screwed up. You really screwed up. But you know what? You're a good man. You've got a great heart and you've done a lot of great things for a lot of people."

We were still sitting there in the golf cart near the seventeenth green.

"I'm Catholic, sir," I said. "Our whole religion is based upon forgiveness. You made a mistake and you've moved on from that. But I look at you in the totality of the great things you've done for so many people in this country and the world. That's how I judge you."

Looking back now, I still can't believe the country was put through so much turmoil just so the Republicans could try to score cheap points. I remember during Reagan's second term when you heard a lot of conservatives talking about how the institution of the presidency needed to be respected and conserved. The Watergate scandal had inflicted a mortal wound, they argued, and if Reagan was driven from office because of the Iran-Contra scandal, it would damage the presidency so severely it could take a generation to recover. I'm a patriot and a proud American and I remember giving some credence to that argument, even though the crimes we were talking about in that case were deadly serious: subverting the Constitution and lying to Congress about matters of national security, selling arms to the Ayatollah to pay for the *contra* rebels trying to overthrow the democratically elected government of Nicaragua. Then these same so-called conservatives turned around and pushed a witch hunt against Bill Clinton. We'll see how history remembers the Clinton administration. I'm betting that Clinton goes down in the books as one of our greatest presidents ever.

★

THE MONTH AFTER THE SENATE VOTE, the President and Hillary decided to take a three-day ski vacation to Park City, Utah, to celebrate Chelsea's nineteenth birthday and invited me along. It was just the four of us and this was still a difficult, tense time for the family.

"Would anybody like a glass of wine?" the White House steward asked.

"No," said the President.

"No," said Hillary.

"You bet!" I said. "And leave the bottle right here for me!"

Chelsea was in her second year at Stanford by then, and it was so hard for the President not to be able to talk to her and to see her as much as he always had. Let's not forget that when Clinton decided not to run for President in 1988, Chelsea influenced him as much as anyone, saying she didn't want to lose her father. When she was little, he used to read to her and pretend to fall asleep, because when he really did fall asleep, she would kiss him awake and he loved that. When he was governor he arranged his schedule so that he rarely spent a night away from the Governor's Mansion in order for him to be there when Chelsea woke up and so he could take her to school. He was always very close to Chelsea and still is to this day, but that period was tough on everyone.

Every evening on that Park City vacation, we would sit around and watch TV, like any family with their friend, only this was a little different. Hillary had the remote control and it was amazing watching her click from channel to channel and almost every channel had some ludicrous anti-Clinton craziness. Clinton murdered people! Clinton sold drugs! Jerry Falwell, the cartoonish TV preacher, was hawking a video called "The Clinton Chronicles" that was packed with every blatant lie imaginable. I had never really realized until that point how much junk was out there on cable against the Clintons every single day. It was a bizarre, surreal experience sitting there with them, but none of us said anything. Hillary just kept clicking until she ended up on ESPN, not her favorite, but the President and I were happy and at least they weren't whacking the Clintons. Here we were, just trying to heal this family, and even watching TV was an ordeal. All we could do was laugh it off and agree it was time to think about the future.

Every morning we would all get up early and Hillary and Chelsea would head off to the ski slopes, and the President and I would sit and talk and drink coffee there in Jeffrey Katzenberg's beautiful house on Bald Eagle Mountain. After awhile he would tell me I should go hit the slopes and I would go join Hillary and Chelsea for some runs. He had given up skiing fifteen years earlier after he hurt his knee on the slopes in Sun Valley, Idaho. While we were off skiing Clinton did a lot of reading, including John Grisham's *The Testament* and *Playback* by Raymond Chandler, and when I'd come back early we'd talk some more about how it was time to move on.

Sometimes a vacation changes your perspective so much, you almost feel as if the home you're returning to has changed while you were gone. The feeling on Air Force One was so positive and upbeat coming back from Utah. We all wanted to think about the future. The President still had almost two years in office and had a lot of work left to do for the American people.

We were all focused on his finishing strong and helping get Al Gore elected in November 2000. The way was also clear now to talk seriously about an idea I'd been excited about for months: Hillary running for the United States Senate. The First Lady and I sat together on Air Force One on that flight back from Utah and talked over the fund-raising and different aspects of the campaign, and the more we talked, the more excited we both were. I told Hillary I was sure she'd win.

"Here's to the next United States senator from New York," I said, clinking glasses with her.

"We'll see, Terry," she said.

16

New York Congressman Charlie Rangel had come up with a great idea in November 1998 when he found out that New York Senator Daniel Patrick Moynihan was retiring. He thought Hillary should run. She was flattered but firm in saying no.

"You're crazy," she told Rangel, laughing. "It's not going to happen."

Unlike many on Hillary's staff, I was all for the idea as soon as I heard it. First of all, I didn't put any stock in the worry that Hillary could be caricatured as some kind of carpetbagger, swooping in from out of state with no thought to what the locals wanted or needed. I remembered when I was a little boy in Syracuse, listening to my dad talk about politics, and everyone was so excited about Bobby Kennedy running for the U.S. Senate from New York. Bobby's Republican opponent in that 1964 Senate race, the incumbent, Kenneth Keating, tried to call Bobby a carpetbagger because he was coming in from out of state. He should have saved his breath. The voters didn't care. Bobby won by more than 700,000 votes and was a huge success as senator.

New Yorkers like characters. We like larger-than-life figures with guts and the ability to laugh when you punch them in the gut and say: *Is that all you got?* New Yorkers also, let's be honest, like smart people, so long as it's New York smart, meaning not only well-read and all that, but shrewd and perceptive and open-eyed about how people really are. Hillary was whip-smart, as everyone knew, but from all my talks with her I knew she also had the kind of real-world smarts you've got to have to get anywhere in New York politics.

Still, the political numbers-crunchers tried to warn Hillary that she would do very well in New York City but would get clobbered upstate, which was more conservative. I had to wave my hands at that one and say no way. This was my territory. Knowing Hillary and Syracuse and Onondaga County the way I did, I was sure she could do very well in upstate New York. Anyone who has spent more than a couple of minutes talking to Hillary knows that the caricature of Hillary as some kind of intellectual who can't relate to normal people is just laughable. Like a lot of people from Chicago, Hillary has a no-nonsense, down-home side to her personality, friendly and relaxed, that gave her a great chance in upstate New York, so long as she came across as herself. Also, the agricultural setting of much of upstate New York felt very comfortable to Hillary, who had grown up not far from Illinois farm country and had spent much of her childhood in eastern Pennsylvania, where her father was born.

"Nobody was for me running," Hillary says now. "And for good reason—it was not a smart thing to do if you looked at it. But Terry was all for me running. Early on he said, 'If you're going to do this, money's not going to be a problem.' "

I knew it wouldn't be. Once the impeachment craziness was out of the way, Hillary started gearing up. We all kicked it around a little and the President and I were both strongly encouraging. We knew she would be a star as a senator, a serious student of policy who would quickly earn the respect of her peers. She just had to get a few preliminary steps out of the way, like buying a house in New York and spending some quality time upstate.

The Clintons' annual summer vacations on Martha's Vineyard always attracted a lot of interest. I sat down with the President and Hillary and told them they needed to spend their summer vacation in Syracuse's backyard, a beautiful lake area with the hard-to-spell name Skaneateles (sounds like "skinny atlas").

"Syracuse will be thrilled to have you," I said.

I worked with Capricia Marshall and Patti Solis Doyle on Hillary's staff and set everything up for August 1999. I kept hearing back from my high school buddies in Syracuse about how the whole city was gearing up for the Clintons' visit. My high school buddy Duke Kinney would be out buying his groceries or stopping off for a cold one and wherever he went, it seemed like no one was talking about anything else. The paper even ran an article and a map giving readers advice on PRIME SPOTS TO SPOT CLINTONS. On the

Monday morning Air Force One arrived in town, a crowd of several thousand had gathered out at the airport to be there for this historic occasion. Local TV went live and the reporters doing stand-ups said the Clintons were likely to say a few quick hellos and then zip off in the presidential motorcade.

I had flown in directly from Morocco to Syracuse and arrived the day before the Clintons to make sure everything was lined up. I was standing there waiting on the tarmac as the big bird landed and taxied to a stop near where the crowd had gathered. When the walkway was rolled up and the cabin door opened, the roar was so loud that they could hear it inside Air Force One. The President, Hillary, and Chelsea walked down the steps, waving and smiling, and from the reception they received, you'd have thought they were born and raised in Syracuse like me. The Clintons spent more than half an hour shaking hands at the airport that Monday morning and basking in the excitement of the crowd, loving every minute.

I wanted to start the trip off with a bang, so I'd planned for us to go straight from the airport to the New York State Fair, which I knew the President, Hillary, and Chelsea were going to love. Historically, Syracuse was an important agricultural hub, because of its strategic location along the Erie Canal. The first New York State Fair was held there in September 1841, and since 1890 the fair has been an annual tradition, but no sitting President had attended since New York–born Teddy Roosevelt in 1903.

The motorcade ride over to the fairgrounds was a hoot. There were hundreds of people lining the roadways everywhere we went, waving signs and cheering so loud you felt like you were in the Carrier Dome on game day. The Clintons were swarmed everywhere they went at the fair. It was such an unbelievable mob scene that they had to bring in extra Secret Service and the rope lines kept getting knocked down. We toured the cow barn, the four of us stepping over manure to admire the animals, and through it all Hillary and the President looked like they were having the time of their lives. I took the Clintons by the Byrne Dairy exhibit and bought them all ice cream cones. As we licked our cones in the blistering heat, I explained how my late uncle Billy, whose son Billy Byrne Jr. now ran the company, had started me out in business by letting me buy one of his old dairy trucks for my driveway-sealing business.

We spent about four hours at the fair touring as many exhibits as we could and at every turn the Clintons were greeted by fresh swarms of well-wishers. On the ride to Skaneateles they talked about how raw their hands were from shaking so many thousands of hands that afternoon. We pulled up to Tom and Cathy McDonald's beautiful house on Skaneateles Lake, where we'd be staying for the week, and Tom and Cathy immediately gave us a tour of the grounds. They showed us the big boathouse and then we all walked out onto the large deck area. As soon as we got out there, you could hear so much clicking it was like locusts. A bunch of press people had rented boats and they were all bobbing a ways offshore, pointing their long telescopic lenses at the President and snapping away.

For dinner we headed over to the Sherwood Inn and sat outside on the porch right on the water. Our waiter, Christoff Anderegg, was so nervous when he came over to take our orders that he was shaking like a leaf. We stayed almost three hours and the President was so thankful for the great service, he left a ninety-buck tip on a $205 tab.

Back at the house we played some cards, and the President and I trash-talked each other good-naturedly about who was going to win the next day's round of golf, the first of two days out on the course I'd planned for us.

"I've got the home-field advantage, sir," I kept saying.

★

TO GET AN IDEA of how excited the people in Syracuse were about the Clintons' visit, you just have to hear about Van Robinson, a Syracuse city councillor. The President and I were going to be golfing in a group of eight so we could rotate people around from foursome to foursome and give everyone a chance to golf with the President. Word got out that besides inviting some of my high school buddies, I also wanted to include some local Democrats. I called up the former Onondaga County Democratic Party treasurer, that is, my dad, Jack McAuliffe, and asked who we should invite. He had never golfed with Van Robinson, but knew he was a prominent city councillor.

"Are you a golfer, Van?" Jack asked Robinson over the phone.

"Oh, yeah, I hit it around," Robinson said.

What else was he going to say? *No?* And miss out on a chance to golf with the President?

Even before the President and I had left the house in Skaneateles that Tuesday, a big crowd had started building at Bellevue Country Club, the same course where I was caddying when I had my crisis at age fourteen and decided to start my driveway-sealing business. The President and I had a half-hour limo ride in from the lakeside house in Skaneateles and he was reading an advance copy of *Sick Puppy* by Carl Hiassen. The President loved Hiassen's books, which always made you laugh with their portraits of lovable, steroid-crazed bad guys or hilarious, two-bit businessmen scheming to get away with polluting the Everglades. The President burned through those books in nothing flat and on that ride he finished the book and insisted I read it next. He pulled out a pen to write something in the front and sign it.

To Terry: With thanks for helping me fend off our fair share of Sick Puppies.
                                                    —Bill Clinton

By the time we pulled up, just before 1 P.M., the crowd had swelled to one thousand with a large press contingent as well. It was a great day out there and we were all in high spirits pulling out our drivers and getting limbered up. The crowd had swarmed over to the area around the first tee and all eyes were on us. The President went first and hit a big, booming drive that put him in good position. No. 1 at Bellevue is a long par four that is one of the tougher holes on the course. I was up next and hit a pretty good drive, too, and so did Duke Kinney.

Then it was up to Van Robinson, the city councillor, and he got up there and took a funny little swing, kind of like he was swatting at something, and flat-out missed the ball. Ouch! You hated to see someone whiff. He tried to laugh it off and gave it another try. Whiff No. 2! Finally, he swung and connected and the ball rolled forward about forty yards. We felt bad for the guy, figuring he had to be awfully nervous to botch his first drive that badly. So he walked up to the ball, just in front of the women's tee area, and took another awkward swing, and this time sent the ball maybe forty-five yards. The whole day went like that. This guy was the worst golfer I had ever seen, and, believe me, I've seen some bad ones. But he was having the time of his life golfing with the President.

"All I could think was, please just let me hit it, I don't care where it goes," Van told the Syracuse paper.

Later I asked Van why he'd said he golfed when it was obvious he'd never picked up a stick in his life.

"I've been *miniature* golfing," he said.

I cracked up and we shared a good laugh. What else could you do? You had to respect the man's eagerness to be out there with us.

★

WE FINISHED UP on the ninth green that day and Clinton motioned me over just after taking a call from Bruce Lindsey at the White House.

"Mac, I need to talk to you," the President said.

His face was red and I could tell he was very upset and agitated, which I

almost never saw from him on the golf course. There were people everywhere, so we walked about thirty yards away, where we could speak privately.

"We're going to lose this damn house," he told me. "We can't get the
loan."

Hillary and the President had searched all over New York and finally
found a house they loved in Chappaqua, north of New York City in West-
chester county. By this time, August 31, 1999, Hillary was well on her way
with her Senate bid and had launched her exploratory committee the month
before. Without a house in New York, she couldn't run. The President was
terrified to tell her that because of the exorbitant legal fees, both the house
and her hopes of running for Senate were in danger of falling apart.

The whole home-loan episode was a farce. Everyone knew that once he
left office, Bill Clinton would rake in millions giving speeches and writing
books. Earning power was never an issue. So even with the staggering debt
they had run up because of legal fees, the Clintons should have been able to get
a normal home loan like anyone else and put up 10 or 20 percent. Given the
fun-house mirror craziness of all things relating to the Clintons, however, they
were somehow expected to pay 100 percent up front. The Clintons found out
that week that their $1.7 million bid for the Chappaqua house was one of the
bids being considered and they had to have $1.35 million in an account, in ad-
dition to the $350,000 down payment they were prepared to make. How is that
a home mortgage? The house had zero value? They had forty-eight hours to
get the money together and other options looked like they weren't working out.

Enough was enough. I'd already offered months earlier to help the President on the house.

"Mac, I don't want you involved in this," he'd said at the time. "You've
already done enough."

Reagan's and Ford's supporters bought them houses and said, "Take it,
it's yours." All the Clintons needed was someone to guarantee the loan.

"Mr. President, screw it," I said as we stood thirty yards away from the
ninth green. "I'll help you. I've got the money."

"Terry, the press is going to kill you on this," Clinton said.

I looked at him for a minute.

"Mr. President, let me tell you something," I said. "You are my friend.
Hillary is my friend. Chelsea is my friend. I'm not going to let the press determine who my friends are and how I'm going to act. I really don't give a
damn. I'll do it. End of discussion. Let's move on. Let's get back to golf.
I'm beating you by a stroke!"

That was that, so far as I was concerned. I just wanted to ease the inexplicable predicament in which the President found himself. "Everybody was afraid to guarantee a home loan because they were afraid the Washington press would attack them and the Republicans would attack them," Clinton remembers. "I was at sixty-four percent approval in the polls and we had just won the midterms. They built Reagan a two-million-dollar house. I didn't ask anybody to give me any money. I just wanted somebody to back up my mortgage."

There was no mystery about why this was happening. The Republicans had put together their elaborate scheme to bankrupt the President, harassing him in court at every opportunity, just as he and I had discussed at Camp David the weekend of the *Good Will Hunting* screening. To a degree the strategy had paid off. They had him $10 million in debt. But it was obviously only a short-term setback.

"They had achieved their purpose," Hillary says. "They had bankrupted us totally. We owned *nothing*. We didn't own a car. We didn't own a house. Here we were, fifty years old, and we owned nothing. *No-thing!* All the money we had, which we had brought into the White House, was gone. I hadn't made any money for eight years, so it was really horrible."

★

SANDY BERGER CALLED THE PRESIDENT just after we finished up our round that day and Clinton disappeared for forty-five minutes to talk about the elections in East Timor. He looked relieved to be off the phone when he came out.

"Let's go see your mother," he said.

Millie had just had her fifth hip-replacement surgery and was at St. Camillus rehab hospital, next to my old high school, Bishop Ludden. I got a huge kick out of seeing the way everyone in my old stomping grounds reacted to the sight of an unannounced presidential motorcade rolling up with nearly forty cars. The President and I got out right in front and there was a whole row of people in wheelchairs with oxygen tanks and they were all outside having a smoke.

"Isn't that the mayor?" one old guy asked the guy next to him.

"That looks like Bill Clinton," said the other one and went back to smoking his cigarette.

We walked in and passed hundreds of old people lying around. The President was all smiles and you should have seen the stares he got. You can imagine if you're sitting there in a nursing home waiting for something, anything, to happen and suddenly the President walks up to you with a smile and says hello. Some of the old people burst into tears. One started singing "The Star-Spangled Banner."

We went up to Millie's room and the woman in the next bed, seventy-eight-year-old Ukrainian immigrant Nina Ruckensteiner, was talking to her daughter in Pittsburgh.

"I've got to go. Bill Clinton just walked in the room," she told her daughter, hanging up.

The daughter in Pittsburgh called the St. Camillus front desk right back to give them the sad news that her mother had gone crazy and was delusional.

"She thinks Bill Clinton is in her room," the daughter explained.

"Well, President Clinton *is* here," the front desk said.

The President sat down next to Millie and spent half an hour with her. As Clinton and I had discussed many times, he was always very close to his mother, who was a real character, and he loved that I was close to my mother, also a real character. Millie and my dad were both thrilled when the President dropped by that day, although when Jack popped in on Millie earlier to let her know the President might be dropping by, she was in a panic. "Oh my goodness!" she said. "My hair is a wreck and I'm in my nightgown. Tell him not to come!"

We got back in the limo for the ride out to Skaneateles and Clinton and I were both hungry, so we decided to order some pizzas and bring them back to Hillary and Chelsea at the house. The President and I decided on one large, half-vegetarian for Chelsea, and two mediums, including one to give the press. We stopped and as the President stepped out of the limo to go in and pick up the pies at Mark's Pizzeria on Route 20 in Skaneateles, he realized he didn't have any money.

"Hey, Mac, you got twenty-five bucks on you?" he asked me.

"Jeez, Mr. President," I joked. "I just lent you a million three and you can't even buy me a piece of pizza?"

★

THE NEXT MORNING the four of us were at the Skaneateles house having breakfast, and Bruce Lindsey and Cheryl Mills called to say the money had to be wired within twenty-four hours or the Clintons would lose the house. Hillary was very upset. House hunting had been an ordeal for them and finally the Chappaqua house seemed to be falling into place. Now it looked like Hillary might lose it and this was all happening because the Clintons' enemies were willing to go to such desperate extremes to try to make their lives harder.

"Don't worry," I told Hillary. "I've got the money. I will do this. Let's not worry about it anymore."

Has been fun since the
beginning. Age three.

Thumbs up for the Dems. At four months, with
Tommy and grandmother, Minnie.

Playing Candyland with Minnie.

With Millie after my first communion.
What a little angel!

Celebrating my sixth birthday. Yes, that's
Duke in the sailor suit.

Jack, Millie, and me at Lake Ontario.

In the arena at an early age (five years old). The New York State Democratic Convention, 1962.

My first job in Washington with Syracuse congressman Jim Hanley during my Catholic University days.

Millie and I show off the new truck—thanks to Billy Byrne.

Millie does her rendition of Carol Channing's "Hello Dolly" while I cheer her on.

My father, Jack, and I enjoying a game of cards, a McAuliffe family tradition.

With former President Gerald Ford, in the early Washington days. Obviously, I had only one suit (see photo with Congressman Jim Hanley).

Seconds before the rope comes off and my three-minute ride began—all for only $15,000.

At twenty-three, my first stint at the DNC dialing for dollars for Carter-Mondale in '80.

In four years, I had made it from the Sheraton lobby to the Sheraton Presidential suite.

Celebrating at the finish of my first marathon. November 2, 1980.

Not quite a turkey. At least it had a red head.

Introducing Dick Gephardt at an '87 fund-raiser.

With Walter Shorenstein and Tip O'Neill at the 1984 Democratic Convention in San Francisco—notice the goggles.

Visiting the *contras* on a wild helicopter ride on the Nicaraguan border.

At an audience with Pope John Paul II—I have an engagement ring in my pocket.

Saying good night to South Korean President Kim Dae-Jung before heading back to the hotel for an all-nighter.

I didn't shoot J.R.!

Gentlemen—start
your engines!
1995.

A campaign briefing aboard Marine One.

Flying on Air Force One, with Laura
Hartigan and the President, to Little
Rock from N.J. after our kick-off event.

Headed toward a
second term;
December 1995.

Teaching Al Gore the Macarena—
hard job.

Moments before Dorothy and the
President danced and she lobbied to get
me out of the DNC job.

Jack McAuliffe, riding shotgun, leads
the 1997 inaugural parade down
Pennsylvania Avenue.

My fortieth birthday party: the Vice
President cracks me up.

On the campaign trail with Cicely Tyson
and Chris Tucker at the Oceana naval
base in Virginia.

A "Good Will Hunting" weekend at Camp David. Notice Dorothy's prime seat!

President Clinton and I watching returns of the 1998 midterm elections in which the Dems picked up five seats.

Nailing a drive down the fairway at Lafayette Country Club, and I let everyone on the golf course hear about it!

Sally's first Thanksgiving at Camp David.

Kicking off the 2000 campaign with the next President and Speaker.

At that point I took the phone and told Bruce and Cheryl that I would take care of it.

Hillary was so relieved, it was like a boulder had been pulled off her.

I called my lawyer, Richard Ben-Veniste, to see if there were any legal issues I should know about.

"Don't do it, Terry," Richard said. "Talk about putting yourself back on the griddle!"

"Thank you, Richard," I said. "I hope you're not charging me your normal six hundred and fifty bucks an hour for that advice. You call Bruce Lindsey at the White House and get back to me and tell me legally can this be done."

Next I called my broker at Oppenheimer and told him to be ready to wire $1.35 million the next day.

The Clintons took a four-hour tour of the Finger Lakes region that day, pressed by crowds everywhere. They stopped for fudge and coffee in the morning in downtown Skaneateles and visited the Vermont Green Mountain Specialty Co., where Hillary told a reporter, "I'm having a great time. It reminds me so much of where I spent my childhood. The nights were cool, and the mornings were cool, and it warmed up. It's so nostalgic, I called my mother last night."

I spent that day on the phone with Ben-Veniste going over what we needed to do, which papers needed to be signed and notarized and executed. That night the hot rumors flying around Syracuse focused on where we would eat dinner. Morris's Bar had a sign out front saying, BILL, WE HAVE A SAX GIG FOR YOU. Swaby's Tavern in Auburn was offering a Presidential Happy Hour of free drinks for everyone if Clinton showed up there. A couple thousand people gathered out in front of Krebs and Rosalie's Cucina downtown and when the motorcade drove past, "hundreds of people gave chase, like kids scurrying after an ice cream truck," as the *Syracuse Herald American* put it. We ended up having a great Italian meal at Rosalie's and I went to bed feeling just fine about knowing one day later I'd be light $1.35 million.

The President and I headed out to Lafayette Golf & Country Club the next day while Hillary and Chelsea spent another day out on Skaneateles Lake. We had two foursomes again, including Kate McKenna, the president of the Syracuse Teachers' Association; Michael Bragman, a New York assemblyman; and Bob Congel, a developer. The President walked a lot of the course shaking hands and talking to people and gave McKenna and Bragman and the others enough golfing tips to keep them going for years.

Clinton and I were standing together on the twelfth fairway when the White House Communications Agency (WHCA) golf cart equipped with all kinds of high-tech gear and a secure line came rolling up. This happened just about every time we golfed and it was usually Sandy Berger calling about an international crisis or a world leader like Tony Blair or Boris Yeltsin wanting to talk with the President. I would always walk away and let him have a private conversation.

"Who is calling?" the President asked.

"I'm sorry, Mr. President, it's not for you. It's for Mr. McAuliffe."

That was a first! I'd never taken a call from the WHCA cart. Bruce Lindsey was calling to say that if the money didn't get wired in the next two hours, the Clintons would lose the house.

That morning, Ben-Veniste had given me the word that legally I was fine. Richard is a very tough lawyer, very thorough and smart, and I also knew he was against me doing this, giving him every reason to want to find something, anything, to raise as a legal issue. He didn't find anything and gave me the okay, which meant we were airtight on the legality.

I left the President on the golf course and caught a ride into the Lafayette Country Club pro shop.

"Do you have a fax machine?" I asked Jack Conger, the pro behind the counter. "Can I borrow it?"

Conger was startled to see me there in the pro shop, rather than out on the course with the President, but he waved me into the office and I went to work.

"Richard, let's get the bank on the phone. I need to wire this," I told Ben-Veniste.

It was a crazy scene. I'm sitting there in Jack Conger's chair on a five-way conference call with bankers and lawyers, looking at a PGA calendar and cases of Titleists stacked in the corner. Nobody in the pro shop had any idea what was going on and the fax kept humming with more papers coming in and more going out. I had to sign authorization papers for Oppenheimer, my banker. I had to sign documents relating to the sale of the house. I had to sign a loan agreement with the President stating that he agreed to pay me back with interest. Finally after half an hour of this the banker confirmed he had all the papers and would wire the money within twenty minutes.

"How did it go?" the President asked me back out on the course.

"Mr. President, it's all done," I said. "You've got the money—and your house."

"Fantastic!" he said, and took a practice swing with his five-iron.

Clinton was relieved that he wouldn't have to have any more awkward conversations with Hillary over this and could just move forward, but once it was settled, there wasn't much to say. The President was focused on lining up his approach shot and right away we started talking golf, not money. He was on his way to shooting an 80, one of his best rounds ever.

"What did Dorothy say?" he asked me on the next hole.

"Holy cow!" I said. "I haven't told Dorothy yet. Mr. President, can I borrow the phone again?"

So I took one of the phones and called Dorothy.

"Honey, I want to prepare you," I said. "Be careful how you answer the phone today. We just lent the President almost a million and a half dollars to help buy their new home."

She was all for helping the Clintons out on the house, as I knew she would be, and took the whole thing in stride.

"Do you think the press will be calling the house?" she asked.

"Yeah, I think they might," I said. "They're going to release it in about an hour."

I really didn't know what to expect from the press on this. I was in the bubble, staying with the Clinton family at the house in Skaneateles and not following the news at all. Deputy press secretary Jake Siewert kept shaking his head, saying, "This is going to be big, real big."

Doug Sosnik was chief of staff on the trip, and once again I asked him for his take on how big.

"Networks?" I asked him.

"Terry, this is beyond networks," he said. "We're talking global news. Do you understand?"

I let him talk for a while about how unprecedented the arrangement was and then cut to the chase.

"Doug, if you were in my shoes, would you do it?" I asked him.

"No," he said. "But I'm not you."

★

THAT NIGHT WE HAD a great event planned. Duke Kinney was hosting a fund-raiser for Hillary at one of my favorite spots in Syracuse, an Armory Square sports bar we all called Mully's, short for Mulrooney's Tavern, owned by my high school classmate Joe Rainone. By the time we were pulling up in front of Mully's in the motorcade, the President, Hillary, and I all sitting in the backseat of the limo, a story had moved on the wires about the home loan and I think every editor of every paper in America was saying, "Get a picture of the three of them together."

We stepped out of the limo and a crowd of two thousand had gathered outside. The President shook some hands and waved to different parts of the crowd, getting a fresh round of cheers every time. The cameras went wild and captured that shot of the three of us, me in the middle in a striped shirt, which was in literally every paper in the world the next morning, along with the news that I had lent the Clintons money.

Duke did a great job with the event, bringing in an unbelievable $125,000, and everyone was so jacked up, you'd have thought the people were there to watch the Giants and the Jets in the Super Bowl. That night Hillary knocked it out of the park with a room full of hard-core sports fans at home in a place where football helmets, lacrosse sticks, and baseball gloves were mounted on the walls and a buffalo head hung on the wall near the front door. Even the President did a double-take when he saw that.

"All I can say is this has been a very interesting night," he said. "Duke and Terry throw a little party in an Irish bar and the first thing I see when I walk in besides all of your smiling faces is a buffalo head. Now, I don't know what that means."

The President and First Lady were ready to leave by about 9:30 P.M., when I was just getting started.

"Are you coming with us?" the President asked me.

"No, I'm staying," I said. "These are my people, sir."

I got back to the house in Skaneateles at about 4 A.M. and had to be very careful coming back in the dark to an unfamiliar house. I was lucky I didn't wake up the entire Secret Service and send them running in with their .357 Sig Sauers drawn to find out what all the noise was about.

The press was fascinated by the home loan, but the story didn't have any legs. "It died because there was nothing wrong with it," Clinton says. No one could work up much outrage. I mean, what was the President going to do for me in return? Invite me to a round of golf?

That weekend back at home I flipped on the Sunday talk shows to see what they had to say about the home loan. I was looking forward to hearing the Republicans take their shots at me and the Democrats backing me up. *This Week* on ABC showed a clip from Fred Wertheimer, who was always criticizing me on something, complaining about this.

"I think Mr. Wertheimer, as usual, is hyperventilating," said George Will, the conservative. "I don't think there's a huge problem with this."

"I agree with you, George—let's mark this down," joked Sam Donaldson. "This is not a big deal. . . . I wish I had a friend like that."

Even ultra-conservative Bill Kristol didn't have a problem with it, which left Cokie Roberts and George Stephanopoulos, the Democrats, to cast the arrangement in the most negative light they could.

By the time they were talking I had already received calls from eight different banks offering the Clintons conventional mortgages, 80 percent on the house and 20 percent down, like every other American could get. "We were held to a totally different standard," Hillary says now. "If we'd been penniless but with prospects for good earning, we could have gone out and got a mortgage." PNC Mortgage in Pittsburgh gave the Clintons a conventional thirty-year adjustable-rate mortgage. I immediately got back the money I'd put in an account for the Clintons, and that ended up being probably the shortest $1.35 million loan ever.

Hillary loved her visit to Syracuse so much, it became a yearly tradition. I was just glad I'd suggested they spend their summer vacation in Skaneateles and the Syracuse area. The visit could not have been more of a success and it had people excited about Hillary running for Senate.

17

★ ★ ★

Almost nothing could stop Bill Clinton from finishing a round of golf except an urgent call from the Situation Room. You finished eighteen holes, no matter what. That was true if you got caught in a downpour or if a brutal summer heat wave made the course so baking hot, you felt as if you were swimming around in your golf shirt. I remember one time in 1999 when the President and I went out for a Saturday afternoon round at the Army-Navy Club on Fourth of July weekend. It was so hot, Clinton and I looked like we'd been playing full-court basketball for four hours, not golfing. We should have been in the shade somewhere, enjoying an iced tea, and instead we were out there competing for bragging rights just as intensely as ever.

Afterward we went back to the White House for dinner and a movie with Hillary, but first the President invited me to use his personal shower, which was quite an experience. One of LBJ's great pleasures in life was the shower, and the week he moved into the White House, he directed chief usher J. B. West to bring in plumbers to renovate the President's personal shower. I don't know what kind of water pressure LBJ was used to back in Texas, but he liked his showers fire-hose strong. Engineers had to install a special tank to generate enough water pressure. LBJ was never satisfied, and according to Margaret Truman's book on the White House, the staff finally put in "a complicated fixture that had a half dozen different nozzles and sprays" and blasted you everywhere. I'd never felt anything like it and, to be honest, hope never to feel anything like that again, considering where it was hitting me.

Before the President went upstairs to meet Hillary for dinner, he was nice enough to leave some clean, dry clothes out for me to change into. I got out of the shower, toweled off, and proceeded to put on the shirt and shorts he'd left me. The shirt fit fine, but as I put the shorts on, I realized they were at least three sizes too small, and no matter how much I held my breath and struggled to pull up those shorts, I still had three inches to go. Now it was time to panic. My options were bleak. I couldn't wear my old shorts, which were wet, and I couldn't go up only in my underwear, so I started digging through the President's drawers looking for a pair of shorts that would fit me. I was so afraid that one of the butlers would come in and see me and think I was trying to make off with a presidential souvenir. Finally after a three-minute panic search I found some shorts that fit just fine and went upstairs to meet the President and First Lady, wondering if Clinton would admit to his practical joke, but he never said a word. However, I did pass on dessert that night.

Sometimes I had the feeling that Bill Clinton was never happier than when he was on the golf course. He was so at home there, so at ease and so himself, you couldn't help but share in his enjoyment. Understand, this was private, relaxing time for the President, away from the pressure cooker of the White House, and he made the most of it. Often when he didn't have time to get away for a full round of golf at Army-Navy, he would step outside on the little putting green just outside the White House and work on his short game. When he wanted to talk to me alone, he would suggest we do some putting and we'd head out to the little green and both sink ten-footers as he talked about a problem that had come up or give me a new job to tackle.

It was good he had that time, too, because to be honest, the President's chipping and putting were not the strength of his golf game. His favorite holes were the par fives. He's really got a great drive and was just about always longer off the tee than I was. He loved to let one rip with his big, fluid swing, watch it land just beyond where my ball had rolled to a stop two minutes before, and then climb into the golf cart and kid me about out-driving me yet again as we rode out to our balls.

From the time we hit the first tee until we putted out on eighteen, he would keep talking the whole time, offering pointers on your stance, your grip, your weight shift, your putting style, your technique out of sand traps, your golf glove and whether you had it adjusted correctly, and your bad luck or your good luck. It was a two-way street. He'd ask for your advice, too, and would listen to what you said and think about doing what you suggested, but he was always happiest when he was giving tips to someone else, no matter who they were.

I'm no scratch golfer, but I always felt like one when the President and I played a round. Cameras and reporters were only allowed on the first tee and eighteenth green and you would get up there to hit your drive and there would be dozens of cameras pointed at you and a huge crowd of people. All the members would come out or if there was a wedding, the whole wedding party would come over. Finishing up on the eighteenth, you felt like you were wrapping up a historic round at the U.S. Open or Masters because again everyone would come out and the sense of excitement and electricity in the air was so strong.

Three weeks after we opened Clinton-Gore reelection headquarters in May 1995, the President called me up at the last minute to ask if I could join him for a round of golf with a group including his stepfather, Dick Kelly, and Corey Pavin, the pro golfer. I always kept my sticks at the office along with a fresh set of golf clothes to be ready when he called.

"Mac, can you get over here this afternoon?" he asked.

My answer was always yes. I would carry my golf bag across the street and go tramping through the White House security gates. Everyone knew me, so they would just say hello and wave me through and someone would come out and get my clubs and load my bag up in the presidential limousine. Buddy Carter, the ever-smiling White House butler, would usually bring me a Bud Lite before I even had to ask and I could take it easy while I waited for the President to finish up whatever he was doing.

Pavin met us at Army-Navy for a one o'clock tee time after having played eighteen holes that morning in the Kemper Open, bouncing back with a 68 after shooting 73 on Thursday. His three previous tournaments, he had missed the cut, meaning he wasn't even playing the last two days, so he had clearly been struggling. Plus, he still had to think about playing the next day and then finishing up the tournament on Sunday.

"Corey, aren't you worried?" Clinton asked Pavin. "That's a lot of golf."

"No, no, I'm fine," Pavin said.

The President had a great time golfing with Pavin and receiving excellent tips from him on getting out of sand traps and using his 8-iron around the green. Clinton in turn helped Pavin out with some small tips on the layout of the course, which he knew so well he could play it in the dark. Then again, as a top professional golfer, Pavin had some surprises for us. We got to the tenth hole, a long par four with a sharp dogleg right with a tall row of pine trees guarding the right side of the fairway, and Pavin turned to the President for guidance.

"Just where is the green?" he asked.

"Behind those tall pine trees," Clinton said. "But you need to hit it straight down the fairway because the pine trees are too tall to hit over."

So Pavin stepped up, without saying anything, and blasted this towering shot that flew right over the stand of pine trees and landed near the green. Just shows that advice only goes so far.

That evening the President gave Pavin, his wife, Shannon, and sons, Ryan and Austin, a personal tour of the Oval Office and Pavin was obviously fired up. He went out the next day and let rip with an eight-under-par 63 at the Kemper Open and came back on Sunday with another 68 to almost win the tournament, losing in a one-hole playoff when Lee Janzen sank a twelve-foot birdie putt. A week later at Shinnecock Hills, Pavin was still on fire and won the U.S. Open, his first major title. The President got a huge kick out of that and called Pavin that night to congratulate him.

"I was good luck for him," Clinton jokes now. "I always told Corey I should have gotten a percentage of the purse, I was such good luck for him."

Given that Pavin won so soon after playing with the President, a natural human-interest story, the topic came up at White House spokesman Mike McCurry's press briefing that Monday. You might think this would have been the occasion for a little lighthearted fun as McCurry talked about how the President's pointers must have been pretty good.

These are the questions that were asked of McCurry:

"Is the President claiming credit?"

"So, Corey took Mulligans when nobody was looking?"

"How far from sixty-three was the President that day?"

"Is the President playing too much golf?"

★

AN EVEN FUNNIER EXAMPLE OF Clinton's love of giving sports advice came on September 9, 2000, when he became the first sitting President to attend the U.S. Open tennis tournament in Flushing Meadows, New York. That was a Saturday and the President had been in New York since Tuesday night for the UN Millennium Summit. Dorothy and I joined Sandy Berger, Madeleine Albright, and the President for lunch at the Stage Deli on Seventh Avenue in Manhattan.

Peter O'Keefe, Dorothy, and I were with Clinton in the limousine on the way over to lunch, and crowds lined the street everywhere we went. We walked into the restaurant and the people inside broke out into applause. The place was crackling with energy. We were joined by two great supporters of ours, Doug Teitelbaum and his wife, Traie. They even named a Stage Deli sandwich for the President: "The Bill Clinton," corned beef, chopped liver, and onion on rye.

You couldn't be with the President that glorious day in New York without thinking: *Too bad he can't run for one more term.* He would have been reelected easily. An even bigger throng was pressing in on all sides as we left the deli and people stopped and cheered for the motorcade everywhere on the drive to the Queensboro Bridge. On the way out to Queens we had an amazing discussion of the presidential election coming up in two months. Clinton went through every state Gore would win, giving the number of electoral votes each would bring him, and all of his picks were right, including Florida. That is, Clinton predicted Gore would win Florida—which he did, as we all now know. I still have the card Clinton wrote his picks on, too. Nobody does it better.

We settled into a box at Arthur Ashe Stadium to watch Pete Sampras's three-set semifinal win over a nineteen-year-old Australian, Lleyton Hewitt, and again Clinton got the rock star treatment. So many people were tossing the President tennis balls, hats, and shirts to autograph, the Secret Service moved in and tried to put a halt to the commotion, but people sitting higher than Clinton kept dropping things for him to sign and he kept right on signing. Marat Safin, a young Russian, won his match against Todd Martin, and then stopped by for a visit and asked Clinton for an autograph. The next day, after winning the tournament, Safin talked about what it was like meeting the President.

"I felt like a little child in the presence of him," he said. "A friendly man. It must be hard to be so famous."

John McEnroe came down to the box after he'd worked some of the matches as a TV commentator and sat between Clinton and me with his pigtailed redhead daughter on his lap, and I listened as the two of them really connected. All kinds of people dropped by the box, from Kofi Annan and Senator Chris Dodd to Donald Trump and Pete Sampras, and it felt like we were at a party. McEnroe was the constant. I love the guy. He tells you exactly what he thinks and looks in your eye when he's doing it. He was in a relaxed mood, enjoying some time with his daughter, but he sat next to Clinton and they jumped around from topic to topic to topic. It was fun just listening to them and it's not often I'm content just to listen.

Then they started talking tennis and before you knew it the President was giving McEnroe suggestions on his grip. Clinton actually stood up and held out his arm to demonstrate what he meant.

"You ought to do *this*," the President said to McEnroe, looking up to make eye contact in that way of his.

McEnroe is one of these guys who either respects you or doesn't and lets you know right away. He obviously respected Clinton. He had kind of a little grin as he listened to Clinton's tennis tips, but you could see he was thinking about it. I waited until McEnroe and his daughter left and then turned to the President with a big, disbelieving grin.

"Mr. President, why are you possibly giving John McEnroe advice on his grip?" I asked and everyone laughed.

"And I knew nothing about it," Clinton admits now, laughing.

★

I CAN'T TELL YOU how many times the President and I were over at Army-Navy for our usual Monday round and it would get hard to see the ball as we putted out on fourteen or fifteen and by the time we teed off on eighteen it was pitch black. I'm talking so dark you could barely see your hand in front of your face. Hillary would be back at the White House, sometimes with a group of guests waiting for the President, and he was just like any husband on the golf course getting a call from his wife. Every golfer wants to finish eighteen so you can get your score.

"I'm just coming up the eighteenth fairway, dear, I'll be right home," Clinton would tell her from the fifteenth fairway, turning to wink at me.

"Mac, we need to hustle," he'd say to me, handing the phone off to someone. "That was Hillary and the guests have already arrived. She's going to kill me."

But he had to finish. That was just how it was. And listen, Hillary knew what was going on. She loved it when the President was out on the golf course with me having a good time and relaxing. She knew boys would be boys and we were as competitive as all get-out and had to finish. Often it got to be comical by the time we got to the eighteenth.

When you golf with the President you always have at least thirty people watching every shot and at least half a dozen golf carts trailing you all the time. There would be dozens of Secret Service agents. You had the WHCA cart, which always followed the President to be ready for secure calls, the person carrying U.S. nuclear codes in the so-called "football," and the White House photographer, usually Sharon Farmer or Ralph Alswang, who would bring a Walkman to help pass the time, since they could take only so many pictures of the President and me golfing. Off in the distance you would have guys in black fatigues, specialized sharpshooters with huge binoculars spreading out in the woods.

We would step up to the tee on the eighteenth and everyone would be totally quiet so we could all listen for the sound of the ball landing, because that was the only way we were going to find it in the dark. That was one time when you were sure glad to have dozens of people along with you standing still and listening—and, depending on where they were standing, hoping the first sound they heard wasn't the ball bouncing off their heads!

Sometimes the Secret Service would help us out by parking all their SUVs right next to the eighteenth, a par three, and shining their bright lights out toward the green so we would have a target to shoot toward. Bill Clinton is one of the most competitive men I've ever met. A lot of times it came down to that last hole, and neither one of us was about to quit without seeing who won, which was usually him, but I got him often enough to keep it interesting—and the few times I did beat him, he heard about it, let me tell you. Actually, everybody heard about it for days, and I know it drove Clinton nuts when different people would come up to him and say, "Mr. President, I hear Mac beat you."

I lived for the times when I'd sink a long putt for a birdie and would carry on so much, I would have everyone cracking up. Clinton got a kick out of it, though sometimes he tried not to show it.

"Oh, man, I've got you on the run now, Mr. President!" I'd say, and you could hear me three holes away. "You are done, done, done! God dang, have you ever played with a golfer as good as me, Mr. President? If this were a fight, they'd stop it!"

He would just shake his head and get back in the cart.

We did not golf in the snow. If it was freezing or colder, then we were sidelined, but other than that we would golf in just about any conditions. I have great pictures from one Thanksgiving golfing at Camp David with the President, Dick Kelly, and Vernon Jordan, all of us with hats and gloves on. We played in the rain so many times, it was second nature to us. A few times we'd hear thunder rumbling off in the distance and we'd both ignore it. We'd see flashes of lightning as the storm moved our way and the rumbles and flashes would get closer and closer together and still we would ignore them. One time in the spring of 2000, it got to the point where you could hear the crackle and pop of lightning really close, but I wasn't going to say, "Let's quit," and neither was he.

Rick, one of Clinton's longtime Secret Service agents, pulled me aside. "Terry, you think we ought to quit?" he asked me.

"Listen, you guys get paid to protect him," I said. "I don't. You tell him to get off the course. I'm not going to show any sign of weakness."

The staff of the golf course was in a panic since they would be ruined if lightning fried the President on the twelfth fairway. Someone hurried out from the pro shop in the driving rain.

"Mr. President, you have to get off this course right now," he said.

That was what it took to get us to end a round early.

★

To ME, GOLFING with the President was a great chance to get to know the man Bill Clinton. From the time I sat on the Truman Balcony with the President the night of the 1994 midterm elections and really started to forge a strong friendship, I found myself liking the man more and more as I spent more time with him. There is a pattern in the media that is probably just human nature: A new figure comes along and it's a fun, fresh story to build him or her up, turn that person into a larger-than-life figure, let that play out for a while, and then turn around and tear down this larger-than-life figure the media have built up. I understand that's probably inevitable. People long for heroes but worry they're being naïve when they believe in someone.

That's not my way. I don't long for heroes and I don't worry I'm seeing someone in a more positive light than they deserve. My style is to approach everyone with an open mind. I like people who are unafraid, resourceful, and resilient. I like people who fight to make others' lives better. I like people who don't take themselves too seriously and can make jokes at their own expense. I like people who think big and dream big. I like people who believe in friendship and believe in people. That is why my friendship with Bill Clinton has been one of the greatest experiences of my life.

"This is just my observation, but watching their relationship develop over the years, Bill and Terry have a great relationship and they have a real friendship," Hillary says. "It's almost like a classical friendship. We live in a world where everybody calls everybody friends, but a friend is somebody who is there for you no matter what. A friend is someone who cares about you no matter what and who is there to pick you up when you fall and to give you a call when no one else will.

"Terry understands friendship and he's been such an important part of Bill's life because when you're President, it's hard to make new friends. Once you get to be President, you're cut off from people and you can't have the experiences with somebody that build a base of a friendship. Presidents often have friends with whom they only relax. They play cards or play golf and basically try to shut out the world by spending time with these friends. Kennedy and Truman are great examples of that. Or they have friends who are like consigliores, people who they go to when they need help solving problems, getting them out of jams, fixing issues, or being emissaries who pass on bad news to other people.

"The White House is very lonely and desolate. Truman called the White House the crown jewel of the American penal system. It's really rare to have someone who is both a really close friend with whom you can let your guard down, argue about football, whatever it is, someone around whom you can be totally unguarded, totally open, totally trusting, and somebody that you can say, 'Oh my gosh, what are we going to do about the convention in L.A.? It's a total mess.' Bill and Terry really hit it off, but their friendship kept developing during those eight years and that's really rare. Their friendship was really forged in the White House and I think when history is written, it will be viewed as a unique relationship."

18

★ ★ ★

Sometimes I look back on all the work I did on behalf of Bill Clinton and his political programs and even I can't believe all the phone calls I made, all the thousands of hours I spent flying around the country, all the time I spent away from home fighting for the President's priorities and, sometimes, his political survival. There are even times when I sit in my backyard late at night, smoking a cigar, and ask myself if it was all worth it. Once I frame the question that way, it takes about a millisecond before my answer comes back: *Absolutely! You bet!*

Every day of the Clinton years, I was reminded of how proud I was to be playing my part in giving one of the great American leaders of our times the chance to show people that the government could play a valuable role in their lives and that American power and influence could be wielded around the world in a way that made people's lives better, not scarier, and inspired respect and admiration, not scalding hatred. If you listened only to the right-wing echo chamber, it would be easy to forget that innovative programs like the Family and Medical Leave Act were not just slogans, they were often turning points in individual lives. Clinton signed the FMLA in 1993, which enabled workers to take up to twelve weeks of leave, whether to look after a newborn baby or to care for a sick family member.

It was amazing, I tell you. I would be at a reception in Biloxi, Mississippi, or waiting in line to buy a newspaper at the Kansas City airport or having lunch in Salt Lake City or Portland, Oregon, and people would come up and tell me their stories. At first I was a little confused. Why did these strangers want to tell me so many personal details about their lives? Then I came to understand: They had heard I was good friends with the President, and they were grateful for a chance to have someone to pass on their personal thanks to him. Again and again, I heard stories from people who had decided to take advantage of the provisions of the Family and Medical Leave Act and ended up having a truly life-altering experience. Often they would get emotional as they told me about the time they had spent being there for a close family member, or being at home with their wives and sharing a baby's first weeks of life in a way their fathers never experienced. The FMLA was just one of hundreds of programs enacted in the Clinton years that made a real, palpable difference in people's lives, and every time someone told me, "Please thank him for me—promise me you'll tell him personally, okay?" I walked away with a smile on my face and an extra hop in my step.

No one had to tell me, a son of Ireland, about all the tens of thousands of lives that had been shattered in Belfast and elsewhere in Northern Ireland during what people there stoically referred to as "The Troubles." The clashes between Catholics and Protestants left more than three thousand dead, going back to the 1960s, and each of those deaths violently disrupted the lives of countless others. Bill Clinton was mocked and scorned early on for having the vision to work toward peace in Northern Ireland. As reluctant as most in Washington were to give him credit for his amazing accomplishment with the Good Friday Agreement, on my travels I was constantly meeting people who, again, asked me to thank the President for his brave and visionary work in showing such courage, stepping into a centuries-old conflict that was too daunting a challenge for most American political leaders to tackle. Ireland's booming economy became one of the great success stories in the world, giving people the chance to improve their lives, and it never would have happened if Clinton had not staked his presidency on finding a solution to The Troubles.

The terrible violence that ripped apart the former Yugoslavia was coldly dismissed by some foreign-policy experts as inevitable and unstoppable, but Bill Clinton could not afford to think that way. He always saw every life as valuable and every problem as solvable. Maybe he was too optimistic sometimes, too insistent on always seeing the good in people, but in the former Yugoslavia, he took huge risks and found a way to use U.S. leadership and military power to force the thug Slobodan Milosevic to back down and accept that the time for peace had arrived. It's one thing to read about the importance of the Dayton Accords and something completely different to meet people face-to-face whose own lives were shaped by the carnage and chaos in the former Yugoslavia. They would implore me to please, please, please let Bill Clinton know how much his work for peace meant to them.

I was thankful to Bill Clinton for the difference he made at home and around the world, and also for the opportunity to help in my small way to see that he could continue to tackle the problems of Americans and people all over the world. I never had any trouble charging myself up every morning to work on behalf of Bill Clinton because I believed with every fiber of my being in what he was doing. I could have spent more time at home with the kids or out making money as a full-time businessman. Thanks to Bill Clinton's economic leadership, the 1990s were a booming time when savvy investors could easily pile up huge fortunes, as so many did.

A lot of people preferred not to get involved with public service. They looked after themselves and their own, and I don't blame them for spending their time in other ways, whether it was on long vacations in the Bahamas or sitting around the country club. The higher you get in politics, the more they try to rip you down, and no one wants to deal with that. But to me, sitting on the sidelines just wouldn't have been right. I've always told people I felt like the luckiest man in the world for all the opportunities this country has given me, and I wanted to work on behalf of bringing those opportunities to every American—and, yes, to people around the world as well, so they could have a chance to work their way out of poverty and not have to worry every day about getting shot walking down the street or whether they could afford life-saving vaccinations for their children.

I knew the fights Bill Clinton took on were not just about me and my family. I wanted to do my part to see that when my children have their own families, and eventually their own grandchildren, they will have the same opportunities that I was lucky enough to have. Most important, I wanted to fight to ensure that *all* children would have the same opportunities as my children.

The President was always a fighter, and persevered against long odds, and I was right there with him through many of the fights not only as a fundraiser, as I'd started out, but increasingly as a political adviser. He was locked in a lot of tough fights and he needed me at his side. I was honored by the way that during Clinton's time as President he increasingly came to me with questions on many of the difficult decisions he faced. I became a sounding board for him on a wide variety of issues, far beyond only politics or fund-raising. I was a voice outside the administration he knew he could count on to give him an honest, unvarnished opinion.

I don't know if my advice was helpful, though I hope it was, but I know I never hesitated to tell the President if I thought something was a bad idea and never backed off from making a suggestion that might not have been what the President wanted to hear. I think I was able to help him because we were always on the same wavelength. We were able to communicate very quickly, sometimes almost without words, and I was never afraid to remain positive and optimistic about the future when others were giving themselves over to gloom and pessimism. A lot of advisers make their bread-and-butter by turning simple issues into complicated problems only an expert can understand. Bill Clinton, the quickest study I've ever met, could understand every nuance and detail of a massively complex problem, but he also had a knack for cutting through to simplicity. I think he enjoyed the way I did that as well, almost as if talking about issues and politics was an extension of another passion we had in common, talking about sports. In both arenas, you are constantly tested, you are constantly knocked flat on your back, and the crowd waits to see if you can get back up. If you don't like getting hit, you shouldn't play.

Here's how Clinton put it to me one time, summing up what he knew we both believed in passionately: "Don't let somebody bad-mouth you out of the game and then sit on the sidelines and lay down. Don't let them score without trying to tackle them. If you're going to play, you ought to know going in what to expect. You cannot expect any sympathy from the public in the face of this, because they figure if you didn't want to play this game, you could have gone and done something else with your life. So half the time when you get hit upside the head, people don't necessarily believe it. What they're really interested in is: How are you going to respond? That's how they can get some guidance as to what sort of President you'd be or senator or congressman or governor."

You have to fight for your beliefs, if they're really important to you, and that's why to me, Bill Clinton has always been an inspiration. As we started to think ahead to the years after he was President, I became obsessed with making sure that he could be an inspiration to future generations as well. The Republicans threw everything they had at Bill Clinton, because they knew he was a more gifted and visionary leader than they had seen in a generation, in either party, and in a way those attacks are a tribute to Clinton. Far from subtracting from what he accomplished as President, they were proof that he was making positive changes in people's lives that the reactionaries and fear-mongers vowed to resist at all costs, even to their own decency. We knew these same cowards would keep attacking the President and trying to smear his good name long after he left the White House, and that was why it became my central focus to work toward establishing a forum for a factual, accurate account of the Clinton years that Americans and people all over the world could visit—in person or via the Web—to learn more about the Clinton years and why they were the best eight years of our lives.

The Bill Clinton Presidential Library was going to be our vehicle to establish his legacy. The President and I first talked about his library in 1998, and by early 1999 we met in the Oval Office and he asked me to head up the effort to get the Presidential Library built, and of course I gladly agreed. This was going to be a fight for Bill Clinton's legacy against the same right-wing character assassins I'd been battling for years and I wanted to be on the front lines. I knew in the end we would get a beautiful library built that could inspire people to have optimism and hope about the future, and to spur people to engage in lives of public service, not poison them with fear about their lives, which is, sadly, all that many Republicans seem to know how to do anymore.

I kept saying in all the early meetings we had on the library that we needed to stick to a $100 million budget, and Hillary kept saying, "He's right, he's right." The more we talked, the clearer it became that we would need to raise way more than $100 million. A key issue related to cost was where to put the library.

"We've got to do it in Little Rock," the President said.

That made sense. If not for Arkansas, Bill Clinton would never have been elected President. I had another location in mind, however, which I kept bringing up in the early meetings. New York would have loved to have had the library and it would have been easier to put the money together to build it there, but I was thinking locally.

"Let me just throw out an idea, Mr. President," I said. "I know you're from Arkansas and they've been great to you, but you know what? You've been such a leader of the African-American community and so strong on civil rights. Why don't you put the thing in Anacostia? It would be great for the community and the tourists would line up for blocks outside."

The President heard me out. He saw how great Anacostia could be. This was an underdeveloped area at the south end of D.C., along the Anacostia River, near where it empties into the Potomac, that could really use a lift economically. Georgetown University had offered to give us $30 million if we built in the area and Howard Milstein was ready to donate a prime piece of land right along the river, which would have been beautiful. "Listen, Terry, I own a lot of land in Anacostia right near the Capitol and if Bill Clinton wants to build his library there, I'll give it to you," he said.

Even with all that, I knew this was going to be a hard sell with the President. On December 14, 1999, we had a noon meeting about the library up in the Yellow Oval with our regular team of the President, Hillary, Bruce Lindsey, and Cheryl Mills, and I continued to press the case.

"Sir, your wife is going to be in the United States Senate and you're going to be around here," I said. "You've got all these world leaders in and out of town all the time. No offense, but they're not going to fly to Little Rock."

I knew I was probably going to lose this one, but I kept arguing for Anacostia over weeks of meetings.

My phone used to ring all the time late at night with calls from the White House and usually I would sit there in my pajamas talking with the President about anything from college basketball to our mothers. One night in this period the phone rang after 11 P.M. and it was Operator One at the White House, only she asked me to hold for a call from the First Lady, not the President.

"Terry, forget about Anacostia," Hillary told me. "Bill wants it to go to Little Rock. He wants to go home. He just doesn't want to tell you."

That was the end of my Anacostia idea.

"It would have been a good favor for Georgetown and I would have been doing something for inner-city Washington," Clinton says now. "But I thought I owed it to Arkansas. I wouldn't have become President without them. Furthermore, I thought it would do more good down there because it's in the middle of the country. We had half a million people go through there in 2005 and a healthy percentage of them were swing-state Americans. Even if they're already Democrats it gives them something to go home and talk about. I still think for our party and for our politics it was the best thing to do."

*

ONE THING I LOVED about nights over at the White House was that both the Clintons were equally comfortable with my Syracuse high school buddies or world leaders. The President invited Dorothy and me to spend the night on October 23 to celebrate Hillary's birthday. That afternoon they had hundreds of people in a tent on the White House lawn for the VH1 "Save the Music" concert with Eric Clapton, Garth Brooks, and 'N Sync, shown live on CBS, which raised money for public schools to continue their music education programs.

We also had a small celebration that night for Smith and Elizabeth Bagley's wedding anniversary in the solarium upstairs at the residence. My high school campaign manager Duke Kinney and his wife, Billie Jean, joined us. Dorothy was nine months pregnant with Sally, our fourth, and we were all joking about how Dorothy was going to give birth right then and there.

"Wouldn't it be exciting if it happened right here tonight?" I said.

"Absolutely, I'm ready to assist with the delivery," the President joked.

"Or how about just firing up the presidential motorcade to take me to Sibley Hospital," Dorothy joked back.

The White House staff brought out champagne to celebrate the Bagleys' anniversary. We were still kidding around with each other and after a glass or two of bubbly I asked the President about his vision for his library. Smith and Elizabeth started talking about how important this would be for Bill Clinton's legacy.

"Okay, Smith, what are you going to do for the library?" I said.

"I'm going to do one," he said.

"A hundred thousand dollars?" Elizabeth asked.

"No, no, no," I said. "You're saying a million, aren't you, Smith?"

"Yeah, Terry, I meant a million," he said.

"Great, let's have another bottle of champaaaaaaaagne," I said.

Prince Bandar, the Saudi Arabian ambassador, was having a dinner at his house that night in honor of Nelson Mandela, to which Dorothy and I had been invited, and the President insisted that we go, promising to hold the birthday cake until we returned. "Any time you can have dinner with Nelson Mandela, you do it," he said. We were glad we followed his advice on that. As we were introduced to Mandela, I'll never forget how he put his hand on Dorothy's belly and gave it a nice, gentle little rub. He was so taken, he wrote a card to Sally, only he didn't use her name because we didn't know yet if this would be a Sally or a Peter.

This was the nice note he wrote: "To the new Baby, best wishes to one who may rise to become one of the world's prominent leaders, Mandela."

We put that one in a special place. Then in October 2005 Dorothy and I saw Mandela at a small lunch Clinton hosted for him. He signed a photo of Sally for us, "To Sally," which we have framed next to the original note.

Five days after the dinner at Prince Bandar's, I flew back from a quick trip to London and found out it was time to take Dorothy to Sibley Hospital.

We got there a little after noon and spent the whole afternoon in her room. I was trying hard not to appear restless, but I am not one to sit still for long and soon I was going stir-crazy, which drove Dorothy nuts.

"Isn't there something you need to do?" she finally said.

I told her *The Washington Post* was having a party that evening for Lloyd Grove, who wrote the "Reliable Source" column.

"Go!" she said. "You're like a caged animal here. I'll call you if I need you."

I went flying out the door and drove to the party. I kept calling Dorothy to make sure she was fine. I made the rounds at the party and ran into Marjorie Williams, who was writing a story on me for *Vanity Fair* magazine. She was shocked to see me at the party.

"Isn't Dorothy having a baby today?" she asked.

"That's right," I said, "but she threw me out of the room."

Marjorie just couldn't understand how I could have left Dorothy alone. I almost told her about the night I was born and how my mother wanted my father to stay at home to watch *Thirty Seconds over Tokyo,* but decided against it.

I went back to the hospital after the *Washington Post* party and at 3:33 A.M. little Sarah Swann McAuliffe was born. We immediately took to calling her Sally, which suits her because she's a real spitfire. She and I both have tightly curled brown hair and some people say our curls might be screwed a little too tightly into our heads, which could explain a lot.

★

NO ONE KNEW what to expect on the night of December 31st that year, which was going to be a New Year's Eve like none other in our lifetimes. The papers were filled with speculation about the so-called Y2K bug, which we were told was going to bring epic computer crashes and doom and gloom for the whole planet. Speculation was also rampant about the threat of a terrorist action that night when it would have maximum impact. People were worried that this was going to be some kind of real-life disaster movie unfolding before our eyes on New Year's and it took some persuading to get people to look past the media scare-mongering.

Hillary Clinton, true to form, saw the occasion as an opportunity. After all, this event happened only once every thousand years. She was brimming with ideas on how to throw the greatest party ever on the Mall and at the White House and stage a televised national celebration of the Millennium that we would all remember to the ends of our days. That August she got on the phone with Quincy Jones, Steven Spielberg, and George Stevens Jr. and got them involved, which guaranteed she was going to be able to organize a great event. That meant, of course, that this would have a hefty price tag, and once she and her staff started asking how they could possibly pay for this, the answer was: Let's get Terry!

"Come on over, I need to see you," Hillary said.

"We wanted to do something that would be memorable and thought of having a party at the White House where we invited a thousand of our closest friends and then have a free public event out on the Mall in front of the Lincoln Memorial," Hillary says now. "We loved sharing the White House with people. People attacked us and made fun of us because we tried to have everybody we ever knew over to the White House. Bill and I both had our high school reunions and college reunions at the White House and that was such a treat for people to come to the White House. This was going to be a big final passage, the Millennium, so we wanted to make it a great party that would be a celebration of America with people who have meant something in arts and culture and sports and entertainment, people like Elizabeth Taylor, Sophia Loren, and Muhammad Ali."

Hillary and I met in the stately Yellow Oval Room at the residence and whenever I was brought to a private meeting at the residence, I knew it was going to be very expensive. Hillary laid out her exciting, lavish—and costly—plans and said that of course she and the President didn't want any public funds used so we would need to raise $2 million to $3 million. I knew after hearing her ideas that the price tag was going to be at least $10 million.

"I'll do whatever you need," I told her.

I immediately put together a great fund-raising team of Peter O'Keefe, David Jones, Scott Freda, and David Mercer. I can tell you that over twenty-five years of fund-raising, this was the toughest sell ever. We were running into brick walls at every turn because there just wasn't any excitement out there about the idea of traveling to Washington for the Millennium. People were worried enough about avoiding some kind of catastrophe at midnight, December 31, even if they stayed at home hiding in their basements with stockpiles of bottled water and beef jerky. Traveling to a potential terrorist target like the Washington Mall was not high on anyone's list. In the rare cases where people did work up a little excitement, they felt like they'd already given enough to other causes and shouldn't have to pay for this, too. Corporations, which you would normally expect to line up to back a celebration of America, had already committed all their charitable gift money for the year by August, so we were really starting a year too late.

However, after four months of effort we raised $17 million, helped by a $2 million gift from Vin Gupta, a man who was born on a dirt floor in India, came to this country with nothing in his pocket, started his business with a $100 investment, and was worth more than $400 million after his company *info*USA went public. Danny Abraham, the founder of Slimfast, also gave us a million.

We held a press conference on September 28 to announce that actor Will Smith was going to host the Millennium party, where we expected a crowd of at least 600,000, with music by B. B. King, Aretha Franklin, and Chuck Berry, and a show at the Lincoln Memorial produced by Quincy Jones that included an eighteen-minute film by Steven Spielberg.

★

I KNEW IT WAS GOING TO BE a wild New Year's celebration when I got things started late on December 30 with Jack Nicholson over at the Mayflower Hotel. The thing about Jack is that in person he's exactly like he is on the screen. He talks the same way. He smiles the same way. He raises his eyebrows the same way. I told him that *One Flew over the Cuckoo's Nest* was my favorite movie of all time and he knew I wasn't snowing him. He'd heard it a few times before.

The one thing I couldn't figure was why Jack took me for an art lover. I can't remember the last time I went to a museum for anything other than a political event. Dorothy has long since given up on me. Jack has one of the most amazing art collections around and he was telling me all about it, like how he got his Picasso and why he likes someone named Tamara de Lempicka. Don't get me wrong. It was fascinating. I just didn't have any idea of what he was talking about most of the time.

We sat around telling stories and drinking whiskey until sometime after 2 A.M. and picked it up the next day with lunch over at the Palm with Jack's buddy Rudy Durand. That was a comical scene. Everyone goes to the Palm to people-watch, but when they see big Washington types they usually stay pretty cool. There was a real buzz over having Jack in there that day and Tommy at the Palm snapped a picture of us, which he blew way up and had on display at the front desk for a month or two afterward.

Jack dug into a big New York strip steak and told us about how he got his breakthrough part as the hard-drinking hippie lawyer in *Easy Rider.* He had worked with Dennis Hopper and Peter Fonda on a 1969 cult classic called *The Trip,* which Nicholson actually wrote. A little later Hopper and Fonda were off working on a new movie with motorcycles, but the set was such a mess, the producers felt they needed a calming influence. So they brought in Jack Nicholson. You should have seen Jack's eyebrows and his grin when he told us that one at the Palm as he was finishing up his New York strip.

Now it was time for the big show and Dorothy and I went over to the residence to see the President and Hillary before the evening's events kicked off. I always felt it was important to say thank you to the people who helped, especially on as big and tough an event as this one, so the President and Hillary agreed to have a reception to thank the top twenty sponsors and fund-raising staff.

It was a super-charged evening with a parade of American icons streaming in one by one or in small groups, passing by a throng of reporters pushing them for quotes. We had Bono, Muhammad Ali, Arthur Schlesinger Jr., Itzhak Perlman, Maya Lin, Robert Rauschenberg, John Fogerty, August Wilson, Carl Lewis, Bill Russell, Elizabeth Taylor, Sophia Loren, Robert De Niro, Martin Scorsese, Sid Caesar, Neil Simon, and hundreds of other people who had made major contributions to American life and also happened to be great fun to talk to at a White House dinner.

One of the highlights for me was watching Chelsea take her place next to the President and First Lady in the receiving line, which was a first for her. The mother-daughter resemblance was strong, now that Chelsea was a poised, beautiful young woman, but then you looked over at the President and saw Chelsea's strong resemblance to him as well.

I sat at the President's table near Clinton, who was between Elizabeth Taylor and Sophia Loren. I was two seats from Sophia, sitting between Denyce Graves and Danny Abraham. Also at our table were Les Moonves, the president of CBS, Elizabeth Bagley, Vin Gupta, Jessye Norman, and Walter Shorenstein. Dorothy was at another table sitting between Muhammad Ali and Jack Nicholson, making it a memorable night for her, too.

The stunning Sophia Loren was grateful to have been included that night and had such a flair for enjoying herself no matter what she was doing, it seemed to rub off on everyone sitting near her. She was beautiful, charming, and graceful, and listening to her talk about Italy, the climate, the people, and the food, I was ready to book a family vacation to Rome right away. Sophia really is amazing. Fifty years after she appeared in her first Federico Fellini movie, she still had men falling all over her. *The Times* noted that "when a rather baldly appreciative reporter asked Sophia Loren whether she would be able to keep warm in her low-cut black dress, she said, 'I have a little wrap,' and seemed to gesture toward the diamonds and rubies around her neck."

Buses started pulling up in front of the White House at 10 P.M. to take people over to the area near the Lincoln Memorial for the nationally televised New Year's Eve performance. Having Quincy Jones involved was another highlight of the Millennium celebration. Quincy was the one who picked Will Smith to emcee, and what a great choice that ended up being. If his other careers in music and movies ever start to seem old, he could be a great fund-raiser. Maybe we'll even get him to run for office someday.

Quincy and I hit it off from the first time we met because we're similar personality types. The man always has a smile on his face and gets excited about whatever he's doing. Quincy has lived music the way I've lived politics, even more so. He knew Billie Holiday when she was in her downward spiral, he jammed with Charlie Parker and Miles Davis, he composed the music for *In Cold Blood,* and he was a legend as a producer even before he produced Michael Jackson's 1982 hit *Thriller,* which went on to become the second-most-popular album in U.S. history. "You have to love the people you're working with enough to dig and probe," he told *The Washington Post*, gearing up for the Millennium. "Then you have to create the environment so that they have no choice but to give it up. You hit that button. The emotion notion."

We tried to have something for everyone. Tom Jones belted out "It's Not Unusual," and Bobby McFerrin, Jessye Norman, and Kathleen Battle sang "He's Got the Whole World in His Hands," and just before midnight, Bono sang "One," his ballad celebrating world unity. The best part of the evening, though, had to be watching Mary and Jack sneak up on the President and climb up into his lap. They stayed there all night, wrapped in his arms, next to Chelsea and Hillary.

The party really got rocking back at the White House later on. They had a buffet table that switched over from evening food to breakfast food as the night wore on and every floor of the White House had a different type of music, jazz or rock or classical. I remember after midnight looking out on the dance floor. Everyone was dancing together in a big circle and there at the center of the circle, dancing up a storm, was none other than Secretary of State Madeleine Albright. It was like, "Go, Madeleine!"

"It was such a great party, just fabulous," Hillary says now.

That had to have been the best night ever at the White House. I'm sure we all enjoyed ourselves more than any group ever had in one night at the White House. We expected people to have a great time for a while and then get going, but no one wanted to leave. They couldn't get enough.

Hillary went up to bed around 3 A.M., and the President followed about forty-five minutes later. Very late, around 5 A.M., I started talking to a guy wearing a black fedora so big it almost looked like a cowboy hat.

"What's your name?" I asked him.

"Slash," he said.

"And what do you do?" I asked.

"I'm with Guns N' Roses," he said.

"Never heard of them, but great to have you at the party," I said.

The White House Marine Guards normally have a tasteful and subtle way of closing in on guests to let them know when it's time to leave. By 6 A.M. that morning, all subtlety was gone.

"Sir, I know you're the President's friend," a Marine Guard told me. "But it's time to go."

As Dorothy and I walked out the White House gates, I felt like I needed to pinch myself, a kid from Syracuse welcoming in the new Millennium at a White House dinner, seated at the President's table, my children watching the fireworks sitting on the President's lap, dancing with the First Lady and Chelsea, and rubbing shoulders with icons of American culture that I'd only read about. What a great country.

19

★ ★ ★

Once we moved into 2000 the top priority was to get Al Gore elected President. My relationship with the Vice President had come a long way in seven years. Since I was never a lobbyist, I had never even set foot in Gore's Senate office. In 1988, we'd actually been on opposite sides of the fence when I was Dick Gephardt's finance chairman and Gore was our rival. I really didn't know Al Gore when he was elected Vice President. However, we soon had a chance to work closely together. I spent more time with Al Gore than I did with my own wife in 1993, when I was chairman of the Business Leadership Forum, doing dozens of events with him all over the country to bring in young entrepreneurs as new supporters of the party.

With Gore it was always about the work at hand and I admired that in him. I found him to be extremely bright. It was obvious to me that he loved governing more than he loved politics and he would have been a spectacular President. Gore had a reputation for being stiff, and sometimes he poked fun at himself over that, but I found him anything but stiff with his quick wit and great sense of humor. He could be very sarcastic and had a dry, deadpan delivery that cracked me up. Half the time I would have no idea if he was goofing on me or not.

"Are you serious?" I always had to ask him.

Bill Clinton respected Al Gore tremendously, especially his intelligence and knowledge, and gave him important areas to focus on, like downsizing government, the environment, and Russia, knowing Gore would do a magnificent job. Going into 2000, Clinton had a long list of priorities, with lasting Middle East peace and a breakthrough with North Korea's totalitarian government ranking high, but I guarantee nothing was as important to him as helping Al Gore get elected President. Clinton wanted Gore elected President more than oxygen itself. He knew a Gore administration would bring a continuation of his policies and would ensure that America was in good hands.

As we moved further into 2000, you could feel the dynamic in the White House shifting. The focus and attention were now all moving to the Vice President, and Clinton knew his final days were upon him. He agreed to make fun of himself in a hilarious satiric video for the White House Correspondents Dinner on April 29. The video showed a bored and lonely President wandering the halls of the White House complex, running after Hillary with a bag lunch she'd forgotten as she left for a day of campaigning, watching clothes tumble in the dryer, washing his presidential limousine, and giving an earnest press conference to an audience of one—putting to sleep the normally spry Helen Thomas. For the finale of the video, the President and I were filmed riding bicycles around the deserted hallways. He and I spent fifteen minutes riding back and forth for the camera, laughing at the absurdity of the scene. We were having such fun that even after we wrapped, the President wanted to keep riding.

"Hey, Mac, let's go for a spin around the whole complex," he said.

We raced down one long corridor, competing to see who could go faster and who could ring his bell louder. As we spun around a corner, we raced past six members of the Vice President's staff who had heard the commotion and interrupted their work on an important foreign-policy speech to come out and see what was going on. They had no idea we had been shooting a video, and they stood bewildered as the President and I sped by laughing. They figured that the President had lost his mind.

★

GORE CAME OUT of the 2000 primaries having spent all of his money fending off a primary challenge from Senator Bill Bradley. In early March, just after Super Tuesday, Gore became the nominee of the Democratic Party but had reached his spending cap and had no more primary money left to spend. That left only two avenues. One was the general election federal money, but that would not be available to Gore until he officially became the nominee at the L.A. convention on August 16. Therefore, the only entity that could spend money on his behalf was the Democratic National

Committee, but they were cash-strapped. We were faced with the doomsday scenario of our candidate not having money for more than five months during a critical phase of the election year at a time when the RNC was flush with cash.

The campaign needed someone to pull a rabbit out of a hat, basically. My old friend Tony Coelho had gone to work for Gore as campaign chairman in May 1999. He and Peter Knight, Gore's chief money man and confidant, approached me to ask if I would consider taking over the DNC. At this point I had way too many balls in the air and could not take that on as well, but I compromised and agreed to chair a major DNC fund-raiser to benefit the Vice President. I wanted to do an event that would not only break all financial records but would be fun and give Gore a real shot in the arm politically.

I moved into DNC headquarters for seven weeks to organize the event and borrowed the corner office of Ed Rendell, who was general chairman. The first day the staff came in and asked where I wanted to hold the event. They were a little worried I was going to go too big and recommend the Washington Hilton with its cavernous ballroom seating two thousand people.

Brian Hardwick, the finance director, mentioned that maybe we ought to choose a smaller venue, so the place would look packed. I smiled, nodded, and waited for him to finish.

"We are going to do it at the MCI Center," I said.

The finance staff was horrified. The MCI was the largest venue in Washington, home of the Capitals and the Wizards, and could easily seat 12,000.

"Why would you possibly want to do that?" the event planner Ellen Thrower asked me.

"Because it's the biggest place in town," I said.

People at the DNC were way too jumpy over recent fund-raising controversies and seemed almost to be bracing for failure. That wasn't my style at all. Our work was all about being patriotic and fighting for positive change in this country. I always told people, "If you haven't done anything wrong, you've got nothing to hide and nothing to worry about," and I lived that.

I spent seven weeks in Ed's office making more than two hundred calls a day from Monday to Friday. This was a real team effort. Peter O'Keefe, Brian Hardwick, and Penny Lee, a finance staffer, would have four phones going. They would make the calls, get people ready, and hand the phone over to me and I'd do my thing, keeping an eye on the easels we had placed around the room with key information. They wrote down the names of all the entertainers we'd lined up on one easel, since I'd never remember them on my own.

After a week or two of this I started to get punch-drunk and I'd throw in different names to keep it interesting, like, "We're going to have LeAnn Rimes, Sammy Davis Jr., and Lenny Kravitz!" None of my staff wanted to be the one to tell me that Sammy Davis Jr. had passed away ten years earlier.

Other easels had information about who I was calling and on one we kept a running tally of how much we had committed that day and our overall total. Every time someone made a commitment to give $250,000 or more, we rang the bell, which was so loud it could be heard everywhere on the third floor. Before long the excitement and enthusiasm that emanated from that corner office rubbed off on everyone in the building. People would pop their heads in all the time and just stare in amazement at us. They were too shy to come in and we almost never left, holing up in there all day long and having our breakfast, lunch, and dinner brought in. We started calling by 8:30 A.M. and didn't leave until 9 P.M., when most people on the West Coast had gone home.

When Ed Rendell came back to town, he was so gracious he used another office so we could keep up our prolific fund-raising in his corner office. He didn't want to interrupt this money machine, and we were glad we didn't have to move our bell and easels somewhere else.

Besides the daily calls, we also did warm-up sessions around the country—lunches or dinners where you give the pitch and try to get people to commit. One of my more memorable warm-ups was April 12 at the Westin Fairfax Hotel in Washington with the Vice President and twenty-five top donors. I showed up for the lunch and saw Kit Seelye of *The New York Times* and Ceci Connolly of *The Washington Post* waiting outside. One thing reporters were never allowed to do was to sit in on warm-ups. To some that was like putting a match to kerosene.

I said hello to Kit and Ceci on my way in.

"Can we come in?" they asked me.

"Sure, why not?" I said. "I've got nothing to hide."

Jenny Backus, the DNC press secretary, immediately whispered in my ear that reporters weren't allowed in warm-up meetings.

"They may not be in yours, but they are in mine," I said.

Ceci and Kit were amazed they were allowed to stay and so was everyone else. I stood up to welcome everybody.

"Ladies and gentleman, Mr. Vice President, we have two very distinguished members of the press corps with us today, Kit Seelye and Ceci Connolly, and I want everybody around the table to introduce themselves now," I said.

"And when you introduce yourself, I want you to put the legislation on the table that you want passed. I want these guys to know everything."

Everyone broke out laughing, which really set the tone. My point was: We had nothing to hide. We had found out that the Republicans were having their own big event a few weeks before ours and knew we were going to have a blast contrasting ourselves with the posh, fat-cat Republicans. They were going to have a swanky black-tie event; we were going to have a blue-jeans bash. I went through my whole pitch at lunch, just the way I would with the donors if the press had not been there, and made jokes and kept everyone loose.

"The Republicans are going to have a beautiful black-tie event with candelabras and wine and champagne," I told Kit, Ceci, and the group around the table. "Ours is going to be a barbecue from Tennessee and Arkansas. We're going to be wearing casual clothes, no tuxedos. We want to celebrate what this administration has done."

Then I went around the table and gave all the donors my suggestions on how much they needed to raise. It was a total setup. I knew there was absolutely no way these donors would embarrass themselves by saying no to me in a small meeting with the Vice President sitting right there.

"Okay, Claire Dwoskin, how much are you going to raise?" I said. "You're in for five hundred."

And I wrote "500" for $500,000 in blue next to Claire's name on the seating chart.

"Tommy Boggs, you're in for five hundred. Mark Weiner, you're in for five hundred. Jody Trapasso, I'll put you down for five hundred. Carol Pensky, five hundred is easy for you. And John Merrigan, I'm embarrassed asking you for only five hundred, that's so easy for you. Alan Solomont, five hundred, you could do that in your sleep."

I ended up with around $7 million in commitments right there. The reporters were amazed at how open I was. Kit and Ceci were pool reporters that day and their dispatch began, "Your pool was welcomed with open arms by host Terry McAuliffe."

I welcomed other reporters with open arms, too. Different papers and news magazines had been asking if they could come in and actually sit right there while we made our fund-raising calls. That was something no reporter had ever been invited to do.

"Okay, let's get reporters in here," I said at a staff meeting. "If they want to come in and sit with us during our calls, let them come in."

All anyone could think to say was: "Are you insane?"

The move was not without risk, I'll admit, since you never know what a reporter is going to put in the paper. I didn't care. We had nothing to hide and we had excitement to sell. This was going to be an amazing event, unlike anything anyone had seen, and if that couldn't get them interested, nothing could. *The Washington Post,* the *Los Angeles Times,* and *Time* magazine all sent reporters.

"I want to ask you a question," I said on one call. "If the world blew up tomorrow, would you do five hundred?"

After only six weeks of call time the MCI Center was sold out. We ended up selling over 14,000 tickets and shut down all sales four days before the event. Believe me, I let everyone hear about it.

"We should have gone for RFK Stadium!" I said.

The best part of the *L.A. Times* article was right at the end where it said, "McAuliffe is completely unapologetic . . . he's proud to raise as much as he possibly can." They got that right!

The Republican event was scheduled for April 26, and here was the hilarious part: It was a black-tie event, but candidate George W. Bush had been tipped off that we were going to be mocking the Republicans and was so insecure about his preppy New England roots that he wore a suit so we wouldn't be able to get a picture of him all dressed up in black tie. Out of everyone at their event, he was the only one not in black tie. I hired a video crew and sent them over to get pictures of the Republicans stepping out of their limousines at their swank, hoity-toity event.

We worked hard and were able to line up an all-star list of talent: Lenny Kravitz, Stevie Wonder, Robin Williams, LeAnn Rimes, and Darius Rucker of Hootie and the Blowfish. As usual I didn't know who any of these people were, except Robin Williams, whom I'd met at Camp David. One unforgettable moment for me was my visit to the MCI Center two days before the event to meet all the entertainers who were there doing their sound checks.

Dana Milbank of *The Washington Post* was following me around the arena that day, and we went in to meet seventeen-year-old country singer LeAnn Rimes in her dressing room. I shook her hand and we were starting to talk when the door to the bathroom flew open and her boyfriend came walking out stark naked, fresh out of the shower, holding a towel.

I was taken a little aback.

"How are you, sir?" he said, sticking out his hand.

He wasn't fazed at all.

"I'm fine," I said. "How are you?"

LeAnn was called to do a sound check and the boyfriend, now wrapped in a towel, walked out with us. The boyfriend and I sat in the front row and Rimes was up there singing "Crazy" or "Your Cheatin' Heart" or something, and the boyfriend was kicking back enjoying himself. That towel wasn't covering much, I'll tell you, and the *Post* photographer was nosing around taking a few shots and I kept thinking: *If that photographer gets on stage and takes a picture of me and LeAnn's boyfriend sitting here, from that angle, I am RUINED.*

Next we went to meet Lenny Kravitz in his dressing room and he didn't have a shirt on either, just about six thousand nipple rings! I was at a rare loss for words thinking of all the pain those piercings must have brought him.

"You're the man," I told Lenny. "If you need me up on the mike, man, I'm ready."

"I'll let you know," Lenny told me.

★

THE REPUBLICANS HAD SET A RECORD of $21.3 million with their April 26 black-tie soiree and I was out everywhere on TV saying we were going to top that. Everyone could tell this was going to be huge and the media started picking up on the excitement. C-SPAN decided to cover the event live and one nightly news program called me "the Godzilla of fund-raising," which was a first. My kids loved that one. Three days before our May 24 gala event the *Drudge Report* splashed this headline at the top of its page: MCAULIFFE MIRACLE: CLINTON TO HOLD BIGGEST FUND-RAISER OF ALL TIME. We ended up raising $26.3 million that night, a record that I'm proud to say was exhibited at the Smithsonian Institution with a menu from the event.

One of our obvious worries the night of the event was staying on schedule. Any time you have Bill Clinton involved that's an issue. This time, though, Clinton arrived on time and was there in the building, so everything seemed fine. I was standing and talking to Hillary and Tipper outside the lounge where the President was waiting when it got to be time for him to come out with the Vice President to stand in a receiving line and pose for pictures with some of the guests.

No Bill Clinton. He had gone inside with Al Gore twenty minutes earlier and they were having a private conversation. The last thing I wanted to do was to bust in on them. There had been a lot of undue tension between them over the previous year following seven years of close partnership and meeting every week for lunch. This was the first time they'd had an extended private conversation in months. Finally, after half an hour I popped in on them and said it was time to go. Clinton said to give them a few more minutes. I gave it a while longer and then tried again. Same thing. They were huddled together, deep in conversation, and weren't budging.

"Hillary, we've got to get going," I said.

"You go do it," she said.

Eventually I went in and turned the lights on and off several times.

"Gentlemen, time to go," I said, stepping inside. "I've got fourteen thousand people outside waiting and we've already delayed our whole program forty minutes for the two of you. I'm not leaving until you get up."

My favorite part of the night was poking fun at the Republicans for their elitism. It was all too perfect. Our fourteen thousand guests were loading up their plastic plates with great down-home food flown up from Lindsey's Bar-B-Q in North Little Rock and Sims Barbecue in Little Rock, as well as Charlie Vergos's Rendezvous World Famous Bar-B-Q in Memphis. Makes me hungry just thinking about it now! We had almost fourteen thousand people in blue jeans, including the President and Vice President, and thirteen thousand of our guests that night paid just fifty bucks to get in, compared to a minimum of $1,500 at the Republican event. Our people sat down to eat on checkered picnic tablecloths with buckets of beer, just like we'd do it back home in Syracuse or anywhere else around the country.

"How many people here came to this event in a long, black, stretch limousine?" I bellowed from the podium.

"Who took the Metro? How many people took the bus?" I asked, and you'd have thought we were at a Capitals playoff game, the way the place roared.

"Who here is wearing a tuxedo?" I shouted.

I worked it like that for a while and said, "Let me show you how the Republicans did it last week."

Then on the big screen we rolled the footage of the Republicans getting out of their long, black, stretch limos in their tuxedos. It was so funny, we had everyone in the place laughing.

"And you know who we have performing tonight?" I yelled. "Lenny Kravitz and LeAnn Rimes."

That brought another huge round of cheering.

"And you know who they had?"

We had found a cheesy picture of KC and the Sunshine Band in the Oval Office with Richard Nixon and put that up on the screen. That got another great reaction as people laughed at the idea of a bunch of uptight Republicans in tuxedos dancing to "Shake Your Booty."

"Are you all enjoying your barbecue?" I asked.

They roared their appreciation of the food and then I read aloud from the menu of what the Republicans ate at their April 26 event.

"They had creamy goat cheese medallion baked in a sun-dried tomato bread. Horseradish-crusted filet of red snapper. Karnut and colusuri rices with wheatberry, whatever all that is. And orange meringue mirror cake."

I couldn't believe the Republicans had given me material that good to work with!

"In Syracuse, New York, where I grew up, Millie McAuliffe never made this kind of food," I told the crowd.

Everyone had such a blast that night and the event was such a success financially and politically, Gore came roaring out of the event. I walked the Clintons and Gores to their cars and Tipper told me she loved me and said, "I cannot thank you enough," and gave me a huge hug. I quickly turned around to see if Dorothy was looking.

We decided to take a few hundred of the staffers who worked on the event for a thank-you party at a sports bar called The Rock that would go until past 3 A.M., but before I left the MCI Center I saw Tony Coelho, who thanked me and also gave me a heads-up that I would be hearing from the Vice President about a job he wanted me to do. I didn't ask Tony what he was talking about and didn't want to know. I'd worked hard on that night's event and was going to enjoy its success.

"I want to thank the greatest fund-raiser in the history of the universe," the Vice President said that night.

That's quite a compliment, coming from the greatest Vice President in the history of the universe.

★

SOON AFTER THE MCI CENTER EVENT, Dorothy and I were over at the White House, playing cards with the President and Hillary until at least 1 A.M. We'd all had a good time at the blue-jean barbecue and were still talking about how much fun that had been and how we'd blown the doors off the Republicans' fund-raising record from the month before. We also talked about the latest news from the Gore campaign, which was going to name Bill Daley of Chicago as its new campaign chairman. Daley, part of the great political family, had been commerce secretary up until then. Daley would be a big help to Gore with his excellent political instincts, but Clinton was going to have to find a replacement for the commerce job, which was basically selling U.S. business worldwide.

"Mr. President, don't you think Terry should replace Bill Daley?" Dorothy said, surprising everyone.

"Darn right, Bill," Hillary said. "He'd be great. He can sell anything. He can sell ice to Eskimos. He should do it. He'd be the best."

Bill Clinton wasn't about to argue with both Hillary and Dorothy, and he joined right in, talking about what a good fit the job would be for me.

"Okay, great, I'm for Terry for secretary of commerce," he said.

I was all excited driving home that night with Dorothy thinking about being in Bill Clinton's cabinet as secretary of commerce, and was especially pleased by the prospect of not raising any more money. But early the next morning I got a call from John Podesta, the President's chief of staff.

"Terry, I hear you were up late with the boss," he said. "Listen, whatever the President wants, he gets. He's the President. But jeez, I don't know about sending the President's buddy and biggest fund-raiser in the party through a Senate confirmation hearing right before the 2000 presidential election. They are not going to confirm anyone political for this cabinet job. How about becoming ambassador to England or France?"

"Let me talk to Dorothy and get back to you," I said.

Dorothy and I hardly had to discuss it. We would both love the opportunity to serve in England if I was appointed ambassador to the Court of St. James. We thought it would be a great experience for the kids and only one other Irish-American, Joe Kennedy, had ever served as ambassador to the Court of St. James, so it would have been a big deal in Ireland, too. I was excited by the chance to bring the two countries closer together.

"All right, John, let's do England," I told Podesta the next day.

Podesta called Elaine Shocus, Madeleine Albright's deputy, and asked her to brief the Secretary that the President was going to send my name over as ambassador to the Court of St. James. There were concerns over at the State Department that with only seven months left in the administration, they could never get the paperwork done in time.

"Let me make this very clear," Podesta said in a follow-up call. "This is not a request. This is an order from the President of the United States."

The next day half a dozen FBI agents showed up at my door to start the vetting process and within three weeks the whole thing had been done and I was cleared in record time.

*

I FLEW OUT TO LOS ANGELES in early June as a favor to Tony Coelho and Marcia Hale during the time the FBI vetting process was underway. I knew they were having problems with the preparations for the Democratic National Convention that August in the Staples Center. They said they just wanted me to come out, have a look-see, and offer them some advice. My first meeting in L.A. was a breakfast with Henry Cisneros, the former HUD secretary, Roy Roemer, the former Colorado governor who was chairing the convention at that point, Lydia Camarillo, the convention's chief executive, Rod O'Connor, the chief operating officer, as well as Tony and Marcia.

At that point I was informed that the convention was in a real crisis. The Los Angeles host committee, which had promised funding for the convention, was at least $7 million short of what it had committed. We were looking at not being able to pay the workers to come in and get the Staples Center ready. It was so bad that Roy Roemer was looking at bailing on the convention to take one of the toughest jobs in America, running the L.A. schools. All through our breakfast meeting, Roy kept walking away from the table to take calls on his cell phone, trying not to be too obvious, but it gradually became clear what he was up to.

"Will you take the goddamned job, Roy, we're trying to have a meeting here?" Tony barked at Roemer after the fifth or sixth call.

Now I knew what this was all about. Roy was bailing and they were trying to get me to replace him. Little did anyone know that my future plans were not in L.A., but in England.

We left the breakfast and went over to City Hall for a meeting with the mayor, Richard Riordan. As soon as we all sat down at his coffee table, the mayor turned directly to me and said, "Terry, thank God you're here, you can raise the money. I've done all I can. I need your help."

Actually, the L.A. host committee hadn't done much of anything to close the cash shortfall, even though they had made all kinds of promises. Now everyone was trying to wash their hands of it.

"I'm just in a look and see mode, sir," I told the mayor. "I haven't agreed to anything."

I came out of that meeting knowing the L.A. convention was in a heap of trouble and flew home hoping that my ambassadorship would be done quickly before the Vice President called. Back in Washington, I ran into Haley Barbour, the former RNC chair, whom I considered a friend and admirable opponent. We didn't agree on politics, but I loved his Southern wit and always enjoyed bumping into him. I told Haley confidentially that Clinton was sending my name up to the Senate for confirmation as an ambassador and asked if he would talk to Senate Majority Leader Trent Lott on my behalf.

"You bet," he told me.

Two days later, Haley reported back to me that he had talked to Lott and I was in great shape.

"Bill Clinton is going to send their biggest money man out of the country before the election?" Lott had said. "Tell him I will walk the SOB to the airplane myself."

Unfortunately for me, my assistant, Alecia Dyer, came into my office three days later and told me that the Vice President was calling from Air Force Two. I was hoping he was calling to reminisce about the great MCI Event. My heart was pounding as I waited for Operator Two to connect us.

"Hello, Terry," Gore said.

"Hello, Mr. Vice President," I said.

"Great event the other night, Terry. Tipper and I loved it, and we can't thank you enough."

"Which barbecue did you like better, Arkansas or Tennessee?" I asked Gore.

"Well, Terry, I think the Tennessee barbecue was a little bit better."

"Thank you, sir," I said. "I really appreciate the call. I know how busy you are and I'll let you go, sir."

"Well, Terry, there's one other thing I need to ask you. Listen, we've got real problems in L.A. The city has not come up with the money that they committed and I need you to go out there and fix it and bring some enthusiasm. Will you go out to L.A. and chair the convention?"

"You bet, sir," I said. "I love L.A."

I hung up and knew I didn't dare call Dorothy, so instead I called Tony Coelho and told him he was a real jackass. There was no way I was going to say no to the sitting Vice President when he asked me to save his convention. As much as I wanted to go to England, I didn't hesitate. I was going to do what the Vice President wanted, no questions asked. We all owed it to Al Gore to do everything humanly possible to get him elected.

20

★ ★ ★

On June 13, Peter O'Keefe and I boarded United Airlines Flight 189 for my new home, Los Angeles. That first night I went to dinner at Spago with Lydia Camarillo, Rod O'Connor, and Tom O'Donnell, the deputy convention manager. I was going to do my best to overcome a bad situation and work up some enthusiasm here.

"Are you excited about the convention coming to L.A.?" I asked our waitress.

"What convention?" she said.

"The Democratic Convention is coming to L.A.," I said. "You didn't know?"

"No, I didn't hear anything about that," she said, taking our menus and leaving everyone trying to slink under the table.

"Well, that's why I'm here," I said. "Time for a change! They're going to hear about it now!"

My first day on the job was filled with meetings. I called a staff meeting to say that the time for worrying was over. The papers had been filled with articles talking about how the convention was in a real crisis and how money was going to be a huge problem. The staff was worrying about whether they were even going to get paid and I told them they could put all money concerns aside.

"That issue is off the table," I said. "We owe it to Al Gore to have a great convention. If we don't, that's our fault. It's time to stop wringing our hands and time to start kicking some ass!"

I called all the departments in one by one for hour-long meetings. My message was simple. This was going to be the greatest convention ever, I said. "Tell me how to do that." Conventions are a huge logistical challenge and I spent the time talking in detail with the people who worked on communications, community outreach, hall logistics, political affairs, credentials, hotels, transportation, and security and told them I didn't want to hear about problems, only about how to get this done and get it done right.

One of the key meetings was on the budget and I asked for an in-depth picture of where we were. They told me we were about $7 million down. If we could raise that much, we'd be able to hold the convention. If not, we were in real trouble. If we could raise $10 million, we could do all the little things that would help make it a great convention that people would be talking about for years. Then and there I knew we would just have to find a way to raise $10 million.

"What are our prospects of raising more money?" I asked the finance people. "The host committee is tapped out."

"Well, there are four letters of credit for a million dollars each," Rod O'Connor told me.

"Have they been called?" I asked.

He told me they had not been and I was aghast. A letter of credit was basically the equivalent of a check waiting to be cashed and we needed to find every dollar we could.

"You're telling me we have four million-dollar letters of credit," I said. "How could you possibly not call them?"

Rod said that one letter was from Mayor Richard Riordan himself and the three others were from three L.A.-based billionaires Riordan had brought in, promising them he would not pull the letters—Jerry Perenchio, chairman of Univision, and real-estate magnates Eli Broad and Ed Roski.

"I'll have to have a little talk with the mayor about this," I told the finance people.

I headed over to the Staples Center for a press conference announcing that they were officially handing us the keys to the place, which meant that for the next two months we owned it. Starting that day, we could go in and start laying the 1.5 million feet of cable the convention would require. For weeks there had been all this alarmist publicity about what a disaster our finances were and the press conference was jammed with reporters eager to follow up on that story. So what did I say? Did I pass on the bad news I'd been given about us being $7 million in the hole? Did I try to play down expectations? That has never been my style.

"Money will not be an issue," I declared after I was introduced as the new convention chair. "We will have the money we need in three or four weeks. I'm here to be a cheerleader and make sure we put on the best convention ever seen."

I took the money issue on directly right away and moved on to talking about the convention and how great it was going to be for Al Gore. The reporters were skeptical, but they had to admit I had credibility on the issue of raising money. I had just pulled off the $26.3 million MCI Center event, which was in every paper, including the *Los Angeles Times*, which had recently profiled me. I didn't like the press we'd been getting in L.A. and I decided to head over to the *L.A. Times* offices as part of my major press offensive the next week.

"I think your coverage has been unfair," I told the editors who met with me. "I read all the clips and I think the press has been awful."

My argument was that the convention was good for L.A. Wasn't it in everyone's interests to focus on the positives associated with this great event? I also met with some individual reporters and talked to them about the work we were doing and how high we were going to aim.

I went to see Ron Burkle my first week in town to ask for his help. Ron, a self-made Southern California billionaire, had helped us often before.

"Ron, I need a million," I said.

"Well, have you called in the letters of credit?" he asked me.

I had to admit that we had not done that yet.

"Ron, I'm having lunch with the mayor tomorrow," I said. "I'm going to tell him that I'll give him a week. Unless he can put a financial plan in front of me that makes sense, I'm going to pull the letters of credit."

"Come see me after you call the letters," Ron said.

I was still amazed at the idea that the DNC had committed to L.A. with only $4 million in letters of credit and no rock-solid guarantees from the city. I would never have agreed to that deal and never would agree to something like that in the future, no matter how attractive the city.

I went over to meet Mayor Riordan for lunch the next day at the Pantry, a restaurant he owns downtown. Riordan had been along on that fantastic trip to Ireland in 1995 and he was a great guy, always fun to be around. But we had some tough business to discuss.

"Listen, Mayor, I've got to call those letters of credit," I said.

"Terry, you can't," he said. "These are my friends. I told them the letters wouldn't be called."

"My whole approach to fund-raising is you honor your commitments," I said. "I have no option. I'll give you a week."

We needed action. We now had the keys to the Staples Arena and had to get to work setting up for the convention. The workers had to reroute power. They had to cut through concrete. The contractors were reading in the papers every day that we were broke and they wouldn't work for free. The only thing standing between us and a solution was those letters of credit. Once we had the $4 million, the rest would be easy.

I'd given Mayor Riordan a deadline and by that Friday at two o'clock it had been a week. The office was abuzz with people wondering if I'd really do it. I called Rod O'Connor into my office right at two.

"Has any money come in from the mayor's office?" I asked him.

It had not.

"Call the bank," I said. "We're calling the letters of credit."

While Rod called the bank to execute the $4 million and have it transferred to our accounts, I phoned up Roski, Broad, and Perenchio to tell them I was calling the letters. Those were some strange conversations. I'd never even met Roski and here I was telling him I was claiming a million dollars of his money. He was totally a class act about it and even made jokes.

"I'm sorry," I said. "I hate to be doing this to you, but it is what it is."

"That damn Riordan told me the host committee would have no problem raising the money and the letter would never get called," he said. "I'm not mad at you, Terry, but this is not what I bargained for."

By 2:14 we had the $4 million in our bank account and I called Ron Burkle right away to give him the news.

"Great, come on over to the house tonight," he said.

"Anybody else you got?" I asked.

"I've got a friend of mine named Steve Bing," he said. "I'll bring him over tonight and have you give him the pitch."

We were sitting there at Ron's house and he handed me his check for a million dollars. About thirty minutes later a guy in his thirties walked in wearing ripped-up old jeans and a T-shirt with holes in it. I was thinking: *Who is this guy? Was he out cleaning Ron's yard up? Or is he the pool man?* I went ahead and gave the pitch anyway and told this nice guy in jeans that Ron was giving me a million.

"All right, I'll help you out," he said.

Then he pulled a crumpled check out of his jeans pocket, unfolded it, and had to rub his hand over it a few times to get it straightened out enough to write on.

Ron was watching me and cracking up and this Steve Bing started writing "Democratic National Convention Committee" and "$1,000,000." I was thinking: *Is this thing gonna clear?* Later I found out that Bing was a producer and real-estate developer who was one of the wealthiest men in California.

That was quite a day. We raised $6 million that Friday and it wasn't even that hard. That was the turning point. Once we had the $6 million, I had all the momentum on my side and I knew another money crisis had been averted. We raised another $4 million over the next two weeks and I could concentrate on getting Los Angeles excited about hosting a convention.

On the Sunday before the convention opened, Barbra Streisand hosted a brunch for the Clinton Library at her beautiful home in the Malibu hills overlooking the Pacific Ocean. She was one of the party's greatest supporters, giving concerts for us all over the country. The President loved Barbra, who had become close friends with Clinton's mother, Virginia, phoning her every week up until her death in January 1994. Barbra agreed to host the event and all the preparations were coming along great until we ran into a small problem. Barbra did not like dogs. In fact, she did not want any dogs on her property, not even the Secret Service's bomb-sniffing dogs, which always had to do a once-over of any place at which the President appeared. The Service told me in no uncertain terms that unless the dogs were allowed to do their job, the President was not setting foot on this property.

I met with Barbra in her living room along with her husband, James Brolin, and political adviser, Marge Tabankin.

"We have to let the bomb-sniffing dogs on the property," I said.

"It's not happening," Barbra said. "No dogs are coming on my property."

"Let me make it simple: No dogs, no Bill Clinton," I said. "Please, Barbra. This is important to the President for his library and his legacy. This is the morning of the event. We can't change it now."

She kept arguing, talking about how the dogs were going to get into her shrubs, which she meticulously maintained herself.

"I'll walk around with the dogs and make sure everything is fine," I offered.

"Okay," Barbra finally said, reluctantly. "But I'm going to hold you responsible."

I went out and did my best to observe the dogs in action, but they moved around fast and I wasn't going to start running. Later, I was in the big tent we'd set up, checking on some things, when I heard Barbra screaming my name. I walked out into her beautiful garden to see what the commotion was all about.

"Look at what I stepped in!" she said.

It was a huge property and the one time in her life that Barbra let some dogs roam her property, she ended up stepping in the one place she shouldn't have. She kept looking down at her expensive-looking shoes and I kept laughing.

"I'm sorry, this is pretty funny," I said. "You've got to admit this is funny, Barbra."

"You have a weird sense of humor," she said.

I offered to buy her a new pair of shoes, no matter what the price tag, and luckily that bill never came. Barbra recovered quickly and could not have been a more gracious hostess, and we had a great event for the President's library.

I could never stop thinking about that Spago waitress who didn't even know there was going to be a Democratic Convention in town that summer. I wanted everyone to know we were there and I figured that was going to require me to do something that would have everyone talking. I wanted to jump out of an airplane and parachute down to our press conference the week before the convention opened. Compared to alligator wrestling, skydiving seemed about as dangerous as shuffleboard. But the lawyers were worried about the risks so instead I decided I would try surfing. I went out and bought a wetsuit and practiced and on August 10 I went out with a whole bank of cameras on me and was able to stand up on the board, which is harder than it looks. Pictures of me surfing made it on TV and in the papers and sent the message I wanted: We were having fun with this convention.

★

As we counted down to the final days before the convention, we no longer had to worry about money or about drumming up enthusiasm, which was now in full swing. The nightmare that had us worried was security. We had weekly meetings with the Los Angeles Police Department and the U.S. Secret Service, and they kept alarming us with predictions that protesters were going to be out in full force trying to mar or destroy the convention.

"Chief, I want you to keep in mind that the second you start pulling out billy clubs and firing off tear gas and charging the protesters, that's how this convention will be remembered," I told the chief of police, Bernie Parks.

My security team spent months putting together a very detailed plan, which called for establishing a no-protest zone around the Staples Center. Nine months earlier at a WTO meeting in Seattle, anarchists and anti-globalization protesters had shown up by the tens of thousands and basically taken over the city. We couldn't afford to let that happen in L.A. It would be the 1968 Chicago Convention all over again. Our security plan was overturned in court, however, for restricting protesters' access. Our argument was that the protesters had every right to be there, but they didn't have to be interfering with the ingress and egress of our nearly five thousand delegates. Unfortunately, Judge Gary Feess had a different view and declared the plan unconstitutional, requiring us to allow the protesters right next to the Staples Center. It was crazy. All the delegates coming in were going to have to walk right by a mob of screaming protesters standing only fifty feet away.

"Why doesn't the judge just give all the protesters credentials and let them come inside the Staples Center?" I told one TV interviewer.

After seven weeks of frantic preparation the details were all in place for us to put on a great convention. We'd reached out to the different communities of Los Angeles through the press and had sent thousands of people out to do public-service events. There wasn't a waitress anywhere in L.A. who didn't know the Democratic Convention was about to open.

A police cruiser picked me up on Monday, August 14, for the ride down to the Staples Center for the opening of the convention and I could finally sit back and take some satisfaction in how well all our plans had come to fruition. Everything was set up for Al Gore's convention to be such a success, the Vice President would come flying out of the convention like a turbocharged booster rocket. What a day it was going to be for Al Gore, for the Democratic Party, and for me and my family. It was my duty to gavel open the convention, but I'd asked for a little help with that job.

My daughters, Dori and Mary, and son Jack came up to the podium with me for the big ceremony and they gaveled open the 2000 Democratic National Convention as I stood nearby beaming. I remember looking up at my sky box and seeing my father looking down at us, along with Dorothy, her father Richard, and dozens of other McAuliffes packed into that box. Dorothy said it was one of the proudest and happiest moments of her life.

Everyone knew the convention had been in trouble and I was brought in to save it, and now, working with a great convention team, we had everything in place for a spectacular four days. However, the greatest applause for my speech came at the end when I turned my focus on George W. Bush's ideas and policies, and talked about how the Republicans had used their convention in Philadelphia to pretend they were Democrats. "Governor Bush sure delivered a pretty speech," I said. "But it reminded me of a Texas longhorn: two points with a lot of bull in between."

I finished up and waved to my family and then took my spot up on the podium where I would spend the next four days. I was at the center of the action with a bank of phone lines and television monitors to keep track of everything. Sitting just to my left was the producer who controlled everything that happened on the podium from dimming the lights to cranking up the music. He relayed all the signals.

★

OUR BIG WORRY INSIDE was staying on schedule and that first day a large group of women candidates for the U.S. Senate had such a good time up at the podium, they ended up going thirty minutes too long. We were half an hour behind schedule and the President was scheduled to be the last speaker that night. If he went on late, there was a risk that the networks would cut away when it got to be eleven o'clock East Coast time, or eight o'clock in California.

Doug Band, the President's aide, came up on the podium, tapped me on the shoulder, and said the President urgently wanted to see me. I went downstairs to the room where the President was waiting with Hillary and Chelsea, and the feeling in the room was tense. The President was mad because one of his staff had told him that the Vice President's people were intentionally slowing down the schedule so that Clinton would get pushed back and knocked out of prime time.

This was typical. Throughout the entire campaign there had been constant bickering and back-stabbing back and forth between the staffs of the Vice President and the President.

"Mr. President, that's flat-out false," I told Clinton. "Whoever is telling you that is lying to you. Once again someone on your staff is trying to create issues that do not exist."

Standing with the President, I immediately called Rod O'Connor and he checked with the TV networks, then got back to me and said they assured him they would honor their commitment to stick with the President to the end of his speech, which they did.

I passed on what Rod said to the President and that lightened up the mood. I made a point of sitting down there with the President, Hillary, and

Chelsea for a good fifteen minutes, joking around and sharing a few laughs. I was needed up on the podium, but nothing was more important right then than having Bill Clinton in a great mood. He needed to give a great speech and I wanted him upbeat and positive. I left the Clintons and walked back up to the podium shaking my head and thinking: *We are our own worst enemies. The foolishness we have to put up with! Here we are trying to win the presidency and our own people are trying to sabotage us!*

Back up on the podium, I could feel the energy in the hall building as Clinton's entrance approached. I will never forget the surge of electricity and excitement when the big screens inside showed the President of the United States, Bill Clinton, walking confidently through the back-stage corridors on his way to entering the arena to raucous cheering. The applause was so loud and went on so long, by the time the President was up on the podium, it was as if waves were crashing all around us. Clinton bounced up onto the podium, and walked over and gave me a bear hug.

"Thank you," he told the crowd, trying to quiet them down, and the cheers kicked up even louder and chants of "Thank you, Bill!" rang out.

"America gave me the chance to live my dreams," Clinton said in his mesmerizing speech. "I have tried to give you a better chance to live yours. Now, with hair grayer and wrinkles deeper, but with the same optimism and hope I brought to the work I love eight years ago, my heart is filled with gratitude."

Clearly the President gave one of the great speeches of his life and it was a powerful endorsement of Al Gore and what he could do for the American people as President.

About thirty minutes into Clinton's speech the red light on one of my phone lines started blinking and I began taking a series of frantic phone calls from Rod O'Connor up on the roof.

"Mr. Chairman, we've got a full-blown riot about to break out here," he said. "We can't let the delegates out."

A band called Rage Against the Machine, whose last CD was called *The Battle of Los Angeles,* had whipped the crowd of well over ten thousand into a frenzy, and incited them against the police. Almost all the protesters were there to hear the music and demonstrate peacefully, but a small group of maybe a hundred were hard-core anarchists looking to trigger a confrontation between the police and the crowd of people. The ten-foot-high fence that prevented the demonstrators from converging on the Staples Center was rocking and shaking as people pressed up against it, and the police were not sure it would hold. Some of these lunatic anarchists were using big slingshots to fire rocks and chunks of concrete and glass at the police as well as balloons and bottles filled with ammonia, bleach, and urine. The police fired pepper spray, which wafted over the crowd.

This had all the earmarks of a disaster waiting to happen. Clinton's speech was almost over and once he finished, the plan was to open the doors to the Staples Center and send people streaming outside, where it looked like they were going to step right into a full-fledged melee. None of our options looked good. The Staples Center had 160 glass doors and there was no way we could have locked them all, even if we wanted to try to keep a crowd of 25,000 bottled up. If we let them out in the middle of a fracas, and the police were out clubbing protesters or firing tear gas, we could be sure that both the Democratic Party and the Los Angeles Police Department would get hammered in the press, drowning out the message of our convention.

The police had moved in some SWAT units to exert some control, but a protester had thrown a homemade smoke bomb, which left a cloud of orange smoke hanging over everything and led to false reports in the press that tear gas had been used. We talked it over, all while Clinton was still up on stage finishing his speech, and decided our only hope was to stall. We had to extend the program to keep everyone occupied. When the President finished his speech and started making a brief circuit around the stage before he left, he looked over at me and I gave him a hand signal to keep circling. Always a pro, he didn't waste any time trying to figure out what was wrong, but followed my cue and salvaged the situation. He kept circling and the music kept playing and the crowd inside loved it.

Another red light blinked on my phone console. It was Bernie Parks, the chief of police.

"We're going in with the horses," he told me.

"Do what you have to do, Chief," I said. "Get order out there."

The police sent in a squad on horseback and they quickly started to restore some order. People saw those big horses coming at them and turned and ran away from the area around the Staples Center. The police focused on the small group of anarchists instigating the confrontation, but it was still too hot a situation out there, so I gave Clinton more hand signals to take more laps. "Keep circling, Mr. President," I said. He started to give me puzzled looks, letting me know he was more than ready to leave. After twenty minutes the police had dispersed the crowd, which was running all over downtown.

We wrapped up the program and delegates streamed for the exits and by then, only fifteen minutes after we were on the brink of bedlam, it was calm and peaceful out there and no one knew a thing about how close we had come to a reprise of Chicago in '68. We were all relieved beyond words. We knew we had dodged a bullet. Naturally some in the press wondered afterward why the President stayed up on the stage so long. Some papers mentioned the protest briefly, but few explored it at length, and to this day many people who saw Clinton speak that night have no idea of what was going on outside at the time.

Once we were past the worries of a full-fledged riot on our opening night, I could enjoy myself and have a great time all week, which I did with the help of dozens of McAuliffes who had flown in for the convention. All over town you had McAuliffes—and people claiming to be McAuliffes—squeezing into parties and events. From my spot at the podium I could see more than fifty private boxes and of all of them one stood out as always being the loudest, most crowded, and most wild. That was the McAuliffe box, of course. Jay Leno even did his show from my box one night. My family made so much noise that on two nights in a row the fire marshal shut the box down, putting someone at the door and not letting anyone else inside. I was the only one with a fire marshal permanently placed outside the door of my box.

While the President was still in town, we headed over to Paramount Studios for an event. I was up in the police vehicle and behind us was a whole car load of McAuliffes being driven by my nephew Matt in a big white Cadillac. Matt's older brother Ryan kept complaining about his driving and yelling at him to drive faster to keep up with us. Finally Matt had enough. When they stopped at a light, both doors flew open and they switched places. Now Ryan was driving and not five minutes later when my car stopped at a light, Ryan hit the brakes too late and rammed into us with the big white Caddy. The hood was scrunched into an upside-down V, and smoke was billowing out of where the grill used to be. We pulled up to the front of Paramount and the Secret Service agents waved me to park over by the President's limousine. As we stepped out, the busted-up white Caddy pulled up and parked right near the presidential limo, spewing smoke.

"Here come the Clampetts!" I said.

*

I LOVED MY SPOT on the podium and the unique perspective it gave me on the parade of speakers stepping forward to talk about what a great President Al Gore was going to be. One of the high points was the keynote address on Tuesday night, delivered by the young Congressman Harold Ford Jr., a friend of Al Gore's from Tennessee whose father had represented the same district for twenty-two years and whose family had been prominent in Memphis's African-American community for decades. Harold was only thirty years old at the time but he was composed and eloquent and talked about meeting Al Gore years ago in Memphis and deciding to make him his role model.

We Democrats are proud of our history of representing all Americans, not only elite East Coast families like the Bushes, and the convention was really rocking on Wednesday night when Senator Joe Lieberman stepped to the podium as our nominee for Vice President. From my first days as a fund-raiser for Jimmy Carter, some of the closest friendships I formed were with prominent Jewish Americans, and I couldn't have been prouder that we were making history by putting a Jewish American on the ticket for the first time in U.S. history.

No one expected to see Al Gore on the podium that night, a day before he gave his big speech bringing the convention to its emotional climax, but he was so close to his daughter, Karenna Gore Schiff, he couldn't resist coming out and giving her a hug after she formally nominated him for President.

The fun of the convention is the way everything builds toward the last night when your nominee speaks. This was why we were all there: to nominate the next President. Al Gore is an excellent writer, a former reporter for the *Tennessean* in Nashville, and he wrote his speech himself, working through dozens of rounds of revisions with his staff. He knew he needed a great speech and it was just like Al Gore to work so hard and put so much of himself into composing a masterpiece.

Tipper Gore came up onto the podium to introduce her husband and showed off a series of great pictures from the Gore family photo album, which was the perfect way to set up Gore's speech. He came out to a huge ovation, rising to the moment just the way I knew he would, and talked about the importance of family in his life, starting with the example set by his father, Senator Al Gore Sr.

"My father respected my mother as an equal, if not more," the Vice President said. "She was his best friend and in many ways his conscience and I learned from them the value of a true, loving partnership that lasts for life. . . . My parents taught me that the real values in life aren't material but spiritual. They include faith and family, duty and honor, and trying to make the world a better place."

As the Vice President spoke, the crowd waved blue-and-white GORE signs and chanted, "Go, Al, go!" Watching from the podium, it was thrilling to watch this man capping a life of public service by showing the nation how ready he was to be President of the United States.

"I know my own imperfections," Gore said late in his speech. "I know that sometimes people say I'm too serious, that I talk too much substance and policy. Maybe I've done that tonight. But the presidency is more than a popularity contest. It's a day-by-day fight for people."

Up on the podium I was thinking, *He's done it. Al Gore has given the speech of his life. This man is going to be the next President.* He had convinced whatever skeptical Americans that might still have been out there that he had what it takes to be President.

I'd been saying for eight weeks that this was going to be a great convention, and in the end it was clearly one of the greatest conventions of all time. It was fun and positive and upbeat, we got our message across beautifully, and the public responded. We'd faced a potential train wreck with the convention, given the early worries about the finances, but we had scored big where it mattered: The Vice President got a double-digit bounce in the polls, riding a wave of support from independents, and came out of the convention leading Bush 48–42 in a *Newsweek* poll and 50–45 in an ABC News poll.

21

★ ★ ★

Bill Clinton and I went golfing the last Saturday in October, just nine days before the election. We teed off at 3 P.M. and it was a beautiful fall afternoon with the sun out, the sky clear and crisp, and the leaves falling off the trees and gathering in yellow and orange piles. Neither of us wanted to talk about politics and focused on enjoying our round, but as we were stepping up to the eighteenth tee, the shadows lengthening so late in the afternoon, the President put his tee in the ground and then looked up at me.

"Mac, what the hell am I doing golfing with you today?" he said. "This is the first time in twenty-five years I haven't been out campaigning on the last two weekends before the election."

That's a question I still can't answer. Some of Gore's advisers had made the argument that having Bill Clinton out campaigning would be a negative. What I could never grasp was why they would want to run away from the Clinton-Gore partnership, which brought us the largest peacetime economic expansion in U.S. history. More millionaires and billionaires were created under Clinton and Gore than at any other time in history, and more people moved out of poverty. Everybody benefited. Nobody was upset about the direction of the country, but Gore's advisers urged him to run a populist, us-versus-them campaign. Which made me ask: *Who was us and who was them?*

The Democrats had made the tough choices to balance the budget, create surpluses, and energize the economy, creating a record 22 million new jobs. All the Republicans could offer was their trickle-down economics and out-of-hand deficit spending. Gore's campaign should have been centered on his eight years as the most effective Vice President in U.S. history. By not highlighting the Clinton-Gore record, the campaign cleared the way for Bush, a failed businessman and political lightweight, to run as a peace-and-prosperity candidate.

Not using Clinton also created a negative image for the Gore campaign. The decision raised questions about why Clinton was being held at arm's length, which opened the door for Bush to run as a so-called compassionate conservative who would restore dignity and honor to the White House. Monday morning quarterbacking is easy. However, I find it hard to believe that having Bill Clinton out there would not have garnered us 7,211 more votes in New Hampshire or 537 more votes in Florida. Either of those states was enough to put Gore over the top in the Electoral College. Or how about if Bill Clinton spent the last two weeks campaigning for Gore in his home state of Arkansas? That right there would have done it. All the talk was of swing voters, but they forgot that George W. Bush was at least as controversial a figure as Bill Clinton was. Bush fired up his own base and got them to come out and vote. If you forget your base and worry only about the swing voters, you're in trouble.

★

THE CLINTONS ENJOYED THEIR TIME in Syracuse so much the previous summer, they decided to go back two weeks after the Democratic Convention in L.A. There wasn't much time for relaxation with Hillary in the middle of a tough Senate campaign against Rick Lazio, the Long Island congressman who got into the race for the Republicans late after Rudy Giuliani backed out. We knew the Clinton-bashing Republicans were going to spend buckets of money against Hillary, since they were all deathly afraid of her unlimited potential in politics. Hillary would have to run a disciplined campaign and she would have to fight back hard against Republican attacks even as she was showing she was having a great time out with the people of New York.

Duke Kinney was hosting another event for Hillary at his house and before the First Lady arrived, I walked over to the neighbor's yard where several dozen reporters covering the event were positioned. That week Lazio had visited the New York State Fair and was offered a sausage sandwich at the stand set up by the Dinosaur Bar-B-Que—a Syracuse landmark—loaded up with Gianelli Sausage, which was headquartered in Syracuse.

Lazio, for reasons unknown to anyone, begged off, saying he didn't eat sausage sandwiches. They were "so-so," he said. Or maybe they weren't on his Pritikin Diet.

Talk about a political faux pas! Guys in bars all over Onondaga County asked each other: What kind of *girly-man* doesn't eat a sausage sandwich?

"How about that Rick Lazio?" I called out to the mob of reporters. "Can you believe he came up here and wouldn't eat a sausage sandwich at our state fair?"

I pulled Hillary aside as soon as she arrived at Duke's, and talked to her about her visit to the fair the next day.

"Hillary, the one thing you need to do tomorrow is eat a sausage sandwich and drink a beer."

"Great," she said, "I love sausage sandwiches and I'd love to have a beer."

The next day Hillary and the President went out and gobbled down big old sausage sandwiches loaded with onions, looking happy as clams, and everyone was talking about it. That was a big story to people in Syracuse, who all loved Gianelli Sausage. Lazio got killed on that one and this was the funniest part: He actually had to go back to the fair and eat a sausage, which just made him look desperate after "realizing the error of his regional heresy," as the *Syracuse New Times* put it.

Hillary and Lazio were actually neck and neck in the polls, but I knew she'd take him in the end. It might be a nail-biter, but she would win. Once she and the President stood there grinning and chomping down sausage sandwiches, it really freed Hillary to connect with those voters in places like Syracuse. She did her homework on issues that mattered upstate and talked to people to hear what was on their minds and as a result she had a clear edge over Lazio, who did not. During a September 13 debate in Buffalo moderated by Tim Russert, Lazio blundered and claimed that the upstate economy had "turned the corner," which wasn't how the people who lived there saw it.

The race kept getting more expensive all the time and we had some very tense finance meetings. I love Hillary because of her toughness and her big heart, the qualities that would make her a great President. What I'd always known but discovered anew during the Senate campaign was that Hillary was also a world-class worrier when it came to money. She and her husband were totally different that way. He knew when he had a problem relating to money, but never dwelled on it, figuring a solution would always present itself, which it did. She worried to death. She worried about each and every expenditure. She had never raised money for herself before and had trouble taking anything on faith.

"Hillary, please quit worrying," I told her at one point. "You're driving me crazy. It's going to be done."

"I know, I know," she said, almost apologetically. "That's just who I am."

We gathered in a suite at the Waldorf in New York for a finance meeting on September 8, and Hillary was upset about the state of her fund-raising. Lazio had raised around $10 million in August alone and she knew she had to be able to answer his attack ads with her own TV buys or she was in trouble. Clinton was talking about some of the world leaders he'd met in New York that week during his last set of UN meetings as President and I was briefing him on my meeting that morning with President Pervez Musharraf of Pakistan. Hillary had heard enough of our global discussion and cut us off.

"We're here to talk about fund-raising," she said. "Lazio is raising more than we thought. Terry, how are we going to fix this?"

"We need to raise another two million over the course of the next month," I said.

"Don't worry, Hillary. Terry and I will take care of it," the President said.

"You bet, sir," I said, knowing full well that meant that I had to be making all the phone calls.

"Terry, can I go ahead and spend this money?" Hillary asked me.

"You bet," I said.

I love the fiery side of Hillary's personality and political style. You just do not mess with this woman. If you take a swing at her, she keeps her balance, steps out of the way, and then whacks you back harder. Most important, she didn't run from the Clinton record. She was proud and she let it show, ripping into Lazio when he tried his tired old Washington Republican rhetoric on the people of New York, who saw right through it.

"My opponent goes around saying, 'Eight years is enough,'" Hillary said on October 22. "The first time I heard it, I thought, well, maybe I had misheard. Eight years of a great economy. Eight years of declining crime rates. Eight years of improving education scores. Eight years of expanding health care. Where is he living and who is he representing?"

★

GEORGE W. BUSH BASED HIS CAMPAIGN on a series of staggering falsehoods. His game plan seemed to be to tell such whoppers, the press would be too embarrassed to call him on it. This was a man who was geared up to take a bull in the china shop approach to governing and called himself a uniter, not a divider. He ran as an outsider, even though he was the son of a President. Gore cleaned Bush's clock in the debates, which I'd attended, but because of the Republican spin machine, all anyone wanted to talk about was Al Gore sighing. The press jumped on the Vice President for being too aggressive and feisty, so he toned it down and they ripped him for being too passive. A round of polls that came out just before Election Day showed that by a wide margin voters thought the Vice President was more prepared, more intelligent, and had more experience than candidate Bush. Yet Bush held a slight edge in all the polls.

We were in some ways victims of our success. Bill Clinton had improved the lives of all Americans across the board and as a result people felt more complacent about politics. People weren't interested enough to pay close attention. As a result, they let the press steer them toward turning it into a personality contest between Gore, whom the press mostly didn't like, and Bush, whom the press at that time actually thought they liked. The whole thing became: Whom would you rather sit down and have a beer with? We needed to remind people of how far we had come as a country in those eight years. If Gore had turned his campaign into a celebration of all that he and the President had accomplished for the country through their partnership, he would have won easily.

The egomaniac Ralph Nader exploited this feeling with a campaign that seemed designed to hand the election to Bush. I like independent-minded people and mavericks, and early on Nader's third-party candidacy seemed harmless enough. As Election Day approached it became clear that in places like Florida and New Hampshire, Nader would siphon votes away from Gore and potentially tip those states toward Bush. Nader had become George W. Bush's best friend, and had signed himself up for a lifetime of responsibility for whatever Bush did if he won.

I woke up on Election Day wishing we could get it over with right then and there. I knew Gore deserved to win and felt sure he *would* win, but I knew it was going to be close. Dorothy and I flew down to Nashville and watched the election results at the City Club on the top floor of the Sun Trust Building along with many of Gore's top supporters and friends. The anticipation was excruciating. We knew it would be a very tight race and a long night.

Early on we had great news from New York, where Hillary was elected senator by a wide margin, finishing with 55 percent of the vote to 43 percent for Lazio, thanks to her confounding the experts and winning upstate counties like Cayuga, Rensselaer—and Onondaga. "Sixty-two counties, sixteen months, three debates, two opponents, and six black pantsuits later—here we are!" Hillary told her supporters at the Grand Hyatt with the President nearby wiping away tears of joy.

In Nashville, we were all excited when first NBC and then the other networks called Florida for Gore just before 8 P.M. East Coast time, but after New Hampshire went red we knew the electoral-college math, and Florida was not enough to put us over the top. We needed a small western state, too. We agonized until around 10 P.M. when the unbelievable happened. The networks began pulling Florida back from Gore's column. We all stood around in shock for a while and sensed it was over. Devastated, we took the elevator down from the City Club and walked over to the War Memorial Plaza three blocks away in a light drizzle.

By the time we arrived in the square, where Gore was planning to make his concession speech, it was really pouring, and Dorothy and I actually considered skipping the speech and going back to the hotel. That was how depressed we were. However, we decided we would stand in the rain no matter how long it took. Al Gore deserved that after all he had put into his campaign.

It was a surreal scene out there and rumors started flying that the Vice President, who had already called George W. Bush to concede, was thinking about pulling back his concession. I'd never heard of *that* before, but I liked it! Gore was on his way to the square where we were standing and when he was two blocks away, Bill Daley took a call from Michael Whouley, Gore's national field director, telling him that the margin had shrunk from 50,000 votes to anywhere from 1,000 to a few hundred, so close that Florida law would require a recount. That was when Gore called Bush back and said in fact he was not conceding and told Bush not to get "snippy."

We were stunned, not knowing what to believe, and as I was standing there in the rain trying to figure out what to do next, one of Gore's press people came up and asked me to go on TV to say that the election was not over and we were not conceding.

"We've got to make sure this election is right," I told Tom Brokaw around 3 A.M. East Coast time. "There is all kinds of talk in Florida that several boxes were not counted down in Florida. . . . The word was out everywhere in the state of Florida that maybe the networks and some of the folks on TV called this election too quickly and that as the numbers got closer and closer and it got down to 1,000 or 600 votes, we needed to just step back a minute and to make sure that democracy was working correctly. . . . We want to make sure that all those votes are counted, because at the end of the day we know that when they're all counted Al Gore will be President of the United States of America."

We went back to our hotel and we all stayed up all night. It was like the

Twilight Zone as hundreds of us were milling around the lobby trying to grasp any tidbit of new information.

That Thursday night, two days after the election, the President and Hillary were hosting a reception honoring the two hundredth anniversary of the White House. If there was ever going to be a bipartisan event, this would be it. We were there to celebrate two hundred years of history and democratic tradition. The Clintons invited Lady Bird Johnson, Gerald and Betty Ford, Jimmy and Rosalynn Carter, and George and Barbara Bush. Former President Bush stopped by at one point and said hello.

"How are you doing, Mr. President?" I asked him.

"How do you think I am?" he said. "It's a disgrace what you're doing to my son."

"Mr. President, we're not doing anything to your son," I said. "Let's just count all the votes."

He walked off in a huff and I was surprised. I'd always liked Bush Senior. He was a good guy, easy to talk to, and even if we didn't agree on things, he was always nice to me.

*

EVERY TIME THE PRESIDENT leaves the White House, he's part of a huge motorcade with dozens of motorcycles and cars taking over the road. Now with Hillary elected to the Senate, the Clintons needed a Washington home. So later that month the President and Hillary slipped out in secret one Saturday morning to take care of some private business that they did not want publicized. Instead of the usual fifty-car motorcade, it was just two vehicles, a car for the Secret Service and the limo for Hillary, Dorothy, the President, and me. This was unprecedented and everyone at the White House went berserk once word hit that the Clintons were out in public practically on their own, but I tell you, we had a great time that day.

"We had never done it before, but it was getting toward the end of the term and we had to buy a house in Washington so we snuck out of the White House," Hillary says now. "We didn't know what house we were going to buy and we didn't want the press following along and kibitzing about which house we were going to choose."

We toured around with a real-estate agent looking at half a dozen houses, which of course had been vacated before we arrived. Hillary was negotiating her book deal for *Living History* by then but even with the millions that would bring in, finding a house in Georgetown can be a real challenge. We looked at one house in Georgetown that I liked and so did the Clintons. It was going for $4.5 million and right on a corner, which would have given the Secret Service fits.

"It was about half a square block with a walled garden," Hillary says now. "It was a beautiful house. If it had been one-third of what it was, I might have been able to swing it. But I'm really glad I didn't now because I would have been like the main tourist attraction in Georgetown and since you were close to the street, people would have been just hanging out on the sidewalk."

We toured five or six homes that day. Hillary and Dorothy would be walking around the house studying kitchens and stairways, and talking about moldings and closet space and northern-versus-southern exposure. The President and I would kind of wink at each other and go find the TV so we could sneak in a few minutes of watching college football. We weren't much help to Hillary, I'm afraid.

"That's right, you contributed nothing!" she says now, scolding playfully.

★

ONE THING ABOUT WASHINGTON RUMORS is they're like weeds, wild, annoying, and impossible to kill. The rumors about me taking over as DNC chair had been kicking around for months or years before there was anything to them. They kept up even after Dorothy danced with the President at that White House Christmas party and said, "Please don't do this to my husband, Mr. President." All through 2000 the rumors intensified and I still wasn't about to budge. For one thing, so long as they were counting votes in Florida and justice might be served, I knew my ambassadorship to the U.K. was still a distinct possibility. However, if the Republicans were successful in cheating the American people, and Bush became President, I was staying home.

Dick Gephardt invited me to lunch on December 4, and he and his aide Steve Elmendorf asked me to give serious thought to taking the DNC job. Dick's point was: We were going to have a huge job rebuilding if Bush ended up in the White House, and I was the man to do it.

"Listen, Dick, let's see what happens with Gore," I said. "I still think he will win."

I was set to fly over to Ireland with Clinton's traveling party again one week after I met with Gephardt, but first I agreed to sit down with Tom Daschle, the Democratic leader in the Senate. Dick had asked Daschle to talk to me about being DNC chairman and we discussed that for an hour, but

I remained noncommittal. John Sweeney, the AFL-CIO leader, also called me to ask for a meeting. Gephardt and Daschle had been in touch with Sweeney and other labor leaders, and they were all asking me to run.

"Let's wait and see where we are," I told John and the others. "I'm still counting on Al Gore to win this."

I talked to Minyon Moore, White House political director, and Steve Ricchetti, deputy chief of staff, to brief them on the conversations I'd had with Gephardt, Daschle, and Sweeney. I asked Minyon and Steve not to brief the President about these conversations, because I knew if he got wind of it, he'd be all for it and then I'd really be stuck.

Visiting Belfast with the President in 1995 had been an amazing, electric experience for all of us who were there with him. Five years later, he still had work to do in convincing everyone to stick with the momentum toward lasting peace gained by the Good Friday Agreement. The rock-star excitement he generated in Northern Ireland helped him get his message across.

I was there at the Odyssey Arena in Belfast for the President's speech on December 13 and the crowd of eight thousand started doing the wave to "Brown-Eyed Girl," sung by Van Morrison, who I found out was actually born in Belfast.

"We've still got problems and headaches," Clinton said. "In spite of the overwhelming support for the Good Friday Agreement and the evident progress already brought, opponents of peace still try to exploit the implementation controversies to rub salt in old wounds and serve their own ends."

The Supreme Court ruled that day that it was halting a recount of votes in Florida, in effect handing the White House to George W. Bush. I felt like I'd been punched in the stomach. The Supreme Court was installing George W. Bush as President on a five-to-four vote. This sounded like nineteenth-century Latin American politics, not American democracy.

Just after he gave the speech, I told the President I needed to talk to him in private. He and Hillary were heading to Chequers, the prime minister's country retreat, for dinner that evening with Tony Blair and his wife, Cherie, and I knew I needed to catch Clinton before that. The President and I walked under some bleachers to talk privately and touched on the Supreme Court decision, then I quickly got to the point. I told Clinton about Dick Gephardt and Tom Daschle putting pressure on me to run for DNC chair and said that after this obscene Supreme Court decision, it was time to fight back and build for the future and I wanted to be in the middle of that fight.

"Mac, please do it," the President said.

"Let's give it a couple days and see what happens," I said. "I'll talk to you back in Washington."

Back in Washington the next day, I went to the AFL-CIO headquarters on Sixteenth Street and met with John Sweeney, AFL-CIO president; Andy Stern, president of SEIU; Gerry McEntee, president of AFSCME; and Steve Rosenthal, the AFL-CIO political director. These union leaders represented millions of hard-working Americans and were some of the most influential figures in the Democratic Party. We met in their conference room overlooking the White House, where we could see construction underway on the Inaugural reviewing stand. The labor leaders all strongly encouraged me to become chairman and pledged their support. I'd known Sweeney and McEntee for years. We were all regulars at the annual Friendly Sons of St. Patrick Dinner, where we all proved that we were Irish.

I knew I needed to talk to Al Gore before I moved forward in a serious way. The next night Dorothy and I went to a Christmas party at the Vice President's residence. Everyone felt terrible for Gore, having to endure hosting an event like that so soon after the Supreme Court had robbed him of what was rightfully his. You knew it had to be killing Tipper and him to be stuck trying to put on a happy face for guests. It was awful that night with everyone milling around awkwardly in a tent in the backyard of the residence, and no one having any idea what to say to the Vice President or Tipper.

"Tom, Dick and John want me to become DNC chair, but I don't want to do it unless you're one hundred percent behind me," I mentioned to Gore. "I need to come see you privately, sir."

He invited me for lunch at the residence the next day. That was when the Vice President said he would endorse me, clearing the way for me to move full speed ahead. Al Gore and I were thinking about the future, not the past. Gore wanted the party to be strong in case he was ready to come back in four years and win back the presidency.

"I'm madder than hell about what the Supreme Court did to you," I told the Vice President. "It's time to fight."

As I pulled out of the Vice President's residence, I drove past dozens of Republican protesters out on the street screaming obscenities at the Vice President's mansion and waving signs saying SORE LOSERMAN and GET OUT OF DICK CHENEY'S HOUSE. Why was it that in a city where Al Gore won 86 percent of the vote, we allowed them to win another media war? Here these nut jobs were harassing the Gore family every day, even in the snow. Why was it that we never had one supporter out there? Because we wanted to play fair, sticking to Marquess of Queensbury rules, and leave it to the United States Supreme Court to do the right thing.

I shook my head as I drove off, more determined than ever to get ready for the next battle. I was jacked up and immediately called Minyon Moore to give her the great news on my meeting with Gore.

"How did it go?" she asked me.

"The Vice President's with me one hundred percent," I said. "We're in this thing and we're in it to win."

★

I CALLED MY FATHER before dinner on December 31, to wish him a Happy New Year, and also to give him the latest on my run for DNC chair, which by then was humming along like a top presidential campaign. Jack and Millie had been in town for Christmas, and I brought them over to the Oval Office to see the President along with the Keegans, Gene and Mary, old friends from Syracuse. Gene used to own a local Irish bar when I was growing up and Jack would always take me there. Gene couldn't believe he was in the Oval Office talking to the President and Jack couldn't have been prouder.

"This is a long way from a tavern owner in Syracuse," Gene told Clinton.

I told Jack on New Year's Eve that a majority of DNC members had already endorsed me for chairman, including most of the state chairs and every living former Democratic chair. We knew we had the votes and that I was going to win. Jack, the former Onondaga County treasurer, had devoted most of his life to Democratic Party politics and he kept telling me how proud he was.

"Happy New Year, Jack," I said, hanging up. "Talk to you tomorrow."

Mark and Susan Weiner were down from Rhode Island with their two kids, Zoe and Richard, visiting us for the holidays, and the house was absolute chaos. We finished up dinner around 9 P.M. and the kids were fixing ice-cream sundaes, running all over the place in funny hats, making an unbelievable racket with their noisemakers, getting ready for midnight. I was surprised when the phone rang and it was Millie.

"Jack's gone," she told me.

"Where did he go?" I asked.

"No, he's dead," she said.

My first thought was concern for my mother, who was all alone at the house with Jack. She had tried to call two of my older brothers, but had not reached them. I told her I'd get help and right away called Duke Kinney. He lived two blocks away from Jack and Millie's, and I gave him the sad news and asked him to get right over there. He arrived before the ambulance and when the EMS workers came in, they put Jack on a stretcher and started giving him mouth-to-mouth and then blasting his heart.

"Stop it!" my mother told them. "The man is eighty-three years old. He's gone. Let him go. He went peacefully."

I was deep in shock at the loss of my best friend, someone I talked to every day, when the phone rang again not more than half an hour after Millie had called with the sad news. It was the President.

"Mac, I'm so sorry for your loss," Bill Clinton told me. "You know how much I loved Jack's spirit. Hillary and I will miss him. You should be proud of his service to our country and to our party."

I had a very tough time talking, I was so shaken up, and Clinton didn't know what to say.

"I'll talk to you tomorrow, Mr. President," I finally said after a long silence.

The whole family was shaken up, no one more than little Jack, who was seven years old. He was named for his grandfather and they always had a special relationship. I went upstairs to say good night to Jack and found him in bed cradling a picture of him and his grandfather on the deck of the house we rented in Dewey Beach, and I held him as he cried himself to sleep.

We flew up to Syracuse the next day to start making arrangements for the wake and funeral. As sad as it was, we Irish have a tradition that you turn the passing of someone you love into a celebration of his life. Jack, the unofficial mayor of Syracuse, gave us a lot to celebrate. As Duke Kinney told my brother John that first night, our father didn't die of a heart attack, "It was death by a great life."

The day after I arrived, a big group of us, including my brothers John, Joe, and Tom, decided to honor Jack in a way he would love, going to see Syracuse play at the Carrier Dome, which Jack had helped build as chairman of the Sports Authority. Duke and I were getting hot dogs at Heid's of Liverpool beforehand when we got a call from the White House saying that the President would be coming to the funeral, despite what I knew was an incredibly jammed-up schedule in the last two weeks of his presidency.

A driving snowstorm had moved in on Syracuse, which dropped more than ten inches, and 2,100 people showed up for the wake, some of them having to wait three hours in blizzard conditions outside Whelan Brothers Funeral Home to get their chance to kneel by the casket and pay their respects. My father was a character. Everybody knew him and he knew every bartender

Mary and the President play UpWords at Camp David.

Mary greets Hillary at yet another fund-raising event at our house.

Sharing an intimate moment with Yasser Arafat.

Hillary, Dori, and Mary at another fund-raiser, as Mary plays with her earring.

The President and Jack at the DNC Blue Jean Bash, MCI Arena, Washington D.C.

We were rocking with Southern bar-b-q while the Republicans let loose with horseradish crusted filet of red snapper.

Al Gore and me with Tony Coelho, Gore's presidential campaign chairman and my best man.

Receiving chipping lessons from the President on the White House putting green.

Hillary and Kevin Spacey laughing it up on the set!

President Clinton and me having fun filming a segment of the "Final Days" video—notice I'm winning.

The annual trip to NYC for the Big East basketball tournament with father and brothers.

A long way from the Persian Terrace for father and son.

Firing up the crowd at the 2000 L.A. Convention, attacking Bush's agenda.

Jack McAuliffe's funeral—January 2001.

Just a *little* embarrassed the night before my election as DNC chair—Olivia Newton-John sings "I Honestly Love You."

At the end of the day, it's not personal.

Not sure Marc Racicot is convinced.

Ed doesn't look too excited about what I have to say.

Receiving a gavel made from the USS *Constitution* to celebrate Boston's pick as convention site.

A long day after the 2002 elections. Peter O'Keefe is on suicide watch.

Democratic dignitaries cut the ribbon at the new DNC headquarters.

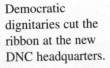

What a night! March 25, 2004.

DNC Unity Dinner, March 25, 2004. Everyone coming together for John Kerry.

President Carter inspiring a new generation of Democrats: Dori, Jack, and Mary McAuliffe.

A special moment with two historic peacemakers.

A handshake with Prime Minister Ariel Sharon at the end of the meeting was just fine—no rubbing of my leg! What—no kiss?

With Sean Hannity and Alan Colmes seconds before Sean "paws" me.

Convention, 2004.

Sen. John McCain gave me a few insights on both John Kerry and George W. Bush at the '04 Republican Convention.

Having fun at Sportsman's Day with West Virginia governor Bob Wise. My press secretary, Elizabeth Alexander—not so much.

Jack wild boar hunting with Prince Andrew in Hungary.

Bird hunting with King Juan Carlos. Because he's king, he gets most of the birds.

Magic Johnson, Quincy Jones, Hillary, Berry Gordy, Clarence Avant, and me at Magic's house for a fund-raiser for Hillary in September 2007.

Nelson Mandela taught us all not to hate.

The McAuliffe clan: Terry, Dorothy, Dori, Jack, Mary, Sally, Peter.

Dorothy and me with the Rolling Stones celebrating President Clinton's sixtieth birthday in NYC in 2006.

in Syracuse. Even in the freezing cold outside, everyone was swapping stories about Jack or telling jokes he'd told around town a thousand times.

That night and into the morning, Jocko Collins, one of Jack's drinking buddies and commissioner of the Department of Public Works, had dozens of snow plows out to clear the ten inches that had piled up by then off the roads. It was a massive snow removal operation. What a fitting tribute to Jack.

Jack McAuliffe was well known for not being a big fan of dogs, and that was why we all ended up having a big laugh at the funeral home the morning of the funeral. They had the motorcade lined up outside with our whole family ready to take the casket over to the Cathedral of the Immaculate Conception, where we'd had to move the funeral because our local parish, St. Ann's, was way too small. You should have seen the look on the face of the funeral director when a team of Secret Service agents came in to check out the casket to make sure it wasn't loaded with explosives. The President was going to be standing right next to the casket during the funeral. First the agents examined every nook and cranny of the casket and one of them actually crawled underneath with a flashlight and studied every square inch of mahogany to make sure nothing looked amiss. Finally they brought in a bomb-sniffing dog and just before they closed the lid of the casket, the German shepherd had to sniff inside the casket. So Jack's last vision on earth was of a bomb-sniffing dog staring him in the face. At that point all four brothers lifted shots of Irish whiskey and toasted Jack.

The day before, the President had attended the swearing-in ceremony for the new class of senators, including Hillary, who was briefly both senator and First Lady. "Don't ever forget it's a team sport," he told the new senators. "You stick with Hillary and you guys will do great things for America." Now the President and Hillary were both in town for this son of Syracuse and the whole city felt honored and awed to have them.

"It was unbelievable," Clinton said later. "They filled the cathedral in Syracuse, which is really one of the most beautiful Catholic churches in America, and there was such a happy, reverent feeling. It was a real tribute to his father."

When it was my turn to speak I laid out the principles that Jack lived by: "Be nice, try to help everyone, always be positive, and never give up."

I talked about how much fun we had attending the Big East Tournament every year and the Democratic National Convention every four years, and joked about how growing up the phone was always ringing every night, interrupting dinner, with people calling to ask for help finding a job or getting a ticket fixed. The timing of Jack's death was no accident, I kidded.

"He wasn't going to go into a New Year having a Republican moving into the White House," I said.

"He was a great spirit. I will miss him greatly. He was my best friend. We talked every day."

Finally, I read aloud from what people had told me about Jack at the wake: "Nobody had more fun."

"He was an adventure in living."

"He always had a smile."

"Thank you, Dad, for being a great husband, father, and friend," I said in closing, before I introduced the President.

"Hillary and I are here because we really liked Jack McAuliffe," Clinton told the hushed gathering at the cathedral. "I'll always be grateful because Jack showed me something about going through life and staying young by never losing your enthusiasm. You know, he didn't take—he was very proud of Terry's role in politics, but he didn't think it meant that he was now too good to do the basic work of politics. He was out there putting up yard signs for Hillary in this campaign when he was eighty-three years old. . . . Terry, of all the things you've done for me, turns out none of them was better than the chance you gave me to be your father's friend."

22

* * *

Clinton flew back to Washington after Jack's funeral in Syracuse and had two weeks left as President. He ran out of time on two giant foreign-policy issues and could have made a major breakthrough on at least one of them if he'd had even a few more weeks. It was big news in July 2006 when North Korea's Stalinist leader, Kim Jong Il, fired off at least half a dozen missiles, including one that could theoretically reach U.S. territory. The Bush 43 policy toward North Korea was to do the opposite of whatever Clinton had done. It was the jealous-of-your-older-brother approach to world affairs. So where Clinton had been modest in his public comments but worked hard behind the scenes, the Bush administration was arrogant and bullying in its comments and in terms of action did nothing, nothing at all, so it could focus on its reckless obsession with taking out Saddam Hussein, and damn the consequences.

Clinton was making great progress with North Korea at the close of his administration. That October, Madeleine Albright became the first U.S. secretary of state to visit Pyongyang, the North Korean capital, and was direct and tough with Kim and said that for the President to agree to a summit, first an agreement on long-range missiles would have to be reached. Kim said he was prepared to do that. "If both sides are genuine and serious, there is nothing we will not be able to do," he said. That was far from a guarantee coming from someone like Kim, but it was worth following up on. Diplomacy takes actual work, not just simplistic speeches about exporting values.

Clinton was ready to spend the last weeks of his administration flying to Pyongyang to negotiate a deal with Kim Jong Il, but he knew that would take at least a week, since he would have to visit other Asian countries as well or risk offending them. The President met with Palestinian leader Yasser Arafat at the White House in November, and asked if there was still a chance of achieving a Mideast peace agreement after all the work at Camp David that year had so nearly produced a lasting peace.

"In a private moment I held his arm, stared straight at him, and told him I also had a chance to make an agreement with North Korea to end its long-range missile production, but I would have to go there to do it," Clinton wrote in *My Life*. "After all my efforts, if Arafat wasn't going to make peace, he owed it to me to tell me, so that I could go to North Korea to end another serious security threat. He pleaded with me to stay, saying that we had to finish the peace and that if we didn't do it before I left office, it would be at least five years before we'd be this close to peace again."

That was a powerful argument and Clinton did not go to North Korea. All through the last months, Clinton and I often discussed the prospects for peace in the Middle East, which was more than an obsession for him. He would hear about the latest outbreak of violence and talk to me about how terrible it must be for these people to live on the brink of chaos. He saw the Middle East first as a moral problem, an unacceptable open wound that needed healing, but he also saw the geopolitical importance of somehow finding a way through to peace. He did not rely on a small cabal of extremist advisers in Washington who saw everything through the lens of 1950s politics and insisted that they knew more than the people on the ground. No, he consulted widely with other leaders and people he met in his travels and understood just how fundamental the fate of the Palestinians was to the future of the Middle East and the entire Muslim world. Clinton was very balanced in his approach. He was sympathetic to the plight of the Palestinians, but he always kept the Israeli security perspective in mind as well. He could do nothing more important to make the world a better place for our children and their children.

One of my good friends was Hani Masri, a Palestinian-American businessman who comes from a prominent Nablus family. If Hani hadn't been born in Nablus, I'd have thought he was from County Cork. He loves everything the Irish love: drinking, enjoying a cigar, and telling endless stories. He was close to Arafat and in April 2000 he hosted a small dinner for him at the Prime Rib restaurant in Washington.

Hani had always been after me to meet with Arafat, urging me to keep an open mind to all sides. He was well aware that I often discussed the Middle East with my friends in the American-Jewish community, including Haim Saban, Danny Abraham, Arthur Schechter, and Ira Forman. I had made many trips to Israel and had known their leadership going back to Shimon Peres and Yitzhak Shamir in the mid-1980s. Hani invited Dorothy and me to join six other guests at the Prime Rib to meet Arafat and discuss issues.

When Arafat arrived at the restaurant, Hani had him sit right next to me. We talked about what was happening in the Middle East and Arafat had all kinds of questions about U.S. politics and of course about Bill Clinton. The dinner soon became somehow comical for me. Arafat would get very animated when he spoke and every time he was making a point, he would lean over and rub my leg under the table. He'd be saying something to the whole table full of people and then he would look right at me, emphasizing a point, and rub up and down on my leg. That is not something that men normally do to me when I sit down to dinner with them. I just couldn't visualize my friend Ariel Sharon rubbing my leg when I talked to him.

Dorothy spent the whole meal laughing at how uncomfortable I obviously was. She knew this was unique for me given my Irish Catholic heritage. What would the nuns at St. Ann's think? As interested as I was in the conversation, after a while it started getting awkward having my leg rubbed so much and I looked forward to the end of the meal. Finally it was time to go and we stood up to shake hands, I thought, but Arafat laid a big ole wet kiss right on my lips. I wasn't ready for that one.

That March, I met Hani for lunch at Morton's, and Hani invited along a man named Mohamed Rachid, part of Arafat's inner circle. That day at Morton's, we discussed the upcoming Camp David talks and it soon became clear that Rachid was meeting with me because Arafat wanted to establish a back channel to Bill Clinton. During the Camp David Summit in July 2000, Rachid called me from Camp David to ask me to relay a message directly to the President, saying that Arafat wanted a few minutes alone with Clinton outside of the group talks. I called the President right up and passed on the request that he meet with Arafat one-on-one.

"And I did," Clinton remembers.

The President invited Arafat over to Aspen Lodge and the two men talked there until midnight. Then Clinton walked Arafat back to Birch Cabin, which happened to be where Menachem Begin stayed during the Carter-era Camp David talks. Clinton pressed Arafat for an answer on whether he would respond favorably to the new proposals from Israeli Prime Minister Ehud Barak, and only later that night did word come back that the answer was no.

Arafat was under pressure from other Arab leaders not to accept a deal just for the sake of a deal, but to fight hard for the best deal possible.

The talks ended on a sour note, but Bill Clinton, understanding the stakes, was not about to give up. He knew that the Camp David meetings would probably not result in an agreement but could move the ball forward. He ordered his team to keep negotiating and pressing for more creative solutions to the intractable problem of forging Middle East peace. The Israeli and Palestinian delegations capped off months of additional work when they met in Washington on December 23 to go over the latest version of what came to be known as the Clinton Plan. Unlike the deal being discussed at Camp David, under which the Palestinians would have had to give up more than 9 percent of the West Bank, the Clinton plan provided for them to retain the equivalent of about 97 percent of the West Bank. Through Clinton's efforts they were also able to resolve most of the territorial and neighborhood issues as well as questions relating to the holy sites.

Arafat's team called Sandy Berger from Gaza at noon on January 1 to say that the latest offer was acceptable to Arafat.

Sandy talked to the delegation for a while and then put them on hold to go talk to the President in the Oval Office. He came back on the phone to ask if they could put Chairman Arafat on the phone, since the President wanted to speak to him directly to hear it for himself. At the end of the call, Arafat offered to send his acceptance in a letter or to visit Washington, if his presence were required. Clinton put Arafat on hold and called in his scheduler, Stephanie Streett, asking her to find an hour and a half on his schedule the next day to meet with Arafat, then got back on the phone with Arafat and invited him for lunch the next day.

That night, Arafat worked the phone and called thirty Arab leaders to discuss the deal, and all of them gave an enthusiastic yes—only two declined to take his call: the presidents of Syria and Lebanon. The leaders of Egypt, Saudi Arabia, Jordan, Morocco, and Tunisia all strongly encouraged Arafat to accept the deal, according to close associates of Arafat's who briefed me.

Arafat flew to Washington on January 2 and was met at the airport by the ambassadors of Saudi Arabia, Egypt, and Jordan. They all went to the Ritz Carlton Hotel, and the mood was upbeat and positive, but no one knew what to expect for sure.

The President was optimistic as a group of twelve, representing the Palestinians and Americans, gathered in the Oval Office for lunch. But as they say, the devil is in the details. Once Arafat got there—even though he had agreed to most everything on the phone with Clinton—he reopened negotiations on specific details and by the end of lunch it was clear that the deal was dead.

I was up in Syracuse for my father's funeral and that afternoon I received a call from Hani Masri telling me that Mohamed Rachid urgently needed to talk to me. It wasn't the best time for me, but I phoned back.

"Arafat needs a meeting with Clinton," Mohamed told me.

"I'm up here in Syracuse, preparing for my father's funeral," I said.

"Please, Terry, this is the last shot we have at peace," Mohamed told me.

So I called Bill Clinton.

"Mr. President, Arafat wants one more shot," I said. "I got a call and was asked to tell you he wants another one-on-one meeting with you."

"I don't know, Mac," the President said. "It didn't go well today. Every time you get in with them, they renegotiate. I feel like we're spinning our wheels."

"I understand, sir," I said. "I'm just relaying the message. They sound really sincere about this."

The phone was silent a minute.

"You know what?" the President told me. "If I have to negotiate until January twentieth, to the last second of my presidency, I'll do it. Tell him I'll see Arafat."

I called Mohamed back to give him the news that Clinton would do the meeting and he was so excited, he put me on the phone with Arafat, who told me in broken English, "Thank you, thank you, thank you."

"Mr. Chairman, this is important for the world," I told him.

"Thank you, thank you, thank you," Arafat said.

CIA director George Tenet went over to see Arafat, whom he had met dozens of times, to try and get him in the best possible frame of mind about the plan. During the meeting, Tenet and one of his advisers went through the specifics of the entire plan line by line, which was read aloud to Arafat both in Arabic and English.

"Yes, I agree to all those terms," Arafat told Tenet.

Tenet sent word back to the White House that it was a go and, later that night, Clinton and Arafat met one-on-one. However, the meeting failed to produce a breakthrough and Clinton was furious. In the end he blamed Arafat for not seizing this last, best chance for peace. The President told me that just before he left office, Arafat gave him a call and praised him as a great man. Clinton almost lost his temper.

"Mr. Chairman, don't try to be nice to me," he told Arafat. "I am not a great man. I am a failure, and you have made me one."

★

THE LAST FULL WEEKEND of his presidency, Bill Clinton invited friends and White House officials up to Camp David for a final celebration and one last chance to relax together at the Catoctin Mountain retreat. We had a big dinner in Aspen Lodge Friday night with the congressional leadership and I sat next to Congresswoman Eddie Bernice Johnson of Texas, the chair of the Congressional Black Caucus. After dinner people started standing up to say a few words to honor the President, and Senator Patrick Leahy got up and talked about what interesting times we'd had during the Clinton years. I elbowed Eddie Bernice and told her it was her turn to speak up.

"Mr. President, as chair of the black caucus, I feel compelled to get up here and thank you for eight great years, but also to thank you for being America's first black President," she said.

Clinton's face lit up like a beacon when she said that. He was so proud, he was just beaming. He fought so hard for everybody, but in particular he fought very hard for the African-American community and they loved him.

Don Henley of the Eagles gave us a small concert over in the chapel after dinner and then we had one last movie screening. Later we headed back down to the two lanes where Nixon used to bowl. Don Henley and the President and I kept bowling until after 2 A.M. and the whole time I kept calling Henley "Donnie."

"You're the first one who has ever called me Donnie in my whole life," he finally told me.

After another late night of Upwords and cards, we showed up at the chapel the next morning and they had me do the reading. Back at Aspen Lodge after brunch, everyone was milling around in the main area and the President came out of his office and said he needed to talk to me privately. It was a sad day. We went into his small office and as we talked about what life held for him after next week, the whole time he was pulling mementos off the walls and taking books from his shelves and putting them into boxes.

Clinton had asked me to join him in his office because he was about to receive a call regarding a settlement offer from independent counsel Robert Ray, Ken Starr's successor. Hillary came in after a while and we all talked on the phone with Clinton's attorney, David Kendall, who was brilliant, tough, and thoughtful with an easygoing, soft-spoken style, to go over what the final deal should be. I was pushing to get this out of the way. I was sick and tired of people mistreating Bill Clinton. Hillary was as tough on it as I was. There were some voices arguing that Clinton should wait and try to get a better deal later after Bush had been inaugurated. I made the point very forcefully that if anyone thought the Bush people were going to cut us any breaks, they were out of their minds. They were going to do everything they could to screw us. My argument was if you've got a deal you can live with now, let's take it, and let's move on. Hillary agreed. We went around the room on it a few times and finally Clinton bit the bullet and decided to take the deal. Kendall said later that if he'd waited until after the Inauguration when the papers were filled with negative stories, there would have been no deal. Good thing we got a decision out of him that day at Camp David.

★

THE BIRD WAITING FOR BILL CLINTON at Andrews Air Force Base on January 20, 2001, officially stopped being Air Force One as of 11:56 A.M. when George W. Bush was sworn in as the forty-third President of the United States, making Bill Clinton the third-youngest ex-President in history at age fifty-four, twenty years after he had become the youngest ex-governor ever. Dorothy and I and a whole group from the administration were onboard the blue 747 with the presidential seal more than an hour before Clinton finally climbed up the walkway for the flight to New York that afternoon. We were enjoying our last hours among the trappings of the presidency as Clinton worked his way through a long line of friends and supporters, none of us knowing then that the Republicans' fear of Bill Clinton and his continuing political strength would lead them to resort to one last massive campaign of disinformation and lies to undermine Clinton. This was the Tonya Harding version of fair play: Have your deadbeat low-life henchmen kneecap someone else to make you look better. Bush came into office promising to set a new tone in Washington and he delivered, all right, giving us years of poisonous character assassination of all enemies and rivals, and in their first days in office the people around Bush gave us a clear blueprint of how this gang would do business.

Clinton was going on only one hour of sleep that day. He'd stayed up all night because he had a pile of work he wanted to get out of the way, but above all because he wanted to make the most of his remaining hours in the White House. He called me over for a final visit that last night and when I showed up in the Oval Office to see him Betty Currie and Nancy Hernreich were in a state.

"Terry, you've got to help me here," Nancy said. "Please, I'm begging you. Do not get into any conversations tonight. He has not packed yet. Say good-bye or do whatever, but please do not tie him up."

I wanted to help her out, I really did, but once I went inside to see the President, we took more time than we probably should have. Seeing him there, I remember thinking that if he could have sat right there at his Oval Office desk until the next day at noon, he probably would have done it.

"Mac, I loved every day in this job," Clinton said to me that night.

He felt so alive those eight years and had worked so hard day in and day out to make people's lives better. If he could have run for President again, he would have done it in a heartbeat. Looking back now, I have no doubt at all that he really did love every single day in that job.

Before the Clintons left for the Inauguration that last morning a piano player gave them a final rendition of "Our Love Is Here to Stay," and the President and First Lady had one last dance, making the most of their remaining minutes in the White House. The Clintons could not leave by helicopter after the Inaugural because of bad weather so instead they rode out to Andrews in a motorcade. It's not traditional for a President to get the kind of send-off he received that day in a crowded Air Force hangar, but he had accomplished so much in his eight years and it was such an emotional day for all of us. There was a full military honor guard, a military band, and a lot of tears and smiles. Thousands came in the rain to pay their respects.

"You know how it is. When you leave the White House, you wonder if you'll ever draw a crowd again," Clinton joked to the people jammed into the hangar, getting a good laugh. "We had sort of a bittersweet good-bye at the White House. We went around and said good-bye to all the staff there, took a last look at all the rooms."

Clinton mentioned that his chief of staff, John Podesta, had looked up at him as they were leaving the Oval Office for the last time that morning and told the President, "We did a lot of good. We did a lot of good. We did a lot of good."

"We should not be sad today, we should be grateful today and happy and full of belief and hope for our country," Clinton said. "You gave me the ride of my life and I've tried to give as good as I got."

I was awed to be part of this historic day with a front-row seat for the transfer of power, dictated by our Constitution, that has successfully continued for almost 220 years. We were there to thank Bill Clinton for all he'd done for the country, to honor this milestone in his life and to celebrate the new phase of his life about to begin. If it had been any other President, the media would have barely noticed the send-off. This was Bill Clinton and some of the networks carried it live with a split screen, half showing Clinton giving his final speech in the hangar, the other half showing Bush going through his first hours as President. Bush stewed over that one for months to come. The media always loved to take shots at Clinton, but they loved covering him and were all over that final scene at Andrews Air Force Base. An NBC reporter pulled me aside and asked me to go on live with him and Tom Brokaw and I told them Clinton loved his time in the White House.

"This week he canceled several meetings in the Oval Office so he could just spend time in there alone and really reflect on the last eight years that he's had as President of the United States," I said.

It was raining cats and dogs outside and we were glad to get out of the rain and up into Air Force One, which was how we all still thought of it, even though technically it's only Air Force One when the sitting President is using it. It was a festive mood inside the cabin, waiting with about twenty of the President's close friends, all of us privately wondering when we would be back on this plane again. Clinton remained back in the hangar, saying good-bye to the thousands of well-wishers.

Finally Clinton's motorcade pulled up in front of the big 747 and the Clinton cabinet, Madeleine Albright and the rest, met him at the bottom of the stairs to say their farewells. They'd planned it ahead of time that Dorothy and I would be the ones to stand at the entrance to the plane and greet Clinton when he came aboard with Hillary, kicking the festive mood up a notch higher. He looked elated but very tired.

"Come on into the office," he said after greeting me with a bear hug.

Clinton took Dorothy and me right into his private office onboard, along with Hillary, and the four of us talked about the rush of events and how much we had loved the farewell ceremony. It was raining so hard outside, Clinton was dripping wet, and as he dabbed off the rain he looked dazed, still trying to grapple with this change in his life. It felt a little weird to be standing with him. He had been the largest player on the world scene for eight years, and suddenly it was gone.

Everyone was waiting in the big conference room and we went back there and joined in the celebration. The TV screens on the plane were tuned to pictures of Bush's Inaugural parade and we watched as thousands of people protested as Bush's motorcade moved down Pennsylvania Avenue. There was so much debris being thrown at the President's limousine, he had to break with tradition and not get out and walk.

We were popping champagne and as a steward carried in a tray of glasses, Sharon Farmer, Clinton's White House photographer, turned around to take a picture and her big lens knocked the tray to the floor. That sent shards into the cake we were all about to eat, so we couldn't drink champagne or eat the cake. We had invited the reporters into the conference room and they were sitting right there when the glasses broke. But somehow that one accident got spun into a giant whopper of a tale about how Clinton and the group traveling with him had trashed Air Force One on the short flight to New York and stolen everything imaginable. Nothing had happened beyond a photographer's mishap. *Nada.* Yet that didn't stop Fox News from indulging in twisted fantasies that were picked up all over the place on right-wing radio and the right-wing media and then leaked into allegedly more responsible media outlets.

"When the loaned aircraft returned to its hangar at Andrews Air Force Base, it looked as if it had been stripped by a skilled band of thieves—or perhaps wrecked by a trailer-park twister," wrote one syndicated columnist in *The Washington Times.* "Gone were the porcelain dishes bearing the presidential seal, along with silverware, salt and pepper shakers, pillows, blankets, candies—and even toothpaste. It makes one feel grateful that the seats and carpets are bolted down."

The Kansas City Star and a small number of other papers knocked that one down, backed up by a subsequent report from the Congressional General Accounting Office, which found there was absolutely nothing to the reports spread by the Bush people behind the scenes. "Except none of it happened," the *Star* reported in May 2001, five months after the fact. "An official at Andrews Air Force Base, which maintains the presidential jets, told *The Kansas City Star* at the height of the controversy that nothing was missing. Bush himself acknowledged the same a few days later."

I'll give Bill Clinton the last word: "The lies they told, it was amazing."

So who was that syndicated columnist who had been humiliated by printing wholesale lies as the truth? Was he hounded from the profession the way that nutty reporter at *The New York Times* was for making stuff up? Did he grovel for forgiveness and vow to reform his ways? Not exactly. It was Tony Snow who wrote that column and now he earns a paycheck using his unique conception of the truth as George W. Bush's spokesman. Tony's actually not a bad guy. I enjoy talking to him when I run into him here and there in Washington and like his sense of humor. But he was dead wrong to put his name over outright lies and smear all of us who were on that final flight that day. To his credit, Tony actually did apologize on Fox News for getting the story so badly wrong, but that was four months later, which even Tony knew was too little, too late, because by then the damage had been done.

Once we arrived at JFK airport in New York, there was another rally, where Hillary introduced her husband, and then Dorothy and I joined Hillary and the President in her van for the ride to Chappaqua. I'll never forget it. As soon as we got inside the van, Clinton's head went down on Hillary's shoulder and he was out, dead asleep, just like that. He was so exhausted, he was passed out the whole ride to Chappaqua, and it was just Dorothy, Hillary, and me talking. We woke him up when we got to Chappaqua and visited a fire station, where they welcomed the Clintons to town, and then I hosted a farewell dinner for everyone who had flown up with us at an old restaurant called the Kittle House built in the 1700s. Most of us had had a few drinks by then and had a warm, elated feeling even as there was also an undercurrent of sadness.

★

THE REPUBLICANS HAD BEEN SUCCESSFUL in their strategy of spending unprecedented millions to build up what was basically a brand name, the myth of the Clinton administration as mired in scandal. If you have trouble believing the scandals were mostly myth, that just shows how effective the campaign was. Call the typical controversies of the Clinton years Potemkin Village scandals: They were built up to the height of real scandals and seen from the right angle, they looked like real scandals, but if you walked around and looked for yourself at what was really there, you saw they were just empty shells. They were, in short, clever fakes. Put a few of these hollow shells in a line together and you just might force the hand of the media: It's a natural weakness of the media that it cannot resist trend or pattern stories and once you give them a list of three of anything, they're ready to bite. We saw it time and again in the case of the Clinton administration when fake scandals would be listed as if lining them up proved something.

Bill Clinton woke up as an ex-President on the morning of January 21 and in the days that followed we were all in for a shock: The smear campaign that had been launched against Bill Clinton long before he ever became President was still going strong. In fact, it had moved into overdrive as part of a strategic decision by the Bush folks to ease his own transition by raising questions about Clinton. They wanted to destroy Clinton's legacy because he was leaving office with unprecedented popularity.

I already covered the myth about Air Force One being trashed, a myth that was carefully spread by Republicans looking to start a fire of controversy around Clinton's last days. Then came the stories about systematic vandalism by Clinton staffers in their last hours at the White House. The truth is that the first George Bush's people had left the White House a mess in 1993, and Clinton's people left it in far better shape than they found it. Incoming Clinton staffers had no workable phones to use. The computers did not work. Drawers and desks were deliberately locked and the keys hidden or stolen. As for things like pens and paper and other supplies, forget about it. They were all gone.

"We had a lot more problems than they did," Clinton says. "But unlike them, we didn't go to the press. We didn't smear Bush. We didn't do all that stuff. I don't believe in that."

In fact, whereas the Reagan administration fired everyone who worked in the Carter White House within the first twenty-four hours, Clinton didn't care about party affiliation. He even allowed Linda Tripp, a vocal Bush loyalist, to stay on and work in the Clinton White House, showing that he regarded service to our country as more important than partisanship.

Outgoing Clinton staffers did play several harmless tricks. In keeping with years-old tradition in Washington about the outgoing staff playing a small prank on the incoming staff, a few individuals had pulled the "W" keys off their keyboards. A few Gore bumper stickers were placed on walls. Not the most clever pranks, but also no big deal. Still, George W. Bush decided he was going to smear Clinton on this. It might not have been something his father would have done, or approved of, but W. had his staffers doing cartwheels to push the story and when he finally spoke up to confirm it was hokum, it was three weeks later and the press had been going snap, crackle, pop over this the whole time.

One aspect of the lies the Republicans spread is that they are usually so outrageous, they throw people off. For example, it's true the White House was trashed the day the Clintons left—it was trashed, that is, by people working for Bush. Capricia Marshall was the last Clinton person to walk out of the White House the day of the transition and she saw construction workers come in with sledge hammers to start knocking down walls and using ripping bars to start pulling up baseboards.

"All this stuff was happening and I was walking through the White House thinking, 'Oh my God, the body's not even cold yet,'" Capricia told me.

One rumor the Republicans spread was that there was grafitti spray-painted on the walls of the White House. Pure fiction, as Capricia saw for herself, along with the weird rumors of porno and what-not. "The condition of the real property was consistent with what we would expect to encounter when tenants vacate office space after an extended occupancy," Bernie Ungar of the General Services Administration wrote in his report to Congress.

"No wholesale slashing of cords to computers, copiers and telephones, no evidence of lewd graffiti or pornographic images. GSA didn't bother to nail down reports of pranks, which were more puckish than destructive."

The whole disinformation campaign was choreographed to a T. Senior White House officials talked to reporters off the record and leaked all sorts of lies about damage done to the White House and then Ari Fleischer, one of Tony Snow's predecessors as Bush's spokesman, kept pulling the classic misdirection. He tried to sound as if he were showing great restraint and not making an issue of the rumors, but of course, that was exactly his intention with comments like, "We're not dwelling on those issues." As if there were issues to dwell on! As if they were somehow taking the high road!

Fleischer worked the story with everything he had. He talked about the phantom acts of vandalism against the White House as if they had actually happened, a blatant lie right there, and then claimed in that just-passing-along-the-facts manner of his that a formal effort was underway to catalogue the damage. This statement—far from being challenged as ridiculous—was passed along by reporters as fact. And the next day, Fleischer revealed that this supposed "cataloguing" consisted of one person allegedly keeping a mental list. Fleischer was treating the press like a bunch of boobs and idiots, and they didn't seem to mind. The Washington reporter's instinct to see everything in shades of gray could not do justice to the garish colors of the press manipulation Bush and his people were already on their way to mastering.

Rich Galen, whom I've debated on Wolf Blitzer's CNN program, wrote in his newsletter on January 24: "Vice President Dick Cheney's staffers trying to move into the Office of the Vice President space in the Old Executive Office Building right next to the White House found the offices had been left in complete shambles by the Gore staff on its way out on Friday and Saturday. Every cord and wire, in many offices—telephone, power, computer and lamp—was slashed. Furniture was tossed."

That got the story going, as Jeff Elliott summed up in a May article at Alternet called "The Trashing of the President": "Hours later, the story was oozing down the same pipeline that had dumped on the Clintons so many times before. There was an item in the *Drudge Report:* 'The Bush Administration has quietly launched an investigation. . . .' It was then quickly picked up by Fox News and the viciously anti-Clinton *Washington Times*. From there, it made the jump to CNN, *The Washington Post*, and other mainstream media sources. Soon the concocted story was being reported with no doubt of its accuracy. From *U.S. News & World Report*, Feb 5: 'It resembled a scene from the movie *Animal House,* where the frat boys from Delta trashed their own house before being thrown off campus. Only this time the frat boys were Bill Clinton's aides.' "

U.S. News had also published a false report that Clinton staffers had received big bonuses, draining half of the annual White House operational budget in the first four months of the fiscal year—but there was nothing to it at all, which soon became clear. The people in charge of the White House went public with a dubious story about the Clintons taking furniture they should not have, a detail that merged with the fuss being made about the gifts the Clintons had received, which were not much more than what the first George Bush had received as President.

Republican senator Mitch McConnell was quoted calling the controversy a "godsend" and gushing, "The comparison is marvelous. It is stark and, from Bush's perspective, a pleasant contrast." Reporters also relayed the story that a senior White House official was heard bragging at the Alfalfa Club in Washington about how well the campaign of lies was working and how "shrewdly" Bush and his people "had taken advantage of the clumsy Clinton exit."

Yes, the Marc Rich pardon was a mistake, but if Clinton's last days in office were "clumsy," as the press reported, then what were the last days of the first President Bush? A train wreck. Bush 41 skated, with not even a hint of congressional hearings to investigate his outrageous pardons, including not only his Iran-Contra coconspirators; he also pardoned Orlando Bosch, a Cuban exile who admitted taking part in the October 6, 1996, bombing of a Cuban civilian airliner, killing all seventy-three people on board.

Now the Republicans wanted to investigate Bill Clinton for his pardons? It was a joke, a big, fat joke. The Republicans were like junkies, going back again and again to their wonder drug of Clinton-bashing, which made them feel good even though in the end it didn't help them with the public, which saw through the lies and distortions.

However, once again the Republicans misjudged the American people. The conservatives couldn't stand that Bill Clinton had the highest recorded job approval rating of any President leaving office, topping their hero, Ronald Reagan. Clinton left office with a 66 percent approval rating, compared to 65 percent for Reagan. Eisenhower was at 59 percent, Bush 41 at 56 percent, Ford at 53 percent—and Bush 43 will be lucky to see 40. There was no mystery why Clinton had such high marks from the people. He had earned it, working during his eight years to compile an unprecedented record of accomplishment:

- Longest economic expansion in U.S. history
- Moved from a record deficit of $290 billion in 1992 to a record surplus of $236 billion in 2000
- Created a record 22.8 million jobs
- Fastest and longest real wage growth in over three decades
- Dropped unemployment from 7.5 percent to 4 percent
- Highest homeownership rate in history at 67.7 percent
- Lowest poverty rate in two decades, down to 11.3 percent
- Child poverty declined a record 28.7 percent
- Expanded the Earned Income Tax Credit, lifting 4.1 million out of poverty
- Created the Family and Medical Leave Act, allowing nearly 9.1 million workers to take up to twelve weeks of unpaid leave to deal with family medical crisis
- Doubled federal funding for child care
- Increased the hourly minimum wage from $4.25 to $5.15
- Created Americorps, allowing 400,000 young people to serve their communities
- Largest investment in education in thirty years
- Created HOPE scholarships, the Direct Student Loan Program, and increased funding for Pell grants, the largest increase in college aid in fifty years
- Created funding for 100,000 new teachers to reduce class sizes
- Created the Technology Literacy Challenge Fund to connect every school to the Internet
- Expanded Head Start funding by 90 percent to assist 900,000 children
- Lowest overall crime rate in twenty-five years
- Provided funding to put 100,000 more police on the streets
- Signed the Brady Bill stopping 500,000 felons, fugitives, and domestic abusers from purchasing guns
- Reformed the welfare system resulting in the lowest number of people on welfare, a 58 percent decline
- Doubled child support collections
- Economic and social policy created the lowest pregnancy rate on record with abortion down 17 percent
- Created 31 Rural and Urban Empowerment Zones and more than 100 Enterprise Communities
- Enacted the most comprehensive Medicare reforms in history
- Extended the life of the Medicare Trust Fund by twenty-six years

- Enacted the single largest investment in health care for children in thirty-five years
- Passed meaningful health insurance reform, allowing individuals to keep their health insurance when they change jobs
- Created four new national monuments, and protected 40 million acres of our national forests—largest amount of land set aside in the continental U.S. since Teddy Roosevelt
- Passed the Safe Drinking Water Act
- Secured $1.1 billion for research and development of clean energy technologies
- Allocated $4.3 billion for biomedical research and completed sequencing of human genomes
- Created the smallest government work force since the Kennedy administration
- Oversaw the lowest level of government spending since 1974
- Eliminated 16,000 pages of federal regulations
- Passed the Motor Voter Law, leading to registration of 28 million new voters
- Brokered the Good Friday Peace Accord in Northern Ireland
- Built a self-sustaining peace in Bosnia
- Restored democracy in Haiti
- Ended violence and protected democracy in East Timor
- Reduced Russian nuclear arsenal
- Eased nuclear tensions between India and Pakistan
- Ratified Chemical Weapons Convention
- Reduced North Korean threat
- Contained Saddam Hussein
- Increased defense spending
- Passed the Africa Growth and Opportunity Act
- Passed NAFTA
- Established the World Trade Organization
- Saved Mexico from currency crisis
- Efforts in the Middle East led to seven years of progress toward peace

Thank you, Mr. President!

PART ★ THREE

THE MAIN EVENT

23

★ ★ ★

My race for DNC chairman really got going on December 15, 2000, the day Al Gore told me he would endorse me. I left the Vice President's residence that Friday afternoon and immediately started working the phones. It cracked me up when people later claimed I was somehow "installed" as chairman, as if I didn't have to work for it. Oh, I worked for it all right, harder than anyone has ever worked a campaign for party chairman. You can never take any race for granted and from day one we always assumed that other candidates would get in the race. In fact, I welcomed the competition. It forced you to come up with proposals and energized your supporters. I've never been one to worry about what anyone else was going to do. I'd made my decision, I was going to give it everything I had, and I was confident we were going to win.

Apparently the first prominent Democrat to give serious consideration to a race against me was Energy Secretary Bill Richardson. He went to see the President in the Oval Office in mid-December to ask Clinton for his support.

"I'm going to run for chair," Richardson said.

"I'm for Terry," the President said. "I endorsed him. I'm going to work for him."

"What if I run?" Richardson asked.

"We will clean your clock," the President told him.

Richardson was taken aback.

"Terry has been one of my most loyal friends," Clinton said. "In my toughest times, he's always been there. But more important, he's exactly what this party needs."

I wanted a few days after my lunch with Gore to get organized and to reach out to people, so the last thing I wanted was media coverage before I could get my ducks in a row. Unfortunately, as is typical in the Democratic Party, someone leaked my meeting with Gore and in a heartbeat John King was reporting on CNN's *Inside Politics* that "just moments ago, as we were preparing to come on air, Terry McAuliffe left the Vice President's residence," where I went to ask for his support. Now everyone assumed I had the job all but locked up.

So much for the few days I'd counted on having to line everything up. Now I had to spend the entire weekend making calls. I wasn't ready to announce until I had my organization put together. One of the first calls I made that Friday was to Donna Brazile, a longtime friend from the Gephardt campaign, who had managed the Gore campaign. Donna was important to my candidacy, given her political skills and her influence in the African-American community. She felt she should have been informed earlier that I was running for chairman, but I felt strongly that I should consult with the Vice President before I talked to anyone else.

"I wasn't consulted," she said.

"Donna, this has happened in the last thirty minutes," I said. "Consulted about what? I'm running. I'm calling to get your support. What do you want to consult on? I'm asking for your vote."

The next morning I called a six-hour meeting of all the top people who would be advising me on the campaign and they all had great Democratic Party credentials: Steve Elmendorf and David Plouffe (Gephardt), Michael Meehan (Daschle), Steve Rosenthal (AFL/CIO), Alexis Herman (Labor Secretary), Harold Ickes, Minyon Moore, Steve Ricchetti, Linda Moore and Doug Sosnik (Clinton), Marcia Hale (Gore), as well as Jenny Backus (DNC), Jeff Forbes (Senate Caucus), Mark Weiner, Peter O'Keefe, Alecia Dyer, David Dreyer, and my campaign manager, Amy Chapman. Our strategy was to take nothing for granted and make the calls and do the outreach work to put together a strong base of support. Starting that day, we went full-time every day except for my father's funeral, and had thirty people in the office all going full tilt. We also knew that the campaign needed money, and my finance chairmen Mark Weiner and Peter O'Keefe went out and raised $350,000 in three days, even with a self-imposed cap of $5,000 on contributions.

Soon after my conversation with Donna she arranged a call with California Congresswoman Maxine Waters and a few DNC members from the South to talk about other possible candidates for chair. They decided to recruit former Atlanta Mayor Maynard Jackson to get into the race.

That was fine with me. It just meant I had to fight harder. But by the time Maynard announced he was in the race on December 21, I already had lined up a majority of the DNC members, and a majority of the DNC Black Caucus had already indicated they would endorse me, thanks to the efforts of Minyon Moore, Alice Huffman, the vice chair of the DNC Black Caucus, and Eddie Bernice Johnson, the chair of the Congressional Black Caucus. I was also honored to have the support of Georgia Congressman John Lewis, the great civil rights leader who had walked the bridge at Selma. Jimmy Carter's endorsement was especially important given Carter's influence in Georgia, where he'd been governor and Maynard Jackson made his name as Atlanta mayor. I knew exactly where I stood with every vote as Julie Eddy and Elizabeth Ann Chandler tracked all my votes on an hourly basis and had all my supporters sign commitment sheets that we released to the press.

★

JANUARY 2001 WAS AN AMAZING TIME for Hillary Clinton. She was not only sworn in that month as a United States senator, she was representing New York, the media capital of the world, and she knew that her every success or stumble was going to get top billing. She had been preparing for this job all her life and was working around the clock that month to read policy briefings and to fill key staff positions to come out of the gate strong. She met regularly with Senator Robert Byrd, who knew the Senate better than anyone, to tap his expertise on what to do and what not to do and how to set about earning the respect of her peers.

Just two days after Bush's Inauguration, Hillary left Chappaqua and flew down to Washington, and Chelsea was busy with her new job, which meant that Bill Clinton was really alone for the first time in his entire life, except for a few aides, including Doug Band, Justin Cooper, and Oscar Flores. Doug has spent the last six years traveling the globe with the President and has become an invaluable asset, dealing with all aspects of the President's life. He and Justin share the incredible travel schedule. The always smiling Oscar Flores runs the residence.

Clinton called me the afternoon Hillary left and seemed down in the dumps. I said I'd fly up to New York the next day and we'd play some cards and have some fun. I'll never forget walking down the main street to lunch in Chappaqua with Clinton the next day. We walked past an ATM and there was a small line of people waiting to stock up on twenties. Clinton looked at the machine, and over at the people, and then back at the machine again and scratched his head. I'm not sure he'd ever seen one before.

"It gives you cash?" he asked.

"Yes, sir, it gives you cash—if you have money in your account," I said.

We walked down the street and as we passed each shop, people inside would come rushing out to welcome the President to town and introduce themselves. This was a little different than walking down the street with the President even just a week or two earlier when he would have been surrounded by hundreds of security personnel. Now they were down to about six.

The warm reception in Chappaqua lifted Clinton's spirits; he loved seeing in people's faces how thrilled they were to have him as their new neighbor. Even so, back at the house afterward it soon became clear that I was going to have to do something for Clinton that I'd never done for anyone, not even my wife, Dorothy. That's right: Against my better judgment, I agreed to go with him to the opera that night at the Met.

Chelsea loved the opera and whatever she loved, the President loved. So there Clinton and I were with Chelsea and her date in the main box at the Met to hear Luciano Pavarotti in Verdi's *Aida,* which, just my luck, runs nearly three hours. They say you know at your first opera whether you're going to be an opera person or not and I had my answer, all right. If I had been sitting anywhere else, I would have nodded off in the first act. There in the main box with the President and Chelsea, with everyone watching, I had to avoid that at all costs. Act One ended and the lights came on, and the crowd at the Met gave Clinton a standing ovation. We headed to the lounge to get something to eat, which I thought might help keep me awake.

Not until the second act did I discover they had installed little boxes to translate the Italian opera into English so you could kind of follow along and get an idea of what was happening. Without that I would have been totally lost. We went backstage afterward to meet Pavarotti, but he was nursing a cold and was on doctor's orders not to talk for too long. In fact, he probably wouldn't have performed that night if the general manager had not told him that with Bill Clinton in the audience, the show must go on. As Clinton and Pavarotti talked, all I could think about was getting back to the house in Chappaqua to play a great twenty-hand card game with changing trumps called "Oh Hell!," which Clinton had recently learned from Steven Spielberg and then taught me.

The papers were erupting that week over the President's pardon of Marc Rich. Once Clinton left the White House, he no longer had his communications team working around the clock on his behalf and no one was defending him. Yes, it was a bad idea to pardon a man who had renounced his U.S. citizenship. That fact alone should have been enough to end any consideration of the pardon, because you knew that in every Veterans of Foreign Wars hall in America they would be saying, "What, are you nuts?"

Clinton had received twenty-one letters urging him to pardon Rich and another fifty letters testifying to his good character. Current Israeli Prime Minister Ehud Olmert, then the mayor of Jerusalem, was one of several world leaders who called to lobby for the Rich pardon. Former Israeli Prime Minster Ehud Barak called Clinton on Rich's behalf four different times. Jack Quinn, Clinton's former White House counsel, was representing Rich, and had sent Clinton a handwritten note passionately arguing that an injustice was being done to this man—and told him that the Justice Department had signed off on the pardon. Clinton told Quinn that Rich would have to waive the statute of limitations in case the government decided, even after the pardon, to pursue a civil case against him. Rich agreed to do that and only then did Clinton issue the pardon.

Quinn was the driving force behind persuading Clinton to grant the pardon and then when most every newspaper in America was viciously editorializing against the President, Quinn was nowhere to be found. I was furious and called him that day in Chappaqua to light a fire under him.

"Jack, you got the President to do this," I said. "You gave him all the legal arguments to do it. This man is hanging out there. You need to get out there and defend him and tell people why you argued he should do it."

"My lawyers are telling me I shouldn't say anything," Quinn said. "They say it wouldn't be good for Clinton."

"Bull——!" I said. "Get out there and tell them why you argued for this."

Bill Clinton didn't know Marc Rich as far as he could throw him and unfortunately relied on people who should have known better. My phone call to Quinn helped spur him to action and he called the press.

"Every word I had with the President was about the legal merits," Quinn told *The New York Times* the next day. "He was not focused on 'Are they Democrats?' . . . He was focused on the distinction I was making about whether this ought to have been treated as a civil or criminal matter."

The article went on to say that Quinn thought he should have come forward sooner with the background on the pardon and "acknowledged making mistakes" and said that President Clinton had every right to be angry with him.

" 'He should be upset,' Mr. Quinn said. 'I'm upset. I didn't anticipate well enough the reaction to this.' "

So here we were, another grand jury being impaneled to investigate Bill Clinton. Millions of dollars of taxpayer money would be spent, and in the end not a single indictment came down because there was no criminal wrongdoing. The Constitution is very clear on the President having unquestioned authority to pardon anyone he or she chooses. Just ask Bush 41, who pushed that authority to the limit with his self-serving Christmas Day pardons of Cap Weinberger and other top administration officials in 1992.

★

THE NIGHT BEFORE THE 2001 DNC ELECTION, we threw one of the great Washington bashes of all time. By then we had 97 percent of the DNC membership and there was no suspense about the vote. We took over Union Station and two thousand people were on hand when Olivia Newton-John called me up on stage, held my hand as she looked into my eyes, and sang "I Honestly Love You." It was one of the few times I've ever been embarrassed on stage. Dorothy had to come up to rescue me.

The day of the big vote everyone was united. I'd offered Maynard Jackson a position as national development director and put him in charge of the Voting Rights Institute, which was a good fit for him. He'd spent a lifetime on these issues and his grandfather had been John Wesley Dobbs, an early civil rights leader. In the end Maynard was actually relieved that he didn't win the election.

"I could never have done this job," he told me about a month later. "This is a young man's game."

We were united and we were ready to fight. I won by acclamation after Maynard withdrew and then I gave a stem-winder of a speech. "If Katherine Harris, Jeb Bush, Jim Baker, and the Supreme Court hadn't tampered with the results, Al Gore would be President, George Bush would be back in Austin, and John Ashcroft would be home reading *Southern Partisan* magazine," I said, earning shouts and cheers.

That was just a taste of what Bush could expect from a revved-up DNC on my watch. I announced we were going to triple the size of our research and communications operations and use them to come after Bush every single day. "The Republicans did that from the day Bill Clinton took office, and George Bush is about to taste that same medicine," I said to the wild cheers of the DNC members. The difference was our attacks would be based on facts, not fiction.

My first official act as chairman was to name Minyon Moore as my chief operating officer. Minyon was one of the classiest, most talented women in American politics, as well as one of the most loyal. She started out in Chicago working with the Rev. Willie Barrow at Operation PUSH, then moved on to Jesse Jackson's 1984 and 1988 campaigns, and later served as assistant to the President and director of political affairs in the Clinton White House. Minyon and I agreed that we were really going to shake up the party together. I don't think anyone at DNC headquarters knew quite what had hit them when I showed up for my first day on the job. The first thing I did was walk around the building, escorted by Brenda Johnson, a beloved figure at the DNC, and introduce myself to every staff member, more than a hundred people. If I already knew them, I still went and talked to them that day. I wanted to spread the word that as busy as I was going to be, if they had something important that needed my attention they could always come to me. I also asked every person in the building from the janitors to the department heads to answer one question for me on a piece of paper: *If you could change one thing at the DNC, what would it be?*

We ended up with more than two hundred recommendations. Some were not very helpful, but most were, even if it was just a simple little thing that should have been taken care of years earlier. For example, someone wrote down as their suggestion that we ought to have caller ID on the phones. Up until then we didn't. Can you imagine? When you're running a political operation you want to know who is calling you. I had that one taken care of by the next day. The staff could see I was taking their concerns seriously and acting on them, and it was great for morale.

"This is going to be a different DNC than we've ever had in the history of the party," I said at my first staff meeting. "You're never going to worry about money again. That's my job. You will have all the money you need. Just don't waste it."

That was a real shocker to people at the DNC who were used to being broke constantly and never being able to pay for anything, no matter how important. I wanted everyone to know that with the money we would be able to raise, we were going to set about rebuilding the party and making improvements in every aspect of our operations from top to bottom. We were not going to throw money away, but we were going to be a lean, mean fighting machine that could take on the Republicans. We were on a mission to energize the party down to the grassroots and equip it for a fight against the Republicans that we knew was going to be tough. We had to use Florida as a rallying cry to remind people of all that was at stake and I told them I was going to keep raising the Florida recount fiasco as an issue, no matter how riled up the White House might get about that.

One of the first things I did was to call over to the White House and ask for Karl Rove, Bush's top political adviser, to give him fair warning that I did not think Bush had won the election and I was going to remind the American people every single day of how Bush had back-doored his way into the presidency.

"Karl, I don't think you ought to be sitting there," I said. "I think we won that election. I wish you luck, but not too much luck."

Rick Berke of *The Times* asked me about that call when he found out about it.

"I'm going to beat them and I want them to know I'm coming," I told him.

Once I started at the DNC, I wasted no time in hammering away at Bush. Ari Fleischer started whining right away about how he found my tough statements "disappointing," which was just what I wanted to hear. Bush and his people might have decided that their talking point that month was going to be bringing a new civility to Washington, but these were the same people who had lied through their teeth about the alleged trashing of the White House and Air Force One. They were as committed to amicable bipartisanship as baseball player Jose Canseco was to clean living.

I was on TV and in the press every day jabbing Bush with reminders to the country that he had not been elected President. If no one else was going to say it, they could count on me. I said it then and I'll say it now: What the Supreme Court did to put Bush in power was a travesty. We would have been fools to forget or let go of our outrage too quickly. I said so many times that Bush had not been elected that *Hardball* host Chris Matthews would kid me about it, and not until the next year, 2002, did I agree it was time to move on and stop raising that point. However, I still remind people of it now and then.

You know you're doing well when the other side starts ripping you and I soon became Rush Limbaugh's obsession—well, his other obsession beyond the pill-popping. He would sputter and snort and whine about "Terry McAwful" all the time and that was music to my ears. I knew I was getting to them. If they weren't attacking you, then you weren't getting under their skin. I used to drive them crazy. And the more they attacked me, the more I enjoyed it. If you're in this business and you're worried about what they're going to say about you, then you're in the wrong game.

And who cares if someone like Rush Limbaugh attacks you? The man is a world-class hypocrite—a morally upright commentator who rails against "the welfare state" but went on unemployment insurance himself in the 1980s, and was so strung out on OxyContin in 2003 that he lost his hearing and had to quit his job as an ESPN analyst after his clumsy smear against Donovan McNabb (the former Syracuse star!). I guess it wasn't just his hearing he lost, because in 2006 he was busted by airport security for having a bottle of Viagra without a prescription. Hey, maybe if this radio thing doesn't work out, Rush can make a nice living as a TV pitchman for the little blue pills.

24

* * *

It was starting to feel like déjà vu. Every time I had tackled a problem for the Democratic Party, I'd come in thinking big and every time I was met with a mix of stares and questioning of my sanity. They'd called me crazy when I was fund-raising for Jimmy Carter and Dick Gephardt. They'd said my fund-raising plan for the Clinton-Gore reelection was pie-in-the-sky and could ruin the President. They'd said my MCI Center event would be a flop and should be held somewhere smaller. Now they were saying I was delusional to talk about raising enough money not only to spend heavily on that year's governors' races and the following year's congressional midterm elections, but also to focus on grassroots organizing and spend $30 million to rebuild the Democratic Party infrastructure from top to bottom.

A lot of sparks flew over my plans. Sometimes that's what it takes for people to give up old thinking, so I was all for it, but there were some tense moments. For example, the DNC was buzzing after a lunch meeting we had with the Democratic Congressional Campaign Committee board of directors on March 20, 2002, with Majority Leader Dick Gephardt and California Congresswoman Nancy Pelosi, the future Speaker of the House. Oh, was it a wild one! I gave my presentation on the need to rebuild the party from the ground up and prepare for the future. At that time we were looking at building a new state-of-the-art headquarters with all the latest technology a few blocks away from the old location. I saw a hand go up at the luncheon meeting and it was Congressman Charlie Gonzalez of Texas.

"Well, Terry, how am I going to get there?" Charlie asked. "It's three more blocks down the street. Will there be a trolley?"

"Charlie, let me tell you this," I said. "You call me and I'll come personally pick you up."

Several of the congressmen in that meeting were dead-set against my approach. Congressman Ed Markey of Massachusetts put his hand up next.

"Terry, I've got to be blunt," he said. "I don't care about any of this stuff. We've got elections coming up in November and that's all I care about."

I was flabbergasted. Not only was I going to fully fund the rebuilding project, we were going to spend more money on the November 2002 congressional elections than the DNC ever had, and we had just committed $10 million to *their* redistricting project, a first. Thinking long-term, the way any good business would, seemed to be alien to a lot of people immersed in Washington political culture who always think election to election.

"Listen, Ed, the Republicans have already done it and we can do it," I said. "The party can't afford not to rebuild."

"You're wrong!" Ed said, standing up. "You want to raise all this money and put it into a building. That's great. But what if we don't win the elections? Let's focus on winning first and think about the future later. If we win, the money will be there to raise funds for a new building."

I stood up, too.

"Ed, *you're* dead wrong," I said. "You're only worried about the election in eight months. I'm worried about elections in eight months and eight years. I'm going to give you more money than the DNC has ever given the House Campaign Committee. But you know what? I'm chairman of this party. My job is to build this party for decades to come. You had nothing to do with raising the DNC's money. We did and we're doing this. And in the end you will see we were right."

We finished lunch and broke up the meeting and I was walking down the hall when I looked back and saw Markey running after me to keep the argument going. It helped that Markey knew I had a lot of respect for him, which I do. It takes a man of integrity to argue that hard for something and then admit later that he was wrong, which was what Ed did. We laugh about it now, but the sparks in the air that day show how hard it can be to build the party for the future.

★

I'D ALWAYS KNOWN the DNC headquarters was in bad shape, I just didn't know how bad. I spent most of my first few weeks as chairman shaking my head over the unbelievable stories I kept hearing. We didn't even have all the staff in the same building. We had a lot of our key people across the street at what was jokingly known as the Stepchild Building, actually the Fairchild Building, which was just a mess, not to mention a financial sink-hole since over the years we'd spent millions leasing space in addition to our DNC mortgage. I'd go over there and visit and they'd be shocked to see me because no one from the main building ever set foot in the dark, dank hole where they worked. They had a better chance of getting a visit from a homeless person than the DNC leadership up until then. I mean that. There was a homeless person who would stop by now and then to say hello. Once a day someone would stand outside their windows and flash them. It was so regular an occurrence that they would ask each other, "Hey, has the flasher been by yet?" as casually as people talking about the weather.

Tracy Sefl, in our research department, was sitting at her desk her first week working for us and a mouse ran over her feet. She went to see Brad Marshall, the chief financial officer, and told him it was gross, not to men-tion distracting, to have mice running across her feet while she was trying to work. If you popped a ceiling tile, mouse droppings fell out.

"Terry won't stand for this," Brad said.

He was right. I had an exterminator in there the next day, which at least made Tracy feel better. That didn't stop the flasher, though.

The phone system was outdated and we paid astronomic phone bills that made no sense. We were paying for the phone calls of people all over the country who had somehow ended up on our account; for example, a doctor in Florida got free phone calls for two years because somehow he had been put on our phone bill and never taken off. An election cycle would hit and someone would order up miles of new phone lines and then when the elections were over, no one gave a second thought to the extra phone lines. They were just left in place and after a few cycles that left us with countless unused phone lines all being charged to the DNC. That was money down the drain.

We had such a variety of outdated software and hardware, it was like we had our own low-rent technology museum. Some of the computers were ten years old. Some had been bought the year before. They were using more than a dozen versions of basic software, which usually were not compatible. The computers were such lemons, they didn't even have enough memory and crashed all the time. It took forever just to store a document you were working on so you didn't lose it when the computer inevitably crashed.

The Republicans already had a huge, state-of-the-art enterprise-level database they could mine for donors. We had nothing like that. What little information we did have was on an expensive set of IBM machines that, unfortunately, were almost useless to us because nothing connected to anything else. The tech people called it a ream of paper on a tractor-trailer truck. If you wanted to move data from one computer to another, you had to print it out and input it by hand.

Our Internet presence consisted of basically an online version of a DNC brochure. It just sat there, never changing, never adding content or updates, and attracted no traffic. I was no tech guy, but I understood what a waste that was. Keep in mind, this was 2001, not 1996. The Internet was fast becoming an integral part of people's lives. Just in the two years from 1998 to 2000, the number of people who used the Internet at home jumped from 57 million to 94 million, according to the U.S. Census, and kept climbing from there. The way to get those people reading about the DNC was to load the site up with useful information presented in a dynamic, lively—and interactive!—way. No one wanted to keep coming back for another look at an online brochure.

Every direction I looked in those first days as DNC chair, the same thought kept hitting me loud and clear: You get what you pay for. The Republicans had invested heavily in developing their infrastructure, dating back to Ray Bliss's groundbreaking work with direct mail in the 1960s, and they had been well rewarded for their foresight. The series of RNC chairmen I mentioned on page 58 brought to politics the discipline and clear thinking of smart businessmen. Having started many businesses, I'd learned a thing or two about what works and what doesn't. We needed to run the DNC like a business and keep in mind a very simple concept called return on investment. The issue was not how much you spent, but what that money bought you. If you made short-sighted choices, you would be doomed to fight the same battles again and again without ever getting anywhere. We had to move beyond that thinking to make return on investment (ROI), our new guiding light. That might not sound like an earth-shaking strategy, but it was new at the DNC.

Our direct-mail efforts summed up the problem perfectly. The DNC raised $1.6 million in 1979 through direct mail. That doesn't sound bad until you hear that it cost $850,000 to bring in that money—53 cents on the dollar. Not much had improved by 1999 when we raised $17 million at a cost of $8 million—47 cents on the dollar. I felt like I was reliving the crisis I'd had at fourteen, walking back from a day of double-bag caddying and realizing I couldn't live with the math.

One of the first questions I asked my new staff at the DNC was how many e-mail addresses we had collected. Remember, Al Gore had received 50,999,897 votes. That was about 51 million people ready to vote for our next presidential candidate and potentially ready to help build our party. I wanted to e-mail those Gore voters to get them thinking about the future, not the painful recent past. I was stunned when my tech people told me we had only 70,000 e-mail addresses in our DNC files. That was one e-mail address for every 729 Al Gore voters out there.

I also was eager to tap our voter files, which were records of individuals' party affiliation, name and address, history of giving, and other useful bits of information. Despite the nearly 51 million Democratic voters out there, we did not have a single voter file at the DNC. Let me emphasize this point: *Not a single voter file!* The system up until then was to let the state parties work with consultants on developing the voter files for each election cycle, and then the consultants would make off with the information for their own purposes after the election was over—even though the DNC had paid for it.

Our list of names for direct-mail appeals numbered 400,000 and it was an old list: the average age of the people on that list was sixty-eight years old. That was a lot of Social Security appeals. The Republicans had a small-donor list forty times the size of ours with an average age of forty-eight. Going back into battle with assets like ours lined up against the Republicans' state-of-the-art firepower was like fighting an M1 tank with sticks and stones. We were an old, dilapidated party, and it was time to fight—and change.

We had been spoiled for eight years. We had a Democratic President and he was such a master communicator, we could overcome whatever problems we had with direct mail or e-mail lists. We hardly noticed the cracks in our party because Clinton could work his magic and fire everyone up. The second he left, we didn't have the megaphone of Bill Clinton anymore and we didn't have the White House. We didn't have anything except a sense of mission about fixing the problem. I wanted every new idea I could find on the table. I was open to any upgrade or revamping that could make us a stronger vehicle for representing the American people and communicating with them how we were going to make their lives better, unlike the Bush plan of recklessly bankrupting the country.

The cycle we'd fallen into was relentless: Raise a nice pile of cash in a presidential year, spend it all as it comes in on whatever seems important that week, and then plunge into debt, which you would then spend the next two or three years slowly paying off. The chickens always came home to roost. The mentality had been that even if you were borderline psychotic in how you spent money, a fresh wave of cash would always roll in during the next presidential cycle when interest and commitment peaked, so why worry?

That was the wrong way to look at it. Too much had changed in politics. We could no longer afford to kiss off the years between election cycles. We had to get past the perpetual struggle to retire debt, and equip the party to hold its own with the Republicans, but it was not going to be easy. Looking at the numbers my first year as chairman, I could understand how paralysis had set in before. We had to take on $11.9 million in debt from years of inefficiencies, and that was on top of our $5.4 million mortgage on our wreck of a DNC headquarters. We were between $17 and $18 million in debt when I came in and we were coming off the devastating outcome of 2000, which had many of our supporters around the country depressed and embittered and in no mood to be generous with a party that they thought did not fight hard enough when the presidency was on the line.

I set a bold goal from my first week as chairman: When I left that job, the DNC would pay for itself. It would be self-sufficient.

That sounded unrealistic to people who had not spent time using ROI as their compass. I knew if I thought only about that $18 million in debt, we would be dead in the water. On my watch we were going to have a two-track system: We would find a way to retire the debt, but at the same time we would be investing in our future. As my heated exchange with Congressman Ed Markey demonstrated, a lot of people thought that was A) impossible, and B) foolish. My belief was that it was foolish and impossible to stick with business as usual.

My approach would have scared some people in a normal year and 2001 was no normal year in politics. The month before I was elected chairman, we were briefed that Congress was likely to pass major campaign finance reform, called McCain-Feingold in the Senate and Shays-Meehan in the House. This is where we have to talk about soft money and hard money. No, it has nothing to do with bounced checks. In politics, soft money is the term for big checks. The idea was that the DNC and RNC needed money for party-building and those funds, called soft money, could come from any source in any amount. Hard money came from individuals and was limited to $25,000 per person to the national party per election cycle.

No one was sure if campaign finance would really pass, but I'd said all along that I favored a ban on soft money. I had a reputation as the king of soft money because of some of the high-profile large-donor fund-raising I'd done during the Clinton years, but over the course of my more than twenty years raising money, more than 90 percent was small, individual checks. The Republicans for years had a devastating advantage over us in hard-money fund-raising because of how well they had developed their technological infrastructure. We'd been able to lessen the gap, thanks to generous support from individuals in a position to write big checks, as well as labor and corporate supporters.

If a soft-money ban was instituted when we were already in trouble financially, $18 million in debt, and had only a shell of what the Republicans had in direct-mail capability, you might as well write our obituary. We would be dead in the water. The Republicans could run circles around us for years to come and dominate the government based on technology and money, not on having a message that was in line with the priorities of working men and women around the country. That was a grim prospect. However, to me it was almost beside the point. We weren't going to be dead in the water, no matter how many times the press kept saying so, because we were going to do the hard work of getting our house in order. We were going to beat the Republicans at their own game.

*

I FACED SO MUCH RESISTANCE from people trapped in a what-can-you-do-for-me-*now*? mind-set, I was deeply grateful to the people who were on the same page as me. ROI was nothing new to Dick Gephardt and Tom Daschle, who recruited me to run for DNC chair precisely because they thought I could get us out of our rut. Dick and Tom were both incredibly helpful in our uphill efforts that first year.

Our single biggest assets, however, were Bill and Hillary Clinton. From day one they took the attitude that they were going to do whatever they could to make my vision come to fruition. They agreed fully that if we tried to do this halfway, we were never going to get anywhere. There were too many obstacles to change for us to build up any momentum without going out as strongly as we could. We couldn't think about just trying to crawl out of debt slowly and upgrade here or there. No, we had to think in terms of getting this party in the best shape it had ever been so that our nominee for

President in 2004 would have every advantage we could give him. If the DNC was like a car the nominee could ride to victory, we had to put our days of being a VW Beetle behind us and have a Ferrari waiting in '04.

I was committed to retiring the debt in one fell swoop and building a whole new DNC with a brand-new headquarters and a new fighting spirit to match. I'd done enough fund-raising to know I could raise the money we would need for a full-fledged capital campaign, which I had asked Peter O'Keefe to head up. But it was going to take a whole lot of hard work and sweat, especially the sweat, as it turned out.

I called Hillary and took her and the President to dinner to brief them on the disastrous state of our party and my plans to embark on a $40 million capital campaign. Hillary was a maniac about infrastructure and planning for the future, and was aghast at what I was telling her. We couldn't rewind the clock, but we could stop wasting time. The Clintons had just moved into their new residence in D.C., a beautiful old house built in 1888, and had not hosted any events yet.

"We need your house," I told them. "I need you there, Mr. President. I need you there, Hillary. We're really going to throw the long ball here. We're going to bring in our top twenty donors, give them a PowerPoint on how we have to rebuild this party, and raise about $40 million. Are you game for it?"

"Absolutely, Mac," the President said.

"I'm in," Hillary added.

We set June 14 for the first dinner, where we'd also have Dick Gephardt and Tom Daschle doing their part, and planned another dinner at the Clintons' house in July. A week before the first dinner the weather in Washington was mild, but it got hotter every day and by the Thursday of the event it was stifling hot. It made me think: *What would we do without air-conditioning?* I found out soon enough. We went over to the Clintons' house near Embassy Row and it felt like walking into the heart of the Amazon rain forest. It was an old house and that afternoon it was so hot, it blew out the air-conditioning system. It was hot enough outside, but indoors it felt like some kind of out-of-control greenhouse effect had taken over the house. The guests had already started to arrive and some of them were in the next room having cocktails. We tried to imagine anyone feeling generous in such miserable conditions.

"Let's move this thing outside," Huma Abedin, Hillary's smart and unflappable executive assistant, suggested. "People are going to die in here."

Once the idea was out there, everyone agreed and you should have seen the commotion after that. It was actually pretty funny, though we weren't laughing at the time. We had all of our top donors there and usually I'd be in making the rounds, greeting old friends, kicking up the energy level. This time we asked everyone to help us carry the tables and chairs outside.

The centerpiece of the night was going to be my presentation of our PowerPoint. We had the tables all set up out back with the glasses and plates and silverware and nametags all in place and then brought out the projection machine and set it up. All we had to do was plug it in and we were set. One small problem: There was no electrical outlet out there and the Clintons did not have an extension cord. Huma saved the day by running over to a neighbor's house to borrow an extension cord. The neighbor was Wayne Berman, one of the finance chairmen of the Bush campaign, and his wife later became White House social secretary. If he'd only known the difference his extension cord was going to make!

Even outside it was still hot. I was mopping my brow as I got up to do the presentation and went through my points. It was important to emphasize the two-track strategy. We were not only planning big for the future, we were also going to do everything we could to win races right away, starting that year. We broke all tradition and decided to help out individual candidates at the local level around the country. The DNC had never done that to this extent, but we wanted to be very aggressive and we wanted to think locally and state by state as well as nationally. We ended up going eight-for-eight in mayor's races, winning in San Antonio, El Paso, Fort Worth, Jersey City, Los Angeles, St. Louis, Omaha, and Jackson, Mississippi. I met with Mark Warner in my office on March 30, and pledged $1.5 million dollars to help him win his race for Virginia governor that year and committed $2 million to Jim McGreevey for his New Jersey governor's race as well. We were also going to think about state legislative races.

I emphasized the positive with a look at what the DNC had already accomplished in 2001:

- House & Senate Election Support
  —Invested $10 million in redistricting
  —Began multi-year technology infrastructure project
  —Launched Voting Rights Institute for electoral fairness
  —Instituted Women's Vote Center
  —Started 10-year Hispanic Outreach Project
  —Funding national message and polling research
  —Launched nationwide Rural Initiative

I explained that the DNC was spending $1.5 million to upgrade state voter files—more than the party had *ever* spent on voter files, even in presidential years—and promised the state parties that we would pay to keep their lists continually updated. As a result, the DNC corrected more than 27 million addresses and phone numbers. Can you believe it? In 2000, 27 million of our potential voters were never contacted by us and asked to vote for Al Gore. In Florida alone we had to fix more than 1.1 million incorrect addresses and phone numbers that the Florida Democratic Party had used during Al Gore's 2000 campaign for President. Don't you think we could have picked up 537 votes if we had corrected that information earlier and contacted 1.1 million more people? We also removed 335,562 deceased voters from the voter files. Just think of it: We were mailing and calling people who didn't exist, and the waste of money was mind-boggling. The end result of cleaning up those lists was a savings of $15 million in mailing costs alone.

I continued on with the sad truth of how miserably we stacked up against the Republicans. One slide showed our decades of disadvantage because of the hard-money gap: The red line for the GOP was always higher than the blue line for the Democrats and when our numbers jumped, theirs jumped more. Our projections for the future were the worst part: A red dotted line for the Republicans literally headed off the chart and a blue dotted line for us that actually started to head downward.

The result of that massive edge in funding for the GOP was a message gap. They had an interlocking system that was stronger at every point than ours and contained elements we didn't even have. The Republicans not only had prodigious e-mail capability, they also were wired to manipulate online polls, as they had done when Vice President Gore debated candidate Bush in 2000. Gore obviously won the debates, but hordes of people organized by the Republicans clicked on the online polls to skew the result toward blinking, confused-looking Bush. Throw in the phenomenon of right-wing talk radio and online message boards, and it added up to a spectacularly effective way both to mobilize voters and to steer the media on major issues and controversies that came up. Their network was big and strong, but also light on its feet and quick to react.

I showed the 2000 electoral map, and took a gulp from my water glass as everyone looked up at the sea of red everywhere except little pockets in the West, the Midwest, and the Northeast.

Another slide gave these three examples from key states in 2000:

Florida, 25 electoral votes: GOP sends nearly 300,000 GOTV e-mails right before 2000 election

West Virginia, 5 electoral votes: GOP multi-media campaign distorts Dem. gun record.

New Hampshire, 4 electoral votes: Dem. voter file had poor phone match. GOP multi-media attacks on environment & defense

The heart of the pitch was a look at the Infrastructure Gap as a result of two decades of GOP technology investment. Compared to our paltry $340,000, they had spent $13 million—Nicholson's investment in the Internet and World Wide Web in the late '90s, Barbour's investment in TV and radio studios in the early '90s, Atwater's investment in opposition research in the late '80s, and Fahrenkopf's investment in voter files in the early '80s. We also faced a daunting Space Gap with the Republicans having 140,000 square feet of office space versus 35,000 for us, even though we were facing a Hard Money Hemorrhage paying for our 35,000 square feet. Since 1985, we had spent $5.4 million for rent when that money could have been much better allocated, as another slide underlined: "Every rent payment eats up valuable dollars we should be using to win elections."

Then, turning to the future:

Democrats' Solutions Lead to Victory in 2004 and Beyond

- *Stop Hard $ Hemorrhage*: Building Ownership
  —*Hard dollar savings 2001–2008 would be $10.5 mil+*
  —House new voter contact initiatives
- *Close the Infrastructure Gap:*
  —Build Email infrastructure to boost hard $ giving
    $9.5 million more if quadruple mail list
  —Negotiating for large data sources and analytical tools to *improve voter files and donor lists*
  —Strengthen State Parties
  —TV-Radio facilities for message creation $ delivery

Then the money shot: An image of DNC HQ in 2004, a sparkling, modern building humming with power and potential. That always earned a round of applause and it did that stifling hot evening in the Clintons' backyard, but not quite as raucous as usual. I was used to firing people up with our PowerPoint presentation. I could grab strangers on an elevator and go through it with them and they'd be fired up. But that night the energy had been baked out of everybody. I thought John O'Quinn, a Texas attorney, was going to pass out, it was so hot. I was sure it was all going to work out fine somehow, but I didn't know what it was going to take.

That was when Haim Saban, media mogul and creator of the Mighty Morphin Power Rangers, stood up to speak after his wife, Cheryl, told him, "Haim, you have to help these people."

"We cannot let them fail on this project," Haim said. "I'll commit up to ten million."

Excellent! That was what I called playing big and it cleared the way for others to follow suit and aim high.

Bernard Schwartz, chairman of Loral Space & Communications, stood up next and talked about why he'd been such a great supporter of the party for so many years and why we had to step up now.

"When my father died, the Democratic Party of New York made sure my mother had a turkey every Thanksgiving," he told us.

He said he was in for $500,000.

When it was his turn, Fred Eychaner of Chicago, who owned a lot of TV and radio stations, stood up and made a commitment that was music to our ears.

"Whatever you're short, I'll write the difference," he said.

We ended up getting a record $7 million from Haim, which had us well on our way right there. Up until that year the record for an individual political contribution had been the $1.7 million Amway gave the RNC in 1996 for their TV studios. Haim blew that away. As for how he came up with the figure of $7 million, he told *The Times*, "We have two numbers in the Jewish belief that are lucky numbers—one is eighteen, and the other is seven. I thought eighteen was kind of too high so I went with seven."

Gerry McEntee, the AFSCME president, was in for a million, Peter Angelos came through with a million, and Bob Johnson, founder of B.E.T., gave us a million as well. Soon other commitments began to roll in from Reg Weaver of the NEA, Terry O'Sullivan of the Laborers, Tom Buffenbarger of the Machinists, Harold Schaitberger of the Firefighters, Ed McElroy of the AFT, Joseph Stroud and Senator (now Governor) Jon Corzine.

We had to sweat it out that night, literally, but we lined up $20 million in commitments and after that we knew we would be able to build the new headquarters. Our second dinner at the Clintons' brought in another $10 million in commitments, and we were off and running with $30 million committed for the capital campaign that was going to build a new Democratic Party. The Republicans had gotten away with an overwhelming advantage for too long and it was time to narrow the gap, as we made clear with that PowerPoint that moved Haim Saban and others to help us so generously.

"When you look at Terry's presentation, you kind of go, 'How can it be that we have two main parties in this country, and one is functioning in the twenty-first century and the other is functioning in the Stone Age?' " Haim told *The Times*.

★

WE WEREN'T LIKELY TO FIND another Haim Saban, but we had to keep looking if we were going to make our deadline and get the new building built. We scheduled a trip out to California the next January to make another big push on the capital campaign, and lined up another meeting with Steve Bing, who had helped save the L.A. convention. Steve's big issue was the environment and he was mad because the Senate had just caved on a bill that would have tightened up fuel-economy standards for cars. He went off on a rant about politicians and how they were never standing up for what they believed.

"I watch cable TV and I see you on TV all the time," he told me. "You're the only one out there fighting."

"I appreciate that, Steve," I said.

I'd done the PowerPoint so many times by then, I could recite it from memory, and I gave Steve the high points.

"We're revolutionizing the party," I told him. "The DNC is a mess and we're in the middle of a capital campaign to rebuild it."

"That's great, man," Steve said. "Terry, let me tell you something."

He sat back for a minute and downed the last of his orange juice.

"I like your fight and I'm going to help you out," he said. "I'm going to give you five."

"Five what?" I asked him.

"Well, five million," he said.

We ordered drinks to celebrate and I couldn't thank Steve enough.

The next morning, we went over for breakfast at the Peninsula Hotel with my old friend Lew Wasserman and his grandson Casey. Lew had helped us so many times but he was now eighty-eight years old. It was great to see him again, and I was in no hurry to cut to the chase. We talked about his health and how well Casey was doing in business. Finally I brought up the capital campaign and how crucial it was.

"Terry, don't be talking money," he said. "I've done this."

"No, Lew," I said. "You've worked too hard for the Democratic Party.

You've got to help us rebuild this party. This is part of your legacy. You can't walk away from us now."

He was trying to dodge it, but he always liked the aggressive stuff, and respected the give and take.

Looking at his grandfather, Casey said, "Maybe we should do a million."

In the end we ended up naming a conference room at the DNC in honor of Lew.

That August we flew to Chicago to have dinner with Fred Eychaner and see about his commitment for the capital campaign. I'm a very punctual person and we were there right on time, but not Fred. We waited half an hour, and still no Fred. Finally he came rushing in and joined us.

"I am so, so sorry," he said. "It's been a very emotional day."

I was thinking, oh no, what a wasted trip this has been. This obviously wasn't going to be the time to talk to him about money.

"Oh no, what happened, Fred?" I asked.

"I just had a little going-away party for the staff at my Chicago TV station," he said. "I've sold WPWR to Rupert Murdoch, so I had to tell them I was leaving and there would be new management."

"No worries," I told him. "I totally understand."

So Fred made himself comfortable and started looking at a menu.

"How much did you sell it for?" I asked him.

"Four hundred twenty-five million dollars," he said.

"Hallelujah, Fred!" I yelled, pounding the table. "Have we got a deal for you."

A few days later a FedEx package showed up at the DNC that was empty except for a small scrap of paper: Fred's check for $3 million.

Sometimes collecting on a commitment is all about just showing up, even when that's difficult. Marty Maddaloni, president of the United Association of Plumbers and Pipefitters, made a commitment to give us a million for the capital campaign. All he asked was that I stop by the annual "Sons of Italy" dinner in Washington.

"Terry, I'm being honored by the Italian-American Foundation," he said. "You've got to come that night and give some remarks."

"Marty, I'm there," I said.

A few months later, the night of the dinner rolled around and Dorothy was back at Sibley Hospital just after delivering our youngest, little Peter. I was there for his birth, then had to fly up to New York for the day, and afterward came back to take Dorothy and Peter home from the hospital. I had to keep pushing back my flight and Dorothy joked to me later that the nurses were murmuring among themselves, "Jeez, isn't it sad that this new mom is here with her baby and her husband is not coming to get her?"

Once I was there, everything was fine. Back at the house the kids were all excited that we were on our way home with their new baby brother. My executive assistant, Justin Paschal, was driving with me in the passenger's seat and Dorothy and little Peter were in back. We pulled out of Sibley and when we came up to Canal Road, where we would turn right to head home to McLean, Virginia, Justin took a left instead.

"Justin, where are you going?" Dorothy asked innocently from the backseat, directly behind me so she could see Justin's face but not mine. "You know we live that way."

Justin sat there gripping the steering wheel and said nothing. I was on my cell phone, so Dorothy thought maybe Justin hadn't heard her.

"Justin," she said again. "Don't we want to head toward Virginia?"

"You better talk to the Chairman," Justin squeezed out.

I was doing my best to get off my call, but it took a few minutes. Dorothy was really upset now.

"Honey," I said, turning back to her. "I just have to do this quick little drop-by, it won't take two minutes."

Dorothy was starting to well up in the backseat. She was having trouble understanding how I could be taking my wife and newborn baby to a fundraiser on our way home from the hospital. We got to the dinner and by then Dorothy was in tears, and I left her with Justin and went inside. Little Peter was sleeping peacefully and Dorothy just sat there and poor Justin didn't dare say a word. He was mortified. I was inside maybe fifteen minutes, said a few nice things about Marty, and hurried back out to the car. I felt bad for Dorothy, but it was a million bucks for the Democratic Party and by the time we got home and the kids had their new little brother in their arms, Dorothy was all smiles and we were one big happy family again. Nobody ever said life with me was easy!

25

★ ★ ★

Bush gave his first State of the Union speech on February 27, 2001, and talked up the big tax cuts he was going to give rich people like me who didn't need any more help from the government. Bush was on a mission to squander the surplus Bill Clinton had built up through years of discipline, even though a poll published that week by *The Washington Post* showed that the American people did not want the surplus paid out as tax cuts—they wanted spending on education and health care, where it was badly needed. I went on fifty-four radio shows and had eight TV appearances after the State of the Union so I could take advantage of the great chance to show how out of step this President was with the American people.

Bush must not have liked the way I was scoring so many points at his expense. In fact, I guess he was a little touchy about it. The 116th annual Gridiron Club dinner was that March 24 and because Jim Gilmore was both RNC chairman and Virginia governor, they put him at the head table with Bush and Cheney. By protocol I had to be up there, too. The Gridiron Club had a private reception beforehand for all of us sitting up on the dais and I was already there when Bush came in with his entourage. I'm not exaggerating when I say he got one look at me and immediately headed for the opposite end of the room. Cheney and Ari Fleischer both stopped by to say hello, but not Bush. Finally as he was leaving he worked his way down a line of people, shaking hands, and I planted myself in the line and stuck my hand so far out he wouldn't be able to get around me without a handshake.

"Mr. President, it's great having dinner with you," I said with my hand out.

Bush just glared at me, grunted, and practically ran down the stairs to get out of there. What was weird about the Gridiron dinners was the way people would get laughs for saying things that were true, too true. Even then, everyone knew Bush had to lean on the Vice President just to handle the basics of his new job. To his credit, he mocked himself, saying, "I hope one day I can clone another Dick Cheney. Then I won't have to do anything." He wasn't only joking, though. Not doing anything was high on his list of priorities. By that August he had spent fully 42 percent of his time as President on vacation, whether at Camp David, Kennebunkport, or Texas.

★

THE BUSH ADMINISTRATION TRIED from day one to tear down everything Bill Clinton had done for this country. Clinton had called for tougher new standards on arsenic levels in drinking water, something you'd think most people could agree was a good idea, but not these pollution-loving Bush people. The new administration came in and Bush decided to block the implementation of the tougher new standards. I'd told the DNC members the day I was elected that I was going to beef up our communications and research teams and now came a test of how serious I was. Michael Meehan and Jennifer Palmieri in communications and Jason Miner in research came to me and proposed going out right away with blistering TV ads on this issue, something the DNC had never done so soon after an election.

One ad would show a cute little blond girl holding up a glass and asking, "May I please have some more arsenic in my water, Mommy?"

I immediately gave the green light. We did another ad at the same time hitting the administration for moving to stop testing for salmonella in ground beef used in the federal school-lunch program, a test that the Clinton administration had instituted. That ad showed a little boy holding up a plate with a hamburger on it.

"More salmonella in my cheeseburger, please," the kid says.

The ads worked because people already knew for themselves that Bush couldn't care less about the environment and had little interest in protecting people from toxic chemicals. The voiceover of the ads confirmed what people suspected: "George W. Bush tried to roll back protections against arsenic in drinking water and salmonella in school lunches. Bush is trying to allow oil drilling in Alaska's National Wildlife Refuge and even in our national parks. George Bush's first hundred days. Brought to you by the oil industry, the meat industry, the chemical industry. The Republicans: These guys aren't for us."

Even my fans at Fox News agreed we had carried the day on this issue. Tony Snow, Bush's future spokesman, thought so. "By all accounts, Democrats have done a successful job of painting President Bush as anti-environmental, specifically with his policy on arsenic standards," Snow said on an April 27 Fox Special Report.

Later that year the Bush administration flip-flopped and decided to stick with the Clinton arsenic standards. Our ads had worked. We demonstrated that the party out of power could still influence public policy. To me the key to this success was keeping people fired up, excited, and eager to keep fighting. It wasn't enough just to pounce on all the huge openings Bush gave us with his reckless policies, we also wanted to make it fun. So I threw a big party to mark one hundred days of Bush, and we handed out 120-page booklets describing the many policy failures of the Bush administration—as well as T-shirts showing oil derricks on the White House lawn over the words: REPUBLICANS. THESE GUYS JUST AREN'T FOR US.

Nothing was more outrageous than Dick Cheney's secret meetings with oil-company lobbyists to rewrite the nation's energy laws. If anyone needed a hint early on about the way Bush would govern, basing everything on what was good for his buddies in the oil industry, this was it. Actually, it was bizarre that Bush would try to get away with such brazen manipulation. He released a big report prepared by Cheney that May and resorted to scare tactics.

"If we fail to act, this country could face a darker future," he said in Minnesota. "If we fail to act, Americans will face more and more widespread blackouts."

That sounded like Bush was against blackouts, didn't it? But his good friend Ken Lay, the Enron boss Bush was so chummy with that he called him "Kenny Boy," had been responsible for the rolling blackouts that hit California that year. This was no fluke or accident. It was definitely not the result of Democratic leadership in California. It was the inevitable result of unregulated energy-company profiteering with Lay and Enron in the lead. A businessman can make an excellent profit without selling out the American people like Bush's buddies thought was their birthright.

The American people knew just what was going on. Having Bush's oil buddies setting policy on energy was like putting a junky in charge of a pharmacy. I went on ABC's *Good Morning America*, and was amazed by Diane Sawyer's pretense of naiveté where these people were concerned.

People were slow to believe Bush could really put the interests of the American people behind those of his buddies in the oil and energy business, but when California Governor Gray Davis requested that the White House intervene with Enron to stop their manipulation of energy supply, they refused to take action, resulting in rolling blackouts throughout California.

"Do you really believe the Bush administration would sacrifice the national interest to oil company profits?" Diane asked me that morning.

"If you just look at the makeup of the Bush administration, it is filled from top to bottom with people from the oil industry," I said. "George Bush's message to California from day one has been 'Drop dead.' "

The intolerance of the Bush administration revealed itself early, if people were paying attention. In July 2001 it was revealed that Karl Rove had been negotiating with the Salvation Army on a plan to allow religious charities to discriminate against gays in the workplace. This was a glimpse of how far the administration would go to do favors to special interests and the Religious Right. But it was amazing how fast Rove backed off of this. He tried to pretend he had barely talked to the Salvation Army and then his own staff flatly contradicted that, saying he was "intimately involved" in the talks. That's pretty embarrassing when your own staff tells the world you're a liar.

I called for congressional hearings to investigate Rove, but I was almost alone in pressing the issue.

"Karl, come clean," I said at the time. "The White House is arrogantly evading questions about its backroom deals, and hiding the part played by Bush's top aides. . . . Rove should come forward, voluntarily, and document his role in all these controversies. If this were a Democratic administration, Republicans would be in their fourth week of congressional hearings and loudly demanding resignations, not explanations. At the very least, Bush has some explaining to do."

My comments bothered the Bush people enough that spokeswoman Mary Matalin tried as her defense to make Rove out as some kind of prince. "For Terry to succeed, they need to create villains," she said. "They had Newt Gingrich, Ken Starr, and Tom DeLay." I had to agree with her. That was an all-star lineup of villains, all right. "Now they're trying Karl and it's not going to work," she added. You'd almost have thought I'd been suggesting Rove was the kind of guy who would undermine national security by leaking the name of a CIA operative, just to exact a little payback against a political enemy. Oh no, I would never suggest anything that vile.

★

EVERY TIME I GAVE that PowerPoint presentation about rebuilding the party, I always talked about voter registration. One lesson from Florida was that we had to be aggressive about continuing to register new voters since the Republicans were going to focus on trying to deny people their right to vote. We started on that project immediately and worked with different state organizations in early 2001 to tackle the problem together. We flew out to California at the request of California party chairman Art Torres for a big operation to register new voters at a naturalization swearing-in ceremony on June 20, 2001, at the Los Angeles County Fairgrounds in Pomona. I was in my element.

It was quite a sight, thousands of newly naturalized citizens streaming out, thrilled to be clutching their new citizenship papers. We had twenty college students out there all having a great time talking to people about our New Voter Registration Initiative, which we launched that day in tandem with the California Party, handing out materials in English and Spanish and urging people to register to vote. The Republican registration effort consisted of two older ladies sitting at a card table under an umbrella, and I guess the ladies got tired of sitting there talking to each other while we had a long line of people waiting to sign up. They called the cops on us, if you can believe it, as if registering Republicans was legal but registering Democrats was not.

"You're going to have to shut this down," a young police officer around twenty-five years old told me. "You're creating a scene and disturbing the peace."

"Officer, we are not creating a scene," I said.

He insisted we were, which was absurd. All we were doing was talking to people about their rights under the Constitution. The cop was in way over his head and I looked him right in the eye and called his bluff.

"Officer, make my day," I said. "Please, put handcuffs on me. I want you to arrest the chairman of the Democratic Party for being out here registering new voters."

By that point I was really having fun, waving to the group of reporters watching me carry on.

"Okay, maybe not," he said. "Just try to keep your kids quiet."

Then he and his partner drove away and the two blue hairs sat there glaring at me. We kept right on signing up new voters and having a great time and it drove the Republicans crazy. That was one of my favorite parts of the job, getting people excited about the democratic process.

★

ANOTHER IMPORTANT PIECE OF our post-Florida strategy was to reach out to Hispanic voters and make sure they knew that we did not take their support for granted. George Bush can apparently say five or six words in Spanish and as a former Texas governor, he pretended to do a lot for Hispanics. As Molly Ivins and Lou Dubose reported in their book on Bush, the main thing he did for Hispanics as governor of Texas was to spend heavily on a Spanish-language ad campaign. "Whatever you say we need to spend, I want you to double it," Bush told the ad man for the '98 elections. "If you say two million, I want you to spend four million. . . . I want to show Latinos there's a lot of opportunity in Texas." When it came to actual spending that could help Hispanics, however, Bush made no mark. As Ivins and Dubose wrote, "Instead of a Marshall Plan of infrastructure, jobs and investment in education and the environment, the border got a martial plan—soldiers deployed by the feds along the Rio Grande."

It was more of the same politics with Bush in the White House. As I told the AP in April 2002, "The sad truth is that the Republicans' idea of Latino outreach is sprinkling a few words in Spanish during a nice White House photo-op surrounded by Hispanic leaders with lots of food."

Democrats care about Hispanics day in and day out, month after month, and year after year, not only on election day, like the Republicans. Of the five thousand Hispanics holding elective office at that point, more than 90 percent were Democrats. Even with Bush out there saying "nachos" and "tacos" as often as he could, Al Gore earned 62 percent of the Hispanic vote in 2000. These were our people and we needed them energized and excited about their future.

Bush had mariachi music at the White House on Cinco de Mayo, but his policies were hurting Hispanics and in May 2001 we announced we would begin running Spanish-language ads on what a disaster Bush's first hundred days had been, talking about his bizarre moves on salmonella and arsenic and his irresponsible tax cuts for the rich.

I flew to San Antonio, Texas, in June 2001 to make a splash by announcing that we were going to spend $10 million on our Hispanic Voter Outreach program with Texas Congressman Sylvestre Reyes as chairman. I made headlines on that trip by saying I was completely open to holding the 2004 Democratic National Convention in San Antonio, as I was. I would have loved to have our convention in George Bush's backyard. We gave that serious study, but our logistics people said there weren't enough hotel rooms.

Our outreach to Hispanics wasn't going to generate any energy unless we made it fun and in April 2002 we held a Hispanic fund-raiser at the MCI Center with Carlos Santana performing. That year we also established our

Hispanic Business Council, modeled on the Business Leadership Forum that I headed up in 1993, to seek out young entrepreneurs and businesspeople to get involved with the party. The HBC raised money for the Hispanic Outreach project and also helped get Hispanics involved in policy issues. "This is by Hispanics, for Hispanics," one of our DNC spokesmen, Guillermo Meneses, announced at the time. "It's a way of highlighting that Hispanics are part of every facet of our party."

★

IF WE WERE GOING TO make a commitment to energizing our party straight through from Election Day to Election Day, with no time off in between, we had to take advantage of our strengths. That was what I had in mind in founding the DNC's Women's Vote Center in March 2001. As I said at the kickoff on June 6, "We know that when women vote, Democrats win." Our goals were not only to reach out to women voters to increase turnout in elections, but also to set up a network of women from all age groups and all regions of the country and all economic and demographic groups. The only way to know what's important to people is to listen and we were ready to do a lot of listening. We also, of course, wanted to get more women elected to office, all the way up to President of the United States.

The following February, I signed up Ann Lewis, who had been communications director in the Clinton White House, to serve as national chair of the center, and she did a great job. Ann made sure that we weren't just proclaiming high hopes, but actively following up on our plans and getting involved with women all over the country. Contrast that with the Bush administration approach, which was to make a few symbolic gestures to try to slow Bush's slide among women voters.

★

WHEN IT CAME TO PRACTICAL LESSONS from Florida, No. 1 for me was always the painful reality that we just didn't fight hard enough. We let the Republicans make off with the prize, despite the wishes of the American people. Another area where we continually let the Republicans fight harder than us was redistricting, or carving up congressional districts in a way that made it easier to win more seats. We'd had too many Democrats who wanted to win their districts with 65 percent or more of the vote, instead of nicking off five or six or seven points and giving it to a neighboring Democrat. They wouldn't do it. The Republicans had cleaned our clocks in this area in recent years, stacking the deck for them, and we had to do something about it.

We decided early in my time as DNC chair that we were going to have to give state parties the resources to work on redistricting. We allocated a total of $10 million to support making a stronger, more strategic effort on redistricting led by Congressman Martin Frost. We hired professional staff to work with state parties and legislative caucuses and provided them with data to help them fight for fair representation. Now we were firing on all cylinders. By September that year all our projects were up and running. We were raising lots of money and hitting Bush very hard. "In fact, there hasn't been an important policy issue on which he has not taken a stand on behalf of the Democrats," Victor Kamber wrote about me in an editorial in *The Hill* on June 20, 2001.

★

I'D LIKE EVERYONE TO REMEMBER that by the end of that summer, Bush was in political trouble and the DNC was on a roll, raising money at a record rate. People were outraged with Bush's recklessness on salmonella and arsenic, his belief in payoffs to the rich through unfair tax cuts, and his lack of leadership. Our strategy of going hard right at Bush was working and it had the White House scared to death. All Bush could think to do was cower down in Crawford, Texas, taking more paid vacation in six months than most Americans get in eight years. This was the same vacation where Bush received a Presidential Daily Briefing entitled "Bin Laden Determined to Attack Inside United States." Did George Bush do anything with this information? Did he alert the FAA? Did he convene an emergency meeting of his top national security officials? No, he went for a walk in the cedar trees with his dog Barney.

The real shocking part of the story was the way Bush treated the CIA briefer who considered this information so important that he flew all the way down to Crawford to deliver this critical news in person. Bush didn't even pay attention and remarked to the briefer, "All right, you've covered your ass, now."

Heck of a job, George.

The other big issue we had that year was Social Security. Bush campaigned all over the country saying that he would not touch the Medicare or Social Security trust funds, and he raided them within his first six months in office to pay for tax cuts for the rich. He lied to the American public. He was just like his father with "Read my lips: No new taxes." This was W's "Read my lips" moment and we were not going to sit back and let him get away with it. We went out with another round of national ads, a totally unprecedented move that had the Republicans crying foul. They had a right to worry.

"Bush inherited the greatest economic expansion in our history," I told the AP in August. "In eight months, he's blown it."

Following my attacks on Enron, a group from the energy company requested a meeting with me at the DNC, and I reluctantly agreed to see them. Ken Lay was a Bush Pioneer in 2000, one of his biggest fund-raisers, and Enron as a company provided over half a million to the Bush campaign. Meanwhile, while I was chairman, Enron had not given a penny to the DNC.

They were mad about the oil-derrick booklet we'd put out and told me I was being too rough. One guy in the group got pretty hot under the collar and tried to bully me.

"You should knock it off," he said. "We've been great supporters of this party and we're not going to help you anymore."

"Good," I said. "I don't want your money."

I always try to be as nice as I can in meetings, but this guy left me no choice. I was going to have to throw them out of my office.

"I will not stop what I'm doing," I said. "I will be fair. If you ever feel that I am being unfair, then please feel free to pick up the phone and let me know. Now this meeting is over!"

As we moved in on the end of the third quarter, we were on track to have the largest first nine months ever for a nonpresidential year. To make sure we really blew the numbers out, I'd asked President Clinton to do a massive direct-mail appeal. This was his first letter since he left the White House and we knew it was going to be very successful. We spent half a million on printing and postage, expecting it to bring in $2.5 million, and our schedule called for us to drop those off at the post office on September 10th, 2001, but something came up at the last minute. No problem, we figured, we can just mail them out one day later.

26

★ ★ ★

I was in my office at the DNC early on the morning of September 11, 2001, getting ready for a meeting in Dick Gephardt's Capitol office with Congressman Martin Frost. When the first plane hit the World Trade Center at quarter to nine I saw the news on the big TV in my office, but like everyone I assumed it had just been a small commuter plane. Frost desperately wanted this meeting to talk with Dick about redistricting and kept calling to make sure I was on my way. I stopped watching TV, packed up my briefcase, and got up to leave.

Just then my executive assistant, Justin Paschal, came into my office.

"Another plane has hit the towers," he said.

This was the day people in the know had been worrying about for years. Bill Clinton had talked to me often about the growing danger of a terrorist threat against the United States. I had no idea who was responsible for this barbaric attack and the death of untold numbers of innocent civilians, but I knew Clinton and Sandy Berger had urged incoming President Bush to take strong action against a group called Al Qaeda and that Bush had ignored them.

Clinton had lashed out against Osama bin Laden, striking at his base camps in Afghanistan in August 1998 in retaliation for the Africa embassy bombings, and cynical Republicans tried to pretend they thought Clinton issued the attack for political purposes, rather than to protect the national security of the United States. Now every American understood how much damage terrorists could do to us even here at home and understood how right Clinton had been to order those air strikes.

This was a national crisis and I knew right away it was no time for politics. I canceled the DNC meeting we had scheduled for two days later in Florida and called Andy Card, the White House chief of staff.

"Is there anything I can do to be of assistance?" I asked Card. "We're all together on this. Just let me know if there's anything I can do or the party can do."

The DNC office was filled with rumors about fires being set and bombs going off in the Capitol. We soon found out that at least two other flights were unaccounted for and people worried that they were on their way to attack the Capitol, which was two blocks away. Forty minutes after the second plane hit in New York, we started seeing smoke out my window. We went out on my balcony and could see fire off in the distance on the other side of the Potomac. We didn't know what had been hit or what would be hit next or how many more planes were still in the air. I called a staff meeting after we found out it was the Pentagon that had been hit, and urged everyone to go home.

As I was in there talking to my staff, Jay Dunn walked in to hand me a note and from the look on his face I knew it was bad. That was when we found out that one of the World Trade Center towers had collapsed. Like Americans everywhere, I felt sickened to know that thousands of people had just died. A whole group of us spent the day in my office, drifting out to the balcony, coming back in to catch the latest on CNN, and wondering what other terrible things were going to happen next.

I soon joined other top Democrats in saying this was a time for all of us to stand together as one with Republicans.

"Throughout our history, the American people have always come together in times of crisis," I wrote in a letter we mailed to all DNC members the next day. "That strength has rarely been needed as much as it is now. There are no partisans today, only patriots."

Andy Card had called me the day after the attacks to invite me to a National Day of Prayer and Remembrance at the Washington National Cathedral on September 14. I was there when the doors opened at 10:45 AM, honored to be included and eager to show my solidarity. "Today we feel what Franklin Roosevelt called the warm courage of national unity," President Bush said, citing a great Democrat, and I nodded in agreement.

Nothing could compare with the sick feeling in the pit of my stomach when Justin and I flew to New York in October and the New York Police Department took us down to Ground Zero. Even then the wreckage was still smoldering. You had to see it to believe it. The great towers had so recently stood filled with people from all over the world going about their workdays, and now there was nothing but a ghoulish landscape of twisted scrap metal. I felt what everyone I knew felt: We had to lash out at the monsters who had done this. By that time we all knew it was Osama bin Laden, shielded by the Taliban regime in Afghanistan, who had inflicted this wound on us, and I stood 100 percent behind George Bush in saying we had to go into Afghanistan, crush the Taliban, and find and kill bin Laden and his Al Qaeda criminals.

As shaky as President Bush was in the hours after the September 11 attacks, New York's political leadership was rock-solid. Mayor Giuliani, to his credit, was the model of calm leadership and New York's two senators, Hillary Clinton and Charles Schumer, both showed toughness, energy, and compassion in helping all of New York come to terms with the loss they'd suffered.

"It will take a very long time before any of us can even find the words to express what this cowardly, evil act meant and did to people we knew and loved, to our city and our country," Hillary said at the funeral of her friend Father Mychal Judge, a sixty-eight-year-old Franciscan priest who rushed to the World Trade Center after the attacks and was administering last rites to a firefighter when he was killed by falling rubble.

Once President Clinton got back from Australia, where he had been traveling, he and Chelsea made several visits to downtown Manhattan to do their best to reach out and comfort emergency services workers and the citizens of New York, helping to hand out food and much-needed supplies and doing their best to be a calming force in the midst of the tragic event. Rather than seeking to divide and scare the country for cynical political gain, as Bush was doing, the Clinton family tried to unite and comfort everyone.

Hillary, as you would expect, also went to work to fight for New Yorkers' special needs in the aftermath. She joined Schumer in fighting for and securing a $20 billion aid package for New York, played a lead role in securing funding to test the health and well-being of the first responders on September 11, who braved horrific conditions to help people—and to this day she works very closely with the families of 9/11 victims on a variety of issues. Hillary has led the fight to see that the Department of Homeland Security provides the appropriate funding for a high-risk state like New York, and the Bush administration has responded by playing politics. Its July 2006 report claiming that Indiana had more potential terrorist targets (8,591) than New York (5,687) or California (3,212) would have produced loud guffaws if this was not so deadly serious an issue. "We don't find it embarrassing," a Homeland Security spokesman told the press, pathetically trying to defend a list that included the following as terrorist targets: Old MacDonald's Petting Zoo, the Amish Country Popcorn factory, the Mule Day Parade, the Sweetwater Flea Market, and a "Beach at End of a Street."

Every single American was deeply and personally affected by September 11. Not every American had the tragedy turn everything upside down at work, too. That was just a fact of life if you made your living leading the Democratic Party. We were, to put it bluntly, out of business. We'd spent months preparing the direct-mail piece with Bill Clinton's words and signature, which was waiting to be mailed out on September 11. Those half a million stamped and addressed mail pieces got rerouted straight to recycling. It was unthinkable to send out any partisan mailings for months to come. In fact, I knew we had to cease all fund-raising because of our commitment to nonpartisanship in a time of national crisis. I wondered if we might have to wait a year before we could send out a single direct-mail piece.

If my father had still been around, I knew he'd have been all for backing the President, and that was my instinct, too. The country needed leadership from the top as we pursued our attackers. Only much later, after we had gone after the Taliban and bin Laden, could Democrats really be Democrats again on the national stage, serving as an opposition party not only on domestic issues, but also on national security and foreign policy.

If not for September 11, Bush would have been gone politically. His approval ratings were sinking and his policies were hurting the country and the American people. He had nothing going for him. After the attacks we knew he was going to get a huge bounce and it soon became clear that the press would come to see its role as making him look good and downplaying any criticism of his administration's fixation on being fast and loose with the facts.

I was one of our party's most visible spokesmen and I had to keep a low profile after the attacks. I was like a caged rat. I couldn't travel. I couldn't make political calls. I couldn't make money calls. I couldn't do anything. I went to my office and worked with my staff to prepare for when we could finally come back out again. That made me feel a little better, but basically there was nothing for us to do in the immediate aftermath.

For the time being, I knew, we would have to preface any criticism of Bush by saying that we fully supported the President on striking back against our enemies. This was in the early days after September 11, when the Iraq obsession of the Bush administration was not yet obvious. We assumed Bush would actually focus on getting Osama bin Laden. But as shaken as the country was, we could not stay quiet for long about Bush's horrendous domestic policies. Too much was at stake. The problem was that after September 11, too many Democrats lost their spirit to fight. Bush and Cheney made it clear that they would brand anyone unpatriotic who dared speak out against them. That quickly cowed almost all opposition.

No one was going to keep me quiet for long. I talked to Will Lester of the Associated Press on September 28, and passed the word that we would soon get active again. "There is not an inch of room between us and President Bush on fighting terrorism around the world," I told Lester, adding quickly that we would still have plenty to say on issues like unemployment benefits for laid-off airline workers and the budget. I said I would be out doing events and campaigning for our candidates for governor in New Jersey and Virginia.

★

ONE OF THE SHOCKING REALIZATIONS after September 11 was just how freely the Bush administration was going to try to redefine reality at every turn. They knew the nation was in shock and I guess they figured people would believe anything they told them. I wasn't critical at the time, because it would have been wrong to undermine Bush's leadership on national security issues, but it was disturbing to hear the details emerging on how Bush spent the day of the attacks.

We've all seen the footage of how Bush reacted when he was sitting with a group of kids at Emma E. Booker Elementary School in Sarasota, Florida, and Andy Card whispered in his ear that terrorists had attacked the World Trade Center. Bush looked so lost, you felt bad for the man, but it's also the job of the commander in chief to get it together and offer leadership to the nation.

Mayor Rudy Giuliani was able to do that in New York City, hitting the ground running and winning praise even from people who were usually harshly critical of everything he did. During the 1963 Cuban Missile Crisis, Jack Kennedy stayed in Washington, even though a nuclear war was more imminent in those days than it has ever been.

No President ever faced a crisis quite like September 11 before, so everyone's first instinct was to cut Bush some slack for not being up to the job. The issue was when the White House started relying on falsehoods to explain the President's whereabouts that day. Rather than flying back to

Washington immediately, which was what any other President would have done in that crisis, Bush didn't seem to know what to do. Air Force One flew from Sarasota to Barksdale Air Force Base near Shreveport, Louisiana, then to Offutt Air Force Base in Omaha, and eventually arrived back in Washington near 7 P.M., almost ten hours after Bush was informed of the attacks.

Even the *Boston Herald,* a conservative tabloid, editorialized that Bush's actions in the crisis "did not inspire confidence."

Embarrassed by Bush's strange behavior, the first line of defense for the White House was to tell reporters that the President had twice said he wanted to come back to Washington but was overruled. That was really their argument. The leader of the free world had twice been overruled—first by the Secret Service and then by Dick Cheney. Didn't they realize how odd that sounded? How could the Secret Service overrule the President? Didn't the Service work for him? And didn't Dick Cheney?

Then came the phantom phone call. Johnny Apple, the veteran political reporter for *The New York Times*, got taken for a ride on the Air Force One story, and did an article the day after the attacks saying that White House officials explained Bush's zigzag path back to Washington by insisting that the White House had received "hard evidence that he was a target of the terrorists."

Apple continued: "Another senior official said that after that plane hit the Pentagon, a chilling threat was phoned to the Secret Service. 'Air Force One is next,' the official quoted the caller as saying. The threat was accompanied by code words that indicated knowledge of White House procedures, the official said."

Karl Rove put his credibility on the line, too, in putting forth the story that a phone call explained everything.

"We are talking about specific and credible intelligence, not vague suspicions," Rove told Apple.

This is one of those stories that looks very, very different from the perspective of five years later. The American public now knows that misdirection and untruth were not occasional lapses during the Bush 43 administration, they were a systematic pattern. Massachusetts Congressman Marty Meehan hit it right on the head when he shared the doubts that so many Americans had about the White House explanation and spoke his mind.

"I don't buy the notion Air Force One was a target," he said. "That's just PR. That's just spin."

He was correct. By late September it had already come out that the administration had backed off the story. *The Washington Post* ran an article on

September 27 headlined, WHITE HOUSE DROPS CLAIM OF THREAT TO BUSH. The AP reported on September 25 that administration officials had admitted they now doubted the call was ever made. The *CBS Evening News* reported on September 25 that the call "simply never happened," and that White House officials "apparently misunderstood comments made by their security detail." That is a long way from the "specific and credible intelligence, not vague suspicions" that Apple passed on to the American people as credible information.

★

THE FALSE STORY bought Bush time. He flew up to New York and visited Ground Zero, and gave the public the picture of a President in control and strong, making small talk with firefighters and talking tough about striking back at our enemies. But he would never have been able to solve the political problem of explaining his whereabouts on September 11 without his closest aides resorting to making up the story. Once the press followed up, two weeks later, no one wanted to talk about Bush's cowardice on September 11 and the story quickly died. We learned an important lesson then, which few took seriously enough, about how little Bush and his team cared about the truth and the real world and about how hard they would work to sell their delusions to the press and the public.

We also found out that Bush's promises not to politicize September 11 were as empty and hollow as the administration's explanation of the so-called threat to Air Force One. The next January, the Republicans showed how committed they were to their pledge not to use a national tragedy for narrow partisan gain. Karl Rove actually came right out and declared in a January 2002 speech to the RNC that Republicans should "go to the country" with the argument that Americans "Trust the Republican Party to do a better job of protecting and strengthening America's military might and thereby protecting America."

Not only did the Bush White House start right away to make explicit political use of the crisis after September 11, they even used the day itself as a tool for fund-raising. We found out the next spring that a souvenir photo of Bush on Air Force One on September 11 was being offered to party loyalists as a historic souvenir—to be had along with two other pictures for $150, payable to the Republican National Committee.

This was a huge opening for us. I went on TV and pointed out how the White House had gone back on its word. To some that might have seemed risky. My attitude was: We have to hold the Republicans accountable.

"We know it's the Republicans' strategy to use the war for political gain, but I would hope that even the most cynical partisan operative would have cowered at the notion of exploiting the September 11 tragedy in this way," I said at the time.

Later that year, I told the *Chicago Tribune*: "All Americans trusted that President Bush would never exploit the national crisis that united us. But we watched as he used September's tragedy to explain away last August's deficits. And then he cynically made 9/11 the cornerstone of the Republican 2002 election strategy."

★

NOTHING SUMMED UP my strategy of taking the fight to Bush in 2001 better than my commitment to working double-time to help local candidates around the country. We knew that the political team at the White House was going to use September 11 as a political weapon, playing on people's understandable fears to turn politics into a gut-level emotional reaction rather than a reckoning of which party could better serve the needs of the American people. For some Democrats, the potency of this approach was paralyzing. They wanted to wait out the crisis atmosphere and pick up the fight down the road. I disagreed strongly. We had to keep up the pressure on Bush every way we could. If that meant flying the leader of the Democratic Party around to get involved in local races, I was all for it.

I especially enjoyed flying back home to Syracuse to campaign for Matt Driscoll, the Democrat running for mayor against Republican Bernie Mahoney. Matt was known in Syracuse for years as the owner of Rosie O'Grady's Tavern on the West Side, which my father used to visit now and then. Like a lot of people, Matt got into politics when he thought the city was ignoring his requests for permits. By 2001, Matt was Common Council President, and when Bush appointed the Republican mayor, Roy Bernardi, as deputy director of HUD that May, Matt took over as mayor for the rest of Bernardi's term. Now he already faced reelection.

I flew up to Syracuse on October 14 for a fund-raiser, joined by Hillary and Chuck Schumer, and also announced the DNC was giving the Driscoll campaign $50,000. Unfortunately, my mother couldn't be there, but I mentioned that she was going to lead the sixty-five-and-older vote for Matt. "Millie promises to do whatever she can to ensure your victory next month," I said.

"I'm not just here today because Syracuse is my hometown," I said, explaining the new role of the DNC on my watch. "We're no longer just a presidential campaign committee. We're about winning elections at all levels. We're tending to the grass roots and reconnecting with local party organizations. We're building a full-service, one-stop shop, providing resources and support to help Democrats win races up and down the ballot."

Dayton, Ohio, was another repeat stop on my circuit that fall. Rhine McLin was running hard, trying to defeat incumbent Michael Turner and become the first woman and third African American to be mayor of Dayton. I flew down on October 9 to support her campaign with $50,000 from the DNC, and then came back on November 4 to go to church with Rhine and Ohio Congressman Tony Hall. Then Rhine and I went and played bingo! That was what you called retail politics and I loved it, sitting there with working men and women having a little fun. Many weekends that fall I spent time with legendary actress Cicely Tyson and comedian Chris Tucker, who were on the road for us doing get-out-the-vote events. The three of us barnstormed through Virginia on October 13 and wound up at the Oceana naval base in Norfolk, where we got a full tour of the facility and served as judges for their annual chili cook-off.

On October 23 I did a press conference with Shirley Franklin, a former aide to Andrew Young who was running for mayor of Atlanta. Two days later I was in Durham, North Carolina, to endorse Bill Bell, an African American who was running against incumbent Republican Nick Tennyson. (Bill ended up winning by only 366 votes, so I was glad I'd done what I could for him.) I also went to Manchester, New Hampshire, in early November to do an event with Mayor Bob Baines, a former high school principal who was running for reelection.

★

LATE IN THE CAMPAIGN for the Democratic nomination for New York mayor that fall, a flyer was circulated that reproduced a *New York Post* cartoon of one candidate, Bronx borough president Freddy Ferrer, kissing the Rev. Al Sharpton's rear end, and word spread that the campaign of former New York public advocate Mark Green was responsible. Mark emerged as the Democratic nominee for mayor, but given the bitterness over the flyer episode, it wasn't clear Freddy was going to accept the result and endorse Green. Mark wasn't worried, though. A Quinnipiac University Poll that appeared on October 24 found Green with a 51–35 percent edge over the Republican candidate, billionaire Michael Bloomberg, and when I met with Mark after the runoff, he was in no mood to listen to my calls for unity.

"You need to call Freddy Ferrer," I told him.

"Terry, I'm up almost twenty points," Mark said. "I don't need him. I don't have to beg him for his support. I can win without him."

"Don't ever say that, Mark," I said. "You know what? Win first. You need everybody."

I met with Freddy and his campaign chairman, Roberto Ramirez, and they showed me the controversial flyer. I'd have been mad, too. This was a big, fat mess. Freddy was furious and so were many of his supporters in the African-American and Hispanic communities. Mark's double-digit lead dwindled in no time. A poll published three days before the election found Green's lead down to 42–37 with 20 percent undecided, a very bad sign for Mark. Bloomberg, meanwhile, was spending his own money freely, flooding the airwaves with his ads.

We did our best to bring everyone together, organizing a big unity rally and unity dinner at the Sheraton on November 2, the Friday before the election, hosted by Miramax chairman Harvey Weinstein. The President and Hillary were both there, hosting along with Chuck Schumer, but unfortunately, Freddy Ferrer and Roberto Ramirez were not. The flyer issue had flared up again when the New York *Daily News* reported that several Green aides held a meeting in Brooklyn on October 4 and allegedly discussed attacking Freddy with the leaflets and other techniques. "It is using racism, racial hysteria, and racial fear, something that we cannot and should not and must not tolerate in the Democratic Party," Sharpton told the *New York Post*, threatening to lead a boycott of the election. "We will not be treated like the bastard children of the Democratic Party."

Harvey Weinstein was furious at Freddy for snubbing him by not showing up at a unity dinner he chaired, but he went to work that weekend trying to broker some kind of behind-the-scenes peace plan between Freddy and Mark Green. Harvey wanted to be the kingmaker and save the day for the Democrats by getting Freddy to endorse Green. So the day before the election, Harvey met at the Four Seasons Hotel bar with Freddy, Al Sharpton, Roberto Ramirez, and Ken Sunshine, a former assistant to New York mayor David Dinkins who went on to be a top PR man, representing Ben Affleck, Justin Timberlake, and Leonardo DiCaprio. Ken explained to me later that the group spent about four hours in the bar, starting around 2 P.M., and then went upstairs to a suite, where they kept drinking and ordered some pizzas. Harvey ate three pizzas himself, Ken said, and as they were eating and drinking the group came up with a plan to have Bill Clinton meet with Harvey, Freddy, and Al Sharpton, to help broker peace so that they could make a dramatic announcement that would get good play on the eleven o'clock news. The plan was always to make a huge splash in the media, as Ken specified to me later.

I knew none of this at the time, however. That Monday we did the last of our many unity events, this time in Bryant Park with Senator Ted Kennedy. That evening I was taking the train to New Jersey for an event at an African-American church for Jim McGreevey, the final event in his campaign for governor. I couldn't wait to get out of New York and when Josh Wachs, Jennifer Palmieri, and I got onto the 6:05 Amtrak train to Trenton, Josh turned to me and said, "Thank God that's over." I shared the feeling.

Soon my cell phone rang and it was the office telling me Harvey Weinstein urgently needed to talk to me.

"I'm in a hotel room at the Four Seasons with Al Sharpton and Freddy Ferrer, and they're going to come out and endorse Mark Green," Harvey told me. "All we need is for Bill Clinton to come to the hotel and bless the deal."

Since I had just seen the President and Mark Green two hours earlier and neither had mentioned anything to me, this all sounded very strange.

I told Harvey I'd get back to him and immediately called the President to check this out. Doug Band got on the line, said Clinton was meeting with Shimon Peres, and asked if I wanted to interrupt.

"No, Doug," I said. "But is he going to an event with Freddy Ferrer, Al Sharpton, and Harvey Weinstein?"

"I think so," Doug said. "We've got our tuxedos on. We've got another event first and then I think we're going to stop by there. Harvey called and asked him to stop by."

"Doug, has anyone called Mark Green to ask him if he wants this to happen?" I asked. "He's the nominee."

"No, Terry," he said.

"Doug, please do not have the President leave that office until I call Mark Green," I said.

I called Mark and asked what he thought. He said it was a terrible idea and could cost him the election.

"Terry, please tell the President not to do it," he said.

So I called Doug back and told him Mark was adamantly against the idea. I was on the train to Trenton this whole time, and Josh and I finally arrived and headed over to the Shiloh Baptist Church for the event. I arrived at the church and the pastor welcomed me and took me to greet a dozen ministers gathered down in the basement beforehand. I kept checking my cell phone and realized I was getting no reception, which was a problem since I knew I had to call Harvey. The pastor said I could use his phone, but the handset was broken and I'd have to use the speaker phone. No problem, I told him as I called up Harvey in the room full of ministers and quietly told him that Clinton would not be attending because Mark Green didn't want him to.

"I'll rip your b—— off!" Harvey screamed at me over the speaker phone, and he was just getting warmed up.

In my entire life I had never been talked to like that. Meanwhile, everything Harvey screamed was coming through loud and clear for the room full of ministers. I was sure these pastors had never heard this kind of language. They all stopped dead.

"You mother f——!" Harvey barked in his Queens accent.

Unfortunately, I can't print most of what he said here, but I'll tell you it seemed like he yelled a long time. I let Harvey vent for a few minutes and then I'd had enough. I told him what I thought of his idea in very colorful language, told him to do something with his anatomy, and hung up. Then I joined the ministers on the altar.

The bottom line was that the President should not have gone to an event if the candidate didn't want him to do it. Clinton was in a tough spot with Harvey, though. This was his buddy, the guy who did things like helping set up that memorable *Good Will Hunting* weekend at Camp David, and Clinton never liked disappointing a friend.

Before long Harvey reached Clinton again and they had a heated conversation. As the two of them shouted back and forth, Clinton noticed the wall art, cupped the phone, and turned to Doug and said, "That's a beautiful print of New York." So they bought it for him that Christmas and now that print hangs in his office.

Doug Band called to tell me the meeting was back on.

"Sir, are you going or not going?" I asked Clinton when I reached him on the phone.

"Mac, they tell me I can go to this meeting and there will be no press," he said.

"Mr. President, I just don't believe that," I said.

"Mac, they promised me no press," he said.

I called Harvey back and said the President would come on one condition—that there would be no press.

"There's no press, no press, no press," Harvey told me.

I couldn't let it go. I called Clinton back once again to tell him one more time I was against this meeting.

"I just don't feel good about this thing, sir," I said. "I think it's a mistake."

Clinton attended his black-tie event and then drove over to the Four

Seasons in a small motorcade with three or four cars. When they pulled up, there must have been at least a hundred press waiting out front.

"Let's get out of here," Doug Band told the Secret Service driver.

So now we had an O.J. situation. The press saw Clinton's motorcade and came chasing after him. Clinton had his Secret Service agent go around the block and this swarm of press was back there chasing after him, the whole thing now being shown live on New York 1, the city's all-news cable station.

I was not surprised to get another call.

"Mac, there's press here!" Clinton yelled at me. "What do I do now?"

"Please leave," I said. "I told you they'd be there."

"They followed us all around the block and we just left," Clinton says now. "God that was awful. That was one of the real low points of my political experience."

Harvey was so mad, he came out that night and endorsed Bloomberg, just three days after he had hosted a Mark Green fund-raiser. He also called all his friends urging them to vote for Bloomberg.

"They wanted me to come meet with them and they would all pull together and support Green and he would pull out the election at the end," Clinton says now. "That was the idea, but if I didn't, it was going to all be my fault. I said, 'Guys, I'm out of this business. Hillary's a senator, for God's sake.'"

I was back in Washington at DNC headquarters on Election Day. Jim McGreevey was on his way to victory in New Jersey, which was great news. I went to New Jersey for his victory event and congratulated him. Mark Warner was going to win in Virginia, too, so we were two for two in governor's races. I drove up to New York and met Mark Green in his suite, which by that point in the night was like a wake. There were about twenty people up there and no official word yet, but Assemblyman Denny Farrell was calling his buddies at polling places and getting numbers and it was clear we were in trouble. There was nothing to do but sit and wait for the final word. When it came, I went downstairs with Mark and stood on stage with him for his concession.

Other than New York, we went ten-for-ten in mayor's races, and after Mark's concession I went back up to the suite and called Matt Driscoll, Shirley Franklin, Bob Baines, Rhine McLin, and all the other winning mayors to congratulate them. Then I called and congratulated fifteen county executives who had won. It was tough to take. We never should have lost the New York mayor's race, no matter that Bloomberg spent $73.9 million on his own campaign. New York was the only big race we lost that day and it was our own damn fault.

27

★ ★ ★

The annual White House reception for the Kennedy Center Honors was always a great event during the Clinton years, because the President and Hillary loved to have a variety of smart, creative, accomplished people around at the White House, and looked forward to hours of great conversation with people they had never thought they'd have a chance to meet. I wasn't sure what to expect on December 2, 2001, when Dorothy and I were invited to the Bush White House for that year's reception because of Dorothy's position on the Kennedy Center Board of Trustees. This was always considered a bipartisan event, a living tribute to John F. Kennedy with Democrats and Republicans well represented no matter who was in the White House.

Considering how hard I had been working to defeat Republican candidates around the country and how tough I'd been on Bush, I knew I hadn't made any friends in the Bush White House. We'd elected governors in two states that previously had had Republicans in charge and the same weekend as the White House event, we found out that we had won the mayor's race in Houston. As *The New York Times* noted that morning, "It was the third closely watched victory for the Democrats in recent months, including gubernatorial victories in New Jersey and Virginia, and it carried the added satisfaction of beating the Republicans in the city where President Bush spent part of his adolescence and where his parents live."

I had sent twenty-five people down from Washington to help incumbent Mayor Lee Brown in the Houston race. The Bush family was so invested in this one, George 41 and Barbara did TV commercials for the Republican candidate, Orlando Sanchez.

"They threw everything at us," I told *The Times*. "This is embarrassing for them. They lost in the President's backyard."

Overall that fall, we won thirty-nine out of the forty-two mayor's races in cities with more than 100,000 people and I knew my quotes in the papers were really going to get the goat of Republicans. I showed up for the reception at the White House, where I had been so many times as a friend of the President during the Clinton years, and I was about as welcome as a Christmas card from the IRS.

However, for me it was great to be back. I got a warm welcome from all my friends on the White House staff and went over to the buffet table, where I had spotted the Vice President camped out by the crab cakes, loading up.

"Terry, how are you?" he said.

"Great," I said. "How'd you like those elections?"

"Well, not much," he said, frowning. "But we'll see what happens next year."

Given all my public criticism of Bush, I debated whether to go through the receiving line for the President and First Lady. It felt awkward going through the line for a man I'd been blasting so much. So many people there that night were speculating on whether I'd do it, I thought they were going to have a pool.

"You ought to do it," Mack McLarty and Vernon Jordan both told me.

I decided the respectful move was to go through the line. It was weird, because I'd been through receiving lines at the White House dozens of times, and they always would announce each guest to the President. Not this time. For some reason the marine escort brought me so close to the President, our heads were only inches apart. Bush had turned away to say good-bye to the guests ahead of us in line and when he turned back around and saw who was standing there, he recoiled and scooted back a few inches.

"Mr. President, it's great to be back in the White House," I said. "Thanks for having us!"

"Great to have you back," Bush said. "Just don't steal the silverware!"

If you've heard Jon Stewart's imitation of Bush's heh-heh, heh-heh laugh, that was how he sounded.

"Like you stole the elections, Mr. President?"

Okay, actually that's not what I said. That was only what I thought. Unlike Bush, I wanted to take the high road. I really had to work at not blurting that out. Pulling punches doesn't come naturally to me. Dorothy cringed, waiting to hear what verbal barrage I was going to launch in response. She could easily imagine me being hustled out the back door by the Marine Guards and maybe worked over for a while.

But I thought: *You know what? I'm at the White House. I'll be a bigger guy than that and this is Dorothy's night.*

"I have no intention of doing that, Mr. President," I said. "I'm just honored to be here."

I discovered that there are actually times when Bush knows he has committed a faux pas. He immediately turned to Dorothy and did his best to show some patrician charm.

"You do know Laura, don't you?" he asked her.

"Oh, of course!" Dorothy said.

He probably would be high-fiving with Rove and Cheney later about being such a petulant frat boy at heart that he had to needle me about the Republicans' success in scoring points against Democrats with big, fat, messy lies. The idea that Clinton people had stolen from the White House was part of the big package of falsehoods that Bush's people had shopped to the press just after the Clintons moved out of the White House. Bush knew it was all a crock, but either he had started believing the lie himself or he made no distinction between reality and fiction. Either way, it didn't say much for him.

One morning a couple of weeks later, Dorothy and I got a laugh over the "Reliable Source" column in *The Washington Post*, which ran a list of readers' alternative comebacks that I could have made to Bush after his silverware crack.

Here were a few:

"That's OK. I'll just get Katherine Harris to steal it for me."
                                        —Matt Erickson
"I have no intention of doing that, sir. I know how much you'd hate having to recount it."
                                        —Eric McHenry
"I'm sorry, sir; have you mistaken me for Mr. Lay?"
                                        —Thantos

★

THE DAY OF THAT RECEPTION at the White House, the Enron scandal had reached its inevitable conclusion: The company had finally filed for bankruptcy on December 2. Enron was the perfect metaphor for the Bush White House. The rich got richer and the little guy got screwed. I'd thrown that group of Enron lobbyists out of my office the previous July, and we found out that after that meeting, with the company's finances in shambles, Enron gave another $80,000 to the RNC on top of $52,000 they'd already given them that year. Even when they were in trouble and their stockholders were taking it on the chin, thanks to the lies of Kenny Boy and the others, they still kept writing checks to Republicans, including one on December 31, 2001, to Tom DeLay's PAC for $50,000.

The Enron scandal was a textbook case of how Bush's embrace of cronyism at the White House could lead to huge problems for ordinary Americans, not only for those who lost their hard-earned nest eggs when the Houston-based energy company went bankrupt, but for all Americans, who needed a government that formed its energy policy by looking out for the common good, not the thick wallets of its buddies in the energy industry. Talk about cronyism!

How about Jeb Bush, the President's kid brother, who invested in Enron before he became Florida governor and turned a profit on his personal $91,000 investment? Under his leadership as governor, the state's pension fund lost more than $300 million on Enron stock—that was the most any public pension fund in the country lost on Enron stock, and Florida, under Jeb, had to work at it. Even after the SEC had already announced in 2001 that Enron was under investigation, Florida—incredibly—kept investing in Enron, with its money manager taking the pension money and buying an additional 2.7 million Enron shares on top of the 4.9 million Florida had already bought. Florida paid between $9 and $82 per share for its Enron stock and cashed out at 28¢ per share.

Jeb was in effect the head of the three-person state Board of Administration trustees who oversaw the pension fund and appointed its members. That made it Jeb's responsibility to protect that pension money, but he had other priorities. He had e-mailed an Enron lobbyist in early 2001 saying he'd "love" to meet with Kenny Boy Lay, close personal friend of the Bush family. Jeb's statements about his ties to Enron turned sadly comical a year later when Jeb kept denying he'd even spoken to Lay—a day after Jeb's own spokesman had already admitted Jeb and Lay had talked. Jeb was rewarded for his loyalty to his Enron buddies at the expense of the state workers whose future was at stake. In January 2002, former Enron president Richard

Kinder hosted a $500-a-head fund-raiser for Jeb in Houston. But at least we can rest assured that the stinking mess of Jeb putting cronyism before the people of Florida was carefully investigated—right? Not quite. Actually, the investigation into the pension fund scandal was delayed at the request of Jeb's chief of staff, who made the request to the then-Inspector General at the Department of Health and Human Services—none other than Janet Rehnquist, daughter of then-Supreme Court Chief Justice William Rehnquist. That's the Republican version of accountability in action.

"How about that Enron story?" I said at our DNC meeting in mid-January 2002. "Folks, it's simply outrageous, and my heart goes out to the employees and shareholders who were victimized by a web of greed and deceit. I do want to be fair though; there's no evidence yet that anyone in the Bush administration did anything improper in this case. But there are interesting parallels between Enron and the administration it so generously supported. Think about it—risky investments, mountains of debt, accounting shenanigans, and a little fuzzy math, then the folks at the top cash in while innocent working people are left holding the bag."

When the scandal broke, Bush panicked, true to form, and denied knowing Lay. An avalanche of evidence of their close friendship in the '90s quickly emerged, including birthday and Christmas cards, and photos of the two together, and the White House spin machine went into overdrive. Bush backpedaled furiously and admitted that he indeed knew "Kenny Boy." I let loose with a massive attack on Bush and his connections to Enron.

"Even before the Enron debacle, President Bush was perceived in polls as closer to corporate interests than to those of common citizens," *The Washington Post* wrote on Sunday, January 20. "Regardless of GOP complicity, the case of Enron—in which thousands of workers lost their savings while executives cashed out—serves as a sort of shorthand for a Democratic class-strife message."

I went on *Meet the Press* that same Sunday and blasted Bush for his ties to Enron, calling on the White House to disclose every contact that Enron had with the administration. I turned up the heat on presidential spokesman Ari Fleischer for his dissembling on Enron, even though as Enron was going bankrupt Lay called Bush's secretary of the treasury and secretary of commerce. In addition, Enron had been represented by Marc Racicot and Ed Gillespie—two men who would become RNC chairmen.

"It does make us suspicious when they say there are no contacts, and then it comes out at the highest levels of the Bush administration they did have contacts," I said on *Meet the Press*. "Put it all out there and people can make the decisions. . . . The President tomorrow should call Ari Fleischer into the Oval Office and say, 'Quit embarrassing this administration. Quit going to the White House podium every day and saying that we've disclosed everything.' . . . Either he's deceiving us purposely or he is totally out of the loop and they need a new White House spokesman."

Before I had even made it back home after my appearance on *Meet the Press,* my assistant, Alecia Dyer, was surprised to get a call for me from White House Operator Thirteen. It had been a year since my last call from a White House operator. How far I'd fallen, going from Operator One to Operator Thirteen. During the Clinton years I didn't even know there *was* an Operator Thirteen. Ari Fleischer wanted to talk to me, but I didn't even call him back. Why bother?

I was at the MCI Center on January 28 watching a Syracuse-Georgetown basketball game with Paul Begala, Mark Shields, and Al Hunt when I got a call from my press secretary, Jennifer Palmieri. Matt Drudge had posted one of his flashing-red-light items talking about my investment in a company called Global Crossing.

"So what?" I said. "That was in *The New York Times* three years ago."

Jeff Gerth did a front-page story for *The Times* on December 12, 1999, reporting that I was able to "turn a $100,000 investment into an almost $20 million windfall."

Now Drudge was quoting a "top White House source" saying, "McAuliffe is a guy who made millions and millions and millions off this Global Crossing stock? And the company goes bankrupt and he has the gonads to criticize anyone on Enron!"

Jennifer asked me what we should do.

"Line up the television interviews," I said. "Let's go!"

You would have thought I'd gone down to Fort Knox and started loading up gold bricks from the U.S. Treasury, the way the Republicans carried on over my investment in Global Crossing. This was their clumsy attempt to get me to back off of the Enron scandal, trying to make me look like an insider, and it was not going to work. If there had been something wrong with my Global Crossing investment, I'd have been thrashed around when *The Times* article came out, but no one cared. Nor should they have. I think it just bothered these Republicans that a Democrat made a smart investment and was rewarded for that. They tried to make it seem like a crime for a Democrat to earn a living or make money. If it had been a Republican, he would have been hailed as a hero, had his picture on the cover of *Forbes* magazine and probably ended up as secretary of the treasury.

There was nothing complicated about my buying the stock. Like many in the late '90s, I was on the lookout for investments related to the Internet. I was approached by my longtime friend Mike Steed in March 1997 about being one of the early investors in a venture to build and lay the first independent, state-of-the-art, high-speed fiber-optic cable connecting the United States and Europe. Because of the explosion of the Internet, it was clear that a lot more cable would be needed to handle that traffic. In fact, the company would end up carrying half the traffic between the United States and Europe. Like all investments in startups, this was highly risky, but I put up $100,000. I was what you call an "angel investor," meaning that I was investing in an idea before a company even existed. It was called Atlantic Crossing then and changed its name to Global Crossing.

The company went public seventeen months later in August 1999 and the value of my stock skyrocketed. No one ever knew how much of the stock I sold, since as a private investor at the time, I was under no obligation to share that information. I made a lot of investments and some worked out, but most did not. Investors in startup companies are lucky if they hit one out of ten. I invested half a million in a company called Value America, an online shopping store, and when it went under I lost the half million. The same folks who invited me to invest in Global Crossing also invited me to invest in Asia Global Crossing and I lost my entire investment of $100,000. Notice Drudge didn't give that one a flashing red light.

Over the next few days after Drudge did his item I was all over TV and radio defending myself against these ridiculous allegations. I had been an early investor in a startup, and put up my own money with no guarantee that I would see a return. Unlike the Enron scandal, where insiders were trading information unavailable to the public, I never worked for the company, I never set foot in their headquarters, and I was not on their board of directors.

Even with the facts out there, the Bush machine kept attacking me. I couldn't believe the stupidity of the White House in going after me when the President's own father was vulnerable. The cochairmen of Global Crossing, Gary Winnick and Lod Cook, were both big Republicans, both members of the board of trustees for Bush 41's library who had made seven-figure contributions. Bush flew more than six thousand miles to Japan and gave a speech touting Global Crossing, and instead of cash, took $80,000 in stock at a sweetheart price of 34¢ a share, which was what I had to pay for it a year earlier when the company had no value, since it was only an idea.

I went on Fox News on January 29 with *Hannity & Colmes.*

"George Bush 41, didn't he take a bunch of stock to go do a speech for this company in Japan?" Alan Colmes asked me.

"Right," I said.

"And we don't know whether he sold it, whether he sold high or low or what he did with that," Colmes said.

"Well, the word is he sold it," I said. "He made about $14 million. But the interesting thing is he got his shares of stock a year after those of us put ours at risk. He got it at a special price a year later. So, let's investigate the former President of the United States."

"Well, you know they're going to try to pin this on you," Colmes said. "They're going to try to make you now a scapegoat and tie you to Enron or make a comparison."

"Listen, I bought stock in a company," I said. "I do it all the time. What can I tell you? It's capitalism. You buy stock and sell it."

"Eighteen million," Sean Hannity said.

"What are you, jealous or something?" I asked him. "I mean, you buy stock. It was a great company."

Within twenty-four hours after I started saying on Fox News that Bush 41 should be investigated, the Republicans stopped pushing the issue and it went away. Oh, and by the way, on April 11, 2006, the SEC ruled after a four-year investigation that nobody had committed any wrongdoing at Global Crossing and no enforcement action was recommended. And we all know that Enron didn't get one of those letters from the SEC.

★

I'D ENDURED SCREAMING MATCHES and stifling heat in working toward my goal of getting the Democratic Party out of debt and building a completely modernized headquarters that could finally compete with the RNC. Normally you figured you needed many years for this large a capital campaign, but we didn't have that kind of time. We were in an eighteen-month sprint from the time I started as DNC chairman, and by February 2002 we were in good enough shape financially to begin planning the work on our new building. We didn't have a single permit or contract, so we were still a long way off, but we were getting there. I'd come out in favor of campaign finance reform, which would not influence our modernization project; so long as the money had been raised before the legislation became law, the money could be spent on infrastructure after the effective date of the legislation. That, at least, was what the Democrats in Congress promised me.

As we approached a vote in the House on Shays-Meehan, the House version of McCain-Feingold, I started to wonder if I could count on the assurances I'd received. I called Dick Gephardt on the afternoon of February 13, as the House was gearing up for a vote, and he told me not to worry.

"Terry, we've got that taken care of," Dick told me. "They won't change it."

"Dick, these guys stick us every chance they get," I said.

"We've got it worked out," Dick said. "As long as you've got the money in, you can spend it to build your building."

Tom Daschle also called me and said I didn't need to worry. The Senate would be voting some weeks later on McCain-Feingold and Tom wanted the legislation to pass. He was worried that if Democrats let the Republicans pull a fast one on us, I might end up opposing McCain-Feingold.

So on the night of the House vote on Shays-Meehan, I went to see a special screening of *The Rosa Parks Story* at the Ronald Reagan Building. As I was walking out of the theater after 11 P.M., I got a call from the office saying that House Democrats were caving. I tried to reach Dick, but he was on the House floor during the furious last-minute maneuvering on campaign finance. I found out later they were referring to me on the House floor, talking about the so-called "Anti-McAuliffe Amendment," which was being put forth by Jack Kingston, the Republican congressman of Georgia, specifically drafted to undermine our effort to rebuild our party headquarters—requiring all money to be spent by the end of the year. This was one of twelve so-called poison-pill amendments put forth—and in the end, the only one that passed, when our own members deserted us. Shays-Meehan passed at 2:43 A.M., banning soft money and also including the Anti-McAuliffe Amendment, which cast our modernization project in serious doubt. (McCain-Feingold passed in the Senate on April 2.)

"I don't blame the Republicans," I told the *L.A. Times*. "If I were them, I, too, would want to stop the Democrats from building an arsenal that will obliterate them for the years to come."

But I did blame the Democrats for once again getting taken advantage of and just taking it. This was so important to the future of the party and now all our plans were in doubt. I met the next day with Leah Daughtry, my chief of staff, and Joe Sandler, DNC counsel, to discuss our next move. Joe was furious.

"We can't build it now," he said.

The Republicans thought they had me in a corner. There didn't seem to be any way to spend all the money before the deadline. But I decided we were going to hire my friend Al Dwoskin, a big northern Virginia developer, to handle the whole job, and we were going to pay him all $20 million up front in one lump payment. I told Joe of my plans.

"Terry, interesting idea," he said, "but they may come back and sue you."

"Let them sue me!" I said. "Who cares? What other option do we have?"

So I got Al Dwoskin on the phone. Al and his wife, Claire, had been great supporters of the Democratic Party for years, and he said he'd be glad to help me out pro bono.

"I should alert you, though," I told Al. "I may get sued and you may get sued, too."

"Terry, we've got to do this for the sake of the party," Al said. "Count me in. I'm with you on this all the way."

So I put the phone down and had Joe Sandler wire Al the money. Fortunately, the Anti-McAuliffe Amendment forced us to get Al Dwoskin involved, and Al was phenomenal. He builds strip malls for a living, and became the owner's rep for this new building project. It was the best thing that ever happened to us. We had to move out of the headquarters in December and into temporary space on Sixteenth Street for one year. We were on schedule to move back into the new, modernized headquarters in late January 2004, just in time to get ready for the 2004 primaries.

28

★ ★ ★

We knew that in the 2004 elections we were going to be facing an incumbent President with an unlimited war chest running at a time of war. Bush could be beaten, but it was going to take a tough and smart campaign. We would have to be willing to use new strategies, and early on I decided we would be smart to rethink our primary schedule, recognizing that we weren't going to change Iowa and New Hampshire's first-in-the-nation status but needed to have some states that reflected the rich diversity of our party early in the process. My goal for the new primary calendar would be to have an early nominee who would be battle-tested in all regions of the country.

I loved Iowa and New Hampshire and the retail politicking those states required. There was a lot of romance associated with the special status of Iowa and New Hampshire. People remembered how Jimmy Carter revolutionized primary politics in 1976 by coming out of nowhere to win in Iowa after devoting more time and energy there than anyone ever had before. Many had read Teddy White's *The Making of the President, 1960,* which sketched a romantic picture of Jack Kennedy campaigning in the snows of New Hampshire. Iowa and New Hampshire were all about going door to door and showing up in donut shops and beauty salons to talk one-on-one with as many people as possible.

However, Iowa and New Hampshire were lacking in diversity. The African-American community votes for our candidates 92 percent of the time but accounts for less than 1 percent of the total population of New Hampshire and 2 percent of Iowa. I thought it was important for us to have a state like South Carolina with a large African-American population hold its primary earlier in the process. Likewise, the Hispanic community supports our party 66 percent of the time and with a growing population, so it was important to bring in states like Arizona and New Mexico.

Our plan became very controversial. Some people thought any change was bad. Others thought we were not shaking things up enough. Leading the charge for more radical alterations in the primary calendar was Michigan Senator Carl Levin, who thought Iowa and New Hampshire should not have exclusive rights on voting first and that it was time for other states to have a turn. He had pushed unsuccessfully for change before the 2000 elections and was back in full force this election cycle. He made it very clear on the telephone that if I allowed Iowa and New Hampshire to go first, then Michigan was going to act on its own and put its primary first.

Carl and I had many heated discussions. I have great respect for Carl and broke tradition and allowed him to argue for a rule change before the full DNC meeting on January 19, 2002. Levin came and made his pitch to end the monopoly of Iowa and New Hampshire and he was given a full hearing. We took a vote on his proposal, and his motion was unanimously defeated. After the vote, the issue was settled in my mind—however, not in Carl's.

I got a call on February 1, 2003, from Carl, John Dingell, and John's wife, Debbie, a DNC member. They told me they were going to hold the Michigan primary before New Hampshire's, which would have led to complete chaos since New Hampshire has a law stating that it must hold the first primary and the DNC had already voted on this issue and settled it.

"If you do that, I will take away fifty percent of your delegates," I told them.

They thought I was bluffing. But it was my responsibility as chairman to take action for the good of the party, and taking away half their delegates was well within my authority. Now all the presidential candidates were upset. They were getting calls from Iowa and New Hampshire asking them to pledge to come to their states no matter what Michigan did, putting the candidates in an impossible position. The whole primary calendar was in danger of spinning out of control. The candidates kept calling me and asking what was happening with the schedule, and I made it clear that I was not going to let Michigan throw the entire process out of whack. Finally I'd had enough and scheduled a meeting in Carl's Senate office for April 2 to settle this once and for all.

As I was escorted into Carl's office with my staff, Debbie Dingell and Carl's chief of staff, David Lyles, were already sitting there waiting with Carl. Sparks flew when I sat down with Phil McNamara and Josh Wachs and immediately complained about all the leaks to the press, which led to finger-jabbing and shouting back and forth between various people in the meeting. Soon Carl and I were going at it.

"I'm going outside the primary window," he told me definitively.

"If I allow you to do that, the whole system collapses," I said. "We will have chaos. I let you make your case to the DNC, and we voted unanimously and you lost."

He kept insisting that they were going to move up Michigan on their own, even though if they did that, they would lose half their delegates. By that point Carl and I were leaning toward each other over a table in the middle of the room, shouting and dropping the occasional expletive.

"You won't deny us seats at the convention," he said.

"Carl, take it to the bank," I said. "They will not get a credential. The closest they'll get to Boston will be watching it on television. I will not let you break this entire nominating process for one state. The rules are the rules. If you want to call my bluff, Carl, you go ahead and do it."

We glared at each other some more, but there was nothing much left to say. I was holding all the cards and Levin knew it.

"Well, that was a good meeting," I told my shell-shocked staff on the way out of Carl's office.

I never argued that the calendar we had in 2004 was a template for the future. You have to use the calendar to face the unique circumstances of each election cycle. Every four-year period is different. Eventually we worked out the 2004 calendar to most everyone's satisfaction. Iowa and New Hampshire would lead off in January and on February 3, seven states would vote— Arizona, Delaware, Missouri, New Mexico, North Dakota, Oklahoma, and South Carolina. We would have a very regionally balanced calendar reflecting the true diversity of our party and we were on track to have a nominee chosen by mid-March 2004, so everything would be lined up and we could have the most united Democratic Party in years.

★

THE DOWNSIDE OF TRAVELING so much as chairman was being away from my family, and having to miss ball games, recitals, and special occasions, so I valued my precious time with my kids and I tried to take them to as many events as I could. I also loved to go all out celebrating the kids' birthdays. I've got a thing about birthdays: For years I've made a point of starting just about every day by calling one or two people to sing "Happy Birthday"—it ain't pretty, but people appreciate the thought. I call my cousins, former staffers, former Presidents, old buddies from Syracuse and around the country, you name it.

For Jack's eleventh birthday, I played Super Dad and rented some rooms at the Embassy Suites in Tysons Corner so Jack could have an overnight pool party with seven of his buddies. The boys were up almost all night, running around and roughhousing. I was so scared they were going to access the adult channels on the TV that I didn't get a wink of sleep until the boys finally conked out at 4 A.M., a few hours before it was time to load the whole gang up and drive off to the Fox News studios in Washington.

"This is Fox News!" I told the boys as we piled out of my SUV. "You drink everything they have in the refrigerator and eat all their food!"

We made quite an entrance once we got there.

"Fair and balanced!" I hollered as I walked down the corridor past the makeup room.

That was my usual greeting to the Fox News crew, only this time I had eight eleven-year-old boys swarming around me, ready to go on a rampage. I brought them into the Green Room to wait, and they were literally bouncing off the walls.

"It's all yours, boys!" I said.

They took me at my word. I was off in makeup, and they were all cramming three or four cans of soda into their pockets and stuffing powdered donuts into their mouths. We went into the studio and they started running back and forth. Poor Chris Wallace, who had recently started as host of *Fox News Sunday,* was not sure what to make of these boys racing up and down his hallways. RNC chair Ed Gillespie, my competition for the day, got a kick out of seeing these rowdy, laughing boys in the studio.

Ed was the third of three RNC chairs who served opposite me during my four-year tenure. In 2001, I went against Virginia Governor James Gilmore, who lasted only a year. It was great fun going on TV to debate Jim because he had done to Virginia's economy what Bush was doing to the country's—running up gigantic deficits.

Next up for a year was Marc Racicot, former Montana governor, a nice guy who admitted to me every time I saw him that he hated the job. He was slated to become Bush's first attorney general, but was passed over in favor of the ultraconservative John Ashcroft, who was so extreme in his right-wing views that his Justice Department thought it necessary to spend $8,000 to cover two partially nude statues that had been in the building since it opened in 1930.

Then came Eddie, my favorite of the three. He and I had more in common than most people knew. We both came from big Irish Catholic families. We were both close to our dads, each named Jack, each a veteran of some of the fiercest battles of World War II. And both of us named our sons Jack in honor of their granddads. But that didn't stop Eddie and me from slugging it out on television several times a week. Sometimes after the cameras went off we would sit down and have a beer and cigar together. He wasn't going to change my views and I wasn't going to change his, but that didn't mean we couldn't be friends.

That Sunday with Ed on Fox News, Chris Wallace kept asking questions to try to make John Kerry look bad, and after fifteen minutes I'd had enough.

"I know this is Fox News, but you got any tough questions on George Bush today?" I asked.

The whole time we were doing the show, the boys were carrying on. It was going to take the Fox people quite awhile to clean up the Green Room after Jack and his friends had at it. But Chris was a good sport and invited the kids up on the set for a picture.

My children liked Tim Russert's show the best, because he freely handed out souvenirs and would invite them up on the *Meet the Press* set after the show for a big spread of food. However, Sally's favorite was CNN. She had been going there since she was two years old and knew right where to find the hot-chocolate machine, which she would hit as soon as we arrived and within minutes had chocolate all over her shirt. George Stephanopoulos outdid everyone by bringing in a chef in a white hat to cook omelettes before his Sunday show, but no one wanted to eat a heavy meal just before going on national TV—or splatter grease on their ties.

One of the best trips I took with Dori and Jack was out to Des Moines for the Iowa Caucus on January 19, 2004. As soon as we landed, we went to the governor's office in the Capitol to see Tom Vilsack. He couldn't have been nicer to the kids and gave them a personal tour of the Capitol and then we went back to his office to talk about that day's caucus. Tom and I had worked closely because of his role as chair of the Democratic Governors Association. He was a very progressive governor who had made a real difference in Iowa with his investment in education and his $800 million Values Fund program, which created or retained 20,000 high-paying jobs in two years. Tom presented a great image for the party as Iowa's first Democratic governor in three decades, and was a great American success story. He was orphaned as a baby and liked to tell the story of his adoption. His future mother came in to inspect a lineup of babies and chose little Tom because he was the plumpest, reddest, healthiest-looking baby in the lot.

As Tom and I sat down for coffee in his office, I asked him how he thought the caucus would shape up later that day. These were his picks:

John Kerry first.

John Edwards second.

Howard Dean a distant third.

Picking Kerry and Edwards first and second was not a surprise, but putting Dean at a distant third was. Dean had been leading in *The Des Moines Register* poll the previous July, then fallen to second in a November poll. Two days before the caucus, a new *Register* poll had Kerry (26), Edwards (23), and Dean (20) bunched up together. Nothing distant about that. I was amazed that night when the results rolled in and Tom had nailed it: Kerry, 37.6 percent, Edwards 31.9 percent, and Dean way back at 18 percent. Tom knew his state.

★

I WAS PROUD OF THE WORK the DNC had done to unite the party during the heat of the campaign leading up to Iowa and the primaries that followed. We had been able to defuse one potentially explosive problem: The proliferation of primary debates. In 2003 the candidates were all besieged with countless requests to appear in different debates around the country. They hated to say no and risk alienating the different groups looking to sponsor debates. However, they couldn't do them all or they would never have time for anything else, considering all the hours required to prepare, travel and participate in the debate itself.

That was when I stepped in. I convened a meeting in my office with Josh Wachs, Traci Siegel, Debra DeShong, Jim Mulhall, Teresa Vilmain, Josh Earnest, and Daniella Gibbs to tell them that we were going to sponsor the primary debates ourselves. No one had ever attempted to do this before, and everybody was worried about taking on such a logistical nightmare. I was asking the DNC to be a gigantic fire hydrant in the middle of a dog pound. However, I knew we needed to take on the responsibility.

In the end we ended up sponsoring a series of debates all over the country from September to December 2003 in Albuquerque, New York City, Phoenix, Detroit, Des Moines, and Durham, New Hampshire. We held a meeting with the managers of all ten campaigns, and as we gathered in the big conference room at the DNC, they were all sizing each other up. This was historic and unprecedented, bringing ten campaign managers together.

"One of you will be representing the next President of the United States and we all have to be together at the end," I said. "We've got to keep everything we discuss today to ourselves. We can't be reading about it in tomorrow's paper. I will take the hit on this stuff. You can blame it on me and say, 'Terry won't let us do any other debates!' But we have to do this as a team. If one campaign breaks off, the whole thing falls apart."

It was only later that Josh told me one of the campaign managers was pounding away on his BlackBerry right there in the meeting, e-mailing *The New York Times* to pass on everything I said.

We knew that once the meeting broke up, the campaign managers would immediately start calling reporters and trying to spin their own versions of what was said. The campaigns were especially worried about Joe Trippi, Howard Dean's campaign manager, and what he might have to say. So to slow him down a little before he started spinning, Kerry campaign manager Jim Jordan and Gephardt campaign manager Steve Murphy invited Trippi out for drinks after the meeting and did their best to get him drunk. Unfortunately, their plan fell apart because they ended up having to match Joe drink for drink. They ended up getting so sloshed, they decided it would be a *great* idea to call *New York Times* political reporter Adam Nagourney together to give him a full download on the meeting. So much for keeping the meeting out of the press. Nagourney reported the next day on "three campaign managers" making a "joint telephone call from a bar near the White House, where they had retired for drinks."

Everyone held together and the debates brought us great exposure around the country. Some political reporters got tired of covering so many primary debates, but every time we went to a new city, we generated local and regional coverage for our candidates. The debates also helped all the candidates and campaigns get to know each other, which helped us to avoid the divisiveness of the 1988 and 1992 Democratic primaries.

It was fascinating to look at the various ways different candidates approached the debates and also to get a unique glimpse of what had them worried. I was very careful to stay completely neutral between candidates, and we went to extreme lengths to make sure everyone was treated the same across the board, down to the last detail. Given how hard we worked to be scrupulously fair, I was amazed to get a call from one of the candidate's top advisers after the first debate complaining that Howard Dean and Dennis Kucinich had been given stools to stand on behind their podiums, to make themselves look taller.

"You've got to be kidding me," I said. "They're short. They wanted stools and we gave them stools. Who cares? So what?"

As a neutral observer with inside access, I would walk around to each of the candidates' dressing rooms before every debate, just to check in and wish them well. I took the Arizona Democratic state chairman Jim Pederson and his wife, Roberta, along with me when I made the rounds before the Phoenix debate on October 9, and we walked in on John Kerry as he was getting dressed. He had no shirt on and was just pulling up his pants, but he was very relaxed and friendly. However, Roberta was mortified and scampered out of the room, leaving Jim and me there to wish John good luck. Roberta took a pass on going to the rest of the dressing rooms.

As much as I loved the debates, Al Sharpton did give me my share of heartburn. He was always the last to arrive, sometimes seconds before the cameras went on. He would be in the elevator on his way to the podium and he'd be surrounded by a small crew working on his makeup and hair, getting him ready, and he would literally walk onto the stage thirty seconds before the debate started. I was always glad he made it, though, as he came up with more than his share of memorable one-liners and kept everyone loose.

A lot of people grumbled at me for allowing all ten presidential candidates to participate in the debates, depriving "top-tier" candidates of valuable TV time, but if you were a declared presidential candidate, then you were entitled to come to the debates. It wasn't my job to determine who the top-tier candidates were. That was up to the primary voters—and no one had voted yet. No matter what tier each candidate might have been on, everyone up there spoke to someone in America.

By the time the campaign kicked into high gear with the Iowa Caucus, people around the country knew our candidates' positions on all the issues. Even with a Republican President dominating the news at a time of war, we were able to cut through the fog and get our candidates invaluable exposure and publicity. Best of all, we came together as a party. I hope the Democratic Party continues the tradition of hosting primary debates, because it was really the smart thing to do.

John Kerry followed up his win in Iowa with a strong showing on January 27 in New Hampshire, winning with 39 percent of the vote, followed by Howard Dean with 28 percent, General Wesley Clark with 26 percent, and

John Edwards with 12 percent. From there it was only another week to Almost-Super Tuesday, as some political reporters took to calling February 3, when Arizona and Delaware and five other states all voted. Soon it boiled down to a two-man race, John Kerry and John Edwards, and it was all the same to me who won just so long as we had our nominee by my target of early March.

29

★ ★ ★

On October 7, 2001, I joined Americans everywhere in cheering the start of the U.S. air war against Afghanistan, and that November I said, "We all support the President. We support him now more than ever." When the Northern Alliance routed Taliban fighters in the battle of Tora Bora on December 17, 2001, my first reaction was that it was a great day for the United States. My only concern was that we didn't go far enough. We had our chance to capture Osama bin Laden that month, but instead of sending in more of our crack U.S. special forces, the best in the world, we outsourced the job to untrustworthy Afghan surrogates because Bush and his war planners were obsessed with their coming war of choice against Iraq. Don't take my word for it. Gary Berntsen, the CIA field commander at Tora Bora and author of *Jawbreaker*, was devastating in his criticism of Bush.

"We needed U.S. soldiers on the ground!" Berntsen told *The Washington Post*. "I'd sent my request for eight hundred U.S. Army Rangers and was still waiting for a response. I repeated to anyone at headquarters who would listen: 'We need Rangers now! The opportunity to get bin Laden and his men is slipping away!!'"

Bush claimed that we never knew bin Laden was there at Tora Bora, but that was patently false, Berntsen said, no matter what Bush or General Tommy Franks might choose to say.

"In Berntsen's view, the Afghan militia that Franks relied on was 'unreliable' and 'cobbled together at the last minute'—certainly not the army to trust with nabbing the man who had ordered the 9/11 attacks," *The Post* reported. "By Berntsen's telling, he could have gotten Osama bin Laden—if only they'd given him the troops and the time to get the job done. Berntsen says he knew exactly where the 1,000-man jihadist force had fallen back in the mountainous region near the Pakistani border. An Arabic-speaking Jawbreaker team member reported hearing bin Laden speaking on a radio taken from a dead al Qaeda fighter. The terrorist leader exhorted his followers to keep fighting and, at one point, apologized 'for getting them trapped . . . and pounded by American air strikes,' Berntsen writes. By his estimate, there were just forty Special Operations soldiers and a dozen other Special Forces on hand to head off bin Laden's potential flight 'across hundreds of miles of caves and mountain passes.'"

That was a travesty. By January 29, 2002, Bush was building up the "Axis of Evil" of Iraq, Iran, and North Korea in his State of the Union address without so much as mentioning bin Laden, the man he'd vowed to capture dead or alive.

Like a lot of Americans, my first instinct was to stand behind the President's push for war against Saddam Hussein. As suspicious as I was of Bush, as painfully aware as I was of his willingness to deceive the American people, I thought he was at least getting the best intelligence estimates from the best people in government. When he said on August 16, 2002, that he would be "making up his mind based upon the latest intelligence," it seemed like even Bush could not be lying to us about something as important to the future of the country as waging a war.

Top administration officials were putting all their credibility behind doomsday scenarios, especially the notion of Saddam obtaining nuclear weapons.

"We do know with absolute certainty that he is using his procurement system to acquire the equipment he needs in order to build a nuclear weapon," Dick Cheney said on *Meet the Press* on September 8, 2002.

"We don't want the smoking gun to be a mushroom cloud," Condi Rice said on CNN that same Sunday.

Unlike the administration of Bush 41, which carefully put together a broad-based international coalition before moving against Saddam in the Gulf War, the Bush 43 administration took the view that it couldn't care less what our closest allies had to say. The administration had the support of British Prime Minister Tony Blair, a thoughtful leader who had worked very closely with Bill Clinton to bring the world together and could normally be counted on to do the smart thing. Blair's support gave Bush cover—but Blair was on his own, exposed to withering criticism at home for supporting a war on a false pretext, as the infamous Downing Street Memo later demonstrated.

The same month that Cheney and Rice hit the talk-show circuit to scare the daylights out of the American people, I happened to be over in Spain attending the wedding of Prime Minister Jose Aznar's daughter, Ana, at the Escorial Monastery in the Sierra de Madrid, a sixteenth-century basilica. At the reception I was standing there having a casual conversation with King Juan Carlos, my occasional hunting partner, when we were joined by Blair and his charming, outspoken wife, Cherie, and Italian Prime Minister Silvio Berlusconi. Soon conversation shifted from the beautiful setting, a magnificent converted horse-breeding stable, to the Bush administration's ill-fated push for war against Saddam. The king, being a king, left the partisan political talk to the rest of us, but not being a monarch, I was free to say whatever I wanted. It soon became obvious that I was standing with two prime ministers ready to back Bush to the hilt, even if there were no facts to back up the Bush argument that Saddam posed an imminent and growing threat to his neighbors—and to the United States.

Cherie Blair was holding her tongue, but I had no doubt that she was on my side on this one. Then, just as we were being called in to dinner, she had a question for me.

"Terry, what do people in America think of my husband on this issue?" she asked coyly.

We were all having such a good time talking, but I decided what the heck, I'd tell them the truth.

"With all due respect, Mr. Prime Minister, most people think you're a lapdog for George Bush," I said. "No offense, sir."

At that point Cherie slapped her husband on the shoulder and said, "See, I told you so, Tony."

I knew I liked that woman.

★

MY WORRY WAS THAT in Bush's fixation on toppling Saddam Hussein, to do what his father had decided not to do, he was selling the American people short—and not taking care of business at home. That was why two million people had lost their jobs, Bush had dipped into the Social Security trust fund he had promised not to touch, and Americans were worried sick about the economy. I kept making that point in my public appearances. However,

I backed off of questioning the President's approach on Iraq, figuring as commander in chief, he ought to get a chance to make his case.

"Iraq is not a partisan issue," I said to thirty reporters at the *Christian Science Monitor* breakfast on September 19, 2002.

A lot of Democrats felt that way. To this day, there is some controversy over the congressional votes that fall authorizing Bush to use force against Iraq. Let me repeat that: Congress *authorized* Bush to use force, it did *not* declare war on Iraq. The idea was to give Bush a stick to use in U.S. negotiations with Saddam, so the Iraqi dictator would be forced to let the United Nations weapons inspectors under Hans Blix back into Iraq to continue their work in a serious way, not just for show. As much as Bush and his team demeaned the U.N. weapons inspectors, the fact was that they had destroyed more Iraqi weapons through their work than the U.S. military destroyed in the Gulf War. All Americans soon realized that Bush had no intention of letting the weapons inspectors do their job and waiting for them to come back with a report.

Democrats in the House and Senate assumed the administration was dealing with them in good faith, but soon discovered that was far from the case. Only six days after the Senate joined the House in voting to authorize force against Saddam, the news broke that North Korea had restarted its nuclear weapons program and had "nullified" the 1994 agreement negotiated with the Clinton administration to freeze its development of nuclear weapons. Not only that, it emerged that the Bush administration had learned all this twelve days earlier—six days *before* the Senate vote on October 11—and had not shared the information with Democratic senators, who would have raised difficult questions about why the administration wanted to focus only on Iraq when North Korea was a more urgent problem.

Not until January 2003 did it become clear just how fraudulent the Bush case for war was. Germany and France had announced on January 22 that they would work together to block Bush's plan to invade Iraq, unless they were persuaded that Saddam posed an imminent threat to his neighbors. Then in his State of the Union address on January 28, Bush cranked it up, declaring, "The British government has learned that Saddam Hussein recently sought significant quantities of uranium from Africa."

That one was hard to believe, very hard to believe. It was sad to watch Colin Powell go to the United Nations on February 5, 2003, to make a case for war relying on a ragtag collection of flimsy evidence. That was all he had? I always admired Powell and respected his service to our country. I couldn't understand why he would risk undermining his own good name to promote a case that was looking weaker all the time.

Once U.S. troops went into Iraq on March 20, 2003, it was time to support our men and women in uniform and hope the fighting would soon be over. Saddam Hussein was a monster who had tortured his own people. True, back when Saddam was gassing his own people in March 1988 during the Iran-Iraq War, he was being propped up with assistance from the Reagan administration. Reagan sent Donald Rumsfeld to Baghdad in December 1983, where he shook the dictator's hand and talked with him for ninety minutes, paving the way for U.S. military support.

I couldn't believe my eyes on May 1, 2003, when Bush landed on the deck of the USS *Lincoln* aircraft carrier, three weeks after the fall of Baghdad, and stepped out in his green flight suit. It was a shameless attempt to produce stirring footage that Bush could use in his reelection campaign. Stung by the public outcry over spending taxpayer dollars to let Bush copilot a jet when a helicopter would have worked just fine, the White House said the aircraft carrier was too far out to sea to be reached by helicopter. However, this turned out to be another lie, just like the whopper his aides told on September 11 about a threat being called into the White House against Air Force One. The aircraft carrier was so close to shore, the San Diego coastline was clearly visible from the deck.

I challenged the White House that week to pledge to the American people that it would not use the footage of this media stunt for Bush's 2004 reelection campaign. That, I said, would be too crass even for Bush, given the cost to the taxpayers and the use of U.S. servicemen and servicewomen as extras when Bush stood on the *Lincoln* that day with a "Mission Accomplished" banner in the background and declared that "major combat operations" were over. On May 1, 2003, when Bush said the war was over, 138 brave Americans had already died in the Iraq War. By October 2006, more than 2,800 Americans had been killed in the war, which has already dragged on longer than World War II, making Bush's stunt on that aircraft carrier even more obscenely disrespectful to our troops in retrospect.

By May 2003 the American people could see that the Iraq War was none of the things Bush had said it would be. He rushed off to war under false pretenses and set off a chain of events that has made this country far less safe. Ask yourself: Are you safer now than when George W. Bush was inaugurated in January 2001? Do you *feel* safer? Instead of sticking with the tough job of fighting the war on terror, Bush pulled most U.S. troops out of Afghanistan well before long-term stability had been established. That country soon reverted to a simmering cauldron, ruled by war lords and heroin smugglers, where our enemies can operate with impunity, and the Taliban has made a comeback. Iraq turned into the biggest terrorist training ground the world has ever seen. Bush gambled with our security and lost—big time. Heck of a job, George.

The questions I had on June 17, 2003, speaking in Oklahoma, were: "Where are the weapons of mass destruction?" and "Where is Osama bin Laden?" I'm still asking those questions today—along with millions of other outraged Americans.

The following month, we started getting a clearer picture of just how far Bush had gone to distort reality in his push for war. Former ambassador Joseph Wilson, who had served in both Republican and Democratic administrations, wrote an Op-Ed article in *The New York Times* on July 6 saying that the Bush argument for war against Iraq was founded on faulty information. "Based on my experience with the administration in the months leading up to the war, I have little choice but to conclude that some of the intelligence related to Iraq's nuclear weapons program was twisted to exaggerate the Iraqi threat," Wilson wrote.

"[Q]uestioning the selective use of intelligence to justify the war in Iraq is neither idle sniping nor 'revisionist history,' as Mr. Bush has suggested. The act of war is the last option of a democracy, taken when there is a grave threat to our national security. More than two hundred American soldiers have lost their lives in Iraq already. We have a duty to ensure that their sacrifice came for the right reasons."

Dick Cheney was so upset about the article and the threat it posed to his credibility, he scribbled notes all over the article and took part in an attempt to discredit Wilson. According to Cheney's former top aide, Scooter Libby, Bush himself gave the order to leak classified information to reporters in an attempt to discredit Wilson's argument. Wilson's wife, Valerie Plame, had been working until then as a covert CIA agent, but the administration leaked her identity to reporters in an attempt to smear Joe Wilson. Libby later lost his job and was indicted. Not only was Valerie Plame's cover blown, but also that of her CIA front company, Brewster-Jennings & Associates, outing several dozen other CIA operatives around the world who were using the same fake business name, as a CIA agent I met at a dinner in Michigan told me.

I was on vacation in Maine when Wilson sent shockwaves through the Bush administration with his *Times* Op-Ed. Dewey Beach was never really Dorothy's action and in the summer of 2003 she rented a house in Kennebunkport, Maine, for most of July. Our good friends, John and Cynthia O'Hanlon and John and Ann Raffaelli, had homes there. The idea was that Dorothy would be there with the kids and I would spend as much time with them as I could, and I'd be close to Boston, allowing me to work on our upcoming Democratic National Convention. We arrived in Kennebunkport on July 3, and I was in town relaxing for several days before I had to get back to Washington for a speech to our national convention of Young Democrats on July 9.

Later that month, I cranked up the full power of the DNC behind a campaign to tell the American people the truth about Bush. We sent out five million e-mails, mailed out a letter to millions of our supporters, and paid for a full-page ad in *The New York Times* exposing Bush's lie on Saddam and uranium.

"America took President Bush at his word," the ad read. " '. . . Saddam Hussein recently sought significant quantities of uranium from Africa.' But now we find out that it wasn't true.

"The CIA knew it. The State Department knew it. The White House knew it. But he said it anyway. It's time to tell the truth."

Twice when I was in Kennebunkport that month, little Peter and I arrived around 7 A.M. at H.B.'s Provisions to pick up the morning paper, just a few minutes after Bush Senior had stopped by for worms. That was an amazing coincidence, since I spent barely a week in Maine that month. I was disappointed I hadn't bumped into the former President. I'd have liked to talk to him and ask how he thought the war was going. Bush's best friend, former national security adviser Brent Scowcroft, opposed the war and wrote a *Wall Street Journal* article arguing "Don't Attack Saddam." Later he told *The New Yorker* magazine he thought the war was a diversion from the much more important war on terror and said of the Vice President, "I consider Cheney a good friend—I've known him for thirty years. But Dick Cheney I don't know anymore." I would have loved to ask Bush about Scowcroft.

John Raffaelli was at a party in Kennebunkport at the end of the summer and ran into a woman who was close friends with Bush Senior and Barbara.

"It was the worst summer the Bushes have ever had in Kennebunkport," this friend told John.

That was quite a statement considering Bush Senior had been summering in Kennebunkport since the 1920s and his grandfather, George Herbert Walker, bought Walker's Point in 1902.

What was the problem? Had a sewage line ruptured near the Bushes' rocky shoreline, befouling the waters? Had rats or roaches overrun the house? Had Bush Senior's golf game suddenly gone south?

"Why was their summer so bad?" John asked this close associate of the Bushes.

" 'That *awful* Terry McAuliffe was up here the entire summer,' " Barbara Bush huffed to her friend. " 'He ruined my summer. Who does he think he is, coming up to *our* town?' "

★

WE WERE ALL IN A MOOD TO CELEBRATE on March 2, 2004, when John Kerry sewed up the nomination by sweeping the Super Tuesday primaries. This was the night we had been working toward for three years. Finally we could focus all our energies on defeating George W. Bush and sending him home to Texas full-time. I had remained totally neutral in the primaries and often wore an "ABB" button on my lapel to sum up my philosophy: Anyone But Bush. Now that John Edwards was dropping out of the race, ending any last suspense on who our nominee would be, the DNC was in the best shape it had ever been.

"Memo to Democratic National Committee Chairman Terry McAuliffe," UPI Senior News Analyst Martin Sieff wrote the next day. "Pour yourself a good large glass of Johnnie Walker Blue Label Scotch. You've earned it. Your party's revamped primary process has delivered the goods exactly the way you wanted it to."

The staff immediately went out and bought me a bottle of Johnnie Walker Blue and put it on the center of my desk.

★

WE HAD $30 MILLION sitting in the bank for the exclusive use of the nominee, so he could hit the ground running. We had the party out of debt for the first time. We had built a new DNC with the kind of technological capability we could only dream of up until that year. Thanks to Doug Kelly and Lina Brunton, our e-mail lists and voter files and direct-mail capabilities had moved light years forward from where they were when I was elected chairman. We were more united than we'd been in decades. All that we had to do was keep pounding away at Bush and be ready for the inevitable Republican smear tactics, and I was sure John Kerry would be our next President.

We'd even kicked off an innovative grassroots fund-raising drive, hiring thousands of college students to go door to door and stand on street corners asking for money. The students not only raised $25 million for the party, signing up 700,000 new donors, they also had a huge political impact, hitting the streets in red DNC T-shirts and engaging millions of people in the political debate. We were in great financial shape and had set fund-raising records, thanks to Maureen White, Andy Tobias, Jay Dunn, Dave Dogan, and the entire finance team, and also because of the discipline we instituted in running the DNC like a business. I'd been launching into tirades about the role of political consultants as far back as my first meeting in the Oval Office in 1994. It had evolved that media consultants were given a percentage of the media buys, which was a clear-cut conflict of interest. They had every reason to push for more media buys, so they could bank more fees. I was not going to stand for that and everyone knew it. As a fund-raiser, I knew just how hard we worked to raise every dollar. I felt I owed it to the many grassroots donors who were sending in crumpled-up dollar bills because this election was so important to them. I was not about to let this insanity continue. I knew we were going to spend more than $135 million on media in the next six months and there was no way in hell I was going to let a media consultant skim off 10 percent of that and pocket $13.5 million to go buy a villa in Italy. Not under *my* chairmanship. We were raising that money to elect John Kerry, not build villas.

As we prepared for the 2004 election, I hired Leslie Kerman, a Virginia attorney who had been representing campaigns on finance matters. Leslie was going to negotiate our media buys and promised me that she could hold the fee to 1 percent, which would clearly be historic. Leslie, who was working for free, thus became our biggest fund-raiser. Some of my staff worried that for 1 percent, we wouldn't get the best talent. I said that was a nonissue. Everybody wanted to work on this presidential campaign, and sure enough, seven top firms ended up competing for our business and agreed to the 1 percent contract. The gravy train was over for Democratic political consultants.

We were all sitting at Café Milano the night Kerry wrapped up the nomination, and a group of top Kerry campaign people came in and I sent over a bottle of champagne to congratulate them. I had called John half an hour earlier to congratulate him on becoming the nominee of our party and he thanked me for all the work we had done at the DNC and said, "Let's go!" The group of Kerry aides drinking the champagne I sent over raised their glasses to toast me from a few tables away to thank me for the bottle. I raised my glass to them as well. Not until later did someone come to me and reveal what was being said over at their table.

"Now we can get rid of McAuliffe and get control of the money," a drunk Kerry fund-raiser from Rhode Island said loud enough to be overheard.

A top Kerry media consultant nodded, but held up his hand to silence the inebriated Kerry fund-raiser.

So as they were drinking my champagne, they were already plotting how to get their hands on the DNC bank account. The media consultant leaked to the media that the Kerry people wanted to take control of the DNC, and once that story was out there, it created a few days of controversy.

I couldn't believe Kerry's people could be so foolish. We were as unified as a party as we had been in years and within hours of John becoming the nominee they were already tearing that down. It blew over within a few days, but the episode demonstrated what a destructive force consultants play in the party. We kept control of the bank account and the 1-percent contract stayed. People doubted that we would line up top talent, but in the end the firms of David Axelrod and Steve Murphy did such a good job on the DNC ads, John Kerry later told several of us at dinner that the DNC ads were far better than the Kerry campaign ads. Not only did we get a great price, we got great ads. Thank you Leslie, Josh Wachs, Ellen Moran, David, and Steve.

On March 10 John Kerry's motorcade pulled up in front of the DNC, and 350 staff members gathered on the steps to cheer his arrival. He came upstairs for a meeting with my staff to go over the campaign. The year before, every Democratic candidate for President came to my office for an hour-and-a-half briefing on what the DNC would have ready for the nominee. Despite that earlier briefing, I think John was a little surprised to realize just how potent an operation we had built.

"John, everything we promised you is done," I told him.

We went over all the details of what we'd be putting at his disposal, the $30 million war chest, the plan to raise $300 million more, the unprecedented e-mail and fund-raising capability, and the technological sophistication that we Democrats had only been able to dream about for so many years. Finally, I asked the staff to leave so I could talk to the senator alone. The tone of the meeting was very upbeat. We were united that day on wanting to do everything in our power to put John in the White House and put the government back to work making a difference in the lives of all Americans.

"Terry," John asked me. "What are you worried about?"

"Let me tell you something, John," I said. "We'll have more field and we'll have more money than we've ever had. I don't worry about any of that. But these Republicans are mean and tough. I'm worried about what they are going to try to do to you."

I think John had been expecting me to say something like that. He looked me right in the eye and tried to ease my concerns.

"Terry, don't you worry about me," he said. "If they hit me, I'm going to hit them back harder."

"Great," I said. "I'm pumped up."

I made it clear that I hoped we could avoid repeating what I saw as one of the big mistakes of the 2000 campaign.

"How much do you want President Clinton campaigning?" I asked.

"Terry, get him as much as you can get him," he said. "All hands on deck. I need him."

Then I briefed John on something we had been discussing in secret and carefully exploring. Smith Bagley had brought the idea to Harold Ickes, who brought it to me: That was the option of delaying his formal acceptance of the nomination until some time in early September so the Kerry campaign could continue to raise and spend primary money all the way through August, up until the time of the Republican Convention. At the time this was a bold new idea. I'd had Joe Sandler, the DNC counsel, trying to figure out if there was a legal way to change our convention procedures and not have the candidate formally accept the nomination.

"Joe is still researching it," I told John. "But I wanted to alert you that we're at least looking at this. It is very secret. Only three or four people know about this. If it leaks out to anybody, the ramifications would be very serious. We're in final negotiations with the networks and if they get wind of this, they might pull out and not cover much of our convention."

John heard me out, but didn't say much about the idea one way or the other. Once John became the nominee, his fund-raising spiked. Through the Internet, he was able to raise $26 million in March alone. He started to see the wisdom of looking for a way to change the usual procedure, and his campaign held a meeting at Kerry headquarters to discuss the idea. No one from the DNC was there, but I'm sure they stressed to the ten people in that meeting how important it was that those talks stay secret. However, within minutes after their meeting broke up, the story had hit the AP wire. Someone must have been inside leaking the information before the meeting was even over!

That was the worst possible scenario. The idea was half-formed and needed careful planning to have any shot at success. The public response once it had been leaked was very negative. People thought it made John look sleazy, as if he were trying to game the system. The networks immediately called us and raised holy hell. John had no choice but to announce within three days that the idea was dead. What could have been an important weapon in our arsenal, allowing John's campaign to raise and spend money for six more weeks during a very critical period, was killed because one of his own staff members couldn't keep quiet, and leaked it to the press.

I was livid when my press secretary, Elizabeth Alexander, informed me that the story was on the wire. We'd secretly been working on this for six months and it didn't last through one meeting at the Kerry campaign. I immediately called John on the road and expressed my bewilderment and disgust.

"Terry, how did this get out?" he asked me.

"All I know is there were ten people in a meeting room in *your* headquarters, John," I said.

"Who wrote the story?" he asked me.

"Nedra Pickler," I said.

"I know who did it, then," he said.

He never told me who the leaker was, but that wasn't even the point. One staffer who wanted to curry favor with the press—or to sabotage our plan—had stabbed John in the back. (And Nedra, dinner for you at Café Milano if you tell me who the leaker was!)

★

MY GOAL WAS ALWAYS TO WORK toward having the Democratic Party as united as it had ever been, and no frustration over yet another leak to the press was going to get in the way of that goal. The Republicans had been eager to protect the massive technological advantage they'd built thanks to the contributions of forward-thinking RNC chairmen like Frank Fahrenkopf (voter files), Haley Barbour (TV studios), and Jim Nicholson (Internet), and by trying to sabotage our project to modernize the DNC. But they had failed. I'd gotten around the so-called Anti-McAuliffe Amendment, paid Al Dwoskin up front, and by March 2004 we were ready to cut the ribbon on the glorious new building. We were set to mark the dawn of a new era in Democratic politics, not only of state-of-the-art technology but also of unprecedented Democratic unity, which we would celebrate on March 25, the day of the ribbon-cutting, with a big Unity Dinner that would be attended by Jimmy Carter, Bill Clinton, Al Gore, and all the 2004 presidential candidates. When I called President Carter in December 2003 to invite him, he graciously accepted and said this would be his first DNC fund-raiser since he left the White House twenty-four years earlier.

The ribbon-cutting that day was spectacular. They closed off the street in front of our beautiful new building and it was packed out there. Everyone came, and after the ribbon-cutting we had a big party inside our new building. I invited Judy Woodruff and her CNN camera crew inside for a personal tour of the new building, and Judy was amazed at how high-tech we had built the place. The TV studios were better than what they had at CNN, she told us.

I introduced Judy to Laura Quinn, an outside consultant I had brought in to oversee our technological upgrades. Laura was more responsible than anyone else for rebuilding the infrastructure of the party. She designed and built the TV and radio studios, rebuilt the computer and telephone infrastructure, including a specialized research search engine, revamped the Web site and online fund-raising, and helped build the voter file. Thanks to her aggressive style, she was able to renegotiate existing contracts and save the DNC hundreds of thousands of dollars every year.

The highlight of the day was the big Democratic Unity Dinner that night at the National Building Museum. No one had brought all the top Democrats together like this before and I remember we were all gathered in the holding room beforehand, and you had Hillary Clinton and Bill Clinton and Jimmy Carter and Al Gore and all the Democratic candidates all standing around talking, and it was just an incredible dynamic. You could see Hillary talking to Jimmy Carter or the Rev. Al Sharpton telling a joke to General Clark and it felt like there was so much Democratic Party energy in that small room, it was about to explode.

"Tonight we stand united behind John Kerry," I said during my speech. "We have two hundred and twenty-two days till the election. We need your heart. We need your soul."

The emotional high point of the night may have been when Jimmy Carter came up to speak and was greeted with a standing ovation. Carter flashed that famous smile of his, but was tough on Ralph Nader, whose third-party run kept Al Gore from winning outright. Thanks to Ralph, the Supreme Court got involved.

"This is the most remarkable unity I've ever seen," Carter said. "Tonight I have some advice for you, Ralph. Go back to umpiring softball games or examining the rear end of automobiles, and don't risk costing the Democrats the White House this year as you did four years ago."

Carter and Bill Clinton brought down the house that night and had the room buzzing. Everyone was solidly united behind John Kerry, the energy in the building was incredible, and with our new building and our new unity, we were ready to stand shoulder to shoulder and make George Bush work if he was going to get four more years. This spectacular evening ended with an event Justin Paschal put together at the Dream nightclub for five thousand young people, all yelling and screaming as they watched Jimmy Carter and Bill Clinton moving and grooving to Ginuwine and Q-tip.

30

★ ★ ★

The fight to host the 2004 Democratic Convention was intense, given the importance to us of putting together an exciting, energetic convention, and given the stakes for the cities hoping to host the convention. The winning city would attract worldwide attention as well as millions of dollars in economic stimulus. In 2001 I had asked former DNC chairman Joe Andrew and Alice Huffman, vice chair of the DNC Black Caucus, to head up a thirty-person site-selection committee that would make a recommendation to me. Nine cities indicated initial interest, but the field was soon logistically narrowed down to four: Boston, New York, Miami, and Detroit, and they all had powerful boosters.

Boston was represented by the powerful senior senator, Ted Kennedy, who has been a towering influence across the board on everything from education, children's health issues, and looking out for working families to foreign policy. Soon into my chairmanship Ted started dropping by my office with his Portuguese water dogs, Splash and Sunny, and he had one thing on his mind. He wanted the Democratic Convention in Boston. Ted's main concern was that the selection process be fair, since Boston pushed hard for the convention in 2000, and in the end felt mistreated by the system. I gave Ted my word the selection process would be fair and also said no city would be considered unless its financing was nailed down. I still couldn't believe

Los Angeles was awarded the 2000 convention without guaranteeing its financing, and I was not about to let us make that mistake again.

Ted got the message. He would show up for his weekly visits and we would have fun telling stories as the two Portuguese water dogs sniffed around my office, and he kept bringing high-powered groups down from Boston to show their commitment to raising money. He came with business leaders like Fred Seigel, Alan Leventhal, and Elaine Schuster, who as Ted well knew were good friends of mine and who for years had been top donors. Also leading the effort was Boston mayor Tom Menino, who visited me often and worked closely with Ted in lining up twenty-five letters of credit for a total of more than $12 million. It was soon apparent that money was not going to be an issue with Boston. Mayor Menino even went so far as to arrange for me to have 00001 as my race number for the Boston Marathon.

Miami had an obvious advantage: I'd have loved to return to the scene of the crime. Unfortunately, the city just couldn't get the money put together. Chris Korge, a longtime fund-raiser from Miami, told me they were having a tough time getting the corporate community behind the effort, so Miami was out. Detroit would have been great. I liked Kwame Kilpatrick, the dynamic young Detroit mayor, and really liked the idea of having our convention in an industrial state like Michigan, but Detroit had half the hotel rooms we would need, since they were still in the process of greatly expanding their hotel capacity leading up to the 2006 Super Bowl. That left New York as the other serious candidate, and money would obviously not be an issue there, primarily because of the leadership of billionaire Mayor Michael Bloomberg.

The lobbying from New York was intense. I was bombarded with calls from Hillary Clinton, Chuck Schumer, Eliot Spitzer, Carl McCall, and the entire New York fund-raising community. The issue with New York was exclusivity. We always have specifically laid out in our bid package that any city that hosted our convention could not also host the Republicans. We wanted a city 100 percent devoted to our preparations, which by necessity would be shrouded in secrecy. We didn't want the city simultaneously working with our opponent and thought there was a good chance Karl Rove would want to play the September 11 card and go to New York for their convention in 2004, which would rule out New York for us. I'll give Mayor Michael Bloomberg credit, though. He gave it everything he had.

"Terry, let me be very clear," he said in May 2002 over dinner at Jimmy's in Harlem. "Money will not be an issue. If I have to write a check myself, I will."

He meant it, too. A week before we were due to make the decision, he called me and said, "I've got to see you privately." So he flew down in his private jet and met me for dinner at the Capital Grille in Tysons Corner on November 10. Before we had even ordered, he pulled out his checkbook and a pen, and was ready to start writing.

"Terry, how big does this number have to be?" Bloomberg said, pen poised in the air. "I'll write it right now."

I was impressed. I loved the man's style, but not enough to make a decision that would hurt our party.

"Mayor, you keep avoiding me on my main issue," I said. "If we pick New York, will you say no to the Republicans?"

"Terry, Karl Rove has already told me they're coming," he said. "I've got the Republican Convention. I'm not going to mislead you. I want both."

"Mayor, thank you for being straight with me," I said. "I'm sorry, but I just can't do it. You want the RNC and DNC spending a year together working out of the same office in Madison Square Garden preparing for our conventions? It just won't work."

Ted Kennedy, never one to be outdone, called me at midnight the night before the site-selection committee's vote and made a blunt appeal, saying, "Terry, what does the Kennedy family have to do to get one Democratic Convention in Boston?" He didn't have to remind me of all his family had sacrificed for the Democratic Party over the years. The next day's vote was unanimous for Boston and we all stood on stage—Ted Kennedy, John Kerry and the site-selection committee—and called Mayor Menino to say Boston would be hosting our 2004 convention. Two weeks later I flew up with my son Jack to sign the official contract and we were met at the airport by thirty police motorcycles that escorted us to the Fleet Center with sirens blaring, and Mayor Menino gave Jack a hockey stick used by Jumbo Joe Thornton and signed by all the Bruins. Ted Kennedy had presented me with an oak-and-copper gavel made from the USS *Constitution*, which was one of only two made, the other having been presented to my favorite former Speaker of the House, Tip O'Neill.

★

PLANNING A CONVENTION is the ultimate team effort. The party organization takes care of all the logistics, everything from building the podium to credentialing, hotels, transportation, and security.

I checked on our progress every week with the team running the convention—Rod O'Connor, Alice Huffman, John Donoghue, Tom O'Donnell, Lee Satterfield, Dennis O'Brien, Erica DeVos, Cameron Moody, Alan Rose, David Medina, Peggy Wilhide, Cindy Lott, and Zoe Garmendia. Most people don't understand the importance of the podium—the stage, the video monitors, the banners, the moving flags. It's all about the imagery and stage-craft and how the party presents itself to the millions of people who tune in to watch on television. It takes more than a year to design and construct, and both parties shroud their plans in the same kind of secrecy as the papal selection.

We had done most of our work on the hall and the podium in Boston be-fore John Kerry even emerged as our nominee. Once he had, we showed him the designs of the podium and he thought it looked great. The nominee and his team decide on the message and thematics for the convention, and set most of the speaking program.

On May 25 I met with my speechwriter, Andrei Cherny, and communi-cations team, Elizabeth Alexander and Jano Cabrera, to begin working on my speech for the opening night of the convention. I'd speak right before former Presidents Carter and Clinton, and figured it was my job to light up the crowd and lay out the many failures of the Bush administration, leaving it to the former Presidents to make a concrete case for John Kerry, the old one-two punch. We spent three hours talking at that first meeting and laid out the framework of a tough, hard-hitting critique of George W. Bush. God knows we had plenty of ammunition.

Two weeks later Andrei came back to my office with a first draft of the speech, and I loved it. This would definitely get the convention fired up. It jumped out to a strong start, beginning, "My fellow Democrats, we're here with a message for George W. Bush: Pack up the boxes. Rent a U-Haul. Forward your mail. The Democratic Party is going to reclaim America's fu-ture. And our march to victory begins today." I gave specifics on Bush's failures, including one of my favorites: "No President since the Great De-pression has a worse record when it comes to jobs." I emphasized the need for change with what I knew would be a great applause line. "For four years, Democrats have tried to convince George Bush to change course," the first draft said. "He hasn't seen the light—so come November we're go-ing to show him the door."

We went through several drafts of the speech over the next two weeks, fine-tuning and sharpening. When we were all happy with it, Andrei submit-ted the text to the Kerry campaign, which was reviewing all speeches for the convention. Twenty-four hours later, Andrei came back into my office look-ing ashen and shell-shocked. The Kerry people had chopped out three-quarters of the speech Andrei had written. He was given instructions that no one was to attack George Bush—or his policies!—at the convention. As Andrei explained all this to me, I kept looking around my office for the *Candid Camera* crew to jump in, I was so sure he had to be pulling my leg—but this was no joke. The message gurus of the Kerry campaign had come down with the marching orders that swing voters don't like partisan politics and thus two words were banned from the 2004 Democratic Convention: "George" and "Bush."

More than anyone at the convention, I should have been able to go after Bush, which I had been doing on national television for four years. But the Kerry people pushed us further and further on my speech to the point where I read one watered-down draft and was so frustrated, I threw the pages up in the air.

"This is worthless," I said. "Why don't I just say, 'George Bush is a great President, but we can do better?'"

Poor Andrei. I thought the decision to back off of any real criticism of Bush was one of the biggest acts of political malpractice in the history of American politics. People wanted to see us fight. If people don't see you fighting for yourself, they won't believe you're going to fight for them. Sure, our first goal at the convention was to convince the American people to vote for John Kerry. But that was only half the equation. We also wanted to make a strong case that George W. Bush did not deserve four more years. We had to sharpen the contrast and give people a reason to want change.

★

FINALLY, AFTER TWO YEARS of preparations, convention week arrived and it was spectacular. The *Boston Herald* had been filled with negative articles for the entire year, whipping people into a panic with worry about everything imaginable from imminent terrorist attacks to Martians attacking from space to gridlock traffic. One day I even made the tabloid's front page when I said traffic would not be an issue and they went so far as to compare me to "Baghdad Bob." Then came convention week and the weather was great, the city had prepared beautifully, and traffic was nonexistent, despite the doomsday predictions. I had been in Boston since the Tuesday six days before the convention opened, talking to a dozen different groups a day, and doing nonstop TV and radio interviews. I threw a staff party at 10 P.M. that Saturday night and I had already lost my voice, two days before the convention opened.

We began our convention as the most united Democratic Party ever and there were no challenges to our credentials committee, our platform committee, or our rules committee, which was unprecedented. We went into the convention with Kerry-Edwards holding a narrow lead over Bush-Cheney, and knew we needed a good bounce in the polls. As the party in power, the Republicans were holding their convention after ours, which in baseball is called "last licks." Little did we know how appropriate that term would be.

I gaveled open the convention at 4 P.M. on July 26, and tried to go easy on my voice, leading up to my speech that night. Every morning that week, starting just after 6 A.M., Kandy Stroud, our radio guru, and I would make the rounds of Radio Row, which was several hundred radio talk show hosts all crammed into the Fleet Center. I'd walk down the hallway and producers and talk show hosts would be screaming at me, pleading with me to come on their show for "Thirty seconds!" or "Two minutes!" It was the funniest thing. Just total insanity. Picture the New York Stock Exchange, with everyone yelling at the same time, and you get a sense of what it was like.

At 8 P.M. I took the podium to kick off the evening speaking program. I talked about what a true American hero John Kerry was, not only volunteering to serve on the front lines of Vietnam but also having the courage, when he came home, to run for office and give "a voice to those our government has forgotten." And I talked about how John Edwards had lived the American Dream, a mill worker's son who had risen to be a senator and devoted his life to standing up for those who needed a champion. I also reminded the delegates that we were facing a tough and determined opponent.

"The Republicans will throw everything they've got at us—but we are going to win," I said. "So for the next ninety-nine days, work hard, knock on doors, call your neighbors, keep the faith, don't let up, don't back down, don't stop, don't rest. We've put people back in the shining center of the people's party. Now let's put people back in charge of America." As instructed, I held off and did not attack George W. Bush—for the first time in four years.

Mark Leibovich, then a reporter for *The Washington Post,* asked if he could follow me around for a day to do a profile on me. I agreed to do the story on one condition: Mark had to commit to me that he would do the whole day from start to finish, and he said, "I can handle you." He met me in the hotel lobby at 5 A.M. and shadowed me for the whole day, late into the night, but to this day I love to tease him about how he embarrassed himself and his newspaper by bailing out two hours before I went to bed after 3 A.M. Jeez, what a wimp.

"When a reporter who had been following him all day asks McAuliffe if he can beg off from the last late-late night events and go to bed—at 1:15 A.M.—McAuliffe smirks and shakes his head and expounds on the reporter's lameness," Leibovich wrote in *The Post*. "And McAuliffe, of course, will remain at the party—for young Democratic activists—at a downtown nightclub. When last seen, he will be dancing on a bar with his jacket off and his sleeves rolled up, screaming to the sweaty throng of young Dems that they are really, really, really lighting things up. There is no better way to end the best day in the history of political conventions."

Damian Williams, my personal aide and body man, probably had it the toughest during convention week as he was the first one to meet me in the morning and the last to see me at night. He did an incredible job of getting me to hundreds of events on time. He spent seven days with me going on one hour of sleep a night and was constantly being besieged by calls and e-mails requesting everything from credentials, hotel rooms, and speaking roles to passes to hot parties. He had to wear five BlackBerries and three cell phones on his belt, all of which were beeping and lighting up twenty-four hours a day. He joked that he would never have children because of all the radiation pulsating throughout his body from all the devices. He was relieved when the convention ended and he could enter the tranquil world of Yale Law School.

Another one who could never sleep, so long as I never did, was my crackerjack scheduler, Yael Belkind. From the moment she started in August 2002 to my last day as chairman in February 2005, she averaged about three hours of sleep a night. Every day in the command center brought a new adventure, and she always kept a cool and efficient manner and never stopped smiling. However, I wondered sometimes how anyone could get that excited about Travelocity.

I was having fun at the convention, but it still ate at me that we were missing an opportunity to give the American people a vivid reminder of all that was wrong with the Bush administration. This was the future of the country we were talking about! Who knew how badly Bush and Cheney could screw up the country and the entire world with four more years to ride roughshod over the Constitution, inflame our enemies in other countries, push the poor deeper into poverty, and bankrupt the country to hand out tax cuts to the rich?

I ran into my good friends James Carville and Paul Begala at the CNN studio and they busted my chops for going easy on Bush.

"Terry, was your speech supposed to be at the Republican Convention in New York?" James asked me.

"You're the chairman of *which* party?" Paul chimed in.

I blamed it on Andrei, joking, "The man has lost his edge." I knew I didn't have to tell them the truth, because they knew it.

John Kerry had called Paul many times and pleaded with him to join his campaign. Paul agonized and finally decided to give up his lucrative contract with CNN to go work full-time on the Kerry campaign. He went to campaign headquarters to accept John's offer, and the top campaign official responded with disdain, telling Paul that she wasn't sure she had a role for him, but would get back to him. To this day, Paul is still waiting for that call.

Finally on Wednesday night I couldn't hold in my frustration anymore. Wherever I went, people would come up to me and ask, "When are you guys going to go after Bush?" I was standing downstairs under the podium talking to the Rev. Al Sharpton, who had livened up the debates so often with his fresh approach and was just about to go up and give his speech to the convention. Like most of the speakers I talked to that week, Sharpton was incensed over having to tone down his speech. He felt like we were letting our people down by missing this great opportunity.

"You know what, Al?" I said. "If you really want to go attack Bush by name, go ahead and do it."

"You really mean it?" he asked.

"I don't give a damn what Kerry's message gurus think at this point," I said. "You go do it and you tell them I told you to do it, okay?"

So he went up and let loose with a great speech that had more applause lines than anyone had all week, including one about the Supreme Court that had everyone talking.

"I suggest to you tonight that if George Bush had selected the court in '54, Clarence Thomas would have never got to law school," he said.

"It, to me, is a glaring contradiction that we would fight, and rightfully so, to get the right to vote for the people in the capital of Iraq in Baghdad, but still don't give the federal right to vote for the people in the capital of the United States, in Washington, D.C.," he continued.

"As I close, Mr. President, I heard you say Friday that you had questions for voters, particularly African-American voters," Sharpton called out. "It is true that Mr. Lincoln signed the Emancipation Proclamation, after which there was a commitment to give forty acres and a mule. . . . We never got the forty acres. We went all the way to Herbert Hoover and we never got the forty acres. We didn't get the mule, so we decided we'd ride this donkey as far as it would take us."

Jimmy Carter gave a great, tough speech noting that the Bush administration had "gratified its enemies by proclaiming a confused and disturbing strategy of 'preemptive' war" and that the Middle East peace process had come to a screeching halt under Bush 43 for the first time since Israel became a nation. "Ultimately, the basic issue is whether America will provide global leadership that springs from the unity and the integrity of the American people or whether extremist doctrines, the manipulation of truth, will define America's role in the world," Carter said. "At stake is nothing less than our nation's soul."

Bill Clinton was a great hit with his "Send me" riff, talking about how John Kerry had stood up to be counted when George W. Bush was ducking his National Guard service. "During the Vietnam War, many young men, including the current President, the Vice President, and me, could have gone to Vietnam and didn't," Clinton said. "John Kerry came from a privileged background. He could have avoided going, too. But instead he said, 'Send me.' When they sent those Swift boats up the river in Vietnam, and they told them their job was to draw hostile fire, to wave the American flag, and bait the enemy to come out and fight, John Kerry said, 'Send me.'"

A year earlier, I was in Maurice and Vietta Johnson's backyard in Chicago with two hundred people for an African American Leadership Council event organized by AALC director Kevin Jefferson. I always had a great time at those events, with so much energy and hope for the future in the air, and I remember a younger man walking up to me to introduce himself, shaking my hand and telling me, "I'm going to be the next United States senator from Illinois." I almost chuckled, because I heard that kind of thing so often, but this young man, a state senator at the time, was poised and smart and I figured: *Why not*? Later, he and I met for breakfast several times on my trips to Illinois and became good friends.

So I was very excited for Barack Obama when he took the podium that Wednesday night as our keynote speaker, giving a speech on the "Audacity of Hope." A star was born that night.

"People don't expect government to solve all their problems," he said. "But they sense, deep in their bones, that with just a slight change in priorities, we can make sure that every child in America has a decent shot at life, and that the doors of opportunity remain open to all. They know we can do better. And they want that choice."

The key question in the elections, Barack said, was, "Do we participate in a politics of cynicism or do we participate in a politics of hope? . . . It's the hope of slaves sitting around a fire singing freedom songs; the hope of immigrants setting out for distant shores; the hope of a young naval lieutenant bravely patrolling the Mekong Delta; the hope of a mill worker's son who dares to defy the odds; the hope of a skinny kid with a funny name who believes that America has a place for him, too. Hope in the face of difficulty. Hope in the face of uncertainty. The audacity of hope!"

We were united and we were optimistic about beating Bush and Cheney. The frustration over backing off at the convention on hitting Bush hard on his leadership did not extend to gloom and doom about our chances in November. We were going to win. We just had to come out of the convention fighting. We had to ride the wave of energy and keep it going.

John Kerry's message in his speech on the last night of the convention was that he had been tested on the front lines of Vietnam and that he was a strong leader who could be trusted to carry the nation through difficult times. He actually used the words "strong" or "strength" seventeen times in his speech, but he was contrasting the strength of wisdom and balance he would bring to the job with the recklessness and panic of the Bush years.

"I know what we have to do in Iraq," John said. "As President I will fight a smarter, more effective war on terror. We will deploy every tool in our arsenal—our economic as well as our military might; our principles as well as our firepower. In these dangerous days, there is a right way and a wrong way to be strong. Strength is more than tough words. After decades of experience in national security I know the reach of our power and I know the power of our ideals. We need to make America once again a beacon in the world. We need to be looked up to, not just feared."

It was a strong way to end the convention and should have given us the bounce we needed. Instead, the Republicans once again showed that they had no scruples about exploiting the pain of the nation after September 11 for political gain. Again and again the Bush team had manipulated the color-coded system of terror alerts for partisan purposes. If they wanted to change the subject, they whipped up fear over a pending terrorist attack and it worked every time. Even three years after the September 11 attacks, many around the country still felt a raw fear that we would be attacked again.

Tom Ridge, the Homeland Security Secretary, held a press conference at 3:30 P.M. that Sunday, August 1, just three days after the convention had concluded, hyping a security threat that was never adequately explained.

"This afternoon we do have new and unusually specific information about where Al Qaeda would like to attack," Ridge said in comments carried live on TV.

The administration was so brazen that Ridge's warning strongly echoed the language White House aides had used on September 11, 2001, to explain George Bush hiding from his duties that day, especially Karl Rove's comments to the press when he said, "We are talking about specific and credible intelligence, not vague suspicions."

Ridge raised the threat level to orange, ensuring that instead of focusing on John Kerry and the Democratic Convention, media coverage would be dominated by more scare-mongering over terrorism. To this day no credible information has emerged to justify this clumsy political trick, any more than any credible information has been produced to explain assurances of a phone call to the White House on September 11, warning that Air Force One was being targeted.

"The latest elevated alert—specifically for financial buildings in the New York area and Washington—was issued three days after the Democratic National Convention, as Sen. John Kerry was hoping to bask in the headlines from his nomination," the *Chicago Tribune* editorialized on August 8. "The timing provided fuel for skeptics who have suggested Bush has purposely used homeland security announcements to change the nation's conversation during times of unsettling news for his administration."

Then on August 5, 2004, a week after the last day of our convention, the "Swift Boat Veterans for Truth" ads hit the airwaves, generating hour after hour of media coverage.

With a one-two punch, with Tom Ridge putting politics before his job, and with John O'Neill and the Swift Boat group putting politics and score-settling before the truth, American politics was captured by a skillful round of media manipulation. The Kerry campaign defended itself when the ads first hit, but immediately backed off, hoping the storm would pass. Their argument was that the Swift Boat folks were only putting up a $300,000 ad buy and if you commented, that only generated more attention. They hoped it would go away, but it didn't—and the damage it did to Kerry's standing in the polls gave Bush the opening he needed. The next year I was in London, speaking at a conference with Mark McKinnon, Bush's media adviser, and Mark told the assembled group that the Bush campaign calculated that in the end the $300,000 ad buy was worth $30 million in free media. Mark said the Bush campaign was shocked and amazed that the Kerry campaign just sat there and took it. They were also overjoyed.

"Americans would never believe that John Kerry would defend them when he couldn't even defend himself," Mark told me. "No one but Kerry could have responded, because it was his credibility and integrity on the line."

The Republicans held their convention in New York from August 30 to September 2, and engaged in nothing but vicious, ugly attacks on John

Kerry and the Democratic Party. There were two words they used every other sentence: "John" and "Kerry." They were so intent on attacking Kerry, it was clear they had no positive message of their own, but I'll say this for them, they sure looked like they were enjoying getting down in the gutter.

One unfortunate aspect of Vermont Senator Jim Jeffords's decision to leave the Republican Party to become an Independent, denying the Republicans their majority, was that we became a majority in name only. Tom Daschle became Senator Majority Leader but he never had a true majority because so-called Democrat Zell Miller had abandoned the Democratic caucus. The Republicans used the situation to label us as obstructionists and to blame us for everything that went wrong.

Zell was such a disgrace to the Democratic Party, I even called Tom Daschle and urged Tom to go on national television and announce he was throwing Zell out of the caucus. The man had no convictions, which was why behind his back people from *both* parties called him "Zig-Zag Zell." He changed positions more than a weather vane.

Who was Zell Miller to be lecturing anyone on values? Talk about a sordid past. As Georgia governor, Zell got awfully cozy with lobbyists. That sure was a nice new SUV he started driving around in right about the time he left office—the one he reportedly sent back until it was fully loaded with *all* the options. That new truck wasn't bad, either.

Zell also took money from the good citizens of Georgia. The ABC affiliate in Atlanta, WSB-TV, conducted an investigation into Miller's sleazy history, and reported that in 1999 during his final days as governor, Miller took more than $60,000 in taxpayer funds that were budgeted for expenses at the Governor's Mansion, not for Zell's retirement fund.

Bill Shipp, the most respected political commentator in Georgia, noted in a column that, "In essence, Miller says he was technically eligible to take the mansion money as his own because no one said he could not. . . . Never mind that every other living governor from Jimmy Carter to Sonny Perdue . . . did not consider the mansion money theirs—and they would not have taken it. The cash was meant for use at the mansion, not for lining the occupants' pockets."

Zell was always attacking me for being a Northerner, saying that since I was born and raised in New York, I couldn't understand his Southern roots. First of all, I married a Southerner. Dorothy was born in North Carolina, and her grandparents came from old Southern families. One grandfather was born in Alabama and the other—you're going to love this, Zell—was born in Georgia.

In fact, two of my all-time top ten heroes in politics both come from Georgia—Jimmy Carter and John Lewis, two of the most honest, decent, idealistic men I've known, and who always reflected the values of the Democratic Party.

Lewis called Zell's words and actions "a shame and a disgrace," noting, "This is the same Zell Miller who said forty years ago that President Lyndon Johnson had sold his soul when he signed the Civil Rights Act of 1964."

Miller got his start as executive secretary to Lester Maddox, the infamous racist Georgia governor who, as *The Washington Post* reported, "chased African Americans out of his restaurant with an ax handle." Following the tragic death of Martin Luther King, Jr., Maddox refused even to afford the great civil rights leader the honor of having flags in Georgia hung at half-mast. Zell obviously learned a lot about values from his mentor. Running for Congress in 1964, Miller vowed that he would vote against Johnson's historic Civil Rights Act and even attacked LBJ as "a Southerner who has sold his birthright for a mess of dark porridge."

Zell, I don't care what part of the country you come from—North, South, East, or West. That's hateful and revolting.

Jimmy Carter said that when Democratic governor Roy Barnes appointed Zell to the U.S. Senate in 2000, it was "one of his worst mistakes" because Zell had "betrayed all the basic principles that I thought he and I and others shared."

Miller must have felt right at home giving the keynote address at the 2004 Republican National Convention, where he questioned the patriotism of Democrats, but it made my stomach turn.

If Miller had been honest, he would have said in his speech that the high-tech military that had proved so effective in the war in Afghanistan and in the first phase of the Iraq War had been built not by George Bush, but by Bill Clinton. It was during the eight years of Clinton's presidency that almost all the spectacular new military technology was developed. Bill Clinton's leadership prepared us to go to war, if forced into it. But Zell Miller went out and attacked John Kerry for voting against some weapons systems. "This is the man who wants to be the commander in chief of our U.S. Armed Forces?" Miller taunted. "U.S. forces armed with what? Spitballs?"

Miller seemed to be going through some kind of personal crisis or meltdown right before the country's eyes.

"What has happened to the party I've spent my life working in?" he asked. "I can remember when Democrats believed it was the duty of America to fight for freedom over tyranny. . . . But not today. Motivated more by partisan politics than by national security, today's Democratic leaders see America as an occupier, not a liberator. And nothing makes this marine madder than someone calling American troops occupiers rather than liberators."

And nothing makes this artillery officer's son madder than someone questioning my patriotism, so I blasted Miller right back as a loose cannon who had hurt his party with his wild-eyed extremism. Our crack team in our rapid response room for the convention couldn't believe Miller's speech was so filled with opportunities to blast him. He was leaving himself wide open. At first they were laughing, but after a while it just seemed pathetic to witness this man going off the deep end. They immediately put out a detailed list of all the times Dick Cheney had voted against the same weapons systems as John Kerry, and CNN and later MSNBC used some of that material to force Zell to answer some tough questions. I've had some heated sessions with Chris Matthews on MSNBC, but nothing like what he and Zell got into in the famous on-camera meltdown everyone was talking about that week—and still are to this day.

"I wish we lived in the day where you could challenge a person to a duel," Zell told Chris, and later, "You get in my face, I am going to get back in your face."

Most important, Zell would never answer Chris's main question, which was: *Do you really believe John Kerry does not want to defend America?* Miller was completely discredited that night, and it was an important lesson in how you have to invest in having a savvy team of rapid-response researchers ready to pounce.

I'd already known for years that Zell was the kind of man who talked tough on TV but couldn't handle it when you came after him. He'd been questioning my positions as DNC chair since 2001, so I thought we ought to sit down and talk man to man, since he'd never met me and knew nothing about my values. I figured it could get interesting to have this mighty former marine squaring off in a room against a former boxer, Mad Dog McAuliffe. I called his office to arrange the meeting and Zell refused to meet with me—how's that for Profiles in Courage? To this day I still chuckle to think that Zell would challenge Chris Matthews to a duel but was scared to sit down with this New Yorker.

I couldn't believe how often these extreme Republicans engaging in character assassination had the sleaziest sort of motivation. I ran into John O'Neill, the man behind the Swift Boat group aligned against John Kerry, in the Green Room at MSNBC later that summer. When he saw me he walked right over to shake my hand and talk to me. You'd have thought I was his best friend, the way he was talking about my strong public stands against Bush.

"Terry, you're a real fighter," O'Neill said.

"Do you believe all that stuff you say about John Kerry?" I asked him. "Do you really believe it?"

He was taken aback and didn't know what to say.

"You really don't believe that John deserved those Purple Hearts?" I asked him.

He claimed he didn't, but I had my suspicions.

"You really just don't like John, do you?" I asked.

"No," O'Neill said.

He went off on a tirade that only proved my point. This was about a man willing to tear down American democracy so he could tear down a man he resented.

★

ON SEPTEMBER 1, just after I boarded a shuttle from New York back to D.C., Doug Band called to tell me that President Clinton was being taken to the hospital for emergency heart surgery. This came as a huge surprise to me because the night before, when I talked to the President on the phone for nearly an hour, he sounded great and we joked around a lot. The plane was already backing away from the gate and I asked Doug if I should try to get off, but he assured me the President's life was not in immediate danger, so I should take the flight and he would give me frequent updates.

That Monday, Clinton went into quadruple coronary artery bypass surgery lasting from 8 A.M. until noon. Doug and I talked at least twenty-five times that day and he reported that the operation went well, and Clinton's doctors and medical experts all agreed his prospects for a speedy recovery were excellent. The first call Clinton received after going into recovery was from George W. Bush.

"That was really funny," Clinton remembers. "He said, 'You know, this is very serious surgery you had. You need to recuperate and it'd be very bad for you to get out and start campaigning too soon.'"

Even Bush knew what an asset Bill Clinton was to the Kerry campaign. He wanted him on the sidelines as long as possible.

"Let me be honest, Bill," Bush told Clinton. "This Kerry campaign is the most inept group I have ever seen in politics. Don't let them ruin your reputation."

31

★ ★ ★

I'd whipped up a hornet's nest earlier in 2004 on Super Bowl Sunday when I told George Stephanopoulos on ABC that "I look forward to that debate when John Kerry, a war hero with a chest full of medals, is standing next to George Bush, a man who was AWOL in the Alabama National Guard." Now the debate was finally here. I flew down to Miami, Florida, for the first of the Kerry-Bush debates on September 30, and I couldn't wait to see John Kerry take Bush apart like Muhammad Ali dancing circles around some slow-footed palooka and pummeling him. This was going to be great.

Justin kept reminding me as we arrived at the University of Miami for the pre-debate media sessions that we did not want to be late.

"We have to be in our seats on time," Justin said.

"Ah, we've got plenty of time," I said.

I loved working the media room at debates, especially when George W. Bush had given us so much ammunition. I walked past row after row of reporters sitting at their desks, did interviews at every turn and also went on half a dozen radio and TV shows.

"Mr. Chairman," Justin said. "Time to go!"

He was right. We had to get moving. Finally we got inside and Justin wanted me to head for my reserved seat right away, but I was working the room and shaking hands. Finally Justin and I walked up the left aisle to where my assigned seat was and saw that it was taken. A woman bedecked with jewels had camped out there and I did not want to make a scene and ask her to leave. I was ready to watch the debate standing on the side. I'd have to leave early anyway to do a conference call with talkers and bloggers all over the country, giving them a rundown on what we wanted to emphasize in our post-debate comments.

"Let's go up *there,*" Justin suggested.

He was looking toward the two front rows where the families of the two debaters had been carefully arranged for the cameras. They put a lot of time into picking exactly who they wanted sitting there, since the podiums were angled so that every time Bush or Kerry looked up, those were the faces they would see.

"There's an empty seat," Justin said. "I'll grab it for you."

There was one empty seat up in the second row, directly behind First Lady Laura Bush and the twins, Jenna and Barbara. John McCain was sitting next to them.

"I don't know, that might be pushing it, don't you think?" I asked Justin.

"We've got nothing to lose," he said. "George Bush is going to look at his wife all night and see you sitting there. You've got to go up there."

I had to think it over. This was a big deal, going over and sitting right behind the First Lady of the United States. This was taking it to the edge, and I spent several tense moments mulling it over.

"All right, let's do it," I told Justin.

In the two minutes we had stood there discussing it, a woman Secret Service agent had moved in and sat down in the empty seat.

"Too bad, Justin," I said. "We lost our chance. There's an agent there now."

He flashed a quick smile.

"Watch this," he said.

If you've never attended a presidential debate in person, it's great theater. We were seconds away from going on the air, the lights were up, and a hush had come over the auditorium. Moderator Jim Lehrer had instructed everyone to stay absolutely quiet. So when Justin started walking up toward the stage, every eye in the place was on him, wondering what he was doing. He marched up to the second row, right in the heart of the Bush family area.

"Ma'am, you are seated in the chairman's seat," he told the Secret Service agent.

"I'm so sorry," she said, and jumped right out of her chair.

For all we know she thought Justin worked for the chairman of the Joint

Chiefs of Staff. That obviously was not the assigned seat of the chairman of the Democratic National Committee.

I walked up, careful not to smile, and sat down in the seat Justin had cleared for me. You could hear murmuring, and people started shifting in their seats to take a look. Laura Bush turned around to see who had just sat down behind her and immediately wished she hadn't. It was like that scene in *The Shining* where Jack Nicholson cries out "Here's Johnny!" Talk about horror-stricken! I'd been on TV every day for four years turning up the heat on her husband—and she knew it. She and the twins were whispering back and forth among themselves and sneaking quick, indignant looks.

Soon it was clear to everyone that something was wrong. Kerry and Bush should have walked out to their podiums by then. Something was holding up the show. I found out later that I was that something: Bush and his team were sitting there in the Green Room and the TV monitors showed Laura and the twins with my big head right between them. If I could ruin Barbara Bush's whole summer by setting foot in Kennebunkport, just imagine how Bush felt about seeing me right behind his wife all through the debate. He was furious and refused to leave the Green Room unless I was removed.

"Get McAuliffe out of that chair!" was the order, and all the TV cameramen heard it over their headphones.

I knew I'd have to move when they sent a huge agent out to get me. This guy made some linebackers look small.

"I need you to move," he told me.

"No," I said. "This is my seat."

"Mr. McAuliffe, I know who you are," the agent said. "Please do me a favor and move."

What could I say? The guy had handcuffs and a huge gun, and the entire nation was waiting for this debate to start. I walked back and watched the debate with Justin, standing over on the side. I was disappointed I didn't get to sit up there, which would really have messed with Bush's head. As Bill Clinton likes to say, "All great contests are head games."

We'll never know for sure what had Bush off his game that night. Maybe his dazed and confused look at the start of the debate had nothing to do with the fuss over having me moved. You had to wonder when the only excuse the campaign could come up with was that Bush had spent too much time riding his bike that day. The important thing was Bush came out and got clobbered in the debate. Bush looked distracted and lost, as if he had been expecting to go mountain-biking and found out at the last minute that he had to do battle with that old enemy of his, the English language.

Asked about the chances of our being hit by another terrorist attack, Bush gave a rambling answer, eventually saying, "People out there listening know what I believe. And that's how best it is to keep the peace. . . . In Iraq, no doubt about it, it's tough. It's hard work. It's incredibly hard. You know why? Because an enemy realizes the stakes."

John Kerry cut right to the point with his reply.

"I believe in being strong and resolute and determined, and I will hunt down and kill the terrorists wherever they are," he said. "But we also have to be smart, Jim. And smart means not diverting your attention from the real war on terror in Afghanistan against Osama bin Laden and taking it off to Iraq where the 9/11 Commission confirms there was no connection to 9/11 itself and Saddam Hussein, and where the reason for going to war was weapons of mass destruction, not the removal of Saddam Hussein. This President has made, I regret to say, a colossal error of judgment, and judgment is what we look for in the President of the United States of America."

We were all proud of John for the way he took it to Bush and I hated to leave the audience early, but had to head over for my meeting with Kerry advisers Michael Whouley and Joe Lockhart on what our response would be. Bush was defensive, annoyed, arrogant, and angry, and that was what we decided to talk about afterward. He pursed his lips and glared and smirked. We produced a bruising video immediately after the debate showing Bush's "Faces of Frustration," giving people the full range of Bush's unpresidential looks. Back in D.C., under Howard Wolfson's direction, our rapid response team posted the video online and delivered it to the networks, furthering the story line about Bush's agitation and discomfort. As I told reporters in the Spin Room afterward, "It was crystal clear that George Bush does not react well to a challenge."

I was overjoyed when Howard joined the DNC right after the Republican Convention in early September 2004. He is as good and tough a communication strategist as we have in our party. He led our tough attacks on Bush in the last months of the campaign. Had Howard been running Kerry's communication strategy when John was nominated, we would never have backed off on our AWOL attacks—and could have pinned Bush to the mat for the entire campaign.

The Republicans had used their techniques of manipulation to convince the public that Bush had somehow gotten the better of Al Gore during their first debate four years earlier, all because the Vice President sighed a few times. As if Gore were the first one ever to sigh after listening to Bush speak. This time around, we wanted to get out the truth—that Bush was prickly and easily flustered. Before the debate, my director of technology, Doug Kelly, met with the Kerry campaign to brief them on what we'd be doing for the first debate: We'd be sending out an e-mail to our entire list of 3.8 million people, asking them to watch the debate, and giving Web sites they could visit after the debate to vote in online polls. I also encouraged them to write letters to the editor and call talk shows.

"We don't want to politicize the debate like this," one of Kerry's people told Doug.

"Listen, are you serious?" Doug said. "Do you remember what they did to Al Gore after his first debate with Bush? Terry is going to do this. If there's a problem, you can blame it on the DNC."

We also bought $400,000 of online ads and timed it so that the ads would pop up on people's screens right in the middle of the debate. This was a great opportunity for us to use our new technology and I thank Laura Quinn for suggesting it. People no longer waited to read their news when their newspapers landed on their doorsteps the next morning. Many of the people who watched the debate would immediately go online to see what others had to say about Kerry and Bush. When they did that, using Yahoo! or other Web portals where we'd bought ads, they'd run right into our ad— which emphasized how presidential and strong John Kerry looked, and how weak and irritable George Bush looked. People were literally road-blocked by these ads.

We had a gigantic load of traffic coming through the DNC Web site, clicking and voting in Web polls, and thousands of letters to the editor were sent out all over the country. Gore had won against Bush four years earlier and then lost the online polls due to the Republicans being smarter, and tougher, and having better technology. I had vowed that we were never going to let the Republicans steal another debate and sure enough, Kerry won all the online polls.

"On Thursday night, it was Bush's aggravated demeanor that contributed to the impression that Kerry won the debate," Dana Milbank wrote in *The Washington Post*. "Bush has flashed such expressions—and worse— at reporters when they ask him hostile questions. But the public has generally not seen the President's more petulant side, in part because he is rarely challenged in a public venue."

A *Newsweek* poll found that Bush's eleven-point lead over Kerry had "vanished" and Kerry now led 49 percent to 46 percent. Of the 74 percent of registered voters who said they watched the debate, 61 percent saw Kerry as the clear winner, compared to only 19 percent who thought Bush won.

Also important, Bush's approval rating dropped below 50 percent for the first time since the Republican Convention that summer.

The Republicans were so used to winning by manipulating the process, it shocked them when they couldn't spin Bush's embarrassing performance in the first debate into the perception of a victory. If they couldn't manipulate reality, they had real problems. We knew they would try their old standby tactic of scaring the people, and the vice presidential debate between Dick Cheney and John Edwards on October 5 was going to be a key test of whether they could gain any traction with that.

Justin and I flew to Cleveland for the debate and went to check out the layout at the Veale Center at Case Western Reserve University, where Edwards and Cheney would be going at it a few hours later. We were so early, the room was empty except for a few technicians setting up their television cameras.

"Hey, Mr. McAuliffe, where are you sitting tonight?" one of the technicians asked me.

I wasn't sure I knew what he was talking about.

"You saw where I sat at the last debate?" I said, chuckling.

"Are you kidding me?" he said. "Do you have any idea the controversy you caused?"

"No," I said.

That was when I found out what a commotion I'd caused in Florida before the first Kerry-Bush debate.

CNN was reporting that the Bush-Cheney campaign was complaining about me having sat behind the First Lady and that Vermont senator Pat Leahy had been asked by the Kerry campaign to sit in the second row that night at the vice presidential debate. That June, Dick Cheney had a very un–vice presidential moment on the floor of the United States Senate. Earlier, Leahy had raised questions about Cheney's ties to energy conglomerate Halliburton, which had made a fortune with its contracts in Iraq through mismanagement and over-the-top profiteering. This was the first chance Cheney had to confront Leahy directly.

"Go f—— yourself," said the Vice President.

You would think the Republicans would have wanted to avoid reminding voters about Cheney's outburst, but instead, they complained to the press about our having Leahy in the second row, right smack in the middle of Cheney's line of sight.

"Now the Bush campaign is crying foul, saying, 'Look, they did the same thing in Miami last week when you had Terry McAuliffe sitting right behind Laura Bush,'" CNN reported.

Asked for comment, Kerry spokesman Joe Lockhart said, "Look, we know these debates can be extremely stressful situations and we wanted to make sure there was a friendly face there for Dick Cheney."

All great contests are mind games!

I guess Cheney and the campaign had good reason to worry. John Edwards, a former prosecutor, won the debate easily, scoring points on the substance and maintaining his composure.

"While he was CEO of Halliburton, they paid millions of dollars in fines for providing false information on their company, just like Enron and Ken Lay," Edwards said in the debate. "They did business with Libya and Iran, two sworn enemies of the United States. They're now under investigation for having bribed foreign officials during that period of time. Not only that, they've gotten a $7.5 billion no-bid contract in Iraq, and instead of part of their money being withheld, which is the way it's normally done because they're under investigation, they've continued to get their money."

The Vice President looked grumpy and befuddled, and got caught playing fast and loose with the facts. He was trying to belittle Edwards as an upstart and a lightweight.

"The first time I ever met you was when you walked on the stage tonight," Cheney told Edwards during the debate.

Oh really? I was so proud of my team that night. Tracy Sefl was working in our D.C. war room and knew as soon as Cheney said that, he was lying. Phone calls and e-mails started coming in within seconds confirming that Cheney and Edwards had definitely met before. Tracy alerted some producers to Cheney's clear falsehood, and worked with the rest of the crew in our war room to get a video of Cheney meeting Edwards. Once the video was out there minutes later, providing Technicolor proof, the story got even bigger, reminding people that as my parents always warned me, if you lie about the little things, it makes it easier to lie about the big things.

After the debate, John's wife, Elizabeth, reminded Cheney that he had met her husband at a prayer breakfast and the Vice President said, "Oh yes, you're right."

Once again, the polls backed up what we all knew: Edwards won the debate handily. A CBS poll of uncommitted voters found that 41 percent thought Edwards had won, compared with only 28 percent for Cheney.

The momentum continued through the last two debates between Kerry and Bush, which once again John Kerry won. Out in Tempe, Arizona, after the final debate on October 13, I did my usual round of TV and print interviews afterward, and went on Fox News with Sean Hannity. Sean's style is to keep badgering you on the same point again and again, and it was pretty funny actually.

"It's very simple, Sean," I said. "If people think that George Bush has done a great job in this country creating jobs, then vote for him."

I started to continue, but he kept putting his hand on my shoulder, and finally I'd had enough.

"Please don't touch me," I said, as he jerked his hand back.

No one could believe I'd actually said that to him, least of all Sean himself. In March 2005 he asked me to fill in for his partner, and he rolled the footage of me telling him not to touch me.

"You know how many people have asked me about that segment?" he said.

"Well I got asked a lot, too," I said. "But listen, the point was you kept touching me. If you're into touching guys, I was fine with that. I mean, the issue is—that just isn't my deal."

The cameraman and a bunch of other people on the set all burst out laughing. Sean loved to badger other people, but was at a loss when someone needled him.

"That's a nice way of saying, 'Shush, answer the question,'" he whined.

"You kept pawing me," I said. "I didn't know what to do."

Two days after the last Kerry-Bush debate, I called Ken Strasma, a consultant to the Kerry campaign who specialized in computer modeling on voter turnout.

"Where are we, Ken?" I asked.

"We're at three hundred twenty electoral votes, fifty more than we need," he said.

"Holy smokes!" I said.

"We're going to win Ohio, New Hampshire, Wisconsin, and Florida," he told me.

The Friday before the election, Osama bin Laden gave the Bush administration just what it needed to change the subject. Up until then Bush was in trouble, reeling from the latest round of bleak economic news and the hammering he was taking for the stunning revelation that U.S. forces in Iraq had somehow failed to secure 380 tons of high-grade explosives. They allowed these fanatics to just walk off, in effect arming the terrorists for thousands of attacks on our soldiers. Bin Laden knew he had a friend in the White House in George W. Bush. Young would-be terrorists were streaming into Al Qaeda from all over the Muslim world, enraged by Bush's clumsy decision to cast the war on terror from day one as a "crusade."

Bush could have finished the job in Afghanistan, but instead he left it in chaos—still raging today—so he could go after Saddam Hussein. Then he turned Iraq into a quagmire and a breeding ground for more terrorists. Bin Laden wanted four more years of Bush, and his bizarre videotape released on October 29, 2004, his first video in a year, served once again to get people scared and worried about the threat of terrorism. That was Bush's only hope: If swing voters were scared and emotional, they wouldn't think as much about all the harm Bush had done to the country.

Bin Laden's taped message four days before the election freaked people out, especially the undecideds whose support we had won. Bin Laden said that Bush 41 was impressed by monarchies and military regimes, jealous of them for staying in power for many years, and "found it good to install his children as governors and leaders." He also mocked Bush 43 for his weird stalling the day of the September 11 attacks, saying, "It appeared to him that a little girl's talk about her goat and its butting was more important than the planes and their butting of the skyscrapers. That gave us three times the required time to carry out the operations, thank God." No American wanted to hear the President of the United States mocked by a shameless killer, and bin Laden's cutting criticism was a surefire way to prompt people to rally behind the President.

Just seeing bin Laden's face flashing on TV was enough to trigger all the old September 11 fears that Bush and Karl Rove had worked so hard to exploit for political gain, and to distract from the disturbing reality that Bush's incompetence and recklessness had made America less safe after 9/11. I had a chance to talk to a senior CIA operative late in 2006 and asked if, bottom line, Bush had made Americans safer or less safe. His answer shocked me. This was a respected veteran who had run many of our black-box operations, a lifelong Republican, not some left-wing pundit. His expert opinion was that we were five times less safe because of Bush's mistakes. Five times! Bush should have had to answer for that in the 2004 campaign, but bin Laden gave him a golden opportunity to use his old bait-and-switch tactics and get people dwelling on their fear, not on Bush's failure to capture bin Laden and his disastrous record of putting all Americans more at risk.

*

EVEN AFTER THE BIN LADEN TAPE, I was still optimistic going into Election Day. We had come up with an excellent strategy to force Bush and Cheney to be held accountable. Left unchecked, the President and Vice President could fly around the country to smaller markets and say just about anything, no matter how big a whopper, and not be challenged on it. However, if I was there in a particular market first, raising tough questions, it guaranteed that the press would ask Bush or Cheney about some of the points I'd raised. The last month of the campaign, we organized the "Kerry-Edwards Truth Squad," headed up by Josh Earnest, and any time Bush or Cheney was going to give a speech, I showed up first, either that morning or the day before. If Bush was talking about education in Minnesota, for example, I would preempt his message with facts about Bush's weak record on education—and I would have people by my side who had felt the sting of Bush's cuts to education, which he had under-funded by $33 million. If we were talking about the military, I was joined by retired four-star generals Tony McPeak and Wes Clark. We all had blue "Kerry-Edwards Truth Squad" jackets, and my visits generated great press and helped set the record straight on issue after issue.

We flew up to New Hampshire on November 1 for the last night of cam-paigning, and finished up with a great rally in Nashua with more than a thousand young people screaming their lungs out. The New Hampshire Democratic Chair, Kathy Sullivan, really put on a show. We hadn't planned for such a big crowd. My voice was shot, so Elizabeth Alexander found a bullhorn and handed it to me and gave me a chair to stand on. I got up there and looked out at all these young faces and gave one last full-throttled speech on what John Kerry was going to do for our country. They were chanting and singing, and I felt so much energy surging through the crowd, it was amazing. I knew we were going to win.

"What a great way to end," Justin told me after I'd finished up. "We started here and we finished here."

I got up early on Election Day to do a final round of morning talk shows and then went back to the hotel and called our national field director, Karen Hicks, and Teresa Vilmain, our general election strategist, to ask how all our preparations had shaped up. They gave me the great news that our field op-eration was firing on all cylinders and they were both sure we were going to win. The unprecedented work and resources we had put into our field oper-ation meant that we had 233,000 volunteers who knocked on 11 million doors to talk to people about why this election was so important for work-ing men and women and the future of our country.

We made 38 million volunteer phone calls to voters and another 56 mil-lion calls from phone banks we funded. We sent over 69 million pieces of mail and 322 million e-mails to get our message out, and also deployed sur-rogates on over 2,000 trips, and produced 9,383 radio interviews and 1,388 TV interviews. We spent more than $131 million on TV ads, which was 90 percent more than what the DNC spent on TV ads in 2000. Keeping in mind the lessons of the 2000 election, which we allowed the Republicans to steal, we deployed 17,000 voter-protection attorneys in key precincts and had them in place, ready to fight attempts by the Republicans to disenfranchise voters.

I also called Brad Marshall, our CFO, to check up on how we had done getting money out the door to where it was needed in the final weekend of the campaign. Four days earlier, I had quietly arranged to borrow $10 million for an extra final round of spending. I hated debt and after decades of the DNC being debt ridden, I was reluctant at first to commit another $10 million, on top of the record-setting totals we'd already committed, but Michael Whouley, John Sasso, and Josh Wachs had made a strong case that given how close the election was likely to be, we badly needed a last-minute surge of spending. I knew that with the powerhouse fund-raising machine we had built, we could easily pay off the additional $10 million by raising more money in my remaining time as chairman, and going all out was the right thing to do. Brad confirmed for me on Election Day that we had moved all our money out the door, including that last infusion of $10 million, and again I hung up feeling confident knowing that we had done everything we could.

32

★ ★ ★

I hate Election Days. I always feel as jumpy and powerless as I had when Dorothy went into the hospital with each of our five children. Your work is done. All you could do is sit and wait and try to stay positive. We were all gathered in a big hotel suite and I sat there that morning in my gym shorts and a T-shirt, wishing there was something more I could do. Someone put a movie on, but I couldn't tell you a thing about it. No one was paying much attention, just staring blankly at the screen. I was driving Justin and Elizabeth crazy, asking them every two minutes, "What are you hearing? What are you hearing?" and they had nothing new to tell me. "I was talking to my dry cleaners," Elizabeth finally said, and they left me alone to pace by myself.

Finally around noon the first exit poll numbers started coming in and the news was great. We were up in Ohio 52 to 48, up 50 to 49 in New Mexico, and up in Florida 51 to 48. Bush was so nervous about Ohio, he made a surprise visit that day after he voted, and we could see why. Our BlackBerries were all chirping with different exit polls and even though we tried to remind ourselves that early exit polls were often wrong, it was impossible not to get swept up in the moment. I always say: real or not, it's better to be up than down.

Dorothy caught an early afternoon flight to Boston from Washington with Dori, Jack, and Mary, our three oldest. The kids were all feeling good about the election. A student vote was conducted the day before at The Potomac School and John Kerry had beaten George Bush in a landslide. Jack wore a John Kerry watch to school every day and had a Kerry baseball cap on top of his locker, which he touched for good luck before a test or quiz. Boarding their flight, which was loaded with Democrats flying up to Boston, people were in a great mood as their BlackBerries lit up with the early exit polls and some even started cheering.

As it got to be four o'clock and then six o'clock and the numbers were holding up, you figured by then they were more reliable. We knew there was a huge turnout, which going in we had seen as the key to the election. I am always the ultimate optimist and tried to keep myself in check, but by seven o'clock I knew we had won the election. John Kerry was going to be the next President of the United States and John Edwards was going to be Vice President.

Someone brought in a bottle of champagne, which we put on ice, but as much as we thought about popping the cork, we held off for the time being. I was going to be opening up the program down in Copley Plaza, so we had Andrei Cherny write my speech. I started practicing and everyone was so jacked up, they'd cheer every line. I was basically declaring victory.

"You know, I can't give this speech," I said. "This is *too* optimistic even for me. The polls will still be open on the West Coast and people will think they don't need to vote."

What a role reversal, *me* having to tone *them* down! We spent some time dialing back the speech and then Malik Husser, who worked in the finance department and was also the son of a pastor, led all twenty of us in a group prayer. Dorothy and the kids were right there with me and it was such a great feeling in the room. Then it was time to make our way over to Copley Plaza. We started driving and after one block it was just gridlock, so we hopped out of the car and walked the rest of the way. I'd been on TV practically every day for four years and people kept coming up to me and giving me high-fives.

"We did it!" people would yell.

"Bush is gone!" someone else would shout, and everyone would cheer wildly.

I had camera crews following after me. We had won. It was as clear as day. Ted Kennedy and I spent the night doing a round of television interviews and we were both surprised when a producer told us that the Republicans had even started refusing to go on television, a clear indication to us that they thought they had lost. People in the White House were e-mailing Democrats they knew to congratulate them.

We stopped off in our little hospitality room and had something to eat and watched the TV coverage, which showed a bunch of red states, like South Carolina and Alabama, but that was no concern. Then word started percolating out that the early numbers were inflated. I wasn't worried. I walked over to Copley Plaza to open the program at nine o'clock and it was pouring rain, but there were thousands of people. Even in the cold driving rain, the mood was electric.

I was due back on stage at 10:30 to introduce the Black Eyed Peas, who we'd scheduled to ramp up to the victory celebration, and then at the end President-elect John Kerry would arrive. I was standing with Jack, Dori, and Mary, talking to Sheryl Crow and Lance Armstrong, Jack's hero, when Justin came over and told me I had to take an urgent call. I went into a back room and it was Josh Wachs calling from the Kerry boiler room.

"Florida is gone and we're dropping in Ohio," Josh told me.

I walked back out after taking the call and just by the look on my face, everyone knew that it now looked bad for us. It spread from person to person, this feeling of getting kicked in the gut. It was beyond shock. I had to go out to introduce the Black Eyed Peas and, standing there in the pouring rain, trying to keep up appearances, I felt like I was sleep-walking. I knew we were in trouble, but kept praying for a miracle.

I took Dorothy and the kids back to the room where my staff was assembled, and could hardly stand to watch the TV coverage.

"I think it's gone," I told the kids.

Dori, Jack, and Mary were all devastated. Jack was especially discouraged after having done so many events with me and putting his heart into it, like the others, just the way I had as a kid his age working with my father on Onondaga County Democratic politics. How do you explain to an eleven-year-old that sometimes the wrong side wins?

Jack started to well up and I sat him down for a talk. There were cameras everywhere outside and the McAuliffe family was going to walk out with our heads held high, proud of John Kerry and the race he had run, and proud of the Democratic Party.

"Jack, when we walk out those doors there's going to be hundreds of cameras trained on us," I said. "We can't give up, buddy. Put a good face on. Do it for your dad, okay? Keep your head up high. We know we gave it everything we could."

I was so proud of my family that day. For four years they had endured their father and husband being gone most of the time, out fighting for the Democratic Party, and we all had so much invested in this race. We walked out past the press, and all the kids were great and did their best to hold their heads up and smile. We could still hope that somehow the election would be ours, and in the meantime we were going to show our pride in the Democratic Party and all the work we had done on behalf of helping people in the future, not just leasing out the government to a privileged few looking out for themselves at the expense of the vast majority of Americans.

★

AFTER TWO HOURS OF SLEEP I woke up the next morning hoping it was all a bad dream. It wasn't. As bad as it was, for me the disappointment in 2004 did not sting as much as what I felt after the 2000 election. I knew that in '04 we had done everything we possibly could to win. We had every player on the field and we had all the resources in place to give our all to the campaign. We didn't let the Republicans fight harder than us or work harder than us. I was mad after 2000 because they stole it from us and we let them. This time around I was satisfied there was nothing more we could have done as a party, and we had gotten a lot of young people involved who would be voting Democratic for years to come. We were building for the future and I was sure that once the Republicans could no longer use September 11 and the Iraq War to distract from other issues, we would have our time. However, I'll be honest: I'm glad those early exit polls were wrong. I had the ten greatest hours of my life.

Even in defeat, we felt vindicated for all our hard work at the DNC. We had delivered on everything we promised. Four years earlier, the Gore campaign had to pull out of Ohio because it ran out of money. They didn't have enough money to mount an effective campaign in Gore's home state of Tennessee. This time out, we showed the Democratic Party could learn from its past mistakes and modernize for the future. We raised $100 million in the month of October and finished that year having raised $348 million in 2004, compared to $247 million for the RNC, the first time in modern history the Democrats had raised more money than the Republicans—and this was even after the passage of campaign finance reform, which everyone said was going to bury us! We doubled our hard-money totals over 2000. We had five times more field staff than ever before, spending $80 million in field organizing, an increase of 166 percent over 2000. We also gave $65 million directly to state parties, doubling the number from 2000. We knocked on 41 million doors, had 10 million volunteers on the street on Election Day, and spent $20 million on base vote activities, three times what was spent in 2000.

We had been saying all along that our priority was voter turnout, which was important not only to turn the election but also to get people involved in the democratic process and to build for the future. Our hard work paid off and helped spur a dramatic increase in voter turnout over 2000 with 9 million more people going to the polls for us. We saw gains across the board—2.1 million more Hispanics; 2.2 million more young people; and more than 13 million first-time voters—a key group, which Kerry won 53 percent to 46 percent, four points better than Gore had done four years earlier. Had we shifted 59,000 votes in Ohio, we would have beaten an incumbent wartime President for the first time in modern history.

The morning after the election, I called my staff into my hotel suite for a 7 A.M. meeting to analyze where we were. A lot of people were still hoping that Ohio could swing from the Republican column to ours, putting John over the top as the remaining uncounted votes were added up, but we had been informed by the Kerry folks on the ground in Ohio that we could not win. If there had been any hope, I'd have been ready to fight on for years, if that was what it took—but Kerry's Ohio people were sure. We had lost and it was time to move on.

Jano Cabrera, our DNC communications director, told me that the National Press Club wanted me to do a press conference with RNC chair Ed Gillespie to give a postmortem on the presidential election. Jano was dead set against me doing it. He said he would quit on the spot if I did. He argued that the Kerry campaign people should be the ones to talk about our defeat, since it was their campaign and they had not involved me directly in their strategy or planning. I'd gone out in 2002 and taken the heat after that year's elections, even though the DCCC and DSCC were the committees that ran our House and Senate campaigns. I finally agreed with Jano and called Ed to tell him I would not be participating in the press conference.

"Why aren't you coming?" Ed asked.

"Ed, how many times do you think I was invited over to Kerry campaign headquarters?" I asked him.

He did a few quick mental calculations. He was part of the group that met with Karl Rove for breakfast every week to talk detailed strategy, and he knew how important that close coordination was.

"I don't know, Terry, thirty or forty times?" he said.

"Not once, Ed," I said. "I was not invited to attend a single meeting."

"Jeez, Terry, I had no idea," Ed said. "That sounds like the Dole campaign in 1996. That's what they did to Haley Barbour and the RNC. I wouldn't do the press conference either."

Dorothy and I were there in the fourth row at Faneuil Hall with its white columns and air of history when John Kerry gave his concession speech at 2 P.M. The five hundred of us gathered to hear him speak were all emotional and John's voice broke several times during the poised, dignified speech. He took the high road and talked about how in a democracy, no one loses because the next morning, "We all wake up as Americans." As soon as he finished, he came right over and thanked me. It felt strange to fly home with Dorothy for a quiet dinner with the kids that night and disengage from politics, but as much as I hated to lose, I loved that we had gone down as fighters. I knew my father Jack McAuliffe was up there somewhere, probably with a glass of Scotch in his hand, smiling down at me, very proud of his son.

Our five-year-old Sally wasn't sad after the election loss, she was mad. Sally, as I've said, is a real spitfire, and we had been careful throughout the election not to tell her that her cute little friend on her soccer team—whom I'll call Lilly—also happened to be Dick Cheney's granddaughter. Knowing Sally, she would have had something to say to little Lilly at some point. That first day back home after Kerry's concession speech, I was sitting there in the kitchen reading the morning papers and Sally walked over to see what I was doing. She spotted a big front-page picture of the Bush and Cheney families on stage greeting supporters the night before at the Ronald Reagan Building.

"Dad!" Sally cried, doing her best to rip the paper out of my hands. "What in the heck is Lilly doing with George W. Bush?"

We all burst into laughter and somehow the loss didn't feel so bad, so long as we were raising a new generation of fighters for the future.

That Sunday, Dorothy and I flew up to Chappaqua for a Clinton Presidential Library dinner. I sat next to Jon Bon Jovi and even I'd heard of him, since he was one of Jack's favorites and he had done a lot of work for the party. I called Jack from dinner and put Jon on with him for a few minutes and Jack thought that was pretty cool.

Dorothy and I were spending the night and long after all the guests had left, we sat with the President and Hillary talking about the elections. No one better understood how much we needed to get the government fighting for working men and women again than the Clintons and all four of us were devastated at Kerry's defeat. We also talked strategy, as we always did, and in particular focused on how successful the Republicans had been once again in using wedge issues against us. They inflamed their strong supporters with emotional talk of abortion and gay marriage and tried to paint us as somehow not moral and weak on defense. We talked about how important it was to fight those tactics aggressively and defiantly, and to connect with people's real concerns on those sensitive issues.

We got a few hours of sleep and then picked up where we'd left off over breakfast, talking two more hours until Hillary had to leave to give a speech. It would have been easy to sink into gloom, given the prospect of four more years with Bush and his crew in charge, but gloom was a luxury we could not afford. The challenge was to keep planning for the future and find a way to win back the political power we would need to undo the damage of the Bush years.

★

I STARTED HEARING disturbing reports that the Kerry campaign had sat on its war chest and left many millions in the bank. I couldn't believe it was true. Thanks to the Internet, the campaign could raise millions more overnight if an emergency arose after the election, like another recount controversy. But I finally found out it was true: The Kerry campaign had $15 million left over in the bank. I was flabbergasted. No one ever gave any credible rationale for hoarding that money when it could have made such a difference in the field. You want to tell me that John Kerry would not have found the 59,000 votes needed to carry Ohio if he had spent an additional $15 million running ads there the last month before the election? Of course he would have. That would easily have gotten us the votes needed to swing the state our way. It was gross incompetence to hoard that money when the race was bound to be so close and the outcome was so pivotal to the future of all Americans, and I will never understand how that mistake was made.

I kept getting calls from supporters who were horrified to hear about the extra $15 million. The DNC had asked the Kerry campaign to transfer $5 million six days before Election Day for last-minute get-out-the-vote activities, but was told they were broke and could only squeeze out $1.5 million. Later I heard from people who worked inside the campaign that they were so short on cash at headquarters that they took to selling extra Kerry campaign signs on eBay. Top Kerry-Edwards fund-raisers like Bob Farmer, Lou Sussman, Fred Baron, and Hassan Nemazee told me they'd had no idea any money was left over. I kept thinking back on the Friday night before the elections when Ted Kennedy, Hillary Clinton, and Tom Daschle all called me pleading for another $1 million for close Senate races. I hated having to tell them that all the DNC's money was out the door, including the $10 million I had just borrowed for last-minute campaigning. Now I was finding out that the Kerry campaign was sitting on $15 million the whole time? Un-f——-believable!

We had planned everything so that when we had a nominee in March 2004, our candidate would be able to hit the ground running like no Democratic presidential candidate in memory. We had the money in place so that state directors and codirectors could be sent out to target states almost as soon as we had our nominee. The money was sitting there, ready to pay their salaries—but the Kerry campaign wasted the opportunity. Most of those people were not in place for four or five months when they could have been on the ground organizing throughout April, May, June, and July. I asked John about that later and he guessed they'd been in place within a month or two after he sewed up the nomination. He shook his head sadly when he found out the truth.

That November, I announced that the DNC was spending $500,000 to hire a team of experts to fan out in Ohio and examine the voting data, as many questions had been raised about fairness and accuracy. I asked Donna Brazile to head the effort and months later her task force reported back that there was no evidence of widespread fraud, but that there were serious problems with the number and age of voting machines in Democratic-leaning districts. Something was definitely wrong when students at Kenyon College had to wait ten hours to vote and a few miles away in predominately Republican districts there were no lines.

There had been a lot of talk after the campaign that John Edwards had not been a visible enough presence on the campaign trail. That December, I sat with Edwards at a Kennedy Center dinner, and I asked him why he wasn't out attacking Bush more. The question made him mad.

"Terry, they wouldn't let me," he said. "I wanted to go after the Swift Boat guys. I wanted to go after Bush. They wouldn't let me."

The Kerry campaign sent him to small, secondary markets where he could say anything he wanted and still not generate major media coverage, he said. In fact, the Kerry campaign wouldn't even share polling data with the Edwards campaign, he told me.

Edwards' explanation was at odds with what Kerry told me later when we had dinner to discuss the election for this book. He told me that he was frustrated that Edwards was not out campaigning harder. Kerry said that Edwards told him several times, "Watch the news tomorrow! I'm really going to go after Bush." Then Kerry would watch the news the next night, and Edwards was nowhere to be seen.

I also heard that Kerry believed Edwards had promised him that if

Kerry wanted to run again in 2008, Edwards would sit the race out. But if you asked the Edwards people about it, they said there was no way any such promise had been made.

As I used to say to my staff all the time, what a s—— show!

★

WE HAD TO THINK about the future, which was why I was so thrilled that we were gathering later that month in Arkansas to celebrate Bill Clinton's legacy of using government in new ways to help people. I had worked for six years raising money to build the Clinton Presidential Library because I knew it would offer an important resource for getting the word out to people about all the accomplishments of the Clinton-Gore administration. If we forgot our successes, we were never going to make a convincing case to the people that they needed to vote out the Republicans and let democracy work for them with Democrats in office.

The day of the library opening, it rained so hard, everyone was drenched. I had never seen so many former heads of state and ambassadors so wet, including Jimmy Carter and both President Bushes. Al Gore and Tipper were seated next to me. Al had no slicker on and was soaked right through. I hardly noticed the rain. I was in a great mood, finally seeing my six years of hard work bear fruit. The library was fabulous and even though it cost us about $75 million more than we had planned on during those first meetings in the Yellow Oval, it was worth every minute of work to see the results. All the great work and achievements of the Clinton administration were now available for everyone from around the country and around the world to see and study for generations to come. After the dedication we all went into a large tent for lunch.

Karl Rove came over to me with a napkin draped over his arm and said, "May I take your order, please?"

I looked up and saw it was Karl and said, "Yeah, how about sixty thousand more votes in Ohio?" and everybody broke out laughing.

Both the current President Bush and the former President Bush stopped by my table and said hello.

Bush 41, the father, said, "Terry, that was a tough, tough, tough, tough campaign." He said "tough" four times in a row.

Bush 43 was gracious.

"Boy, Terry, you threw a lot at me," he said.

"Yes, I did, and you took it and you won this election," I told him. "Congratulations."

"Darn right," he said as he turned and walked away.

I remember worrying about Bill Clinton that day. He was proud and thoughtful, reveling in the moment, just what you'd expect given how long we'd waited for this day, but if you knew the man well, you could see that two months after his heart surgery something wasn't right. I'd be spending more time with the President the following week. Before the election, Hillary saw Dorothy and invited the entire family down to Punta Cana in the Dominican Republic to stay at Julio Iglesias's spectacular oceanfront estate over Thanksgiving.

"Terry has been away so much these last four years, it's perfect timing, right after the election," Hillary told Dorothy. "We really want you to come with us."

"You're too nice," Dorothy said. "But are you two sure you really want us with all five kids? We aren't the most relaxing family to travel with, as you know."

Dorothy was worried that the President really needed some quiet time as he continued to recover from his surgery. Our brood is anything but quiet. They're McAuliffes!

"Terry has been on the road so much, he deserves a nice getaway with you and all the kids," Hillary insisted. "You have to come."

So we did and that trip to Punta Cana was one of the best family vacations we've ever had. People often ask me what the Clintons are like on vacation and I have a two-word answer: Great fun! Julio had a beautiful lagoon-shaped pool and every day during the four days we spent down there, I'd see Sally in the pool playing mermaid with Hillary, directing her to do this and do that, and Hillary was happy to obediently take orders from a five-year-old. I'd never seen anyone order Hillary around the way Sally did.

I like to get up early, but on that trip the President would be up before me every morning and I would find him sitting with Mary, then ten years old, the two of them deep in conversation over a board game or playing cards in the beachside pavilion where we ate most of our meals. They would talk for hours. Mary had studied Africa in school and they had long exchanges about the President's travels in Africa and his work there through his foundation. They talked about anthropology, architecture, and geography. The President would also tutor Mary and all the kids in strategy for word games like Upwords and our favorite card game, "Oh Hell!" It was great to see him so at ease and so happy sitting for hours with Sally teaching her to play Upwords and to spell all at the same time.

Another thing I remember from that trip was Oscar de la Renta telling us that top runway models earn up to $20 million a year, which had me urging my thirteen-year-old daughter, Dori, to go for it. Why not? She's pretty, elegant, and stylish. So every time I saw Dori and Oscar talking on that trip, I'd suggest that Dori ought to be a runway model, which of course embarrassed the heck out of her, and I teased Oscar that he ought to make her an offer in a few years. The President laughed every time I said it, but Hillary and Dorothy were against the idea, saying Dori should put her beauty *and* brains to work. Still, $20 million a year. Not bad. I hope she's still considering it.

Our youngest, little Peter, has had a thing about clothes ever since he was a toddler: He doesn't like them. Peter loves to strip naked and run around the house. I can't tell you how many times little Peter has come flying out of nowhere, fully naked, and jumped onto someone's back. That week in Punta Cana, Oscar joined us for cards most every day, driving over in his golf cart, just the picture of the elegant gentleman. One afternoon two-year-old Peter came darting out of nowhere and hopped on Oscar's golf cart stark naked, screaming with glee, and the two of them drove around, elegant Oscar and nude little Peter. The President and I will never let Peter live that one down.

Hillary, Huma, Dorothy and I went down to Mikhail Baryshnikov's beach villa one afternoon. Misha was a longtime friend of the Clintons, going back to Chelsea's interest in ballet when she was younger. He told us great stories about his fabled career and fascinating life, especially his early days as a young star of the Kirov Ballet in Leningrad and his dramatic defection from the Soviet Union, and then showed us around his dance studio and led us all in a round of stretching. Misha was so limber he could raise his foot over his head and touch the top of the doorway. Then it was my turn. Let me put it this way: after fifteen marathons and a million-plus miles on airplanes, it was evident that I will never become a ballet dancer. I couldn't even get my foot up to the doorknob. Hillary, Huma, and Dorothy totally showed me up!

Misha was also a great golfer, and every day on that Punta Cana vacation, he and I would hit the links with the President and Doug Band. I couldn't help noticing that something was wrong with the President. This was a man who finished a golf round no matter what, only now he was quitting after twelve holes and going back to the house to take a nap. Never in the countless rounds we'd played together had I seen that. In the evenings Dorothy and I would go for a walk along the shoreline with Hillary and the President. Even strolling on the sand, he would get winded and occasionally he broke into chills—and this was a Caribbean paradise! Hillary was really worried. She and I kept talking about the President not seeming like himself. Of course, he swore he was fine.

"He'd had his bypass on Labor Day and the doctors and everybody I talked to said it starts to get better slowly but surely and by six months he'll be fine," Hillary remembers. "We were taking all these walks and doing everything you're supposed to do, but to me Bill did not look good. He looked gray. He did not have good color. I just didn't see what I'd been told would be improvements. I kept saying, 'Bill, I don't think you're making progress.' But he would have these blood tests and he would go get examined and the doctors all said he was making progress, which I didn't believe."

I agreed with Hillary and told her so. "He doesn't look like himself," I said on that Punta Cana vacation. I think she was relieved to hear I agreed with her.

"I kept trying to convince somebody besides me that there was something wrong," she says now.

Hillary was convinced that something physically was not right with the President, even though the doctors kept telling her that the recovery from bypass surgery could be slow and deliberate. Finally, after the tsunami on Christmas Eve, when Bush called and asked President Clinton to work with Bush 41 on disaster relief, Hillary had to take a strong stand. She was not going to sit back and watch her husband fly off to Indonesia and Thailand without first making sure he was all right. At her urging, Clinton's doctor called to see if he wanted to come in for a checkup.

"I don't need to come in," the President told his doctor. "I'm getting better."

Clinton didn't want to admit that his recovery was slower than it should have been. Hillary insisted he go in for another checkup and that was when they found that the lower half of his left lung was impaired. So in March 2005 he had to go back in for a second operation, four and a half hours on the table, and they stripped off the scarring on his lung. He told me later it was like putting a piece of leather on top of a sponge and trying to get air through it. The important thing was, thanks to Hillary's insistence, the President had the problem taken care of. Soon he was himself again, playing golf with me even long after dark, intent on finishing every round.

Another time at Punta Cana, the four of us were sitting around in the living room of Oscar de la Renta's house talking and the President started flipping through Oscar's CD collection. We'd had dinner that night with Julio Iglesias, and the President put on some of his music and asked Hillary to dance. They were laughing and whispering to each other as they swayed around the room. It was nice to see them so relaxed, enjoying the moment, but unfortunately, it left Dorothy and me no choice but to join them. The four of us danced for more than an hour. Dorothy loved it, but I have to be honest, I was dying to go play some cards. Every time I thought we were going to get a game of "Oh Hell!" started, the President would go put on another CD and we'd all dance some more. We didn't hit the cards that night until way after midnight.

★

BACK IN WASHINGTON after our great Thanksgiving vacation with the Clintons, I met with my fund-raising team to assess our financial condition. Jay Dunn and David Dogan reported that even after the election, we were still raising money at a steady rate, which was an amazing departure from the usual pattern. Normally donations completely evaporate following an election, but we had planned to build the DNC into a year-round operation, and thanks to our massive improvements in infrastructure and data building, that was exactly what was happening. We had brought in so much money in November and our projections were so strong for December and January that we could quickly pay off the $10 million that I had borrowed for last-minute spending before the 2004 elections.

I didn't need to worry about the upcoming New Jersey governor's race, where Jon Corzine, a self-made multimillionaire, could spend whatever he needed, but I committed $5 million to the upcoming Virginia governor's race. That was the single largest donation the DNC had ever made to a candidate for governor. I wanted to show our commitment to a Southern state and I also knew it would be a huge shot in the arm, coming off the disappointment of 2004, if we won a big governor's race in 2005, setting us up for a comeback in 2006.

I've always believed in saying thank you to the people who help you, something that too often gets overlooked in politics. We put together a forty-six-page PowerPoint detailing all our political and fund-raising activities and I spent the first two weeks of December flying around with Jay and our political team, thanking people in person. I wanted everyone to know that we appreciated their support, first of all, but also how spectacularly their investment in the party had paid off. We were strong going into the future because of their vision and support.

I kept getting calls asking me to run for another term as DNC chairman, but I'd made my decision and it was final. I had announced in my hometown paper, the *Syracuse Post-Standard*, on February 26, 2004, that I would serve only one term, saying at the time, "I have five little children and you know what? I miss ballgames." One term was the norm and was definitely right for me. I loved the job, but felt that I had done everything I promised and it was always smart to leave on top. A Hotline poll of DNC members that December found I had a 92 percent approval rating, so I also had the satisfaction of knowing that the membership I had so energetically courted four years earlier was overwhelmingly behind me and the work we had done on my watch.

On November 11, I went to Northern Virginia for a press conference with Tim Kaine, our candidate for governor, and announced the $5 million commitment. I personally handed Tim a check for $2.5 million on the spot. I left money in the bank for the next chairman, whoever he or she was, to hand over the remaining $2.5 million, since the election would occur during his or her tenure. We gave $250,000 to Christine Gregoire's recount fund to help her win the Washington state governor's race, we gave $250,000 to the New York state party for upcoming elections, and also wrote checks for $1 million to the Democratic Senatorial Campaign Committee and the Democratic Congressional Campaign Committee. This was definitely a first, giving out any money, let alone millions, within months after a presidential election.

Republicans started traveling to Washington from all over the country to gather for Bush's second Inauguration on January 20, 2005. They would arrive at their hotels, turn on their TVs, and see an ad with me talking to Bush, saying, "Democrats are eager to work with you, but make no mistake: We will not abandon our long-held principles." It was, as analyst Bill Schneider commented on CNN, a clear signal that "Democrats are standing their ground, and they're saying, we're going to fight this President." I decided to do the DNC ad during Bush's Inauguration week, breaking with precedent, because I knew we had to send a strong signal that Bush had squeaked through to another close victory and did not have a mandate. "So as you swear to uphold the Constitution, we will be standing with you, making sure you keep that promise for all Americans," I said at the end of the ad.

One of my favorite reporters in Washington had always been Michael Weisskopf of *Time* magazine, who was tough on me at times, but always fair, and always kept his sense of humor. That February he invited me to come with him on a visit to Walter Reed Hospital, where many Iraq War veterans were being treated for serious injuries. Michael was an embedded reporter during the fall of 2003, which put him right in the thick of some of the heaviest fighting of the war. One day he was startled to see that a grenade had been tossed into his Humvee. Michael had only an instant to react, no time to think, but risked his own life to grab the grenade and fling it out of the vehicle. Michael saved several soldiers with his act of bravery that day, but the grenade blew up and he lost his right hand. Knowing the kind of guy Michael is, I'm sure he'd do the same thing again in a second.

I will never forget how positive and upbeat these young men and women at Walter Reed were, even though, like Michael, they had received severe injuries. One of the more remarkable women there was Tammy Duckworth, an Illinois National Guard helicopter pilot who lost both legs and full use of her right arm in 2004 when a rocket-propelled grenade hit the Black Hawk she was flying over the Tigris River. She was determined to get back into the pilot's seat and fly again. Instead, she ended up running for Congress in the western suburbs of Chicago—I am proud to say as a Democrat.

The night before my final DNC meeting as chairman on February 11, we had a farewell party at the National Building Museum with two thousand people, including Bill Clinton, John Kerry, and Al Franken. "Terry McAuliffe can talk an owl out of a tree but he also has the heart of a lion and he works harder than almost anyone I've met in my life," Clinton told the crowd.

The next day at the DNC meeting I had Dori, Jack, Mary, Sally, and Peter come out on stage and lead us all in the Pledge of Allegiance, which was one of my proudest moments ever. I told the members I'd made a lot of promises four years earlier when I took over as chairman, and thanked them for their incredible support. We had paid off the party's back-breaking cumulative debt of $18 million, including the mortgage on our building. We'd achieved a sevenfold increase in our donor base from 400,000 to 2.7 million, boosted our e-mail list from 70,000 to 3.8 million, and built our voter file from zero—a big fat zilch!—to 178 million. We raised $248 million in 2004 from small donors, up from $35 million in 2000, brought in $70 million online, and built a new, state-of-the-art headquarters that doubled our work space, gave us a modernized database and Web platforms, built a satellite TV studio, updated IT backbone, and added training facilities and a conference center—and paid for it all in cash.

Dorothy gave a speech introducing me and she had the whole room laughing. "I often hear it said that my husband has been the greatest chairman in the history of the Democratic Party," she said. "And each time I hear it, my reaction is the same, 'Yes, dear. I know.' "

She thanked the members for putting their trust in me and working so hard, and also thanked the many people who had talked to her about how hard it must have been having me on the road so much with the five kids at home.

"As you might imagine, even a house with five young kids seems kind of quiet after you're used to having Terry around," she said.

"Though we weren't along for the plane flights that took Terry to all fifty states—twice—we were along for the ride," she said. "He would come home and tell us about the people he had met and how much they meant to him. About all the work people were doing to make sure the Democratic Party could stand up for people without a voice. Our children didn't sacrifice— they got the greatest lesson in what is important in life that any parent could ever hope to teach their children. And as much as Terry inspired you and so many others, I can tell you that *you* inspired *him* and kept him going."

As Washington focused on Bush's State of the Union on February 2, I'd had dinner with Howard Dean, the incoming DNC chairman, and told him, "You are about to become a human fire hydrant. You will get blamed for every loss. You will get zero credit for any win. But it's still a great job because you have the ability to help so many people." Up on stage with Howard as I handed over the gavel at my last DNC meeting, I gave him that day's money sheet, which showed the DNC with no debt line and $4 million in the bank, a first for any DNC chairman in modern history. I walked off that stage a proud man and felt that I had done my small part to help Democrats win elections and fight for the little guy for years to come.

As we all walked out front after the meeting, my assistant Addisu Demissie pulled up the car to drive us home to Virginia, as he had done hundreds of times. I told him to move over and ride shotgun. I wanted to drive us home. It was time to start the next chapter in my life!

EPILOGUE

★ ★ ★

On November 7, 2006, a political earthquake occurred in America. Democrats were united and won at all levels in all regions of the country, in red states and blue states, not only reclaiming the House and Senate but also adding Democratic governors in six states and picking up statehouse majorities in nine more states. The die was cast for the Republicans when Bush made the mistake of boasting after his razor-thin 2004 reelection about all the political capital he had earned. He was disconnected from the voters and unwilling to listen to any alternate views or strategies on Iraq, discounting the advice of his own generals. Now the voters have offered their answer and put Democrats in control of Congress. The victory was sweet, but we Democrats know that with victory comes responsibility. We are on notice that we'd better waste no time rolling up our sleeves and getting down to work for the American people. They gave us the keys to the car, and now they want to see if we can offer a steady hand on the wheel.

I said early in this book that Republicans were wrong to claim they had a monopoly on patriotism and love of the uniform. Bush, Cheney, and Rumsfeld were also wrong to insist that any criticism of their approach to the war in Iraq was defeatist and dangerous and offered aid and comfort to the enemy. The American people put an end to all that nonsense. They united against Bush's incompetent handling of the war, and his insistence on repeating all the same mistakes over and over and trying to package his stubbornness as principle.

With Democrats in Congress upholding their constitutional responsibility to perform oversight, the American people will get the truth about how much this war has cost us and how we could have been so wrong about weapons of mass destruction. Last year, Bush received a grim report from sixteen U.S. intelligence agencies spelling out in black and white that his war in Iraq had made Americans less safe, actually creating more terrorists. Confronted with this overwhelming reality check, the administration chose to offer the American people fantasies about all the progress being made in Iraq when they knew better and saw the truth for themselves every day on the news.

On Bush's watch, North Korea has tested long-range missiles that can reach U.S. territory, enriched enough plutonium for seven to nine new nuclear weapons, and shocked the world by actually detonating one. Iran has started a nuclear program, Hezbollah has fired thousands of rockets into Israel, and now the Taliban has staged a comeback in Afghanistan, controlling much of the country outside of Kabul, and poppy production is at its highest level ever.

Congressional Democrats have a responsibility to work in a bipartisan way to find a solution to the mess Bush has created in Iraq. We need to set up benchmarks to hand off security responsibilities to the Iraqis. Democrats in Congress will push to implement all the recommendations of the 9/11 Commission, to protect our ports and actually make Americans safer. They will work to make quick progress on vital issues like raising the minimum wage, providing tax relief for middle-class Americans, and revamping our health care and educational systems, not just promising to do so.

Above all, we will bring back fiscal responsibility. Bush inherited a huge surplus and soon ran up gigantic deficits that our children and grandchildren will still be paying off. The voters delivered a loud message in November 2006. Voters all over the country were fed up and energized, and they turned out in record numbers, especially young people, reminding every citizen from coast to coast just how much his or her vote matters. Time and time again, from Florida in 2000 to Ohio in 2004 to Virginia and Montana in 2006, we keep seeing outcomes determined by only a few votes. There can be no denying that your vote matters—it's your voice; you've got to use it.

The American people are ready to give Democrats the job of leading the country. If we are smart and unified, we will take advantage of this opportunity for a historic realignment. When we produce, and when we get results, people who have drifted away from the party will come home and join us in the work of rebuilding this great country. I call that an exciting opportunity and an exciting challenge for everybody in the American political process. Now let's get to work!

ACKNOWLEDGMENTS

★ ★ ★

More than anyone, I want to thank my wife, Dorothy, who has been a true partner in every aspect of this book, as she has been in my life for more than twenty years. I always knew it's not easy being married to someone as involved in politics as I am, and now I know how tough it is to be the wife of an author. She helped me put the right perspectives and touches on my stories, and her influence is felt on every page. Also, thanks to Dorothy's vigilance, this book can be recommended to high school students interested in a close-up look at American politics. I'd have sprinkled in some more colorful language, but Dorothy was always there attempting to reel me in, sometimes with success.

I also want to thank my children, Dori, Jack, Mary, Sally, and Peter, for never making me feel bad that I had to spend so many nights on the road fighting for the party. I hope that this book will give them a better appreciation of what their dad was doing and why I believed the time away was important, though it wasn't ever easy to miss a game or school event. Evie (Bebot) Overton and Alicia Reyes kept the chaos at home manageable with warmth and devotion to our family.

While I often thought about writing a book, it was my agent, Bret Saxon, who convinced me to actually do it. My friend Alex Zakrzeski introduced me to Bret, and for that I am grateful. I knew I'd get along with my publisher, Tom Dunne, a fellow Irishman, because we both love to talk politics and tell stories. Tom, I apologize for handing in the manuscript four months late. However, I had to work at least four times harder than I ever thought I would. Thanks to Ellis Trevor, whose professionalism, attention to detail, and good cheer made all the difference. It never seemed like work with John Murphy, another Irishman with a gift for shameless promotion, who got the word out on this book with infectious enthusiasm and all-out style.

There is a small group of people who have lived and breathed this project over the last year, and who were the backbone of putting this book together. Peter O'Keefe, my Irish consigliere, provided invaluable insights on our many years in politics together and helped me remember the details of stories I'd half forgotten. My longtime assistant, Alecia Dyer, took on the daunting task of organizing trunkloads of information going back to 1979 to build my book War Room, and lent her sharp eye to numerous reads of the manuscript. Yael Belkind kept the War Room humming with her contagious energy, and Tracy Sefl, our crack researcher, was on call 24/7 and offered helpful interpretation and context.

And of course, special thanks to President and Hillary Clinton, who have both been a constant source of information, advice, and encouragement for this book. They were very generous with their time and I value their friendship.

Last but not least my cowriter, Steve Kettmann. When Steve and I started he was a ghost writer and we thought this project would take about twelve weeks. Unfortunately for him, it took fifty-three weeks and took over his life. Over the course of the project, he lived in our home for more than seventy-five days. He immediately became part of our family and happily endured the insanity of a house with five children. He put in twenty-hour days and pulled ten all-nighters—something he hadn't done since college. He went from writing about steroids to needing them. Thank you, Steve, for helping me put a voice to this book. Your creativity and talent brought my stories to life.

Interviewed for the book:

Huma Abedin, Elizabeth Alexander, Madeleine Albright, Kevin Allen, Lance Armstrong, Jenny Backus, Elizabeth and Smith Bagley, Doug Band, Governor Haley Barbour, Bob Beckel, Paul Begala, Yael Belkind, Richard Ben-Veniste, Sandy Berger, Steve Bing, Tommy Boggs, John Boland, Lina Brunton, Father William Byron SJ, Jano Cabrera, President Jimmy Carter, James Carville, Bill Carrick, Amy Chapman, Rashid Chaudary, Andrei Cherny, President Bill Clinton, Chelsea Clinton, Senator Hillary Rodham

Clinton, Tony Coelho, Sheryl Crow, Tom Daschle, Chairman Howard Dean, Addisu Demissie, Brian Detter, Debra DeShong, Evan Dobelle, Dave Dogan, Tom Donilon, John Donoghue, Jay Dunn, Alecia Dyer, Julie Eddy, Tom Edsall, John Edwards, Nancy Eiring, Janice Enright, Bob Farmer, Tim Finchem, Ira Forman, Ron Fournier, Mike Fraioli, Scott Freda, Dick Gephardt, Ed Gillespie, Marcia Hale, Laura Hartigan, Alexis Herman, Karen Hicks, Denise O'Leary, Elaine Howard, Malik Husser, Harold Ickes, Brooks Jackson, David Jones, Doug Kelly, Peter D. Kelly, Peter G. Kelly, Leslie Kerman, Monsignor William Kerr, Senator John Kerry, Kamran Khan, Duke Kinney, Nate Landow, Penny Lee, Boyd Lewis, Phil McNamara, Art McZier, Mark MacKinnon, Hal Malchow, Chuck Manatt, Thomas Mann, Congressman Ed Markey, Brad Marshall, Capricia Marshall, Millie McAuliffe, Michael Meehan, Jason Miner, Minyon Moore, Hani Masri, John Mills, Jim Mulhall, Dennis O'Brien, Rod O'Connor, Tom O'Donnell, John O'Hanlon, Peter O'Keefe, Norm Ornstein, Jennifer Palmieri, Justin Paschal, Scott Pastrick, Chris Petersen, Roberto Prats, Amy Pritchard, Laura Quinn, Mohamed Rachid, John Raffaelli, Steve Ricchetti, Governor Bill Richardson, Ed Rogers, Paul Rothstein, Haim Saban, Marty Salanger, Joe Sandler, Lee Satterfield, Arthur Schechter, Peter Scher, Marc Schloss, Mike Schneider, Tracy Sefl, Al Sharpton, Doug Sosnik, Stephanie Streett, Kandy Stroud, Richard Swann, Joe Sweeney, George Tenet, Andy Tobias, Teresa Vilmain, Tom Vilsack, Josh Wachs, David Wade, Mark and Susan Weiner, Michael Weisskopf, Maureen White, Michael Whouley, Damian Williams, Howard Wolfson, David Yarkin.

A special thanks to the real stars of this book: the countless number of people whom I have worked with in Democratic politics. Although I have done the best I can to include everyone, inevitably I couldn't remember everybody and for that I apologize:

Morra Aarons, Steve Achelpol, Bart Acocella, Christy Agner, Tom Albert, Barbara Allen, Luis Alvardo, Chris Anderson, Tony Anthony, Aswini Anburajan, Samir Arora, Kathy Baczko, Danielle Baierlein, John Balduzzi, Staria Barnett, Greg Bates, Richard Bayard, Elizabeth Baylor, Mikhail Belgorodsky, Joshua Belkind, Cecil Benjamin, Scott Bennett, Cheryl Benton, Paul Berendt, Stephanie Berger, Emily Berman, Mike Berman, Achim Bergmann, Jesse Berney, Jim Bernhard, Joe Birkenstock, John Blandford, Robert Blunt, Amy Bodette, Micah Bonaviri, Hannah Bond, Carolyn Boyce, Rick Boylan, Robin Brand, Mark Brewer, Travis Brock, Erica Brooks, Jennifer Brown, Leslie Brown, Kristopher Brown, Mike Brown,

Tanya Brown, Lina Brunton, Melissa Brunton, Bill Buck, Ruthanne Buck, Deb Burger, Bill Burke, Thomas Burke, Nancy Burke, Justin Burkhardt, Pam Burns, Dan Burrell, John Bushman, Jeremy Button, Randy Button, Jennifer Cafiero, Kevin Callahan, Deroy Callands, Rodd Campbell, Spencer Capp, Maria Cardona, Carolyn Carlson, Joe Carmichael, Yvettte Carnell, David Carroll, Jay Carson, Nick Casey, Ida Castro, Gerry Cavanaugh, Waynette Chan, Elizabeth Ann Chandler, Emma Chappell, Rosalind Chapman, Namrita Chaudhary, Dan Chavez, Josh Cherwin, Roger Chiang, Claudette Chidi, Parag Chokshi, Brook Colangelo, Brent Colburn, Bonnie Watson Coleman, Edda Collins, Patrick Colwell, Lori Congleton, Peggy Connolly, Chealsa Cook, John Coombs, Justin Cooper, Angela Courtin, Adam Crain, Joe Crapa, Bob Crowe, Kim Cubine, Brandon Cull, Charles Curry, Greg Curtis, Amin Cyntje, Joe D'Angelo, Leslie Dach, Megan Damiano, Myra Dandridge, Leah Daughtry, Michael Davies, Clarence Davis, Crystal Davis, Joseph Dennison, Erica DeVos, Meredith Jones-DeWitt, Melissa Diaz, Tom Dickson, Evan Dobelle, Clay Doherty, Jean Doherty, Tene Dolphin, Kerry Donley, Eileen Donohue, Mae Dove, Wayne Dowdy, Patti Solis Doyle, Randy Dresser, Chris Duda, Judy Olson Duhamel, Kharye Dunlap, Donald Dunn, Linnea Dyer, Atarrah Dymally, Josh Earnest, Jim Edmunson, Nancy Eiring, Rahm Emanuel, Connie Sanders Emerson, Rob Engel, Mike Erlandson, Joe Erwin, Amy Everitt, Matthew Farrauto, Denny Farrell, Will Federspiel, Matt Felan, Robert Fernandez, Kathy Finnie, Patti Fiorello, Ann Fishman, Patrick Fn'Piere, Tina Flournoy, Todd Floyd, Leigh Foley, Eric Folley, Brian Foucart, Sarah Foy, Marty Franks, Scott Freda, Will French, Vince Frillici, Vincent Fry, Cecilia Fucuy, Maria Galdo, James Gallagher, Mary Gallagher, Brickwood Galuteria, Clare Gannon, Maureen Garde, Ramon Gardenhire, Leigh Garland, Zoe Garmendia, Nadia Garnett, Chris Gates, Lawrence Gates, Michael Gelber, Dan Geldon, Alice Germond, Mike Gierau, Kris Van Giessen, John Giesser, J. Rufus Gifford, Eureka Gilkey, Harold Gist, Major Glick, Curtis Glover, Matt Gobush, Maya Goines, Andrew Goldberg, Parisa Golkar, Kathleen Gomez, Andres Gonzalez, Stephen Goodin, Lila Gracey, Elizabeth Gramling, Jonathan Gramling, Kerry Greeley, Jim Green, Kellie Green, Janice Griffin, Angela Groehl, Steve Grossman, Gabrielle Guevara, Saurah Gupta, Carla Gutierrez, Nicole Gyfori, Susanne Haessler, John Hagner, Emily Hajek, Franklin Hall Jr., Patrick Hallahan, Charles Halloran, Brian Hardwick, Karen Harmel, Nathan Harris, Rogette Harris, Joyce Harrison, John Hart, Patrick Hart, William Hart, Wendy Hartman, Fred Hatfield, Shaun Hayes, Jewelle Hazel, Megan Hedman, Kate Henningfeld, Russ Henry, William Herrin, Rick

Hess, Shiloh Heurich, Bob Hickmott, Victoria Hight, Alyce Hill, Gail Hoffman, Ben Holzer, Mike Honda, Linda Honold, Philip Hood, Dana Howitt, Drew Hubbard, Barbara Hurd, Buck Humphrey, Malik Husser, Rebekah Hutman, John Interante, Bob Irving, Carlos Jackson, Kevin Jefferson, Ben Johnson, Brenda Johnson, Jennifer Johnson, Jua Johnson, Mark Johnson, Rochester Johnson, Phil Johnston, Geneva Jones, Natalie Jones, Alan Julson, Robert Kahn, Cameron Kalunian, Ariel Kastner, Danny Katz, Maura Keefe, Rosemary Kelanic, Doug Kelly, Dana Kennedy, Chris Kenngott, Joan Kenny, Stacy Kerr, Frances Kidd, Ji Kim, Julie Kim, Jennifer Kinder, Jeff King, Lalla King, Tom King, Craig Kirby, Hilary Kline, Peter Knight, Bobby Koch, Joshua Kravitz, Lori Kreloff, Ben Labolt, Amanda LaForge, Victoria Lai, Clarinda Landeros, Jarel Lapan, Hoa Ledinh, Denise Lee, Gretchen Lee, Daniella Gibbs Leger, Bridget Leininger, Doreatha Leonard, Robert Leonard, Rick Lerner, Ann Lewis, Peter Lewis, Terry Lierman, Wanda Lockridge, Jamie Long, Kimberlin Love, Bridget Lowell, Jerry Lundergan, Bari Lurie, Bill Lynch, Sandra Lyon, Ana Ma, Christy Mach, Michael Madigan, Scott Maddox, Michael Mahdesian, Peter Mallary, Jonathan Mantz, Rodney Margol, Peter Maroney, Dwayne Marshall, Wayne Marshall, William Marshall, Brendan Martin, Adriana Martinez, Michelle Mayorga, Erin McCann, Joshua McConaha, Alicia McDonald, Kathleen McGlynn, Jason McIntosh, Monette McKinnon, Dan McLaughlin, Kiki McLean, Natasha McMahan, Maura McManimon, Matthew McNally, Phil McNamara, Heather Meade, Greg Mecher, Michael Meehan, Belen Mendoza, Guillermo Meneses, James Metcalfe, David Mercer, Brandi Mercurio, Kate Michelman, R. Anthony Mills, Laila Mohib, Gloria Molina, Jon Monger, Robby Mook, Carolyn Moore, Patricia Monroe, Albert Morales, Ellen Moran, Mary Morrison, Jonathan Murray, Justine Mwebaza, Andrew Myers, Amy Nachtomi, Ted Nakata, Shwantae Nelson, Terri New, Sam Newman, Tracy Newman, Ali Nikseresht, Nancy NiNardo, Dave Noble, John Noonan, John Norton, Matt Nugen, Courtney O'Donnell, Josephine Odukoya, Becky Ogle, Eric Ohlsen, Sara O'Keefe, Ramona Oliver, Ron Oliver, Sandy Oreste, John Orlando, Lina D'Gornaz-Orr, Denise Outlaw, Liz Packard, Holly Page, Amanda Pardo, Dan Parker, Kevin Parker, Helina Burton Parks, Jay Parmley, Mona Pasquil, Mark Paustenbach, Erica Payne, Jim Pederson, Sally Pederson, Laura Pena, Kerry Peoples, Hilda Perez, Alexander Perkins, Brenda Peterson, Jay Petterson, Tom Petrillo, Reed Petty, Dan Pfieffer, Anne Pfrimmer, Dave Phelps, Michael Phillips, Michael Pinnick, Christopher Pipa, Redding Pitt, Vincent Pla, John Plaxco, Erich Potter, Roberto Prats, Chris Prendergast,

Alicia Kolar Prevost, Amy Pritchard, Peggy Propst, Carrie Pugh, Brad Queisser, Laura Quinn, George Rakis, Rene Rappaport, Bob Ream, Phillipe Reines, Rene Redwood, Neil Reiff, Nelson Reyneri, Christina Reynolds, Ted Richane, Brian Richardson, Hannah Richert, Monique Richardson, Gabrielle Riggio, Andy Rivera, Tori Robbins, John Robinson, Fabiola Rodriguez, Isabelle Rodriguez, Jennifer Rokola, Christine Romero, Sabine Romero, Xavier Romeu, T. J. Rooney, Cheryl Parker Rose, Erica Rose, David Rosen, Adam Rosenberg, Simon Rosenberg, Joshua Rosenblum, Stella Ross, Cynthia Jasso-Rotunno, Ann Rowan, Lisa Rowan, Melissa Roy, Jamie Rubin, Audrey Russakov, Tricia Russell, Melina Sanchez, Joe Sandler, John Sasso, Miti Sathe, Kristina Sauders, Don Schmanski, Griffin Schultz, Janet Scott, Terry Scott, Jen Scully, Jake Seher, Josh Sellers, Lottie Shackelford, Faiz Shakir, Jackie Shapiro, Nicholas Shapiro, Rodney Shelton, Paul Shone, Alexa Daniels-Shpall, Bridget Siegel, Traci Siegel, Kate Sienicki, Lesley Sillaman, Alicia Simmons, Angela Simpkins, Bill Singer, Ruth Singer, Matthew Slutsky, Kathryn Smiley, Iwona Barton-Smith, Steve Snyder, Charles Soechting, Jeff Sollender, Andy Spahn, Campbell Spencer, Mark Spengler, Rebecca Star, Eric Stern, Eric Stoltz, Gail Stoltz, Jason Strautman, Larry Strongin, Kimball Stroud, Lauren Supina, Adriana Surfas, Kathy Sullivan, Richard Sullivan, Jeanne Sutter, Laurie Syms, Mark Swansiger, William Swenson, Ari Swiller, Corrine Tapia, Donna Tappin, Tanya Tarr, Davidia Burnette-Taylor, Jed Taxel, Mark Thomann, Jeff Thompson, Linda Chavez Thompson, Jeri Thomson, B. J. Thornberry, Ellen Thrower, Brenner Tobe, Andy Tobias, Oreta Togafau, Art Torres, Jody Trapasso, Pam Traxel, Cassie Trotter, Susan Turnbull, Dan Turrentine, Thomas Tutt, Kathy Tuttle, Greg Twomey, Chinyere Uzoukwu, Rachelle Valladares, Estela Vallarta, Grace Van Cleave, Maju Varghese, Dag Vega, Joe Velasquez, Kathy Vick, Maketa Void, Mary Jane Volk, Elizabeth Wainwright, Fran Wakem, Jennifer Waldman, Sue Walitsky, Richard Walker, Jennifer Waller, Mark Walsh, Simone Ward, Josh Warren, Kimi Washington, Ervin Webb, Wellington Webb, Jacob Weigler, Lauren Weiner, Tony Welch, Cheryl Ann Welsh, John Wertheim, Wanda Wheeler, Denny White, Jeff Wice, Erin Wiley, David Wilhelm, Jacqueline Williams, Carol Willis, Jackie Wilson, Roger Wilson, Steve Wilson, Joceyln Woodards, C. R. Wooters, Amy Wojciki, Lauren Worley, Pam Womack, Peggy Wortham, Annie Wuerth, Chuq Yang, Victoria Yang, June Yates, Mohammed Yilla, Amy Young, Benjamin Young, Jamaal Young, Bob Zanlungo, Ivan Zapien, Yuming Zhang, Jonathan Zucker.

INDEX

★ ★ ★